APR - - 2011

W9-BON-844

WITHDRAWN

MONEYMAKERS

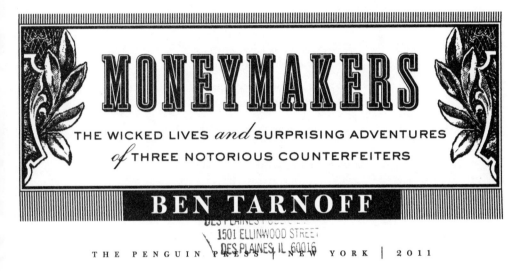

MONEYMAKERS

THE WICKED LIVES *and* SURPRISING ADVENTURES *of* THREE NOTORIOUS COUNTERFEITERS

BEN TARNOFF

DES PLAINES PUBLIC LIBRARY
1501 ELLINWOOD STREET
DES PLAINES, IL 60016

THE PENGUIN PRESS | NEW YORK | 2011

THE PENGUIN PRESS
Published by the Penguin Group
Penguin Group (USA) Inc., 375 Hudson Street, New York, New York 10014, U.S.A. •
Penguin Group (Canada), 90 Eglinton Avenue East, Suite 700, Toronto, Ontario, Canada
M4P 2Y3 (a division of Pearson Penguin Canada Inc.) • Penguin Books Ltd, 80 Strand,
London WC2R 0RL, England • Penguin Ireland, 25 St Stephen's Green, Dublin 2, Ireland
(a division of Penguin Books Ltd) • Penguin Books Australia Ltd, 250 Camberwell Road,
Camberwell, Victoria 3124, Australia (a division of Pearson Australia Group Pty Ltd) •
Penguin Books India Pvt Ltd, 11 Community Centre, Panchsheel Park, New Delhi – 110 017,
India • Penguin Group (NZ), 67 Apollo Drive, Rosedale, North Shore 0632, New Zealand
(a division of Pearson New Zealand Ltd) • Penguin Books (South Africa) (Pty) Ltd,
24 Sturdee Avenue, Rosebank, Johannesburg 2196, South Africa

Penguin Books Ltd, Registered Offices:
80 Strand, London WC2R 0RL, England

First published in 2011 by The Penguin Press,
a member of Penguin Group (USA) Inc.

Copyright © Benjamin Tarnoff, 2011
All rights reserved

Library of Congress Cataloging-in-Publication Data

Tarnoff, Ben.
Moneymakers : the wicked lives and surprising adventures of three notorious counterfeiters /
Ben Tarnoff.
p. cm.
Includes bibliographical references and index.
ISBN 978-1-59420-287-2
1. Counterfeits and counterfeiting—United States—Case studies.   2. Counterfeits and
counterfeiting—United States—History.   I. Title.
HG336.U5T37 2011
364.1'334092273—dc22
2010029617

Printed in the United States of America
1   3   5   7   9   10   8   6   4   2

DESIGNED BY STEPHANIE HUNTWORK

Without limiting the rights under copyright reserved above, no part of this publication may be
reproduced, stored in or introduced into a retrieval system, or transmitted, in any form or by
any means (electronic, mechanical, photocopying, recording, or otherwise), without the prior
written permission of both the copyright owner and the above publisher of this book.

The scanning, uploading, and distribution of this book via the Internet or via any other means
without the permission of the publisher is illegal and punishable by law. Please purchase only
authorized electronic editions and do not participate in or encourage electronic piracy of
copyrightable materials. Your support of the author's rights is appreciated.

For my parents

Blest paper-credit! last and best supply!
That lends corruption lighter wings to fly!
—ALEXANDER POPE

CONTENTS

MONEYMAKERS

INTRODUCTION

O N A NOVEMBER NIGHT IN 1876, two men passed in silence under the granite obelisk that rose a hundred feet above the tomb of Abraham Lincoln in Springfield, Illinois. Below the obelisk stood a statue of the slain president, the bronze silhouette glistening in the moonlight as the men moved swiftly by. Trying to make as little noise as possible, they entered Lincoln's burial chamber and approached the marble sarcophagus. The men drew their crowbars and, straining against the handles, managed to push the large tablet that covered the coffin over the side. Inside was the cedar casket that held Lincoln's corpse. Reaching into the sarcophagus, they began lifting the wooden box.

Suddenly a gunshot sounded outside. The men froze: the first shot was followed by another, then another, until the volley seemed to come from every direction. They dropped the casket and darted out of the tomb, fleeing the cemetery as bullets whistled past Lincoln's final resting place.

The men were caught several days later. They confessed to trying to kidnap Lincoln's body, which they planned to exchange for the freedom of their gang leader, a counterfeiter named Ben Boyd. The Secret Service, which had nabbed Boyd a year earlier, learned of the plan, and sent agents to lie in wait for the grave robbers. The officers sat watching the tomb for hours before the two men arrived. But before they could arrest the criminals, one of their pistols went off by accident. The others, thinking they were under attack, started firing wildly and the robbers escaped in a hail of bullets.

The irony of the scene was surely lost on the raiders of Lincoln's tomb. The robbers hoped to exchange a counterfeiter's freedom for the remains of a man who had done more than any other president in history to eliminate counterfeiting. Maybe they didn't know enough history to make the connection; the Secret Service agents lying in the bushes nearby certainly did. Before the war, state-chartered banks across the country printed notes of various designs and denominations, which made counterfeiting fairly easy. Under Lincoln, the government began phasing out these banks and creating a uniform national currency. A few months after Lincoln's death in 1865, the Secret Service was created to crack down on counterfeiters. Over the next several decades, the agency aggressively pursued its task, and by the end of the century, counterfeit cash amounted to just a slim fraction of the currency in circulation. The counterfeiters who flourished in the nation's infancy and adolescence would almost entirely disappear, victims of an unprecedented centralization of federal authority. The golden age of counterfeiting was over.

FEW COUNTRIES HAVE HAD as rich a counterfeiting history as America. In the centuries before the Civil War, the absence of a strong central government, an anarchic economic system, and the irrepressibly entrepreneurial spirit of its citizens helped make the country a haven for counterfeiters. Counterfeiting gave enterprising Americans from the colonial era onward a chance to get rich quick: to fulfill the promise of the American dream by making money, literally. Stories of their rise and fall thrilled their contemporaries, who traded tales of these criminal adventurers in taverns and devoured the reports that appeared in the pages of local newspapers. Although the memory of early America's moneymakers was preserved in local legends, by the twentieth century they would fade from public view, relics of an unrulier era in the nation's history.

American counterfeiters had an early advantage over their European counterparts for one crucial reason: the British colonies in North America were the first governments in the Western world to print paper currency. Paper notes appeared in response to the severe shortage of precious metals that was a persistent problem of colonial life. The British government limited the export of gold and silver to the colonies, and although an array of foreign coins circulated—pieces of eight, reals, doubloons, mostly of Spanish and Portuguese origin—there weren't enough to meet the demand. Colonists developed a range of different strategies to deal with the problem. Starting in the seventeenth century, American settlers tried using an Indian currency called wampum that consisted of beads of shell strung together on a thread, but widespread counterfeiting soon made it worthless. Since blue wampum was more valuable than white wampum, Indians often dyed their shells to sell them at a higher price, and diluted the threads with pieces of stone, bones, and glass. Colonists also tried using food commodities as money: in the seventeenth century, Massachusetts adopted corn as its official medium of exchange, and in Virginia, tobacco circulated as the common currency.

Coins would have been more convenient, but the paucity of precious metals in North America made coinage difficult. Unlike Latin America, whose gold and silver deposits provided the Spanish and the Portuguese with more than enough raw material to mint their currency, British settlers in the Atlantic colonies found little to work with. Even when colonists acquired precious metals through trade, the idea of a coined colonial currency met with opposition from home. Massachusetts began minting silver coins in 1652, but by 1684 the British government had ordered the colonists to stop, citing their violation of the royal right of coinage.

A growing colonial population and an expanding continental market demanded more credit, and with precious metals scarce and the home government hostile to coinage, paper money offered a solution. In 1690, the Massachusetts legislature started printing bills of credit to pay its debts. The authorities promised to retire the bills by levying future taxes payable in the new notes. But the colonists weren't concerned: relieved to have something resembling a functioning currency, they treated the notes like money, and Massachusetts kept the credit engine going by printing new issues to supersede the old ones.

The colonists had discovered a loophole in British regulations. Paper money didn't infringe on the home government's monopoly on coinage, and since the Massachusetts bills of credit were not redeemable by the British Crown, they weren't officially considered money. South Carolina started issuing bills of credit in 1703, followed by New Hampshire, Connecticut, and the remaining nine colonies over the next several decades. By 1764, the colonies had become so dependent on paper money that when the British Parliament passed legislation prohibiting bills of credit, it sparked an uproar, further souring relations between the colonists and their transatlantic rulers.

Paper money may have satisfied the colonial craving for credit, but it also exposed the economy to new vulnerabilities. Unlike gold or silver, which can be traded as commodities, notes have no market value aside from being a medium of exchange. Without anything "hard" to fall back on, paper can become worthless overnight, more useful as wallpaper or kindling than as money. Bills are only pieces of paper inscribed with a promise—the promise to be received for public debts like taxes, to be redeemed for a certain quantity of precious metals, or, as is the case today, to be accepted for all debts, public and private.

Paper money had other disadvantages. Excessive printing of paper caused inflation, which became an endemic problem in the colonies. The crude quality of most colonial currency also made counterfeiting relatively easy, and since many colonists were illiterate, spelling errors on fake bills often passed unnoticed. But in spite of its drawbacks, paper money became an indispensable part of the American economy from its debut in seventeenth-century Massachusetts through the Revolution and beyond.

When the Continental Congress needed to generate revenue to fund the war against the British, it printed paper notes called continentals, whose value fluctuated with the public's confidence in the promises of the new political leadership. In the early days of the Republic, debates over paper currency preoccupied prominent people like Benjamin Franklin and Alexander Hamilton, who tried to shore up the finances of a country that had few natural resources and little political or economic leverage. The decades before the Civil War saw the rapid proliferation of different currencies, as banks and a host of other state-chartered companies like insurance firms and railroads flooded the country with paper that constantly oscillated in value. By the time the federal government began regulating the money supply, there were more than ten thousand different kinds of notes circulating in the United States.

Paper helped entrepreneurs secure capital on credit and catalyzed commerce, but it also made the economy highly volatile and vulnerable to periodic fits of inflation. Perhaps the biggest beneficiaries of this financial chaos were counterfeiters, who thrived in a virtually unregulated economy that ran mostly on faith. These moneymakers were characters worth remembering—people like Mary Peck Butterworth, a housewife from Rehoboth, Massachusetts, who during the early eighteenth century ran a counterfeiting operation out of her kitchen with the help of a hot iron. Butterworth would cover a note with a strip of damp muslin and run her iron over it, transferring the bill's design to the fabric, which she then imprinted onto a blank piece of paper. She made a fortune selling the notes to her husband's friends. When the authorities learned of Butterworth's activities and came to arrest her, they couldn't find a shred of incriminating evidence, just an ironing board and a few burnt scraps of muslin in the fireplace. Another counterfeiter named Peter McCartney had less luck eluding arrest but earned a reputation as a talented escape artist. According to one story, he once bet the chief of the Secret Service that he could break out of an Illinois jail. When McCartney showed up at the chief's hotel room that evening, he told the astonished detective that he was calling to pay his respects and would return to his cell presently. "I merely wished to show that some things could be done as well as others," the counterfeiter explained. McCartney eventually went to prison for twelve years. "He was not an ordinary man," wrote Allan Pinkerton, the founder of the country's first private detective agency, "and when he disappeared suddenly, it was as if some great wreck had gone down at sea." The counterfeiter died in an Ohio penitentiary in 1890 at the age of sixty-six, having forged more than a million dollars.

Counterfeiters owed their success in large part to the patronage of their fellow citizens, who often didn't discriminate between forgeries and the genuine article. They were grateful to get a note that could hold its value until they could pass it, regardless of its authenticity. The men who printed the genuine bills and those who counterfeited them were opposite sides of the same coin: both hoped to inspire trust in pieces of paper whose value relied entirely on the confidence that people had in them.

It was this faith that enriched three of the most colorful counterfeiters in American history: Owen Sullivan, David Lewis, and Samuel Curtis Upham. Owen Sullivan (c. 1720–1756) was an Irish immigrant whose extraordinary talent for earning people's trust made him among the most notorious counterfeiters of the colonial era. After stints in Boston and Providence, Sullivan settled in a sliver of swampy land on the lawless border between New York and Connecticut, where he forged tens of thousands of pounds' worth of colonial currency. David Lewis (1788–1820) was a charismatic counterfeiter and robber who prowled Pennsylvania's Allegheny backcountry. His legendary acts of charity catapulted him to prominence as a populist folk hero, a Robin Hood who dispensed his ill-gotten gains to the poor while punishing the greedy. Samuel Curtis Upham (1819–1885), a Philadelphia shopkeeper and former California gold prospector, sold counterfeit Confederate currency from his storefront during the Civil War. Upham's "mementos of the Rebellion" proved enormously popular, and the influx of these fakes into the South drove down the value of Confederate currency, infuriating Southern leaders.

The biographies of these men tell the story of a country coming of age—from a patchwork of largely self-governing colonies to a loosely assembled union of states and, finally, to a single nation under firm federal control. Each responded to the political and economic realities of his era, propelled by a desire for profit and fame. They belonged to a class of criminal that overran America for much of its history, as integral to the country's financial past as those who printed its many kinds of legal currency.

Moneymakers didn't just infiltrate the money supply—they embodied the nation's speculative spirit. The American economy rose and fell on a tide of paper credit, fueled by notes that tended to promise more than they could deliver. As long as everyone believed something had value—whether a colonial bill of credit or a stock certificate—it did. But when that faith faltered, mistrust spread throughout the system, triggering a panic. Americans had a confidence problem: they either had too much of it, taking risks as everything surged, or too little, fleeing the market as everything crumbled. By feeding America's appetite for paper currency, counterfeiters helped stoke this cycle. They made fake money in a country where real money's value was often just as imaginary, bluffing their way to wealth in the casino of American capitalism.

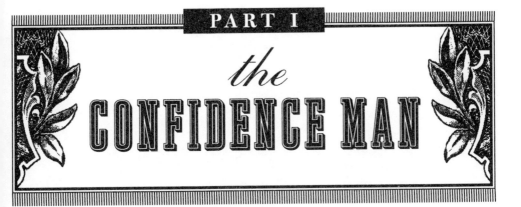

PART I

the

CONFIDENCE MAN

I F YOU HAD SPENT THE SUMMER OF 1749 in Boston, you likely would have heard that a gardener grew a twenty-eight-pound melon—the biggest anyone had ever seen—and invited thirty of his friends over to help him eat it. You might have heard about the mulatto boy who had been bitten by a rattlesnake at Stoughton and died twenty-four hours later, or the Irishman in yellow buckskin breeches who had hired a horse and then absconded with it to Rhode Island. You certainly would have heard about what the North End merchants were selling that season: Choice Lisbon Salt, the Best Burlington Pork, a Good Brick House, a Healthy Strong Negro Man—and at the printer's over on Queen Street, the latest selection from a fiery Calvinist preacher named Jonathan Edwards.

The printer couldn't have picked a better time to publish the preacher, whose best-known sermon, "Sinners in the Hands of an Angry God," warned parishioners that God could toss them into hell at any moment. After a summer in colonial Boston, everyone would have had a pretty good idea of what hell felt like. An oppressively hot sun singed the flesh, the air's humidity smothered the skin like a damp blanket, and the sour smell of sweat mixed with the fish stink wafting down from the piers of the harbor. The inferno couldn't have felt very far. An unchristian season, summer encouraged slothfulness, stirred lust, quickened the temper.

One day in late August, a local silversmith could be heard fighting with his wife. Their voices reverberated through Boston's corkscrew streets and into the ears of inquisitive neighbors in houses of timber and brick listening through thin walls and open windows. The wife was drunk; the silversmith probably was too. The words were indistinct; perhaps they slurred their speech. Suddenly a phrase, howled by a woman hoarse with rage, could be heard clearly above the din: "You forty-thousand-pound moneymaker!"

The silversmith's name, the neighbors would tell the authorities, was Owen Sullivan. Presumably this wasn't the first time the couple had quarreled: both he and his wife drank heavily, and they were angry drunks. Lately Sullivan had been seen with large quantities of cash, which he spent lavishly, conspicuously, arousing envy and suspicion. When officers came to arrest him on August 28, 1749, they found more than thirty counterfeit ten-shilling Massachusetts notes on the silversmith—not £40,000 but still a considerable amount of money. The print on the forgeries was too black, making his bills easily detectable as fakes when placed alongside genuine notes. Discovered in Sullivan's chest were printing materials, ink, and pieces of paper with his attempts to imitate the official signatures that appeared on the colony's currency.

They carried Sullivan off to jail, but the silversmith didn't intend to stay long. Once inside the prison, he passed a message to his partner John Fairservice, who agreed to secure his freedom in exchange for a plate for making counterfeit currency—not Massachusetts money, Fairservice specified, but New Hampshire. Since Sullivan's tools had been seized, he would have to make the plate from scratch. He would need a few things: a New Hampshire note to work from, a sheet of copper, and a small metalworking chisel. Fortunately, jails in colonial America were poorly guarded, making it easy for Sullivan to smuggle in whatever he needed. He could bribe a warden to pass packages for him or enlist one of the jail's many debtors, who were allowed to leave the prison grounds whenever they liked as long as they returned at night. Once Sullivan had obtained the materials, he set to work.

New Hampshire's forty-shilling note was printed on a rectangular piece of paper, and the text read from top to bottom, like a page out of a book. The bill was adorned with a large royal seal and various images: columns of acanthus leaves wreathed its borders, scrolls coiled and unfurled across the page, a pine tree stood at the center. The note's designers had introduced these flourishes to dissuade counterfeiters, who couldn't reproduce such elaborate designs without real technical skills. These details had another, more abstract purpose: they gave the bill a certain gravity, so as to reassure people that an inked slip of paper equaled a certain quantity of silver or gold. Aside from discouraging forgers, the intricate handiwork helped bolster people's confidence in the colony's currency.

To make the plate, Sullivan had to engrave everything backward. It was tedious, painstaking work. Each curlicued letter and drooping leaf had to be carved into the copper as a mirror image, so that when the plate was inked and run through a printing press, the resulting bill would look right. He etched the front of the note on one side of the copper sheet and the back on the other. The finished product must have looked peculiar, but anyone who glimpsed it sitting in Sullivan's cell—a brown pane inscribed with delicately executed, illegible glyphs—would have known what it was for.

Satisfied with the silversmith's services, Fairservice paid his bail, and Sullivan walked free for the time being. Fairservice stashed the plate at the bottom of a sled in a barn on Bull Wharf, one of the piers on the south side of town, and started printing counterfeit notes, hanging the newly inked forgeries from a string to let them dry in the wind along the waterfront. When the bills were crisp, he assembled them and headed off to make the sale. Across from the wharf stood a tavern named the Bull, where sailors and sloop masters passing through Boston ate, drank, and traded stories from abroad. These were Fairservice's ideal customers: itinerant men of dubious morals who could be persuaded to purchase counterfeit New Hampshire money, particularly after they had been softened up with a few tumblers of rum. Instead of selling his forgeries for a fixed fee, Fairservice lent the bills on consignment: the patron would keep one-half of the profits made from spending the counterfeits and remit the other half to Fairservice. Perhaps for this reason, the enterprise never really took off. In 1767, after twelve years of marriage, Fairservice's wife, Mary, filed for divorce. She claimed that her husband was financially irresponsible, abusive, and unfaithful; the most damaging of her many charges was that he had conducted "criminal conversation with a Negro Woman Slave in the family." Mary got the divorce.

In the meantime, Sullivan stood trial in the fall of 1750. He pleaded not guilty, but there was enough incriminating evidence found in his house to persuade the jury to convict the silversmith of "wickedly falsely & deceiptfully" forging Massachusetts bills with an intent to pass them off as genuine. On Thursday, September 13, Sullivan was led to the square below the imposing Georgian facade of what is now known as the Old State House and locked into the pillory. He spent two hours with his head and arms fastened between two pieces of wood and his back painfully bent while Bostonians passed on their daily business or paused to get a glimpse of the criminal. The more entertaining spectacle came later, when a sore Sullivan was removed from the wooden frame, tied to a nearby post, and whipped twenty times, his naked back reddening with each blow. Sullivan wasn't the only convict punished that Thursday; on the same day, one man received more than twice as many stripes for stealing. But those who remembered watching the little-known silversmith lashed would later recall the scene when they read reports of a notorious moneymaker named Owen Sullivan in the newspaper. No one could have known it at the time, but in the shadow of the Old State House, the greatest counterfeiter in colonial America had made his criminal debut.

BEING A COUNTERFEITER IN a city was never a good idea. There were always neighbors listening, whether to your drunk wife or to the rumbling of the printing press. Counterfeiting also produced refuse like test prints and bad bills that needed to be disposed of without attracting attention. Most difficult of all, counterfeiting generated wealth that was hard to conceal in a densely populated environment. In a town like Boston, crowded with fifteen thousand inhabitants when Sullivan lived there, neighbors knew a lot about one another, including their trade and income. If the silversmith down the street started living above his means, people would notice. By colonial standards, Sullivan was forging a lot of money. When he was first arrested, the authorities found three hundred shillings in counterfeit Massachusetts notes on him. In Boston in 1749, three hundred shillings could buy you about six bushels of wheat at wholesale prices, enough to feed a family for months. In his barn on Bull Wharf, John Fairservice printed more than twice that in a single day, producing 680 shillings in paper bills. Counterfeiting cash in such large quantities posed a problem. Spending it was risky, particularly among people who had reason to doubt you earned it honestly.

The solution was to let others pass it for you, either by selling them the counterfeits in batches or, like Fairservice, lending the notes on consignment. At the top of the counterfeiting scheme was the engraver: someone like Sullivan, whose metalworking skills determined the success of the whole undertaking. Next came the printer, preferably someone who knew how to operate a press and could obtain the right ink and paper. At the bottom were the passers, who exchanged the fake bills for real money, thus generating the profit that fueled the venture.

This system had a couple of advantages. It protected the heart of the operation—the engraver—by transferring most of the risk to easily replaceable unskilled workers: the passers, who could be arrested whenever they spent the counterfeits. It also meant that one engraver could rapidly recruit a large, decentralized network of accomplices. A single plate was enough to build a diffuse criminal organization consisting of several printers, countless passers, and everyone in between. In reality, the distinction between the different roles wasn't always clearly defined; while primarily an engraver, Sullivan often helped print and pass his forged notes. But his basic business model—the engraver as the vital center of an expanding web of collaborators—remained intact. Without it, he could never have gone from a solitary silversmith to the boss of a major counterfeiting ring.

Sullivan's arrest in Boston in the summer of 1749 marked the beginning of a remarkable criminal career that would span seven years. It was evident early on that Sullivan was more than just a gifted engraver. He also possessed an extraordinary talent for getting others to trust him, a flair for persuasion that helped endear him to the public, recruit partners in crime, and convince the authorities to lighten his punishments. While Sullivan was a skilled forger of notes, his greatest counterfeit was the confidence he inspired in others, from the accomplices who trusted him to produce undetectable fakes to the colonists who believed his bills were authentic. Sullivan had an entrepreneurial streak, a trait that placed him firmly within the commercial culture of his day. Just as the North End vendors exploited Boston's prominence as a port to maximize their returns, he capitalized on the conditions in colonial America that made his venture particularly ripe: the colonies' reliance on paper money, a general craving for cheap currency, and lax law enforcement. In the years following his arrest in Boston, he would distribute his wares throughout the Northeast, peddling strips of paper that cost him little to produce, netting profits that he either spent or reinvested in an enterprise that helped him become the most successful counterfeiter in colonial history.

SULLIVAN COULDN'T HAVE PICKED a more momentous year to become a counterfeiter. Seventeen forty-nine was a turning point in the financial history of Massachusetts, a time when the disputes that had been simmering throughout the colony's fifty-nine-year experiment with paper money ignited into a ferocious public debate. Massachusetts had begun printing paper notes in 1690 after an unsuccessful effort to conquer the nearby French colony of Quebec. The government expected to fund the expedition with plunder, but when the soldiers returned empty-handed and close to mutiny, the colonial legislature quickly issued bills to pay them off. The notes, whose value was secured by future taxes, proved to be a useful medium of exchange, so the legislators continued to print them. Their decision would change the American colonies forever. As the first society in the Western world to establish a public paper currency, Massachusetts became the battleground for a particularly intense struggle over the finer points of economic policy—a struggle fought not just by the elites and the experts but by the vast majority of the population.

On May 1, 1749, a few months before Sullivan's arrest, the rooftop of a magnificent town house in the North End burst into flame. A crowd of lower-class spectators gathered nearby to watch the fire consume the upper half of the building and, rather than running for help, started yelling, "Let it burn!" But someone must have alerted the authorities, because firefighters soon arrived to extinguish the blaze, and to the mob's dismay, the house was saved. The next day, the *Boston Gazette* printed a report blaming the fire on a defective chimney flue. But given the anger evident in the streets, arson seemed like a distinct possibility.

The house belonged to Thomas Hutchinson, the scion of a prominent Boston family and the speaker of the Massachusetts House of Representatives. The son of a wealthy merchant, Hutchinson had been precocious from an early age: he entered Harvard at twelve, graduated at sixteen, and joined the Massachusetts legislature at twenty-six after launching a successful business career. He was also an outspoken opponent of paper money, and early in 1749 had ushered a controversial bill through the legislature requiring that Massachusetts retire all of its paper currency by March 1751. Hutchinson, like most members of his social class, favored a "hard" currency based on silver and gold. This made him unpopular among the colony's tradesmen and laborers, who relied heavily on paper money in their daily commerce. The thought that it would be taken away by one of the richest men in Boston enraged them.

Wealthy Bostonians had clear reasons for wanting money to be made of precious metals. Since many of them were involved in international trade, they needed a universally accepted currency whose value wouldn't fluctuate with inflation in order to do business with their overseas partners. They also tended to be creditors, which made them particularly vulnerable to depreciations of the colony's money. A ten-shilling note could have considerably more purchasing power when it was lent than the same amount a few years later. When the debt was paid, the lender had to sustain the loss of however much value had evaporated.

This state of affairs benefited the debtors, who could essentially get away with paying less. But that wasn't the only reason that Hutchinson's plan provoked such panic among the middle and lower classes, from whose ranks most debtors were drawn. If you made your living trading goods or services in local markets, you depended on paper money. Paper provided people with a shared medium of exchange: it gave the colony's silversmiths, brewers, and printers a way to sell their merchandise and buy what they needed to expand their business. Replacing paper with precious metals would have curbed this commerce, as coin was scarce and what little existed was held by Boston's financial elite. Paper's proponents didn't object to a metallic currency on philosophical grounds. Their concerns were practical: coin was concentrated in the hands of the wealthy. Moving to a metallic currency would effectively hand control of the money supply to men like Hutchinson.

It's possible that Hutchinson's attempt at currency reform was motivated purely by economic self-interest; the crowd that collected opposite his house to cheer while it burned undoubtedly thought so. But to be fair, he had a strong case against paper. Paper was a blessing and a curse: it may have lubricated local markets, but only at the cost of making the economy more mercurial. Ever since Massachusetts started printing its bills of credit in 1690, the currency had been steadily declining in value. As more and more bills came off the colonial presses, the legislature began postponing the notes' retirement. The result was depreciation.

In 1744, a conflict called King George's War broke out between British and French colonists in the Northeast, and the financial situation became even worse. Under the enthusiastic leadership of Governor William Shirley, Massachusetts spearheaded a successful effort to capture the French fortress of Louisbourg on Île Royale, later known as Cape Breton Island, in present-day Nova Scotia. In order to pay for the expedition, the legislature printed large quantities of money. Between June 1744 and June 1748, nineteen new paper issues appeared, and in roughly the same period, the cost of silver in Massachusetts paper money nearly doubled. The steep inflation didn't just hurt creditors; everyone suffered when the colonial currency lost almost half its value in the space of four years.

Although the war had a catastrophic effect on the economy, it also ultimately enabled Hutchinson to follow through with his plan to retire the colony's paper money. After an extended negotiation, Parliament agreed to reimburse Massachusetts for its expenses from the Louisbourg campaign. The settlement, to be paid mostly in silver, represented a large injection of coin into a colony where precious metals were in short supply. For hard-money advocates like Hutchinson, this was the opportunity they had been waiting for. On January 25, 1749, after much wrangling by Speaker Hutchinson, the Massachusetts House of Representatives passed a bill committing the entire Louisbourg reimbursement to the redemption of the colony's paper money. For a single year, from March 31, 1750, to March 31, 1751, anyone would be able to bring paper notes to the Old State House in Boston and exchange them for silver and copper coins; by April 1, 1751, Hutchinson hoped, Massachusetts would finally have a hard currency. Pushing the measure through the legislature wasn't easy, but Hutchinson was satisfied with the outcome. "I am convinc'd it was absolutely our Duty," he wrote, "to bring our wicked Mony to an End."

The approaching elimination of paper money hung over Boston like a dark cloud. In the streets people could be overheard praying that the ship carrying the payment from England would sink at sea: the coin could do far less damage deposited on the ocean floor, many colonists felt, than in Hutchinson's hands. After a five-week voyage, the *Mermaid* arrived without incident in the fall of 1749. Onlookers watched the ship unload its cargo, which was carried to the town treasury and secured in a specially prepared underground vault. The spectators' mood was grim. "Few Tokens of Joy were shewn on its landing," one newspaperman observed, "but on the contrary, an uncommon Gloominess appeared in most Countenances." William Bollan, the colonial official who had spent the last four years in England negotiating the reimbursement, feared that the gloom would soon turn to rage. He urged Hutchinson to hide out at his summer home in nearby Milton until emotions had cooled.

Instead of subsiding, tensions only grew in the coming months. Colonists on both sides of the issue tangled in the pages of Boston's newspapers, which became inundated with dispatches from the money war. Currency debates in local papers were nothing new: back in August, a pseudonymous author in the *Boston Evening-Post* warned that the abolition of paper money would force Massachusetts to return to a barter economy. "[W]e shall have the pleasant Sight of a Housekeeper groaning under the Burden of a Barrel of Flour to Market, to barter for Mutton," he wrote. But now that the silver from England had reached Boston, the issue acquired a new sense of urgency. Readers wrote in, complaining that moving to a hard currency—which would considerably decrease the amount of money in circulation—would make it impossible for them to do business, settle debts, or pay taxes. The opposing camp shot back, responding that the plan would restore order and stability to the colony's economy. Hutchinson himself joined the fray. In a letter to the *Boston Gazette*, he argued that paper money had sown "Fraud, Injustice and Oppression," and, true to form, spoke up for the colony's creditors, who suffered under a system where people paid "their Debts with a less Value than when they were contracted."

As the bickering continued, the fault lines became increasingly clear: between rich and poor, creditor and debtor, town and country. In a satire published in the *Boston News-Letter*, a country trader named Honestus comes to Boston to pay off his debt to Politicus, a wealthy merchant. Politicus tries to interest his longtime customer in the latest imported goods, but Honestus, reluctant to dig himself deeper into debt, refuses. Eager to make the sale, Politicus promises that when silver dollars replace paper notes, he'll have nothing to worry about:

> *Pol.* Fear not *Honestus*—I don't doubt
> When once the Dollars shall come out—
> There'l be no Want of Money then:
> Eager you'l catch the glit'ring Coin—
> And bless the golden Æra when
> This Paper Trash is no more seen.

> *Hon.* Ah! Sir, we hear the Province Bills
> Do lye recluse within the Tills
> Of some great Men, to wait the Time
> The Dollars shall the same redeem;—
> And what is worse than all, 'tis said
> To foreign Lands they'l be convey'd!
> Then what's our Fate—The Silver gone—
> The Paper burnt—and we undone.

The dialogue summed up the anxieties of many colonists. Like Honestus, they feared that Hutchinson's scheme would deprive them of a functioning medium of exchange, and that precious metals—stockpiled by the superrich, tied up in overseas trade—would forever remain out of their reach.

PEOPLE HAD A LOT at stake in the currency crisis of 1749. With their livelihood on the line, colonists took a strong interest in policies that would impact them directly. But while the consequences couldn't have been more concrete, the debate itself often became quite abstract.

At the heart of the squabble between paper and metal was a philosophical dispute between two very different theories of value. Hard-money supporters like Hutchinson saw value as being fixed and intrinsic. They believed that money only had value in proportion to its metallic content, and that silver and gold alone provided the bedrock upon which the edifice of a secure economy could be constructed.

Paper's proponents, on the other hand, thought of money in more utilitarian terms: they argued that money had value because it could fulfill certain tasks, like buying a bushel of wheat or a day's worth of labor. Precious metals weren't intrinsically valuable, but rather derived their value from a cultural convention that made them exchangeable for goods and services. If money was a standard of exchange agreed upon by a group of individuals—defined not by its form but by its function—then a scrap of paper could serve the purpose just as well as a silver coin. Through the power of belief, paper could be magically transformed into money. As one Congregationalist preacher from Ipswich, Massachusetts, pointed out in a widely read pamphlet, life was full of such acts of faith. He likened paper bills to women: "necessary Evils . . . Metamorphised into things called Wives."

Paper money's most articulate advocate came not from Massachusetts but from Pennsylvania. Benjamin Franklin was twenty-three years old in 1729 when he published "A Modest Enquiry into the Nature and Necessity of a Paper-Currency." His immediate reason for writing the pamphlet was to convince the Pennsylvania legislature, which had been printing paper money since 1723, to put more currency into circulation. But while he was on the topic of currency, the young printer couldn't resist engaging in the philosophical wrangling that so preoccupied his fellow colonists to the north. The true value of money, Franklin claimed, was its ability to purchase another man's labor. "The riches of a country are to be valued by the quantity of labour its inhabitants are able to purchase," he wrote, "not by the quantity of silver and gold they possess." Since labor was what made money valuable, there was no reason to prefer precious metals to paper. Both were arbitrary instruments of exchange, but paper provided a more plentiful and convenient material.

Increasing the quantity of paper money would have a number of positive effects, Franklin argued. It would prevent wages from declining, keep interest rates low, and decrease dependence on European exports. He made a convincing case. His essay was widely read, and succeeded in persuading the Pennsylvania legislators to authorize another issue of paper money. Two years later, the Assembly hired him to design and print the notes. In his *Autobiography*, Franklin recalled the episode with characteristic immodesty. "This was another advantage gained by my being able to write," he observed. As Pennsylvania's official money manufacturer, Franklin came up with creative ways to thwart counterfeiters. He intentionally misspelled the word "Pennsylvania" on his bills, hoping to catch forgers who corrected the error. He also added botanical motifs by casting real leaves in lead and then printing them directly onto the notes, creating intricate patterns that were difficult to duplicate.

Better than anyone, Franklin understood paper's potential. Faced with a scarcity of coin and an abundance of entrepreneurs, colonial America needed a way to convert the ambitions of its inhabitants into real economic growth, and paper currency met that need. Paper let ordinary people—not just the privileged few with access to precious metals—participate in the buying and selling that fueled local markets. Franklin's defense tackled the core question of the currency debate: What is value and how is it created? By putting labor at the center of economic value, he cast the laboring classes as society's most important members—the shopkeepers, artisans, and small businessmen that in Franklin's view represented the soul of colonial America. Paper reflected hard work, ambition, and enterprise; it offered a practical alternative to the idolatrous fever for precious metals that afflicted the Old World.

Franklin's greatest insight was that for money to have value, people have to believe in it. Money can't do anything by itself; unlike a gun or a banana, it has no utility other than as a medium of exchange agreed upon by a group of individuals. This is most obviously the case with paper money: it depends entirely on confidence, which is why it can become worthless overnight if people lose faith in it.

The intangible nature of paper money caused its detractors in the Massachusetts money war to condemn it in unusual terms: not just as financially unsound but as immoral and even supernatural. One Protestant minister compared printing paper bills to the "Popish Doctrine of Transubstantiation," a false metamorphosis that preyed on the laity's will to believe. Substituting paper for silver and gold was not only deluded, it was blasphemous. Another hard-money supporter extended the religious argument even further: paper money, in usurping the role traditionally reserved for precious metals, represented "an abomination to the righteous GOD." Silver and gold were eternal, God-given measures of value. Spurning them in favor of something man-made disrupted the natural order of things, and betrayed an unholy desire to play God.

According to this logic, paper money's sinful origins meant that its use inevitably encouraged immoral acts, like debtors cheating their creditors and speculators exploiting the volatility of value. Paper was a kind of illusionist's trick with potentially catastrophic consequences, an intrinsically deceitful medium that bred bad behavior as it spread like a virus through the body politic. Both the officials who printed money legally and the counterfeiters who forged it were sorcerers of a sort, inspiriting otherwise worthless paper with the power to be exchanged for goods and services.

The oft-repeated charge that paper money was unnatural revealed a deeper, more tangible fear. Paper posed a very real threat to the traditional class system of colonial America, an order that its self-appointed stewards liked to think of as natural. While hard currency tended to be concentrated in the hands of rich merchants, paper money was more widely distributed and changed hands more frequently. As a fluid and fickle form of wealth, paper's dynamism undermined a static social arrangement built around fixed classes and a fixed currency. An entrepreneurial class buoyed by credit clearly unnerved traditionalists, who were terrified of an economy where value had been sublimated into something spectral and slippery. Their alarm at the "ghost" of paper money had a metaphysical aspect: what they really feared was a world where appearances no longer reliably corresponded to reality, where a piece of paper could equal a pile of gold or an uncultured tradesman could become a powerful member of society. No one typified this phenomenon better than counterfeiters, who made a fortune capitalizing on the interval between appearance and reality. They were the most extreme exemplars of paper money's corrosive effect on social conventions: men of simple origins who became rich and famous riding the coattails of an incorporeal currency.

IF THE PHANTOM OF PAPER frightened men like Thomas Hutchinson, then Owen Sullivan was the flesh-and-blood fulfillment of their fears. In many respects, he was their worst nightmare: a hard-drinking Irish immigrant who used colonial America's dependence on paper currency to become as wealthy as a prosperous Boston merchant. It was an exercise in immorality that only an economy built on paper could produce.

The only account of Sullivan's early life is a pamphlet that appeared posthumously entitled *A Short Account of the Life, of John— alias Owen Syllavan*. He probably dictated the narrative just before his death to someone who transcribed and printed it. Although his embellishments and omissions, or those of the pamphlet's printer, are impossible to know, the sequence of events he describes fits the chronology outlined by colonial records and newspaper accounts. Printed in twelve pages of thick black type, the confession recounts Sullivan's life, beginning with his childhood in Ireland in the 1720s and 1730s.

Imagine a child cowering in bed while an invisible spirit floating somewhere within the lightless room calls his name for several minutes before disappearing. It starts each night at eleven o'clock, and continues for days, weeks, months: ministers from local parishes come to pray alongside the boy's bed, begging him to repent of his sins, hoping to dispel the spirit with prostrate displays of devotion. Word spreads, drawing hundreds of visitors from near and far to the child's room to get a glimpse of the afflicted boy and convey their sympathies. But the spirit keeps returning, now calling so loudly that the windows of the house shake, and when the child falls ill, the voice becomes even more powerful, and the boy, lying in bed, feels a hand press the skin between his shoulders as if the specter, after three months of nightly visitations, were at last reaching down to pry his soul from its mortal cavity.

Sullivan started hearing voices as a young boy. Born and raised in a seaside village in southeastern Ireland, he became a troublemaker early, perhaps out of boredom, perhaps on the advice of the demon that haunted his sleep. "[F]rom my youth I was always in all kinds of Mischief," he confessed, "so that I never minded Father nor Mother, Sister nor Brother; but went on in all Manner of Vice." He tormented his parents, who tried desperately to discipline their unruly son. First they locked him in his room with only bread and water, then they sent him to live with a schoolmaster. Neither reformed his ways.

At the age of thirteen, Sullivan ran away from home. He roamed the countryside, wandering westward. The landscape he traversed must have offered countless scenes of the poverty endemic to Ireland in the middle of the eighteenth century. Tenant families farmed potatoes on rugged plots of a few acres each, living in windowless cabins made of dried mud. Inside were single rooms lit by slow-burning peat fires, livestock dropping dung on earthen floors, a few broken stools. In 1727, Jonathan Swift deplored the "miserable dress and diet and dwelling of the people, the families of farmers who pay great rents living in filth and nastiness upon buttermilk and potatoes, not a shoe or stocking to their feet." Two decades later, little had changed. In an impassioned 1748 editorial published in the Dublin periodical *Reformer*, a nineteen-year-old Edmund Burke wrote that tenant farmers wore "clothes so ragged, that they rather publish than conceal the wretchedness it was meant to hide . . . it is no uncommon sight to see a half dozen children run quite naked out of a cabin, scarcely distinguishable from a dunghill, to the great disgrace of our country with foreigners, who would doubtless report them savages."

Anglo-Irish Protestants owned most of the land, and as the country's population rose precipitously over the course of the eighteenth century, they raised rents and further subdivided their estates, forcing more people to live on less acreage. A series of laws passed by the British Parliament severely restricting Irish trade had made farming essentially the only livelihood, and the island became almost wholly dependent on agriculture. To make matters worse, the harvests failed regularly, causing devastating food shortages. A famine in 1740–1741 killed hundreds of thousands of people, emptied whole villages, and left the roads littered with unburied corpses.

A young face amid the scruffy sea of beggars and landless laborers then tramping around the country, Sullivan drifted about a hundred miles from home before meeting a rich man riding along the road. The teenage runaway made up a tearful story about being the orphan of poor Dubliners, and the performance was so convincing that the gentleman, affected by the tale, brought Sullivan back to his estate to work as an errand boy. He ended up staying six years, enjoying what must have been a life of relative comfort. But as he grew older he began to feel homesick, and vowed to visit his parents at the next opportunity.

He soon had his chance. One day the gentleman gave him a letter to deliver, and after riding twenty miles to drop off the message, Sullivan continued for another fifty at breakneck speed, arriving at Waterford, a port town near his home, at four o'clock in the afternoon. Flushed and sweaty after a full day of travel, he ducked into a tavern to drink a tumbler of wine. But instead of cooling him down, the wine made him sick, and he had to lie down. Sprawled on a bed waiting to feel better, he was only thirty miles from his parents' house—he had traveled more than twice that distance in a day but couldn't finish the last leg of the journey. During his convalescence people asked Sullivan who he was, where he was headed; but he refused to reveal his true identity, perhaps fearing that news of his presence might reach his parents.

Once he had recovered, he unaccountably lost all interest in returning home. "After I got well I went down to the Wharf," Sullivan reports, "where I saw several Passengers going on Board of a Vessel bound for Boston, in New-England." Finding the captain, he negotiated to pay his passage with an indenture of service for four years, and after a few days, the ship set sail. Perhaps Sullivan couldn't face seeing his parents after all those years, or was suddenly tempted by the promise of the New World; his motivations are unclear, but his destination was New England, three thousand miles across the ocean. By Sullivan's own account, the most important decision of his life—his emigration to America—appears to have been completely spontaneous.

Within the first few pages of the counterfeiter's tale, a personality emerges whose outlines are immediately recognizable from later accounts: impulsive and impatient, marked by a hustler's itch for a better angle and resentment of anyone who stands in the way. Sullivan's hostility toward authority of any kind would only increase in the coming years, as the early tyranny of his well-intentioned parents became the tyranny of a government trying to capture and kill him. He followed his instincts, and often appeared to act without thinking, yet his resourcefulness rarely failed him, and he seemed to know intuitively how to get what he wanted. Sullivan was the kind of man it would have been easy to underestimate. He was a drunken Irishman who, in the language of the period, fell victim to vice; but he was also indisputably ambitious, driven first across the Irish countryside and then across the ocean by something greater than just pleasure-seeking.

IN THE FALL OF 1741, a sloop named the *Sea-Flower* floated off the coast of Massachusetts. Its mast had split in a gale, and the boat drifted helplessly with the current. On deck, emaciated men and women, tongues swollen from thirst, sat staring at the horizon with bloodshot eyes. Many of their companions had died of starvation and sickness. The corpses that hadn't been thrown overboard or left decomposing in the hold were sitting half-digested in the stomachs of the survivors: chunks of putrid muscle and brittle bone, carved in desperation from the withered bodies of former friends and relatives. The passengers ate six carcasses altogether. While cutting into the seventh, a vessel appeared, a British warship under the command of Captain Thompson Commander. Commander boarded the *Sea-Flower* and found that the ship had departed Belfast for Philadelphia months earlier.

Fifteen days into the voyage, the *Sea-Flower*'s captain had died, followed by the first mate; the mast snapped off, and the supplies of food and water ran out. Commander loaded provisions onto the ship and put one of his midshipmen on board to navigate the *Sea-Flower* into port. About a week later the survivors spotted the flickering candles of Boston's lighthouse. By the time the *Sea-Flower* arrived in Boston Harbor on October 31, 1741, it had been at sea for sixteen weeks, and 46 of the original 106 passengers had died. The survivors were taken to a hospital to recover, but no one seems to have seriously considered releasing the half-starved servants from their indentures. A month later, on December 1, an advertisement appeared in the *Boston Gazette*: "Just arrived in the Sloop Sea Flower, from the North of Ireland, several likely Men Servants, both Tradesmen and Farmers, their Time to be disposed of, for four years, by Capt. John Steel, at the North End of Boston."

While an extreme case, the *Sea-Flower* was fairly typical of transatlantic journeys for indentured servants at the time. Sullivan probably boarded a boat at the Waterford pier in 1742, a year after the *Sea-Flower* disembarked from Belfast, and often went hungry during his nine-week passage. He cut a deal with the captain to fill his empty stomach: in exchange for adding three more years to his indenture (for a total of seven years), he would be allowed to eat as many biscuits—bread designed to survive long sea voyages—as he could in the span of ninety minutes, as timed by the ship's hourglass. The skipper burst into laughter when he heard Sullivan's offer. He agreed to it on one condition: the Irishman couldn't have any water for the hour and a half he was eating. The captain upended the hourglass and Sullivan stuffed the biscuits into his mouth, the parched bread ground down to a semi-edible paste of flour and saliva by his teeth before being forced down his throat. A few dozen biscuits were worth this little piece of sadistic entertainment, the captain figured, even if he lost some servants to starvation as a result.

The reason for the nightmarish conditions aboard these ships was simple economics. People like Sullivan who were too poor to afford the trip to America sold contracts of their future labor for a certain period of time, usually between three to five years, to the ship's owner, who recouped his expenses by retailing the contracts to customers in the colonies. Merchants tried to maximize profits by cramming as many servants as they could into their ships and keeping costs low by feeding them as little as possible.

Even if a quarter of their cargo died, the traders reasoned, enough would survive to turn a profit. Provisions consisted of heavily salted bread, meat, and cheese calculated to last for twelve weeks, although a ship making several stops along the British Isles and the Continent before departing for America could be at sea for much longer. Even if there had been enough food, it would have been nearly impossible to stay healthy under such circumstances. One observer who inspected the servants' quarters on a ship in the middle of the eighteenth century described foul odors, vomiting, seasickness, fever, dysentery, constipation, boils, scurvy, and mouth rot.

If Sullivan came to America hoping to find the good life, he would soon be disappointed. When the ship arrived in Boston, the captain sold Sullivan's seven-year indenture to a man named Captain Gillmore, who put the Irishman to work clearing wooded land on his estate near the St. George River in Maine. Maine in the 1740s was still mostly wilderness, beset by severe winters that kept its settlements rugged and small. It was also a major battleground, perhaps the bloodiest in North America, aggressively contested by the English, the French, and local Indian tribes for more than a hundred years. The fighting had been ruthless, with atrocities committed on all sides—villages burned to the ground, civilians massacred, corpses scalped. By the time Sullivan arrived, however, Maine had been relatively peaceful for almost two decades. While tensions still ran high—British colonists along the St. George River complained that they frequently lost horses and livestock to Indian raids—no major hostilities erupted.

The next conflict, when it came, would last for four years and yet leave the political map of North America virtually unchanged. It would also set in motion the chain of events that led Sullivan to counterfeiting and, along a parallel path, enabled Thomas Hutchinson to eliminate paper money from Massachusetts. It began in Europe, triggered by the unexpected death of the Holy Roman Emperor, Charles VI. One rainy night in October 1740, after returning from a hunting trip, Charles ate a meal of sautéed mushrooms. He spent the night vomiting, became feverish, and died nine days later; although there was never a conclusive diagnosis, most people blamed the mushrooms, which were said to be poisonous. Charles's death posed a serious problem, since his succession was disputed: he had decreed that the crown would pass to his eldest daughter, Maria Theresa, but not everyone accepted her as legitimate, partly because of an ancient Frankish law forbidding royal inheritance by a woman. Prussia took advantage of the confusion by invading Silesia, an Austrian possession, in December 1740. The invasion eventually ignited the War of the Austrian Succession, with Prussia, France, and Spain on one side and Austria, Britain, and Russia on the other. As Voltaire recalled in his memoirs, "This plate of champignons changed the destiny of Europe."

Despite heavy fighting on the Continent, war was not officially declared between England and France until the spring of 1744. The news reached the French at Louisbourg on May 3, a full twenty days before it reached Boston. Emboldened by the element of surprise, the French wasted little time, striking British positions in Nova Scotia and dispatching privateers to capture British ships. This began the North American phase of the War of the Austrian Succession, named King George's War after Britain's King George II, the same conflict that would soon force the Massachusetts legislature to boost its production of paper money. When Sullivan's master, Gillmore, heard of the French attacks, he decided to move his family to safety in Boston, fearing a wider war in the Northeast. He sold the remainder of his servant's contract to Captain Jabez Bradbury, the commanding officer at a nearby fort along the St. George River.

Bradbury was a veteran of colonial Maine. He had spent the last thirty-odd years living in trading outposts along the northeastern frontier, and was almost fifty when he took command at the St. George River in 1742, where he had the unenviable task of manning an isolated garrison in territory inhabited by mostly hostile Indian tribes. He hated it, and in his correspondence with the governor of Massachusetts, William Shirley, he frequently requested to be reassigned, or "diliverd from this place of torment," as he put it in one such letter. By the summer of 1744, around the time that Sullivan got there, the mood at the fort must have been extremely tense. Now that the British and the French were officially at war, it was only a matter of time before the Indians, many of whom were allied with the French, emerged from the dense cover of the Maine forest and attacked the garrison. When he arrived, Sullivan found a fort full of frightened soldiers commanded by an aging officer who loathed his job.

WHILE SULLIVAN AND BRADBURY'S MEN waited, their superiors in Boston set their eyes farther north, to another fiercely contested strip of terrain, Nova Scotia. The British had controlled mainland Nova Scotia since 1713, but Île Royale, the landmass that capped the peninsula, remained in French hands. Its main settlement, Louisbourg, was a heavily fortified seaport and one of New France's most important trading hubs. Hoping to consolidate British control over the North Atlantic, Governor Shirley started building support for an ambitious plan to capture the fort. The proposal, approved by the Massachusetts legislature in February 1745, was wildly impractical. It involved using three thousand poorly trained New England militiamen to stage an amphibious assault that even an elite British regiment would have found challenging. When operations began in the spring of 1745, the campaign started stumbling right away. Discipline among the New England militias, whose ranks consisted of plunder-hungry colonists with little to no military experience, was nonexistent. They made all sorts of mistakes, like loading the siege cannons with multiple shots, thinking that doubling the ammunition would pack twice the punch. Instead, the iron siding of the cannons burst, and the shrapnel from these explosions caused a significant number of casualties on the New England side. If the battlefield was chaotic and carnivalesque by day, the camps at night were no different. The men sat around the fire drinking, singing, and roasting hunks of meat carved from poached French cattle.

Remarkably, though, the siege succeeded. On June 26, exhausted by more than a month of fighting, Louisbourg's forces surrendered. The report of the fort's capture had an electrifying effect on New England. This was their victory: it was the colonials who had defeated the French, not those pompous "lobster backs," the red-coated British regulars. The reality, of course, was more complicated, since British soldiers had fought alongside the militias and a Royal Navy blockade played a key role in the victory. But in the jubilant outpouring of Yankee pride that swept Massachusetts in the summer of 1745, the finer points were lost. Americans of all classes took part in the festivities, toasting the triumph with copious quantities of liquor while fireworks burst against New England's night sky. "The churl and niggard became generous and even the poor forgot their poverty," reported the *Boston Evening-Post*.

Not everyone greeted the fall of Louisbourg with joy. The news enraged the pro-French Indian tribes in the woods near the St. George River. One day in the middle of July, Bradbury's men heard the crackling report of gunfire followed by the shrill sounds of a woman screaming. They looked out and saw a woman running toward the garrison: she was bleeding from a bullet wound in her shoulder, with some seventy Indians in pursuit. The soldiers fired on the natives, slowing them down long enough for her to sprint to safety within the fort's gates. When the battle was over, Bradbury found that the Indians had killed around sixty of the settlers' cattle and taken a man prisoner; they discovered his scalped corpse about a week later.

Sullivan witnessed the attack, and the several that followed, before leaving the fort in 1746. After serving Bradbury for two years, he chose to enlist in an infantry regiment bound for Louisbourg, departing for the newly captured town about a year later than most New Englanders. While Sullivan still had three years left on his indenture, servants were allowed to enroll in the military, albeit with the provision that their wages went to their masters. Sullivan's enlistment proved decisive for his future as a counterfeiter, since in Louisbourg he became his regiment's armorer, a position that taught him the metalworking techniques he would later use in engraving plates for forging currency. He seems to have enjoyed his time in the military, recording in his memoir that he "took great Delight in the Discipline, which pleased my Officers exceedingly."

Perhaps for someone so impetuous, the rigor of martial life was a relief, a forced vacation from his capricious nature. But if that was the case, he joined the wrong army. The wildness that the New England militiamen had displayed during the siege didn't disappear in the months after they took Louisbourg; if anything, it worsened. Tensions between the American colonials and the British regulars, pervasive before, now threatened to erupt into outright revolt. The royal troops hoarded the plunder for themselves, enraging the Americans, many of whom had signed on to the expedition exclusively for the spoils. Bad housing and poor sanitation, combined with Louisbourg's damp climate and brutal winters, produced epidemics among the soldiers; by the summer of 1746, an estimated twelve hundred soldiers had died of sickness. The expedition's commander in chief, William Pepperrell, increased the rum ration to tamp down discontent, and the men drank heavily to numb themselves to the cold and forget their frustrations. The Louisbourg that Sullivan saw didn't look like the thriving Atlantic seaport that had been so prized by New France and so coveted by New England. It was a foggy, isolated outpost that held within its walls a volatile mix of mutinous Americans, supercilious redcoats, and defeated, demoralized French.

During the two years Sullivan spent there, he honed his metalworking skills, got married, and became a drunk. Nothing is known about his wife other than the unflattering description he provides in his confession, and after their loud fight in Boston, they seem to have permanently parted ways. "I unhappily Married a Wife, which proved a Torment to me, and made my Life uncomfortable," Sullivan says, "and she was given to take a Cup too much, and I for my Part took to the same." His drinking took its toll on his work in Louisbourg, and his behavior worsened to such a degree that his superiors demoted him. Provoked by his wife's "aggravating Tongue," Sullivan squandered his privileged position as an armorer and had to serve out the rest of his time as a common soldier.

Fortunately for Sullivan, Louisbourg didn't remain in British hands much longer. On October 18, 1748, after months of preliminaries, delegates from the major European powers met in Aix-la-Chapelle to end the war that had begun eight years earlier with Charles VI's deadly dish of mushrooms. They agreed to restore the map to the prewar boundaries, which meant among other things that England had to return Louisbourg to France. When news of the treaty's terms reached New England's shores in early 1749, people were livid. After mounting a successful siege against almost impossible odds, after enduring the frigid Louisbourg winter, a savage epidemic, and the condescension of British officers, the Americans now had to pick up and leave the fortress they fought so hard to capture. Partly in the hopes of calming the Americans' anger, Parliament agreed to reimburse the New England colonies for their role in the expedition, and Massachusetts was slated to receive the lion's share: more than £183,000, mostly in silver. Thomas Hutchinson planned to devote the sum entirely to retiring the colony's paper money by exchanging everyone's notes for coin, thereby putting enough silver into circulation to end Massachusetts's dependence on bills of credit.

While the windfall delighted hard-money advocates like Hutchinson, who saw Louisbourg as a long-awaited opportunity to finish off the specter of paper currency, it was the final insult for the men who actually went to war—farmers and laborers who relied on paper to trade goods and pay taxes. If any of the soldiers at Louisbourg had a twisted-enough sense of humor, it would have made a good joke: England's payment for the war, rather than being used to reward the men who fought it, would eventually deprive them of the currency they needed in their everyday lives. The incensed militiamen stationed at Louisbourg took a souvenir with them back to Massachusetts, a last bit of booty to commemorate their voided victory: the wrought-iron cross adorned with fleurs-de-lis that stood in the citadel's Catholic chapel. The cross remained in Massachusetts for centuries, and hung on the walls at Harvard University before it was returned to Canada in 1995 on the 250th anniversary of the siege.

Sullivan returned in 1748 or 1749 to Boston, a city he had last visited as a half-starved Irish immigrant waiting to be sold to the highest bidder. Now he was a free man with a marketable skill set, namely, a talent for metal engraving that he had perfected in the military. Sullivan found work as a silversmith but soon discovered a more lucrative outlet for his expertise: counterfeiting Massachusetts money. After his arrest in 1749 and his conviction and punishment the following year, he could have stopped forging notes and returned to the life of a craftsman. Instead, he resolved to become a moneymaker, and left Boston for Providence, Rhode Island, to start building his counterfeiting empire. Sullivan's reasons weren't complicated. He didn't think of himself as an alchemist infusing worthless paper with the value of precious metals, or as a class warrior trying to unseat colonial elites with a flood of cheap currency. He didn't counterfeit out of a metaphysical conviction or an allegiance to a particular social group. His reasons were simple. "I thought it was an easy Way of getting Money," he explains in his confession, a sentence that reflects how deeply American Sullivan had become during his seven years on the continent.

O N A SUMMER DAY IN 1752, two fugitives galloped through the dirt streets of Providence. The hooves of their horses struck the earth as they rode past the wharves and warehouses that stood along the river, past the taverns where tradesmen chugged tumblers of rum and the market where hawkers cried the contents of their carts. The horsemen didn't stop until they were in the meadowlands a few miles outside town. They dismounted while nearby cows grazed behind stone walls, and took out a pile of paper money that they began dividing up between them. Against such a bucolic backdrop, the man-made notes must have looked out of place—slips of yellow-brown paper inked with arbitrary insignia, as flimsy as the leaves dangling from the locust trees overhead.

When they had finished divvying up the cash, the fugitives got back on their horses and sped away, each in a different direction. Someone would come after them eventually, and the farther they made it into the countryside, the better their chances of escaping. But one of the men, once his partner had ridden out of sight, turned his horse around and returned to Providence. In town he gave himself up, hoping to receive a lighter sentence: he told the authorities he was Nicholas Stephens, a laborer from Dighton, Bristol County, and an accomplice to a counterfeiter named Owen Sullivan.

The Providence jail already held several of Sullivan's gang, who had recently been picked up for passing false £16 Rhode Island bills. On August 17, the *Boston Post Boy* accused Sullivan of engraving the plate for the forgeries—"he is now in the Country with a great Quantity of the aforesaid Bills," the newspaper warned—and promised a large reward from the government for his capture. With a price on his head and his associates behind bars, the counterfeiter decided to make a run for it. He split the remaining money with his partner and took off. He couldn't have known at the time that Stephens would ride back to Providence—toward the modest skyline cast by its taverns, churches, and inns, right into the center of town—and offer to testify against his former friend.

Colonial Americans had an expression for this kind of betrayal: they called it "turning king's evidence." Informants played a crucial role in convicting counterfeiters. The government needed their testimony to prove that the defendant paid money that he knew was false, since without establishing criminal intent, it was almost impossible to secure a conviction. Strictly speaking, spending forged notes wasn't illegal; what criminalized the act was the knowledge that the bills were bad. This convenient legal wrinkle meant that as long as there wasn't an abundance of incriminating evidence—like the plates and ink found on Sullivan when he was arrested in Boston—people caught with spurious notes could always plead ignorance by saying they believed the bills were genuine. Part of what made counterfeiting so hard to stamp out was how abstractly it was defined: the only thing that distinguished the culprit from the dupe was the thoughts passing through their respective skulls at the moment the money changed hands.

Sullivan was caught after a week in hiding. His captors delivered him to the jailhouse that stood near Towne Street, the winding thoroughfare that ran along the eastern shore of the Great Salt River. The seawater smell drifted up from the brine below the banks, and in the distance, ships bound for the West Indies sailed through the brackish tide with hulls full of rum, butter, and horses. Farther south, past the row of houses that lined Towne Street, a wooden drawbridge eighteen feet wide straddled the stream. Across its surface farmers herded livestock to town to be butchered and sold, and underneath, the muddy shells of oysters and clams glinted in the riverbed. The bridge had been there for eighty years, a prized piece of infrastructure in a town that had seen little growth since its founding in the early seventeenth century. As late as 1752, Providence still didn't have a post office, a customhouse, a schoolhouse, a bank, a printing press, or a newspaper. But in recent years local merchants had begun a lively export business, and with greater wealth came a growing population: the number of residents went from almost four thousand in 1730 to more than seven thousand by 1748. On the west side of the river, opposite the piers and storehouses arrayed below Towne Street, stood the shipyard where the boats that carried the colony's wares overseas were built. Despite the increasing amounts of money brought in by these ships, Providence remained what it had been for decades: an agrarian community, a place for people from nearby farms to trade, drink, and worship.

By the time of his arrest, Sullivan had spent two years in Providence forging Rhode Island currency, recruiting coconspirators, and polishing his engraving technique. He had come a long way since his early efforts in Boston, when the ink on his bills was so black that the authorities immediately recognized them as fakes. He had gone from novice to professional; even the *Boston Post Boy* admitted that his Rhode Island notes were "exceedingly well Counterfeited, so that without inspecting very narrowly, few but what may be deceived," a phrase that must have flattered the counterfeiter's vanity. At least two other newspapers—one in Boston, another in New York—reprinted the report, so that as early as the summer of 1752, colonists throughout the Northeast were reading about the moneymaker Owen Sullivan, a name that would become notorious before the decade was over.

Providence provided a good staging area for Sullivan's activities. Its small size and rural setting made his operation easier to conceal. Certain sights and sounds—freshly inked bills drying on a line, the squeaks and groans of a printing press—had to be hidden from inquisitive neighbors, and Providence offered more privacy than a densely inhabited city like Boston ever could. Local politics also worked to Sullivan's advantage. Providence's farmers dominated the Rhode Island General Assembly, where they used their political muscle to push for a plentiful currency. From 1710 to 1751, the Assembly approved nine paper money printings, despite vocal opposition from the merchants of Newport, Providence's more affluent neighbor to the south. The struggle between the two towns over the currency mirrored the money war being waged in Massachusetts at the same time: farmers wanted cheap paper to pay debts and exchange goods, while merchants needed a stable, coin-based currency for international commerce. Who better to satisfy Providence's demand for cash than a counterfeiter, whose infusions of phony capital weren't bound by the dictates of the law or the legislature?

WHEN SULLIVAN ARRIVED at the Providence jail in 1752, he found several members of his counterfeiting ring. These men weren't hardened criminals; they were farmers, millers, boatmen—people who dabbled in passing forged bills in order to earn a little something extra on the side. The prisoners were probably frightened by the time Sullivan got there, and unsure of how to plead their case. The engraver took control immediately: he promised his confederates that if they followed his instructions, all of them would walk free.

There was only one problem. Stephens confessed that he had received money from Sullivan that he knew was forged, which gave the government exactly what it needed to build a solid case against the counterfeiter: a sworn statement from a former accomplice. When Sullivan discovered Stephens's treachery, he was outraged. Not only had Stephens ridden into

Providence and surrendered like a coward, he had squealed, volunteering testimony that would surely convict Sullivan and possibly implicate the others.

Sullivan's anger didn't prevent him from thinking clearly about how to get his gang out of jail. He told them to plead not guilty, and to swear that they had considered the bills genuine. Sullivan would then declare he had intentionally deceived them—that they were his victims, not his collaborators—and enter a guilty plea. What's more, he would announce that he had hidden £4,000 in counterfeit money, and refuse to reveal the stockpile's location until the innocent men were released.

Sullivan had learned enough about colonial courts to know his offer was irresistible. A big bundle of spurious notes, along with a guilty plea and deposition from Stephens, proved too tempting to the Providence authorities, who promptly freed all of the prisoners except for the counterfeiter and the informant. From their point of view, nailing the ringleader was much more appealing than convicting a handful of small fish. The plan worked: once Sullivan's associates had been set free, he delivered the cache of forged money, confessed his guilt, and stood trial.

A grand jury indicted Sullivan, identified as "a Transient Person now confined in his Majesty's Gaol in Providence," of engraving a plate to counterfeit Rhode Island's currency "in order to defraud and cheat" unsuspecting colonists. Stephens had probably described the counterfeiter's activities in some detail, because the charges were unusually specific: the court accused Sullivan of starting to make the plate on June 12, finishing it on August 5, and then using it to produce "sundry false & counterfeit Bills in imitation of the true Bills of Publick Credit." In a puzzling twist, Stephens also faced charges, since he had incriminated himself in his confession. "[F]or the sake of unlawful gain," his indictment read, the laborer from Bristol County "did council and advise Owen Sullivan" in engraving the plate, printing the notes, and passing them. Both men pleaded guilty, and both were convicted.

In September 1752, two years to the month since his last punishment in Boston, Sullivan was led to the pillory across the street from the jailhouse and bolted between its wooden beams. He stood there, overlooking the crowd that had gathered to watch. An hour and a half after Sullivan had put his head and hands into the contraption, the constable emerged with a red-hot branding iron with the shape of the letter R at one end, for "incorrigible Rogue." Although punishments varied by colony, physical mutilation was typically reserved for criminals considered irredeemable, or repeat offenders like Sullivan, who would be forced to carry the mark of their crime for life. In this case, however, Sullivan convinced the authorities to show mercy, so the constable planted the brand above the hairline, where it would be less visible. The onlookers inhaled a strange smell: the stench of burning hair and skin mingling with the sweet odor of fermenting molasses from the nearby rum distilleries. Then the constable took out a blade to crop the convict's ears, but again, Sullivan had prevailed on the authorities to get his penalty reduced. Instead of slicing large pieces off the ears, the lawman only cut the edges, severing bloody strips from the counterfeiter's head while the residents of Providence stood staring.

Stephens's punishment was next. He had received the same sentence and, despite helping convict his former partner, wasn't as persuasive as Sullivan in his appeal for leniency. According to the inscrutable whims of the colonial authorities, Stephens faced the full force of the law: the constable burned the R into each of the criminal's cheeks and cropped both ears. Sullivan, freshly branded and bloodied, had talked his jailers into letting him attend the performance, to gloat over Stephens's suffering. But once he got there, the sight of the snitch so enraged him that he broke away from his keepers, seized a cutlass, and, swinging the sword in the air, urged the constable to do his duty. When the sentence was carried out to Sullivan's satisfaction, he vaulted into the crowd, fought his way through, and disappeared.

Sullivan had escaped in broad daylight while the entire Providence law enforcement establishment looked on. His keepers, whether from fear or incompetence, were incapable of holding him; he did what he liked, and when he fled, they couldn't recapture him. If this wasn't embarrassing enough, Sullivan returned to town a few days later to shame the authorities again. He declared that by turning himself in, he would do voluntarily what they couldn't do: put him in prison. The counterfeiter was promptly hauled back to jail and chained with heavy irons. Within a few days he broke out again, somehow having gotten hold of a sword, and the town officials, determined not to be further humiliated, sent men to chase him. "[T]hey pursu'd me very close, sent Post haste after me, and did all they could to Apprehend me," Sullivan recalls in his confession. But he eluded his pursuers, and traveled 150 miles west through Rhode Island and Connecticut to settle in Dutchess County, New York, where he began planning the next phase of his career.

Sullivan's performance at the pillory and subsequent jailbreaks provided just the right kind of kindling to fuel his burgeoning reputation. It helped that he had a flair for showmanship. There was no reason to return to jail after his first escape other than to demonstrate his daring and his brazen contempt for the law. His theatrics had the quality of a burlesque— taunting, humiliating, and outwitting his captors. But Sullivan wasn't just entertaining; he was also sympathetic. One account of his punishment in Providence called him "a man of good Address" who "found Means to prejudice the Populace in his Favour." It made sense for the crowd to commiserate with the counterfeiter. First his partner betrayed him, then he was punished for making money, an activity that inspired more admiration than indignation among the spectators standing below the pillory. Everyone wanted to make money—Sullivan's method was just more literal than most.

Sullivan also provided a service that many residents of Providence had patronized: cheap currency, virtually indistinguishable from the genuine article. There was always demand for paper money among the town's farmers and laborers, who needed it to pay down their debt and trade in the marketplace. For these people, Sullivan had an obvious appeal. Like them he came from humble origins—an Irish immigrant and a former indentured servant—but went on to make a fortune almost overnight. Many of the men and women standing within sight of the town pillory in September 1752 must have found something moving in the spectacle of an entrepreneur forced to suffer for his success.

Sullivan had more than just the popular desire for paper currency to thank for his growing celebrity. He also owed his fame to the public nature of punishment in colonial America, which gave the counterfeiter a soapbox and a captive audience. In Sullivan's day the government would discipline the convict publicly, in front of his peers, to shame him and to deter onlookers from following in his footsteps. While specific punishments varied by jurisdiction, the sentence passed on Sullivan and Stephens was fairly typical for property crimes; burglars and thieves were likely to face the same penalty. Since long-term imprisonment was rare, jails served mostly as holding areas for convicts awaiting trial and debtors who defaulted on their loans, which helps explain why they were so poorly guarded. Punishment didn't happen within a cell hidden from sight but outside, in full view. The whip, the branding iron, the pillory, and the gallows gave colonists their community rituals—entertaining and edifying theater pieces about the consequences of crime. But as Sullivan understood, once you had the stage you could do what you wanted with it. All it took was a little imagination to depart from the official script and spin a more interesting story line. The treachery of Stephens, the audacity of Sullivan, the helplessness of the authorities—these were the things people remembered from the moneymaker's Providence premiere.

IT WAS IN DUTCHESS COUNTY that Sullivan made his third and final effort at being a counterfeiter. His experiences in Boston and Providence taught him the fundamentals of the craft: how to carve a plate from copper, how to recruit people to print and pass the notes, and, crucially, how to dodge the law. His name had started to become familiar to the readers of New England newspapers, and his antics at the Providence pillory surely enlivened the conversations of more than a few colonists at the local taverns. If Sullivan had stopped then—if he had returned to Providence, served the rest of his jail term, and renounced his criminal past—he wouldn't have left much of an impression on the historical record. He would have been remembered as a minor crook, if at all: just one out of the countless low-level moneymakers who plied their trade throughout colonial America. Instead, Sullivan decided to give free rein to his ambition, assembling a counterfeiting venture on an unprecedented scale. Within the next four years, he would produce thousands of pounds of fake currency, develop an extensive network of accomplices spanning several colonies, and pro-voke considerable panic among the leaders of colonial governments, who scrambled to respond to the Irishman's onslaught.

Sullivan set up his headquarters in an area called the Oblong, a rectan-gular strip of land on Dutchess County's far eastern boundary. Two miles wide and sixty miles long, it ran along New York's border with Connecti-cut, and had been fiercely contested by the two colonies since the early seventeenth century. Although Connecticut officially ceded the area to New York in 1731, the exact location of the dividing line remained dis-puted well into the nineteenth century. Sullivan settled in a place called Dover, a loosely defined region that included a handful of hamlets and settlements scattered along the New York–Connecticut frontier.

Dover presented a number of advantages to anyone who wanted to do something illegal on a large scale. In the early 1750s it was only sparsely inhabited, its settlers few and far between. German immigrants had been the region's first colonizers. By the time Sullivan arrived, poor squatters had taken up residence on East Mountain, scouring a subsistence life from the inhospitable soil of its hillsides and valleys. Farther south, on a smaller hill, stood the meetinghouse of a Quaker colony. Life there was basic: when the young men traveled to Massachusetts to find women to marry, they passed around their only pair of good shoes. In the next few years, homesteaders from New England would start streaming into the area, but in 1752, Dover was still populated principally by enterprising Germans, starving squatters, and barefoot Quakers.

Pioneers are usually too concerned with surviving to be curious about what their neighbors are doing, particularly if their neighbors live far away. Even if they had wanted to check in on one another, the terrain wasn't easy to traverse. Two rivers ran through the lowlands of Dover, watering a large swathe of thickly wooded marshes and swamps. The boggy wilderness offered excellent places to hide counterfeiting tools that would be impossible to see through the layers of foliage. The wetlands' tangled growth also concealed something else: wolves and panthers, which stalked the damp ground in great quantities looking for deer. There were so many of them that the government regularly offered rewards for killing the predators: all you had to do to collect was bring the animal's head and pelt to a local magistrate. In a place like Dover, Sullivan wouldn't have to deal with unexpected visitors. If the forbidding terrain didn't keep people away, the threat of wild creatures lurking behind the trees certainly would.

Another virtue of the region was its contested history, which made the already difficult task of capturing and convicting Sullivan nearly impossible. Since the counterfeiter would operate on the border and forge the currencies of both New York and Connecticut, intercolonial cooperation would be essential for apprehending him. But the disputed status of the Oblong meant that officials from the two colonies weren't inclined to help each other police the area. Whoever wanted to catch Sullivan would not only have to wade long distances through wolf-infested swamps; he would also face the challenging chore of getting two colonies with a history of conflict to work together.

If his choice of location is any indication, Sullivan seems to have thought things through. Once he had a base of operations, he set to work gathering the necessities. One of these was a hideout, and the hills around Dover had many promising candidates: spacious caves that had been carved into the cliffs by rivulets. The size of these caverns was impressive; one of them, known locally as the Dover Stone Church, had an arched portal and a vaulted stone interior that resembled a Gothic cathedral. Sullivan picked out a cave cut into the side of a small bluff, located near a particularly isolated corner of a forested swamp. He camouflaged the chasm's mouth with brush and a tree stump so the entrance wouldn't be visible. Inside, a long corridor led to a sizable room that Sullivan covered with wooden panels, presumably to prevent it from collapsing, or perhaps to lend the interior a cozier atmosphere. His grotto was certainly comfortable. There were tables and chairs, places to eat and to sleep. An opening in the rock formed a natural window, letting in light that illuminated the chamber.

Sullivan also put together a gang to help produce and dispense his forgeries, a criminal crew that would come to be known as the Dover Money Club. Most of these men wore a brand mark on their cheeks or had their ears cropped, and they displayed these disfigurements proudly, as the insignia of their outlaw brotherhood. One of them was Joseph Boyce, an attractive, well-built convict with short black hair. On his hand was a scar in the shape of the letter T, imprinted by a constable's iron several years before for thieving. Originally from Salem, Massachusetts, he and his son, Joseph Jr., had spent the last decade churning out fake bills of various colonies as a father-son counterfeiting team. They were an accomplished pair of moneymakers and had been in the business much longer than Sullivan.

Without the Boyces, Sullivan would probably never have found out about the Oblong; they had been there as early as 1742, counterfeiting currency with a group of accomplices in the rugged wetlands along the New York–Connecticut border. In fact, their undertaking was so successful that within a few years they had aroused the alarm of the governors of New York, Connecticut, and Massachusetts, who exchanged agitated letters about the moneymakers. In early 1745, Jonathan Law, the governor of Connecticut, wrote Governor George Clinton of New York to complain: "the place where this Wickedness is supposed to be carryd on is the Oblong," Law declared, "and it is possible that great Quantities of it are handed about by a confederated Gang." In April, William Shirley, the governor of Massachusetts, urged his counterparts in Connecticut and New York to do everything in their power to capture and convict members of the band. "The Heads of this Confederacy have been bold and daring in their Villanies and have practised the same hitherto with so much success, that it will be next to impossible to Suppress this great Mischief without Suppressing them," he warned.

Despite their tough talk, the governors did little to stop the Boyces. The job was left to the initiative of a private citizen, a native of Uxbridge, Massachusetts, named Robert Clarke, who first encountered the gang when one of its members swindled him. After discovering he had been cheated, Clarke confronted the criminals, who tried pacifying him by offering him large quantities of forged bills. According to an affidavit filed by Clarke in the spring of 1745, the counterfeiters "Endeavour'd to make him one of their party," hoping to secure his services as a passer. He feigned interest and drew himself deeper into the ring in order to collect evidence that could be used against the moneymakers.

Clarke would end up giving the authorities a detailed picture of the Oblong crew's operations: they forged the notes of multiple colonies and enlisted passers, whom they dispatched to distant locations to buy horses, cattle, and other goods that could either be used or resold for genuine money. Clarke swiped two of the gang's plates—one for printing Rhode Island currency, and another unfinished panel for making New York money—along with some printing implements, and resolved to turn the incriminating items over to the authorities. When law officials from New York refused to help, he found a magistrate in Connecticut who agreed to bring the criminals in. Clarke managed to lure the young Boyce and his coconspirator Hurlbut across the border into Connecticut, where they were seized and carried off to the New Haven jail. Hurlbut ratted out his confederates, fingering no fewer than twenty-two of them. While Clarke's efforts succeeded in dispersing the Oblong gang, many of them remained at large, including Boyce and Hurlbut, who escaped from the New Haven jailhouse shortly after their arrest.

A STUDENT OF COUNTERFEITING could learn a lot from the Boyces. The most important lesson was that local governments had a hard time enforcing the law. Nothing resembling a professional police force existed: instead, ordinary colonists were elected or appointed to be sheriff, constable, or justice of the peace. Arresting criminals was only one of their duties; they spent much of their time on more mundane work, like inspecting taverns for drunks, chasing runaway pigs, and fixing potholes in the road. When it came to bringing down a counterfeiting gang tucked away in a remote corner of the countryside, the lawmen simply didn't have the manpower or the money to do the job.

Moneymaking was also more complicated than most crimes. Simple offenses like larceny involved a culprit and a victim, but a counterfeiter's impact was more diffuse. An engraver like Sullivan didn't have to meet his marks to swindle them, and he would never know how many people had touched the paper printed from his plates. If robbery worked in a straight line—a thief stealing something from a shopkeeper—then counterfeiting was a set of concentric circles radiating from a single center. A plate that Sullivan engraved in Dover could be used by printers in several different colonies to manufacture fake bills; passers then put the notes into circulation, where they would continue to defraud people until they were identified and destroyed. Faced with such an elaborate criminal web, it's no surprise that colonial officials weren't up to the task. Like most Americans, they lived in small communities where people knew one another by name and interacted on a daily basis. In a society that still revolved around face-to-face relationships, counterfeiting presented a unique threat. Unlike a shopkeeper robbed by a thief, someone cheated with counterfeit money couldn't confront the real perpetrator, the engraver who had set everything in motion. All the mark could do was to identify whoever passed him the note, and that individual could either be another victim, oblivious to the fact that the bill was fake, or the lowest minion in a counterfeiting venture.

Counterfeiting thrived on anonymity. It reflected colonial America's broader gradual movement toward a more impersonal world, where people who didn't know each other personally could exchange goods in a common marketplace. A seller didn't need to know a buyer's name, history, or reputation to do business: if his money was good—if the notes carried the right symbols in the right places—that was enough. The man who mimicked these symbols could rob people without ever putting a hand on them, dispersing his counterfeits through a chain of proxies.

Anyone who wanted to take down a counterfeiting ring would have to start with a passer and work his way up the ladder. This would be difficult, tedious work, and it took someone as motivated as Robert Clarke to get the job done. He had to gather enough evidence for warrants and convictions, persuade the authorities to help, and capture the culprits. Doing all this within one colony was difficult enough; across several jurisdictions, it was even harder. It didn't help that governments kept trying to dodge responsibility. When the governor of Rhode Island proposed that the colony's legislature offer to pay all costs for apprehending and prosecuting members of the Boyces' Oblong gang, the assemblymen refused, declaring that the expenses should be borne by the government of the colony where the crime was committed.

The governor had good reason to urge the legislators to take action. Rhode Island currency was the Boyces' specialty, despite the fact that the

Oblong lay more than a hundred miles west of Rhode Island. But a colony's currency didn't just circulate within its own territory; it fed into a regional money market that extended over multiple colonies. Paper money was originally intended only for residents of the same colony, but by the middle of the eighteenth century, currencies in New England mingled freely as trade expanded. Money from another colony was usually discounted, except in the cities, where it often preserved its full value. This greatly expanded the opportunities for counterfeiting. It also made the legal situation even murkier. Officials didn't know for sure if a counterfeiter could be prosecuted in one colony for forging the currency of another. In their correspondence about the Boyces, Governor Law of Connecticut explained the predicament to Governor Clinton of New York. "Our chief Justices are in doubt whether ye Matters of fact comitted in your Govt can be tryd here," Law wrote, "so crave your Advice whether they shall be sent for Tryal in your Courts." Extraditing moneymakers to the right jurisdiction was always an option, but the authorities were understandably reluctant to devote their meager law enforcement resources to taking on someone else's problem.

The growing interconnectedness of the American economy meant that no colony could make policy on its own, not even one as populous and powerful as Massachusetts. Under the direction of Thomas Hutchinson, the colony had spent a year retiring its notes. From March 1750 to March 1751, Hutchinson and the other members of the exchange committee sat in the upper room of Boston's Old State House, exchanging colonists' ragged, soiled old bills for silver and copper coins. But eliminating paper currency proved to be trickier than Hutchinson expected. There weren't enough precious metals to redeem all the bills, so the treasury had to issue people new notes to use as provisional currency until they could be fully compensated in coin. In addition, many people simply refused to redeem their paper money, continuing to use the notes among themselves; more than a year and a half after the end of the redemption period, almost £132,000 worth of the old bills remained outstanding. And the money that Hutchinson successfully withdrew from circulation was soon replaced, as notes from neighboring colonies poured in. Foreign paper posed such a threat to Hutchinson's plan that the legislature passed a law requiring anyone elected to office in Massachusetts to swear under oath that he hadn't traded in other colonies' bills.

What Hutchinson realized, and what counterfeiters already knew, was that individual colonies needed to act in concert to get anything done. If one colony tried to print less currency or eliminate paper altogether, the notes of another would start flooding in, as people tried to satisfy the demand for paper credit. As long as colonial governments were incapable of coordinating policy and colonists wanted cheap cash, counterfeiting would continue to flourish. Benjamin Franklin captured the problem with his famous "Join, or Die" cartoon that showed the colonies as cut-up pieces of a snake that would die if they didn't come together. Franklin drew the snake in 1754, on the eve of the French and Indian War, to urge Americans to unite in the face of the threat. Franklin's vision wasn't just useful for fighting the war that had broken out on the border; it was also the only way to combat a formidable internal enemy, the counterfeiters who inhabited the ungovernable gaps in America's loosely strung lattice of colonial authority.

THE INTERDEPENDENCE OF COLONIAL economies wasn't lost on Sullivan, who, during his four years as head of the Dover Money Club, was constantly on the move. He didn't stay holed up at his hideout in the hills; he traveled throughout the Northeast, funneling his bills into a wide range of local markets. The counterfeiter's strategy was simple. First he boarded at someone's house, preferably somewhere rural and remote. There he acquired engraving and printing tools—copperplates, ink, and paper— enlisted locals to help, and churned out fake currency. He kept some of the notes for himself and used the rest to pay everyone off before continuing on his way. As he moved from one place to the next, he left behind engraved plates that his contacts continued to use to print currency long after he was gone. Those who got caught surrendered Sullivan's name or one of his known aliases to the authorities, who slowly pieced together the scope of the counterfeiter's enterprise from the scattered testimony of his operatives.

In the summer of 1753, Jedediah Cady, a Connecticut native in his late twenties, housed Sullivan and a few others at his secluded home in Killingly. Like Dover, Killingly was ideally located to be a counterfeiting haven: it occupied the northeastern corner of Connecticut, not far from the border with Massachusetts and Rhode Island. From Killingly, a criminal could move contraband into three different colonies. Cady helped Sullivan make a pile of Rhode Island money, and when they finished, the counterfeiter paid Cady with £400 in fake bills. Cady buried most of the notes underground and gave the rest to a local Indian to pass, with the understanding that they would split the profits. Cady couldn't have been very discreet in his dealings, because by November, he had been picked up on counterfeiting charges. He admitted his guilt and revealed Sullivan's role in the venture, although by then the engraver had returned to the safety of the Oblong. Cady's ears were cropped and his cheeks branded with the letter C, for "Counterfeiter."

Cady's case wasn't unique. The same scenario repeated itself in many different villages and towns: a man was arrested for spending bad bills, and under examination, confessed that Sullivan had recently visited the area. So many of the people taken into custody admitted a connection to Sullivan that the authorities assumed that every counterfeiting case originated with the Oblong moneymaker. When a farmer from Massachusetts named Joseph Munroe was caught passing forged money in Newport, his captors asked him if he knew Sullivan, to which Munroe cryptically replied that he had "heard tell of such a man." At his interrogation the next day, Munroe revealed that he met Sullivan six weeks before in the forest near his home in Swansea, Bristol County, and received fifty-five notes from the engraver. Some of these he spent, and some he placed in a small sugar box that he hid in a nearby hedge. In the same hedge, Munroe confessed, Sullivan had concealed another sugar box with about a hundred counterfeit bills inside, its lid sealed shut with pitch.

Stashing bills at a secret site made sense, since carrying the notes on your person or keeping them in your house was dangerous. Passers of false currency wanted to minimize risk whenever possible: as the most exposed part of a counterfeiting ring, they lived in constant fear of being arrested. When Sullivan surfaced in the woods near their houses and asked for their help, the temptation must have been overpowering. It would have been hard to resist the lure of making money, the delicious sense of satisfaction as they became richer than their neighbors in a matter of minutes or hours. But once the engraver departed and the passers faced the prospect of spending the counterfeit bills, anxiety set in. There would be no shortage of tense moments, like watching the tavern keeper's face as he squints to examine the note just handed to him—maybe it's a higher denomination than he's used to seeing, or he's had problems with fake money before. Perhaps he read an article in the newspaper about how to detect forged bills, like the ones printed in the *New-York Gazette* and the *New-York Mercury*, and he knows exactly what to look for: a stroke that's too thin or too crooked, an unusually large space between certain letters. Waiting for him to make up his mind couldn't have been easy, but without these everyday acts of daring, Sullivan's notes would never have circulated.

Sometimes the stress proved too much. Ichabod Ide, a laborer who received a stack of fake money from Sullivan in Rehoboth, Massachusetts, decided to get rid of his counterfeits. He had already spent some of them: he bought a horse from his brother and a piece of gold from a tavern keeper in Connecticut, and repaid an outstanding debt. But, "being apprehensive I should be apprehended," as Ide later recalled, he wrapped the remaining notes in a rag, tied a stone to the pouch, and threw it as far as he could into the Seekonk River, on the border between Rhode Island and Massachusetts. He was arrested anyway about a week later, after an accomplice gave him up to the authorities. Ide confessed to his relationship with Sullivan, and explained how the two of them had hidden a plate and printing materials behind a large rock in the woods near Worcester. After pleading guilty, Ide stood in the Newport pillory and lost his ears to the sheriff's sword.

WHILE TRAMPING ACROSS THE COUNTRY, Sullivan lingered in some places longer than in others. One of his favorite spots was the area around the Merrimack River, the swiftly flowing waterway that runs southward through the heart of New Hampshire until veering east through Massachusetts to empty into the Atlantic. The counterfeiter did a brisk trade in the settlements that had sprung up along the river, populated by families who planted crops in the fertile floodplain and fished salmon and shad from the rapids. The valley had recently been the site of a ferocious boundary dispute between New Hampshire and Massachusetts. Emissaries from both sides had petitioned the king to settle the squabble, and when he decided in favor of New Hampshire, the Massachusetts legislature was so distressed that it sent twenty-nine-year-old Thomas Hutchinson—then a rising public official and a loyal servant of the Boston establishment—to plead their case. Hutchinson made useful political contacts in London but failed to persuade the king to reverse his decision, leaving the upper Merrimack firmly in the hands of New Hampshire.

Few people knew the region as well as Robert Rogers, a man who would become the most famous of Sullivan's many collaborators—even more famous than Sullivan himself. Six feet tall and athletically built, Rogers was the consummate frontiersman. Born in a log cabin, he roamed New Hampshire's dense forests from an early age and, as a teenager, saw combat when Indian raiding parties surged across the Northeast after the capture of Louisbourg in the summer of 1745. Rogers served as a scout during the war, a job that required him to tread silently through the woods looking for approaching Indians. The fighting on the New Hampshire frontier left a trail of scalped corpses, slain cattle, and demolished homes. No one was immune to the carnage—not even Rogers's family, who returned to their farm one day to find that the Indians had burned their house, killed their cattle, and hacked down every tree in their orchard but one. Rogers's father survived the war but suffered a bizarre death five years later, when, at dusk on a winter day, he approached a friend's hunting camp dressed from head to toe in bearskin. The dark figure looked so much like a bear that the friend, thrilled to find such large game, shot him fatally. The friend was so upset that he could never again tell the story without crying, but it was a fitting end for a frontiersman, who might have been flattered by the resemblance if it hadn't killed him.

When Rogers went hunting later that year, he found a different kind of creature, something rarer than a bear and considerably more dangerous: Sullivan, who emerged from behind the pine trees to greet him. The counterfeiter showed him a wad of fake bills, and gave him a twenty-shilling note in exchange for pasturing his horse. Sullivan also told him that he wanted to buy three yoke of oxen, and they agreed to meet two days later at the farm of Rogers's friend Ebenezer Martin to make the trade.

Sullivan and Rogers had a lot in common. Both men had learned how to traverse tough ground fighting Indians on the frontier: while Sullivan repulsed attacks at the St. George River in Maine, Rogers was in New Hampshire, weaving his way through the trees to tell settlers of the enemy's movements. Like Sullivan, Rogers was restless. As a young man he dabbled in farming and hunting but couldn't settle on a trade. He traveled widely, wandering the British, French, and Indian quarters of the continent with the same peripatetic spirit that drove Sullivan across the Atlantic and throughout the Northeast. They both preferred the backwoods—inaccessible, unpopulated places that provided a vast and varied haunt for their activities—though, as always, Sullivan's reasons were more practical. He filled the terrain's unfrequented nooks with paper notes and copperplates, covered by rocks or buried in the undergrowth.

Whether by playing to their affinities or to the frontiersman's lust for cash, Sullivan easily seduced Rogers. The eager recruit secured some oxen and brought them to the appointed place, but the counterfeiter never showed up. Undeterred, Rogers sought out Sullivan and became one of his many coconspirators along the Merrimack. He continued until late January 1755, when a warrant for his arrest was issued by Meshech Weare, a justice of the Superior Court in Portsmouth, the colonial capital, and the speaker of New Hampshire's House of Representatives. It warned of an extensive counterfeiting conspiracy, with "Just Grounds to Suspect that there are many Persons Concerned." Written below, in Weare's elaborate hand, were nineteen names, Rogers's among them.

The trial that took place before the Inferior Court at Rumford (now Concord) on February 7 generated many pages of testimony, taken both from the defendants and from witnesses called by the court. By then Sullivan had fled the area, but his name loomed large over the proceedings. People recalled encounters with Sullivan, divulged glimpses of their neighbor's suspicious behavior and snippets of eavesdropped conversations—bits and pieces that together composed a clear view of the counterfeiter's Merrimack outfit. Sullivan had arrived as early as March 1754. His most important contact was Benjamin Winn, a carpenter who housed him for two or three months. The engraver cut a plate for making New Hampshire money while Winn built a printing press, and the two men produced about £15,000 worth of forged notes.

Winn's wife hated Sullivan. She complained that he made unreasonable demands, like insisting on having chicken or fresh meat on his plate every day, and swore that she would never board him again, not even for £1,000. Sullivan's irritability no doubt had to do with his heavy drinking.

He was rarely sober, and his alcoholism made him prone to explosive fits of rage. When one of Sullivan's associates introduced him to a potential new recruit named John McCurdy and McCurdy rebuffed the counterfeiter's advances, Sullivan erupted. "Damn you for a pack of fools," he told his associate. "I never was concerned with such a pack of damned fools before."

Sullivan had always had a hot temper. Fighting with his wife five years earlier led to his first arrest in Boston, after she accused him of moneymaking loudly enough for the neighbors to hear. In Providence, Nicholas Stephens's betrayal had made Sullivan so furious that he publicly shamed his former partner at the pillory. The character sketched by the statements before the Rumford court was just as angry. But the charisma that leavened his wrath seemed to have vanished, replaced by something more brooding and choleric. The loyalty Sullivan displayed at the Providence jailhouse when he committed himself to freeing his imprisoned confederates had disappeared; now he lashed out at them over trifles. His life had acquired the monotony of a professional criminal: he made money and moved on—not with the light step of an impatient, enterprising youth but with the heavy gait of a traveling salesman weary of the road. Perhaps it was the itinerant lifestyle, or the alcohol, or all the time spent by himself in the woods, but the confidence man had lost his charm.

In his examination before the court, Rogers had relatively little to say about Sullivan's temperament. He played naive and tried to persuade the justices of the peace that he barely knew the counterfeiter. When they asked him how he had met Sullivan, he replied in a way calculated to convey his innocence:

> I saw a man when I was hunting in Goffstown near Ebenezer
>   Martin's house that called himself John McDaniel, and had
>   some conversation with him. He wanted to buy a number
>   of fat cattle and told me he would pay me as much as they

would fetch in any market, and give me my money and that
it would go through all the laws in any of the provinces, and
maintained that his money was good.

Rogers explained that he appeared with the oxen at the rendezvous but
Sullivan didn't come, so he sold them to someone else. When the justices
asked if he knew that Sullivan "could make money or plates, or had so
designed any such thing," the frontiersman flatly denied it. "No, never,"
he told the court. "I saw him only that one time."

Rogers was lying through his teeth. Perjury wasn't always a bad tactic,
but in this case it wouldn't work, since other testimony contradicted Rogers by indicating that the two had more contact after their first meeting in
the woods. The Rumford court released Rogers on bond and summoned
him to stand trial before the Superior Court at Portsmouth on February 12.
Rogers was terrified. A conviction at Portsmouth would mean branding,
cropping, or death. Determined to dodge the charge, he traveled the forty-
odd miles to Portsmouth and, with only five days until his trial, considered
his options. What he needed was the protection of a powerful official, but
to win favor, Rogers needed leverage, something he could offer in return.
Fortunately, another war with the French and their Indian allies had broken out, and with it came a window of opportunity just wide enough for
Rogers to make his escape.

IN THE SPRING OF 1754, while Sullivan stalked the shores of the Merrimack, George Washington marched through the Pennsylvania backwoods,
his boots muddy from a night of heavy rain. Then a twenty-two-year-old
lieutenant colonel in the Virginia militia, Washington and his company of
forty soldiers followed their Indian guide over the damp earth until they
reached the rim of a small hollow shortly after sunrise. In the glen below
was a French camp. The Frenchmen had just woken up, and someone

was cooking breakfast; the smell wafted up to Washington's men, perched motionless with their muskets ready. No one knows who fired first, but the brief battle that followed left thirteen French corpses on the valley floor and saw another twenty-one taken prisoner by Washington.

These were the first casualties in what would become a decisive struggle for control of the American continent, the culmination of more than a century of strife between England and France. War had been brewing for several years, and arrived just in time for Rogers, who used it to duck his counterfeiting charges and, later, to boost his personal fame. The Treaty of Aix-la-Chapelle, which ended the last colonial conflict in 1748—the war that had brought Sullivan to Louisbourg—resolved nothing; neither side emerged with significant gains, and it was only a matter of time before the struggle for territory sparked another confrontation. Louisbourg, restored to the French under the terms of the treaty, continued to frustrate British ambitions in the North Atlantic, and tensions soared when the French built a fort on the isthmus linking Nova Scotia to the Canadian mainland, in present-day New Brunswick.

An even more volatile flashpoint lay farther south, in the upper Ohio River valley, where a French military buildup on the western borders of Virginia and Pennsylvania caused growing alarm among British colonists. When the governor of Virginia sent Washington to lead an expedition against the French at the forks of the Ohio River, it prompted the skirmish in the glen that triggered a wider war. The fighting would spread to Europe, eventually engulfing every major European power and their colonies all over the globe in what Winston Churchill later called history's first world war. Europeans called it the Seven Years' War, while the colonists used their enemies' names, labeling it the French and Indian War.

As with the last conflict, England expected the American colonies to contribute troops to the effort. Rogers had enough military experience to convince Major Joseph Frye of the Massachusetts militia to hire him as an enlisting agent. In January 1755, with money that Frye provided, Rogers signed up twenty-four colonists and had them gather in Portsmouth. But he was arrested before he could arrange their passage to Massachusetts, and the men remained there, waiting for him.

While in Portsmouth awaiting trial, Rogers realized that his two dozen recruits were powerful bargaining chips. He contacted New Hampshire's governor, Benning Wentworth, and offered to hand over the men in exchange for his freedom. It was an appealing offer, as Wentworth needed troops for an expedition against Fort St. Frédéric, a French garrison on Lake Champlain. The governor arranged for Rogers's release and made him a captain in the New Hampshire regiment, commanding a company of his recruits. When news of Rogers's defection reached Boston, Major Frye was outraged. Frye complained to Governor William Shirley, who in turn wrote Wentworth a letter requesting the return of the soldiers. Wentworth deflected the plea, replying that the matter was out of his hands.

Rogers so successfully ingratiated himself with his superiors that in April, when fresh evidence of the frontiersman's counterfeiting career surfaced, nothing came of it. The incriminating items had come from Carty Gilman, a shoemaker who was arrested for passing bad bills. When the officer came to apprehend Gilman, he saw the shoemaker put a piece of paper in his mouth and start chewing it into scraps small enough to swallow. The man grabbed Gilman, pried open his jaws, and wrested out what was left, tattered and soaked with spittle. The half-chewed morsel in Gilman's mouth was a letter, still partly legible. "Gilman, for God's sake do the work that you promised that you would do," it read. "By no means fail or you will destroy me forever, for my life lays at your providence. Once more I adjure you by your Maker to do it, for why should such an honest man be killed?" The signature belonged to Robert Rogers. In addition to the letter, two counterfeit notes were found on Gilman. During his interrogation, Gilman swore that Rogers had given him the bills, along with several other fakes.

Rogers presumably wanted Gilman to destroy the evidence and keep quiet about their dealings. Actually, Rogers had nothing to worry about. Someone who knew the terrain of the Northeast as intimately as he did was too valuable an asset to be wasted on the gallows. After a few humiliating defeats early in the war, the British realized they needed to do a better job adapting their forces to the realities of the American landscape. The French and their Indian allies organized units that could fight in the forests, using the cover of the woods to launch guerrilla attacks. Rogers helped develop the British equivalent, drawing on his experiences as a scout and his skills as a frontiersman to create a light infantry corps trained in woodland warfare. These commandos were more mobile and versatile than traditional soldiers accustomed to the European style, which consisted of pitched battles between large, strictly regimented formations.

Rogers' Rangers, as his men came to be called, had many military successes, and by 1759, their numbers had grown to more than one thousand, spread across six companies. Thanks to his tactical innovations and a talent for publicity, Rogers became a celebrated figure at home and abroad. He wrote three books, published in England in the 1760s—his journals, an account of North America, and a play—that helped cement his reputation. To European readers, he offered stories of an American wilderness teeming with exotic savages and devious Frenchmen, an alluring if not wholly accurate vision of the New World. But while Rogers fascinated Europeans, his real legacy was at home. He represented a distinctly American war hero: a white man who fused aspects of both Indian and European fighting techniques to create a new kind of combat. In the centuries following Rogers's death in 1795, his reputation grew. Today's U.S. Army Rangers consider Rogers their forefather and require recruits to read his "rules of ranging," written during the French and Indian War only a couple of years after his trial at Rumford. If it weren't for Sullivan, Rogers might never have organized his Rangers and become a legend to later generations.

While Sullivan shared certain traits with Robert Rogers, he also bore a resemblance to an even better-known American, Benjamin Franklin. Both made paper money, although in different capacities: Franklin printed it, while Sullivan counterfeited it. Both also had a gift for deception that they discovered early in life. When Franklin was sixteen, he wrote a letter purporting to be from a widow named Silence Dogood and slid it under his brother James's door. James, who published the *New-England Courant*, wouldn't have run the piece if he had known its true author, but Benjamin's counterfeit was so convincing—he even disguised his handwriting—that it appeared on the newspaper's front page the following week. Emboldened by the success of his first confidence trick, Franklin went on to cultivate a variety of fake personas; his most famous, Poor Richard, offered aphoristic bits of wisdom in a series of best-selling books. "Let all men know thee," he told his readers, "but no man know thee thoroughly."

Sullivan took the advice to heart. As a counterfeiter, he had experience with false facades, and like Franklin, used pseudonyms to mask his identity. Rogers and the other members of the Merrimack network knew Sullivan as James Tice or John McDaniel. These were just a couple of the many aliases that the counterfeiter used; others included John Pierson, Isaac Washington, and Benjamin Parlon. Even Owen Sullivan was a fake name, although his best known; he reinvented himself so often that his real name is unknown. Aliases helped him remain anonymous. If the townsfolk knew that Sullivan the moneymaker was passing through, they might notify the authorities. Aliases also shielded his accomplices, who, even if they knew the counterfeiter's identity, could deny that they had met Sullivan. Colonial lawmen had few resources for identifying criminals. With no central database to consult and no system for sharing information with their counterparts in other colonies, the authorities relied on a name and a physical description in catching a culprit, an imperfect method at best.

Sullivan's various names reflected how dispersed and disconnected his enterprise was. As James Tice, he made New Hampshire money; as Isaac Washington, he handed out Rhode Island bills. Once he quit an area, he had no control over what happened to the plates and the notes he left behind. The strategy had its advantages. As a colleague rather than a boss, he could concentrate on making as much money as possible without worrying about preserving his authority. But his hands-off approach also meant that he couldn't affect how people used his products. Injecting huge quantities of cash into small communities had consequences. Many spent their new wealth in predictable ways: one purchased a barrel of Spanish wine, and another bought drinks for everyone at the tavern. But Sullivan's money could also empower more desperate men, with more violent minds.

THE SOUND OF GUNSHOTS FROM a nearby estate woke the neighboring farmers in Wilton, Connecticut, on the night of April 26, 1754. When they rose from bed and looked out the window, they saw fences from a field in flames, the wooden posts incandescent against the black sky. As the wind picked up, the blaze grew. A gang of robbers had started the fire after trying to steal cattle and being shot at by the men hired by the cows' owner to stand guard. When the locals ran to smother the flames, the thieves set more fires and escaped. The gang returned a week later to take their revenge. They snuck into the barn where the cattle were, cut the tongue out of one of the cows, and started another fire. The flames were discovered before they could do much damage, but the arsonists got away.

The crew was led by a former collaborator of Sullivan's, David Sanford. The two had counterfeited New York bills at Sanford's home in Salem, a town in the Oblong about forty miles south of Sullivan's Dover headquarters. From the start, money brought out the worst in Sanford. When a couple of fellow travelers on a Connecticut road confronted him about spending fake notes in taverns along the way, Sanford offered them £1,000 each for their silence and, if that didn't work, threatened to kill them if they squealed. "Say nothing," he said as they neared the next tavern, "but go with me, and I will make Gentlemen of you." They didn't expose him then, but the next day, after Sanford was arrested for passing counterfeit money in Waterbury, they came forward to tell the justice of the peace what they knew. Their testimony proved incriminating enough for Sanford to be convicted on counterfeiting charges in New Haven on February 26, 1754. He soon escaped from jail and slipped over the New York border to Salem, where he assembled a criminal ring and swore vengeance on those who had imprisoned him. From Salem, Sanford and his men launched nighttime raids into Connecticut, terrorizing the countryside near the southern tip of the Oblong. They focused on the farmlands between Ridgefield and Norwalk, a gentler stretch of land than the craggy terrain farther north, made up of cascading hills that ran southward to the sands of the Long Island Sound.

Sanford's cronies shared his taste for destruction. One of them, Joseph Nichols, was convicted of forging the deed for his house. He resolved to avenge himself by burning down the house that he had acquired illegally, and then setting fire to the home of the justice of the peace who prosecuted him. When he arrived at his old address, he looked through the window and saw his daughter Abigail inside, weaving. He asked her why she was still in the house, and Abigail replied that she wanted to finish her work. She would pay a price if she did, her father sneered, because he and Sanford would have the building burning by nightfall. Nichols demanded that she hand over all the bullets in the house, and when she refused, he pulled out a gun. Before he left he promised to kill her if she ratted on him. Shaken, the girl worked up the courage to tell a neighbor what had happened, and the alarmed villagers posted men to keep watch. After sunset, the watchmen caught a glimpse of Sanford's dog and knew the criminals were nearby. Soon flames flared in the dark and the residents rushed to extinguish them. They put out the blaze, but not before it did a fair amount of damage.

Sanford's victims, knowing that the authorities wouldn't take the initiative, decided to put an end to the rampages themselves. In May 1754, a posse of young men from Ridgefield cornered Sanford and hauled him to the New Haven jail. Capturing the crook had been a simple, bloodless affair, but holding him would be tricky. The jailhouse was completely insecure—Sanford had broken out of it earlier that year—and Nichols, who was still on the loose, might do something desperate to liberate his friend. The people of Ridgefield and Norwalk petitioned the Connecticut General Assembly, trying to convey the urgency of the situation to the legislators. Sanford and Nichols, they explained, had been "arming themselves in daring and audacious manner, threatening waste and destruction to the persons and estate of sundry," and leaving colonists "greatly terrified and disquieted." The assembly responded by ordering the capture of Nichols and any remaining members of the gang, and went on record to praise Abigail for "Disclosing the wicked Design of certain convicted Desperados." Since her father might return to fulfill his promise to kill her, the assembly placed her under government protection.

Sanford was a different kind of criminal than Sullivan. He was nastier and more vindictive, with none of the Irishman's charm. While Sullivan endeared himself to the populace with his playful defiance of the authorities, Sanford tormented innocent people with acts of violence. He and his gang didn't taunt officers of the law to entertain crowds, like Sullivan at the pillory in Providence: instead, they vowed retribution and destroyed the property of anyone who got in their way. The men who captured Sanford calculated that the fires had caused more than £4,000 worth of damage. The figure wasn't significant compared with the amount of fake cash Sullivan produced, but there was an important contrast between the two men's crimes. Sanford deprived people of their possessions: the crops he incinerated were irreparably lost to the farmers who planted them. Sullivan's impact, on the other hand, was more ambiguous. His counterfeits could defraud colonists of genuine money or goods, but they could also circulate as a useful medium of exchange in local markets starved for cash.

Most people could relate to Sullivan's entrepreneurial motives; cutting tongues out of cows, however, inspired little sympathy. Although powerless to stop Sanford, Sullivan bore part of the blame. By casting a wide net in his search for accomplices, the counterfeiter had indiscriminately enriched a whole cast of characters, some less savory than others.

IN THE FOUR YEARS following Sullivan's escape from Providence, pressure had mounted among colonial officials to take a stronger stand against counterfeiting. Rhode Island, whose frequent printing of paper money had made its economy volatile, was the hardest hit. Its General Assembly offered a £400 reward for capturing Sullivan as early as October 1753, but the legislators were regularly reminded of their impotence by stories of the counterfeiter's exploits. When the authorities arrested five people connected to Sullivan in Newport, the *Boston Evening-Post* reported that the "famous Villain *Sullivan*" ran free despite "[a] great Reward" offered for his arrest. "Our Gallows has groaned for him a long Time," the article added. Sullivan's forgeries so successfully infiltrated the Rhode Island money supply that in 1756, they turned up in an official lottery held to underwrite the construction of a fort. Rhode Island not only had to deal with the counterfeiting of its own money; it also faced a steady stream of fakes from other colonies, particularly New Hampshire, where Sullivan's Merrimack operation was based. New York, the home of the counterfeiter's Oblong gang, became so overrun with forged notes that its treasury published a notice in the newspaper urging anyone holding bills of a particular date to come in and exchange them for new ones.

Colonial governments could put a price on Sullivan's head, but the complicated task of taking the counterfeiter into custody would require the resolve of a private individual. On January 21, 1756, a forty-four-year-old businessman named Eliphalet Beecher trudged through the snow under the leafless branches of New Haven's elm trees to the building that housed the Connecticut General Assembly. It stood on the northwest corner of the town's Green, an unenclosed common overgrown with weeds and marked with the furrows of wagon wheels. Yale students walked nearby, passing through the doors of the newly built Connecticut Hall, a boxy brick structure three stories high. Tracking footprints through the powder, Beecher entered the assembly chamber and introduced himself. A native of New Haven, he had met members of Sullivan's ring near Connecticut's western border while traveling on business. He was eager to put a stop to the counterfeiter's activities, and hoped to obtain the help of both Connecticut and New York. The legislators, relieved to find someone so committed to enforcing their laws, responded enthusiastically. They agreed to bear all of Beecher's expenses and to pay a reward once he finished the job.

From New Haven, Beecher rode northwest past the limestone bluffs of the Housatonic River valley, crossed the mountains near the New York line, and descended into the marshy lowlands of Dover. Traveling roughly sixty miles in winter over rugged terrain wasn't easy, and once he reached the Oblong, he faced more challenges. When Beecher arrested two people he thought were involved with Sullivan and brought them before a pair of justices of the peace, the officials proved completely uncooperative. Citing lack of evidence, they refused to give Beecher a warrant to extradite the suspects to Connecticut and then released the two men on bail, setting their court date for a few months later. In a further insult, the justices made Beecher pay for the time they spent examining and processing his prisoners. The episode upset him enough to send a letter to New Haven to be read aloud on the floor of the Connecticut legislature. The lawmakers responded with a resolution regretting the "many difficulties" caused by "want of the encouragement and assistance of the civil authority" of New York, and demanded that their governor write his counterpart in New York requesting full cooperation.

If he wanted to capture Sullivan, Beecher needed to rethink his approach. Since the prickly, amateurish men responsible for keeping law and order in the Oblong wouldn't help him without hard evidence, he would have to catch someone in the act of passing counterfeit money. Beecher hired eleven deputies, including his son Eliphalet Jr., and set to work. One possible lead was a tavern keeper whom he suspected of conspiring with Sullivan. Beecher decided to set a trap: he entered the man's tavern, handed him some bills, and asked for change. A middle-aged stranger from Connecticut with an outstretched palm full of good money made an irresistible target. Travelers exchanged cash at so many places along the road that even if they discovered they had been cheated, they probably wouldn't be able to remember where they received the forged notes.

The tavern keeper took the bait and slipped a counterfeit bill into the wad of notes he returned to Beecher. Beecher thumbed through the bills, spotted the fake, and, pulling it out, confronted the man. At first the tavern keeper insisted the money was genuine. When Beecher pressed him, he conceded it was forged, but denied he had known when he handed it over. Finally, he confessed he knew the bill was counterfeit but refused to say where he had gotten it. Beecher and his men hauled the tavern keeper to a justice of the peace and, furnished with a counterfeit bill and an admission of guilt, obtained more cooperation this time. In his examination the tavern keeper implicated other members of Sullivan's ring, leading to more arrests. The prisoners divulged details about the Dover organization and, crucially, gave Beecher the location of Sullivan's hideout.

Boggy ground squished under the weight of Beecher's boots as he and his deputies threaded their way across a vast wooded swamp, following a prisoner who had agreed to show them Sullivan's retreat. The guide conducted them through the damp thicket to the side of a small hill. Walking ahead of them, he came up to the bluff and removed some brush and a tree stump, revealing the entrance to the counterfeiter's cave. Beecher and his deputies ducked into the cavern, marching down the rock-hewn corridor. Gradually it broadened into a large, wood-paneled chamber where the sun shone through a crack in the wall. They scoured the room, overturning tables and chairs. Scattered across the floor was the counterfeiter's furniture, places where he had sat, slept, and eaten in recent days. Sullivan was gone.

He couldn't have fled far. Beecher resolved to search the houses of anyone in the area connected to the counterfeiter. He went door-to-door with his deputies; desperate to catch Sullivan before he could run farther, they woke people up in the middle of the night, grilling the groggy tenants for the criminal's whereabouts. At 1:00 a.m. on March 13, Beecher's band arrived at yet another house. The residents answered the door and saw the men on the step, their tired faces lit unevenly by the quivering light cast by their lanterns. Beecher entered with his assistants, examining the rooms for any trace of Sullivan, and interrogated the inhabitants, who strenuously denied knowing the counterfeiter. The late hour hadn't made Beecher's men careless. While inspecting the house, they found a small but significant clue: dirt on the floor that looked as if it had been tracked in recently.

The soil prompted an even more thorough search. Determined to comb every inch, they moved a bed with a woman sleeping in it to examine the ground underneath. There they discovered another clue: a floorboard that, instead of being nailed down, had been broken in half. They picked up the plank and saw a tunnel dug into the earth. The secret passageway led to a cozy burrow lit by a fireplace; the smoke rose through a vent that fed into the house's chimney overhead. One of the men yelled Sullivan's name into the hole, and the counterfeiter, knowing he had nowhere left to go, came forward to surrender.

Sullivan was tired. He had spent the last seven days hiding in the mountains until, starving and exhausted, he came to the home of a friend and asked for help. By the time Beecher's men found him, he was in no condition to put up a fight. But the counterfeiter's fatigue didn't diminish his bravado. He tried bribing Beecher with fake cash, and when his captor declined, bragged about making several hundred thousand pounds of currency over the course of his career. Taking Sullivan prisoner, Beecher and his crew departed for Connecticut. After four days of travel, the entourage reached New Haven and locked up the counterfeiter in the jail overlooking the Green, within sight of the building where Beecher, back in the middle of winter, had pleaded his case before the Connecticut legislators.

It was March 17, 1756: St. Patrick's Day. Thousands of miles away, in a seaside village in southeastern Ireland, Sullivan's parents were likely celebrating: eating and drinking, parading shamrocks and Celtic crosses, while their son sat in his cell. It had been twenty years since Sullivan left home, and fourteen since he boarded a ship as an indentured servant bound for Boston. Now he awaited trial after a four-year counterfeiting spree that spanned five colonies and made him a legend. The "famous Money Maker" was behind bars, the *Boston Gazette* reported, and it wouldn't have happened without the "extraordinary Address and Resolution" of Eliphalet Beecher.

Beecher never revealed what drove him to do it. Personal reasons often played a part: Robert Clarke broke up the Boyces' gang after being cheated by one of its members, and the residents of Ridgefield had a lot at stake in sending their sons to stop Sanford. But in his speech before the Connecticut General Assembly, Beecher didn't mention whether Sullivan's men had swindled him, only that he wanted to bring them to justice. A later statement to the assembly, made after Sullivan's capture, didn't offer any more insight into his motives. Beecher had first discovered the counterfeiters "in the course of his private business, travelling forth & back through the country," he explained, and he simply wanted "to break up a nest of so great Mischief." He wasn't in it for the money. He received a total compensation of £144 from the Connecticut treasury—£134 for his expenses and a £10 reward. Beecher would have made more as a counterfeiter: the Boston authorities seized more than twice that amount in fake Massachusetts money when they arrested Sullivan back in 1749. Beecher didn't divulge his motives, but he did what he promised, and got written up in the newspapers for his trouble.

AT THE END OF MARCH 1756, the Connecticut authorities sent Sullivan to New York to stand trial. Although the Connecticut legislature funded Sullivan's capture, its counterfeiting laws were lenient compared with those of New York. New York had sentenced moneymakers to death since 1720, while Connecticut only cropped the convict's right ear, branded his forehead with the letter C, and put him away in a workhouse for life. Since keeping prisoners was expensive, Connecticut officials usually released counterfeiters after a relatively short period of time. A conviction in New York, on the other hand, meant hanging, a cheaper and irreversible punishment. Letting Sullivan live would cost a lot of money—it would involve feeding, housing, and guarding him for decades. Eliminating the man behind the moneymaking epidemic was the most economic alternative. This presumably sweetened the deal for the Connecticut legislators, who would be willing to forgo the satisfaction of trying Sullivan in their colony if he might swing from the gallows of another.

The men charged with bringing Sullivan from New Haven to New York could travel by land or by sea. The route along the Connecticut coast was rough and rocky; the journey would be difficult, especially with a prisoner who had to be closely guarded. For that reason they likely chose to go by boat, sailing across Long Island Sound and down the East River. Along Manhattan's eastern shore Sullivan would see the country estates of New York's wealthiest families, acres of landscaped gardens at a comfortable distance from the bustling town below. Farther down the island was a more somber sight: a barricade of cedar logs that secured the settlement's northern border. The palisades had been built eleven years earlier, during the last war, but the renewal of hostilities with the French and their Indian allies made defending the town a top priority.

The outbreak of war delighted New York's businessmen. The city became the provisioning center for British forces arriving in America, and local merchants made a fortune supplying soldiers with food, clothing, rum, horses, and anything else they needed. "New York is growing immensely rich," Benjamin Franklin noted to a friend in 1756 with a twinge of jealousy. Selling to the British wasn't the only way for entrepreneurs to cash in on the conflict. They also traded secretly with the other side, running contraband to the islands of the French Caribbean. Others became privateers, preying on enemy ships and capturing valuable cargo. The influx of cash from war profiteering coincided with a flood of new settlers that helped transform the former Dutch seaport on Manhattan's southern tip into a major colonial town. By 1760, New York had eighteen thousand residents, surpassing Boston and second only to Philadelphia in size.

Despite a booming economy and a growing population, New York still didn't have a proper prison, only a jail in the basement of City Hall, a brick building located at the intersection of Broad and Wall streets. The authorities secured Sullivan in its cellar, chaining the prisoner with irons. That didn't hold him long. Somehow he slipped out of his shackles and opened the door to his cell. He would have escaped if it weren't mealtime, as the woman bringing his food saw him and raised the alarm. The incident reminded the authorities that they needed to deal with Sullivan quickly; five days later, he was arraigned before New York's Supreme Court of Judicature, conveniently located in the rooms above the jail. Sullivan pleaded not guilty, but the court produced plenty of incriminating testimony. Among the witnesses called to testify were two people with intimate knowledge of Sullivan's criminal activities: the convicted moneymaker and arsonist David Sanford, who turned king's evidence against his former colleague, and Eliphalet Beecher, who came down from New Haven to volunteer his services. After hearing the statements, a jury of twelve New Yorkers declared Sullivan guilty. On April 29, the court delivered the sentence. "That the prisoner be carried from hence to the place from whence he came, and thence to the place of Execution," it read, "and there be hanged by the neck, until he be dead."

The place of execution stood on the upper end of the Common, a triangular tract of land on the northern end of town that occupied what is now City Hall Park, right beneath the palisades near present-day Chambers Street. Sullivan's hanging was scheduled for the morning of May 7 but had to be postponed. First the hangman couldn't be found, and then someone snuck across the Common in the middle of the night and cut down the rope. No one knew who did it—probably one of Sullivan's friends or admirers. It took a few days for the authorities to string up a replacement and find an executioner; in the meantime, anticipation for the spectacle grew, fueled by stories of Sullivan's showmanship. The final date for his death was set for May 10. "He is certainly to make his exit," the *New-York Gazette* promised.

The best route to the Common was up Broadway, the tree-lined promenade that cut through the center of town. It started near the island's southern edge at Bowling Green, a well-kept park in an expensive neighborhood of Georgian brick houses, and from there extended north toward the tall Gothic spire of Trinity Church, a favorite spot for New York's Anglican elite. Closer to the Common, Broadway passed through a poorer area, blocks of makeshift wooden shanties where the cart drivers, bricklayers, carpenters, and other tradesmen lived—the class that Sullivan, as a silversmith in Boston, once belonged to. The street ended at the Common, the view widening as the town's buildings fell away. On the fields ahead was a tree with a rope dangling from a branch; below, the counterfeiter stood on a cart with the noose around his neck.

There was no guarantee that Sullivan would give a good performance. In the four years since he dazzled crowds in Providence, he had spent a lot of time alone in the backwoods. He was so obsessed with making money, his charm had worn thin: he barked at his associates and when courting new recruits, relied more on their lust for money than on his powers of persuasion. In New York he could have made an angry exit, raging at the men who captured and convicted him, or gone quietly to the gallows, broken by the inevitability of his death. Instead, energized by the onlookers who gathered that spring day on the grass, he mustered an endearing mix of defiance and levity.

First Sullivan boasted about how much money he forged: £12,000 of Rhode Island's currency, between £10,000 and £12,000 of New Hampshire's, £3,000 of Connecticut's, and large amounts of New York's. These numbers were huge by colonial standards: in Manhattan at the time, a single pound could buy about three bushels of wheat or ten gallons of rum. When asked what denomination of New York money he counterfeited, Sullivan refused to say. "You must find that out by your learning," he declared. "All my accomplices deserved the gallows," the moneymaker continued, "but I will not betray them, or be guilty of shedding their blood." Looking out at the spectators, he scanned their expectant faces. "I see none of my accomplices here," Sullivan announced, adding that he hoped they destroyed all the money and plates in their possession, so "that they may not die on a tree as I do." Then, in a final flourish, he put a plug of chewing tobacco in his mouth and, as his saliva blackened, grinned at the people collected below. "I cannot help smiling," he told them, "as 'tis the nature of the beast." As the hangman prepared the noose, Sullivan made one last request. "Don't pull the rope so tight—it is hard for a man to die in cold blood," he instructed before the cart disappeared from under his feet.

A century later, executioners would invent a more humane method of hanging called the "long drop," where a longer rope was used to break the convict's neck, resulting in an instant death. But in the kind of hanging practiced in colonial America, death happened by strangulation and was relatively slow and painful. The cord would dig into Sullivan's neck, searing the skin as the weight of his body pulled him deeper into its grip and he gradually suffocated. The corpse would look nothing like the confidence man who had captivated the crowd minutes earlier. The tongue would be swollen, the eyes bulging in a cold stare.

Killing the moneymaker removed the root of the problem, but it didn't stop people from using what he left behind to keep breaking the law. Long after Sullivan's lifeless body was cut down, they continued passing his notes and printing money from his plates. The authorities did what they could to stamp out the remnants of the counterfeiter's enterprise. In the summer of 1756, New York passed a law intended to punish the accomplices that Sullivan had refused to name at the gallows. "[I]t appears by the Confession of Owen Sullivan," the act read, "that there are sundry Plates" held by his associates "in order to carry on that pernicious Practice" of moneymaking. Anyone found concealing plates, notes, materials, or other implements for forging the colony's currency would be sentenced to death. Along with the harsher penalty came another push for enforcement, as Eliphalet Beecher, fresh from his big success, returned to the backwoods to track down the rest of the Oblong gang. While many of its members eluded him, he effectively scattered the Dover Money Club—he even captured the seasoned counterfeiters Joseph Boyce and his son, although the men later escaped. What Beecher couldn't do, however, was intercept all the paper Sullivan had put into circulation, bills that would take years to work their way through colonial markets.

Sullivan's posthumous paper trail didn't just take the form of forged notes. Printers, hoping to cash in on his fame, published leaflets about him, bringing the events of his life to a wider audience. Within a week of the counterfeiter's death, a copy of his gallows speech went on sale at Henry De Foreest's print shop in New York. By the time the newspaper publisher Thomas Fleet reprinted the text in Boston, it had been expanded into a short autobiography, advertised as "[t]aken from his own mouth"—probably transcribed while Sullivan sat in jail awaiting trial. Curious colonists could learn about his childhood in Ireland, his harrowing voyage to America, his adventures in Maine and Louisbourg—and, of course, the story of how he became a moneymaker. Readers would have found much to relate to: like many of his colonial contemporaries, Sullivan was an immigrant, a war veteran, and a businessman. He died at thirty-three after making a fortune and losing it all. When he stood trial in New York, Sullivan's only possessions were a horse and saddle, together worth a total of £5. The man who had incensed governments and fascinated colonists by imbuing paper with value saw his wealth evaporate almost as quickly as it came. He ended the way he began, an Irishman with nothing to his pseudonymous name but a talent for earning people's trust.

SULLIVAN'S CAREER LASTED only seven years, but it coincided with a pivotal period in America's monetary history. He started counterfeiting in Boston in 1749, the year that Thomas Hutchinson pushed a bill through the Massachusetts legislature mandating the elimination of the colony's paper money within the next two years. Far from following Hutchinson's example, other colonies kept printing currency, inundating Massachusetts with their notes. When Sullivan died in 1756, the outbreak of the French and Indian War had dramatically expanded the paper money supply, as colonial governments approved large issues to cover their military expenses. Hutchinson's dream of weaning America off paper credit vanished under the flood of bills printed to fund expeditions against the French.

Americans couldn't reform the messy colonial monetary system on their own; any meaningful policy change would have to come from England. Historically, the imperial authorities had been reluctant to intervene. Aside from a few cases, they left the colonies' paper currency alone. Citing Cicero's maxim "Endless money forms the sinews of war," England recognized that paper helped finance colonial wars against the French; it also stimulated local trade and facilitated tax collection. Around the middle of the eighteenth century, however, stirred by creditors' concerns about inflation, the mood among the London authorities began to shift. In 1750, the Rhode Island General Assembly, notorious for its abundant issues of paper money, voted to print another £50,000 in response to colonists' demands for easy credit. Panicked by the move, Rhode Island's wealthy merchant class petitioned the Crown for help. The result was England's strongest statement on colonial money matters to date, the Currency Act of 1751. After decades of salutary neglect, Parliament now forbade the New England colonies to print paper currency except when war or other public emergencies required it. Most important, New England paper money would no longer be considered legal tender—that is, a kind of payment that cannot be legally refused.

The legal tender status of paper wasn't a pedantic point; it lay at the heart of creditors' anxieties on both sides of the Atlantic. They feared that debtors would pay debts contracted in sterling with paper money, whose value, unlike silver's, could depreciate significantly. By prohibiting paper from being legal tender, the new law protected creditors from losing money on their loans. But Parliament's greater ambition, to strictly limit America's use of paper currency, had to be postponed when the French and Indian War started three years later. England, eager to wrest control of the American continent from France, didn't interfere when its colonies printed paper notes to fund the war effort. The investment paid off. The conflict ended in 1763 with a definitive British victory: the French handed over all of their territory in North America east of the Mississippi except for New Orleans, ending a struggle that had lasted more than a century. Louisbourg, where Sullivan had served in the military seventeen years earlier, saw its ramparts demolished by British engineers, who used explosives to ensure that even if the French later retook the seaport, they could never again use its fortifications.

After the joy of the triumph subsided, a bad financial hangover set in. The war had invigorated the American economy: commissaries bought provisions, soldiers spent money, and the army put thousands of colonists to work running supply routes and building infrastructure. Once the conflict ended, these revenue streams dried up. A simultaneous financial panic in Europe curbed the flow of credit to American borrowers, triggering a downturn that continued to deepen.

In a case of colossal bad timing, England resumed its efforts to restrict paper money just as the colonies were facing a serious economic depression. The Currency Act of 1764 extended the earlier policy to the colonies south of New England but included even broader language: paper money couldn't be legal tender in payment of "any bargains, contracts, debts, dues, or demands whatsoever." As with the last act, Parliament wanted to prevent American debtors from paying their British lenders in paper. But the law's wording seemed to apply the ban not just to private debts but to public ones as well, like the payment of taxes. If enforced to the full letter of the law, this would have a crippling effect on the colonies. Without paper money, colonial governments wouldn't be able to collect revenue to cover their expenses, as colonists couldn't pay local taxes. Moreover, currency that couldn't even be accepted for tax payments would become completely worthless as a medium of exchange.

Faced with potential disaster, colonists interpreted the 1764 law as concerning only private debts and continued to use paper money for public purposes. Fortunately for their sake, the authorities in London decided it wasn't worth imposing a total ban on paper money, even if the text of the law appeared to demand it. The Currency Act was far from the only unpopular piece of legislation passed by Parliament in the 1760s; the taxes levied by the Stamp Act and the Townshend Acts provoked greater outrage. But it showed how little America's transatlantic rulers appreciated paper money's importance to the colonial economy. That ignorance would prove dangerous when Parliament insisted on meddling in matters that aroused strong feelings among colonists.

On a summer night in 1765, sixteen years to the month since Sullivan's first arrest in Boston, a mob broke into Thomas Hutchinson's town house. They wrecked the furniture, shattered the windows, looted the wine cellar, and almost took the roof off the top of the house before the sun came up. The vandals wanted to punish Hutchinson, now the lieutenant governor of Massachusetts, because they suspected him of supporting the Stamp Act. They also remembered his role in ridding Massachusetts of paper money two decades earlier, an affair that had spawned long-standing grudges. The mob "threatened me with destruction then," Hutchinson noted in a letter to a friend, "and have retained their rancor ever since." Ten years later, when the steady souring of relations between America and Britain provoked the Revolution's first shots, Hutchinson decided to stay in England, where he had been recalled a year before. A die-hard Loyalist, he penned a point-by-point refutation of the Declaration of Independence, which made him even more reviled on the other side of the Atlantic.

However much the rebels hated Hutchinson, they had a lot to learn from him. In seizing the American colonies from the British, they also inherited a volatile and disorganized financial system swirling with multiple currencies. Hutchinson had grappled with the minutiae of the colonial money problem and knew the perils of paper better than anyone. His loyalty to the Crown, however, ensured that America's new leaders wouldn't heed his warnings.

THE REVOLUTIONARIES' FIRST EXPERIMENT with paper came early. Faced with the mounting costs of the war with Britain, the newly formed Continental Congress needed a way to generate revenue. Isolated by a British naval blockade, it couldn't borrow from abroad, and it lacked the authority to impose taxes—it could ask the individual colonies for money, but with no guarantee that its requests would be met. So, in June 1775, Congress decided to print paper money. Since the American revolutionaries did not have a plentiful supply of precious metals, it issued the bills, called continentals, with the expectation that the colonies would later levy taxes payable in the notes. Congress also promised to redeem the continentals for silver or gold whenever their treasurers had enough coin to do so. Benjamin Franklin, by now sixty-nine years old and the world's most famous American, was called on to design the notes. Franklin had experience printing Pennsylvania's colonial currency, but the continentals required a new approach—the royal insignia that adorned many of the old bills, for instance, were out of the question. He took to the task with typical zeal. Never one to squander a potential platform for his views, the author of *Poor Richard's Almanack* emblazoned the notes with emblems and mottoes intended to instill republican virtues of hard work and self-reliance. His $6 bill bore the Latin word *Perseverando* ("By Perseverance"), while his $1 bill read *Depressa Resurgit* ("Though Crushed, It Recovers"); images of beavers, eagles, and cranes accompanied the phrases. As both elegantly executed works of art and cleverly disguised propaganda, Franklin's continentals were the most visually interesting paper money that America had ever seen.

Despite Franklin's graceful designs, gross mismanagement of the currency soon resulted in a financial nightmare. Instead of introducing taxes to retire the notes, individual colonies—after 1776, they called themselves states—made continentals legal tender and threatened retribution against anyone who refused them. In January 1776, Congress condemned people who rejected payment in continentals as traitors; such individuals should be "treated as an enemy of his country," the representatives resolved. But intimidation and patriotism weren't enough to bolster the money's value. As Congress continued to print the notes, the currency started depreciating rapidly. During one period in 1779, the continental dollar lost half its value in just three weeks; the precipitous drop made the phrase "not worth a continental" part of the new nation's lexicon. In March 1780, Congress tried to solve the crisis by issuing a new dollar that was worth forty of the depreciated continentals. This well-intentioned effort to put the currency on a stable footing impoverished the many Americans unlucky enough to be holding the old paper.

Although Congress made the mistake of printing too much currency, the continental's collapse wasn't entirely its fault. Under the new country's first charter, the Articles of Confederation, the national government had very little power. Not only was it banned from imposing taxes; it couldn't even prevent individual states from printing their own money, which they did throughout the war, greatly increasing the amount of inflationary paper in circulation. Neither could Congress effectively curb counterfeiting, which intensified when the British recruited talented engravers to forge the rebels' money and drew on existing criminal networks to distribute the notes in an effort to undermine the American economy. After the British captured New York City in 1776, a notice appeared in the city's newspapers advertising "counterfeit Congress-Notes" for anyone traveling to the other states. "[T]here is no Risque in getting them off," the announcement added, "it being almost impossible to discover, that they are not genuine." Although the British smuggled large amounts of forged continentals into the states and enlisted Loyalists to pass them, the campaign was considered too unseemly for their leaders to admit the operation's existence. In a letter to George Washington, the commander of the British forces called allegations of counterfeiting "too illiberal to deserve a serious answer." Washington didn't need a confession to prove the enemy's guilt, as his soldiers had already seized British warships with printing materials and piles of counterfeit continentals aboard.

The currency crisis profoundly shook the country's Founders. Their first efforts at finance had inflicted real trauma on their fellow citizens. They had more than just humanitarian reasons for trying to fix the mess: financial instability had the potential to undermine the new nation's authority. The disastrous continentals had provoked antigovernment sentiment, causing people to distrust and despise the national leadership for its role in the catastrophe. "I am so angry at this affair that I hardly know what I write," penned one Pennsylvanian during the war. "I sometimes think we don't deserve the liberty we have been contending for, while such miscreants are suffered to breath[e] among us." Once the Revolution had been won, American leaders needed to demonstrate the credibility of their promises and pronouncements, to gain the confidence of their citizens by giving them a currency whose value didn't vaporize overnight.

Antigovernment feeling spilled over into outright revolt in 1786, when Daniel Shays, a decorated veteran of the Revolutionary War, led an uprising of farmers in western Massachusetts. Saddled with high taxes and crushing debt, the insurgents forcibly blocked foreclosures of their lands and shuttered courthouses. Chief among their complaints was the severe shortage of currency that made it impossible for them to pay taxes or debts. After the disastrous experience with continentals, governments and creditors had begun demanding payment in coin rather than in paper, but by the mid-1780s, precious metals were extremely hard to come by. The Massachusetts farmers wanted the government to give them a working medium of exchange by printing paper money and making it legal tender. The Shaysites scattered by February 1787, after an unsuccessful effort to capture a state arsenal killed four of the farmers. But the affair was a vivid reminder of the central government's frailty: bound by the rigid restrictions of the Articles of Confederation, Congress couldn't enforce its will, and the task of squashing the rebellion was left to the Massachusetts militia. The incident contributed to growing calls for reforming the nation's governing document, which eventually brought about the Constitutional Convention in Philadelphia in May 1787.

The United States faced the same problem that its colonial predecessors had struggled with since the seventeenth century. In a land with few deposits of precious metals, what do you use for money? Taxes and trade required a circulating currency, and paper seemed like an obvious candidate. But the crisis with the continentals had been so damaging that virtually none of America's leading men advocated printing paper money. In the turbulent period leading up to the Constitutional Convention, they denounced paper in language that would have made Thomas Hutchinson proud. George Washington condemned paper for its propensity "to ruin commerce, oppress the honest, and open the door to every species of fraud and injustice."

Thomas Paine took a similar view. In a vociferous polemic, he compared paper currency to alchemy, since both were efforts to transmute something worthless into gold and silver. Replacing precious metals with paper, he wrote, "is like putting an apparition in the place of a man; it vanishes with looking at it, and nothing remains but the air." Like the hard-money men in the Massachusetts currency debate almost four decades earlier, these prominent critics saw paper notes as a kind of sorcery, a magical attempt to circumvent the scarcity of precious metals. They feared an economy built on nothing but promises.

At the Constitutional Convention, support for paper was scarce. Only one of the fifty-five delegates, John F. Mercer of Maryland, declared himself "a friend to paper money," although he qualified the statement by saying that under current circumstances, he didn't condone its use. The debate at the Philadelphia State House didn't explore whether the nation should embrace paper currency—the consensus was that it shouldn't—but whether it made sense for the national government to retain the right to print bills of credit, as provided by the Articles of Confederation. Advocates of keeping the clause explained that in the case of a public emergency like war, Congress might need to print paper notes to cover its costs.

Opposition was predictably fierce. George Read, a delegate from Vermont, replied that the power to issue paper, "if not struck out, would be as alarming as the mark of the Beast in Revelations." John Langdon of New Hampshire agreed, announcing that he would rather "reject the whole plan than retain the three words" that gave the government the authority to print money. When it came to a vote, the delegates chose to remove the words. The final document they produced in September 1787 came out firmly on the side of a hard currency under national control. The Constitution gave Congress the right to "coin Money, regulate the Value thereof, and of foreign Coin," and prohibited states from minting coins, printing paper money, or making anything but silver and gold legal tender. While the Constitution didn't expressly forbid Congress to issue paper currency, the assumption among the delegates was that the federal government didn't possess any powers it wasn't specifically given. They hoped that after almost a century of paper bills, the American economy would finally stand on a more solid footing.

They were wrong. The two factors that had caused colonial Massachusetts to print America's first paper currency—the scarcity of coin and the demand for credit—were just as present in 1787 as they were in 1690. As long as the core issue remained unresolved, paper would find a way to return, and with it, the counterfeiters who capitalized on financial chaos. Far from ending the counterfeiting trade, the founding of the American Republic would usher in a golden era of moneymaking. If Owen Sullivan had been alive, it would have warmed his entrepreneurial heart. In the decades following his death, the Irishman's successors enjoyed opportunities he could never have imagined, and took full advantage of the young United States.

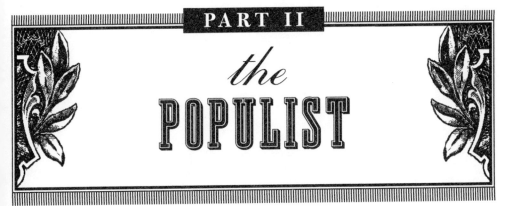

PART II

the

POPULIST

O N NEW YEAR'S EVE 1815, Philadelphia's Methodists crowded into a brick church on the northern end of town. They planned to stay up praying and singing past midnight while less pious Philadelphians caroused drunkenly through the streets. The congregation had a lot to give thanks for. On the verge of its fortieth year, the Republic was surging with patriotic feeling after having fought the British to a draw in the War of 1812. Americans had reasserted their freedom from a foreign power, safeguarding the experiment that had begun with the Declaration of Independence and the Constitution—documents that were signed in the hall of the Philadelphia State House, only a few blocks from where the worshippers stood. The nation was expanding westward and the economy, energized by an increase in foreign trade, was thriving. "Come, let us anew our journey pursue," began one of the Methodist hymns for the New Year, a verse that captured the moment's optimism.

About two hundred miles west, the year's last sunset darkened the sky over Bloody Run, a village in the Pennsylvania backcountry. Under the orange silhouette of the Allegheny Mountains, David Lewis rode up to a tavern, dismounted, and walked in. He had left a horse with the proprietor, Hill Wilson, a couple of days before, with the understanding that

Wilson would either keep it for him or sell it. Now he wanted first to find out what happened, then a tumbler of gin to slake his thirst.

Lewis was a man who made an impression when he entered a room. Close to six feet tall, he held himself straight and walked with an easy, confident step. He had fair features—sandy blond hair and blue eyes—and dressed like a gentleman. His elegant attire would have been enough to attract attention from the other patrons, whose clothes, while less refined, were probably better suited to life in the Allegheny outback. But there was something else in the air that focused people's eyes on Lewis, a palpable undertow of tension that followed him as he walked through the door.

Wilson the tavern keeper was nervous. When Lewis asked about the horse, he said the sheriff had confiscated the animal after discovering it was bought with counterfeit money. Lewis laughed. "I haven't bought a horse in two months," he replied; he didn't even own the animal—he had borrowed it from someone named Leeper. Overhearing this, a local man named Jim Peoples called his bluff. "That was none of Leeper's horses unless he got him lately," Peoples said. "I don't care when the devil he got him," Lewis snarled. "Leeper gave him to me."

Peoples and Wilson didn't believe him. As it slowly became clear that they intended to arrest him, Lewis kept calm. He didn't run; he took off his coat, ordered more gin, and made conversation. He maintained his innocence, laughing off their accusations. Escaping would have ended the moment too soon. He enjoyed sharing drinks with them: the civility of it tickled him, and he took great pleasure in hearing their impressions of him. "What did you think when I came in?" Lewis asked Peoples. "I considered you damn safe and pitied your case. I knew you could not get away," he answered. This rankled Lewis enough for him to drop his genteel demeanor and declare that no man had a right to touch him. He promised to remain peaceable but swore to kill whoever laid a hand on him.

Lewis had been at Wilson's tavern for two hours by the time the sheriff arrived. The officer came in with the man who had sold Lewis the horse to help identify the culprit. After he confirmed that Lewis paid forged notes for the animal, the sheriff grabbed the counterfeiter by the wrist to take him prisoner. Wilson, either out of respect for Lewis or fear that he would become violent, told the sheriff there was no need to use force. The officer relented, and soon the evening's good-natured tippling resumed as everyone settled down to drink more gin. They sat there for an hour before the sheriff pulled himself away from his glass to ask Wilson for a rope. "I must tie this man," he explained. Wilson said it wasn't necessary, but the sheriff insisted, so the tavern keeper reluctantly agreed to go find some cord.

A moment later Wilson heard a sound. He picked up a candle and ran toward the noise. The fluttering flame revealed a shadowy tableau: Lewis was clutching a gun in his right hand, trying to shoot, while Peoples, the sheriff, and another man struggled to disarm him. Wilson rushed to help, and the four of them knocked the pistol out of his palm and restrained him. "Why would you shoot me?" asked Wilson. It wasn't personal, the counterfeiter explained. "If it was my own brother, I would kill him rather than be tied."

The sheriff later described what happened while Wilson had been looking for rope next door. When the boozy socializing came to an end and the reality of his capture sank in, Lewis abruptly changed course. As the sheriff told the court at Lewis's trial:

> Lewis said he had no arms, when I asked him. Put my hand in
> his pocket and pulled out a dirk. He pulled out a pistol, said,
> "Y'r life is mine!" and snapped the pistol. We could not get
> him down. Fletcher struck him 2 or 3 times on the head with
> a stick. Mr. Wilson came in and caught him by the back of
> the neck and pulled him down . . . He said afterward he w'd
> have been sorry to have killed me but he was determined to
> kill any person who would attempt to take him.

Lewis had every intention of murdering the sheriff, and would have done so if his weapon hadn't misfired. After securing the prisoner in the tavern for the night, the men went to bed. In the morning they took the road to Bedford, a nearby town nestled in a valley enclosed almost entirely by the Alleghenies, and locked Lewis into the jail in the county court-house. The building looked nothing like its prim, redbrick counterparts farther north in New England. It had a more rugged feel, with walls of blue limestone quarried from the nearby mountains—solid enough in their construction, the townsfolk hoped, to confine Lewis until he could stand trial.

LEWIS WAS VIRTUALLY UNKNOWN when he arrived in Bedford on New Year's Day. A newspaper report blandly identified the prisoner as "a man calling himself David Lewis." But as he showed at the tavern the night before, he already possessed the qualities that would make him a legend within the next four years. To the men and women of central Pennsylva-nia, Lewis looked like he was from another planet. His polished dress and sophisticated affect dazzled them, and he complemented his refined exte-rior with a personality that immediately inclined people to him. Above all, he was a narcissist. Lewis wanted to know what others thought of him; he loved to see his reflection in his admirers' faces. In less skillful hands, this self-absorption might have been alienating. But Lewis had a politician's gift for letting other people feel like they owned a piece of him, that even in his most egotistical moments, he understood and represented them. This more than anything else is what would make him a folk hero.

Despite his apparent gentility, Lewis didn't come from an eastern city or a southern plantation. He was a native of central Pennsylvania, the youngest son of Lewis Lewis, a Welsh immigrant who then lived about a hundred miles north of Bedford, on the banks of a stream that runs alongside a ridge of the Alleghenies. His father settled in Pennsylvania before the Revolution and became a surveyor, dividing up parcels of land in a region still bloodily contested by Indians and whites. Pennsylvanians had a reputation for being particularly ruthless colonizers. In 1763, a band of white vigilantes who massacred natives on the Pennsylvania frontier became so powerful that they marched on Philadelphia five hundred strong, hoping to kill every Indian in the colony. Benjamin Franklin and others talked them down, but white rage continued to simmer as settlers pushed farther west into Indian territory. Another war broke out in 1774, this time sparked by colonists moving aggressively into the Ohio River country. The conflict began when the governor of Virginia sent land surveyors to explore the disputed area, inviting attacks by Shawnee raiding parties.

Surveying was a risky business: it involved spending considerable time in rugged, unsettled places and eluding Indians who were often enraged at the sight of a white man measuring land that didn't belong to him. Surveyors made easy targets because their task required precision. They used a magnetic compass and a chain of one hundred iron links totaling twenty-two yards to mark out a property's boundaries, and the process could take time. When surveying along the steep flanks of Pennsylvania's Juniata and Susquehanna rivers, Lewis Lewis must have kept a close eye on his surroundings, just in case a group of Indians charged down the valley to ambush him.

Despite the danger, land surveying was prestigious. It was considered a profession of the propertied class; rich Virginia planters like George Washington and Thomas Jefferson both knew how to survey. It also paid well, either in money or in acreage. Lewis Lewis made a good living, earning land grants from the government in exchange for his services and becoming a landowner in at least three counties. When he died, his possessions included enough household items to fill a few homes: rugs, chairs, trunks, teacups, gold ware, spinning wheels, and hundreds of other articles. He also left his compass and chain, the two indispensable tools of his trade.

Lewis Lewis's background suited his distinguished occupation. He didn't come to America as a poor country laborer but as an Oxford University graduate with a proud pedigree; his descendants later claimed George Washington and Meriwether Lewis as relatives. It's not clear why, but after four years as a student at Christ Church college, he left its vaulted halls and manicured gardens for the American colonies. Being the only Oxford-educated land surveyor in central Pennsylvania presumably helped attract clients. It also came in handy when, at the age of thirty-three, he courted a nineteen-year-old girl named Jane Dill. The daughter of Irish immigrants, Dill was famous for her fearless horsemanship and stern Presbyterianism. She fell for the Welshman, and the two married. Together they traveled throughout Pennsylvania, surveying one plot after another.

By the time Jane gave birth to David, the last of their eight children, in 1788, hostilities between Indians and whites had cooled. Although Pennsylvania saw skirmishes until the last decade of the eighteenth century, the frontier line had shifted farther west and so had the battlegrounds. Locals commemorated the bloodshed with place-names that recalled the region's violent past. Lewis's birthplace, Bald Eagle Creek, took its name from one of two Indians, both known as Bald Eagle, who were murdered by whites in the 1770s. Bloody Run, where Lewis almost escaped arrest, had allegedly been the site of an Indian ambush decades earlier. The natives descended on a trading convoy, killing enough men to dye the nearby stream red with the slaughter. The name Bloody Run remained until 1873, when residents decided to rechristen the town with a less sanguinary and more respectable name. They chose Everett, after Edward Everett, the famous orator who delivered the two-hour speech before Lincoln's two-minute address at Gettysburg.

Lewis never had a chance to hear his father's stories about the Indian wars, since the Welshman died when his son was still an infant. Jane remarried an old Dutch widower named Frederick Leathers, who no doubt offered fewer opportunities for adventure than her last husband. But their relationship, cut short by Leathers's death four years later, was happy; in his will, the Dutchman left all his property to his "loving wife, Jane." With enough money to bring up her children, Lewis's mother decided to live on her own for a bit. Around 1800, she moved to the town of Clearfield and, then in her fifties, started a distillery.

Lewis's childhood couldn't have been dull. Raised by a widow turned entrepreneur with a reputation for spirited horseback riding, he grew up in the valleys of the Alleghenies, roaming the landscape that his father had spent years surveying. As a boy he lived comfortably, and as a young man he could have easily chosen to become a respectable citizen. Instead, he counterfeited money and robbed members of the communities that Lewis Lewis had helped map out decades earlier. He learned the terrain as well as his father, but with a different end in mind: not as open land to be carved up and claimed, but as a tangle of camps, hideouts, and trails to transport forged currency or stolen goods.

IN THE FALL OF 1812, a few years before Lewis's arrest on New Year's Eve, General Isaac Brock paced the ramparts of Fort George, a British garrison on Lake Ontario at the mouth of the Niagara River. Over six feet tall and heavily built, he was well liked by his men and admired for his military prowess throughout Canada. Brock loved war: he joined the army at fifteen and remained a soldier—and a bachelor—his entire life. Until recently, however, he had been desperate to leave his post. Eager for action, Brock seethed at being stuck in the colonies while the British fought Napoléon's troops thousands of miles away. But in 1812, as the conflict between Britain and the United States heated up, he chose to stay, hoping to make a name for himself when the fighting began. As the governor of Upper Canada—a colony that comprised present-day Ontario—and the commander of its armed forces, he would soon have his chance. Only a couple of months after war was declared in the summer of 1812, Brock dealt a humiliating defeat to the Americans at Detroit, a victory that earned him the nickname the "Hero of Upper Canada." By October he had moved farther up the Great Lakes to the Niagara River, the strait that divided British Canada from New York.

On the other side of the water, not far from where Brock was standing, six thousand American soldiers were preparing to invade. Brock knew they were there, and wanted to attack. But his superior General George Prevost, the governor of British North America, insisted on a strictly defensive strategy and, as a way to enforce his will, sent Brock a relatively small number of men. His hands tied, Brock waited. The imminent American assault and the timidity of his superior weren't Brock's only problems; he also faced widespread defeatism at home. Despite Brock's celebrated reputation, people in Upper Canada felt an American triumph was inevitable. "[T]he population, believe me, is essentially bad," Brock wrote to Prevost. The Canadian militia shared the public's pessimism; their gloom, combined with poor training and inadequate equipment, made them practically useless. On top of everything else, Upper Canada had become a refuge in recent years for criminals fleeing from the United States: "the most abandoned characters," Brock complained, "seek impunity in this province from crimes committed in the states." The lawlessness they brought over the border further sapped Canada's ability to defend itself.

One of these émigré crooks was David Lewis, whom Brock had caught with counterfeit money and imprisoned at Fort George. Lewis's arrest couldn't have come at a worse moment. While typically an affable man, the British commander was also a firm disciplinarian—and the thought of

Lewis swindling his men, added to his many other frustrations, pushed him over the edge. Brock threatened to hang Lewis on gallows so high that he could see his own country. Given the short distance across the river to New York, the general wasn't exaggerating. An execution might help him maintain discipline in his camp, or at least give his troops a little entertainment to ease the anxiety of waiting for the Americans to make their move.

Fortunately for Lewis, Brock didn't live to fulfill his promise. Shortly before daybreak on October 13, American batteries opened fire on British positions, provoking an artillery exchange across the Niagara. The flash of exploding shells in the gray dawn illuminated the water below, where boats of American soldiers paddled furiously to the opposite shore. They were headed for Queenston, a village about seven miles south of Fort George. Brock hadn't expected them to land there, and now he raced to confront the invaders. While he was leading the charge, a ball from an American musket pierced his chest. He died almost instantly, and his men, shaken by the death of their beloved commander, gathered around the powerful frame lying lifeless on the battlefield. They carried his corpse to Queenston while their colleagues successfully repelled the attack. Upper Canada was saved, but the loss of Brock inflicted a major blow to the British effort.

The battle that killed Canada's greatest general also saved Lewis's life. He sat behind bars at Fort George for weeks after Brock's death, until another stroke of luck set him free. In mid-November, the British started shelling the enemy across the river, and the Americans responded with their own bombardment. The barrage set fire to much of the British garrison, including the mess hall, and did enough damage to the walls of the jail to allow Lewis to escape. As the cannonballs fell and engine crews ran to extinguish the flames, he took advantage of the commotion to slip out of the fort.

Lewis was twenty-four years old when he fled Fort George. The boy from rural Pennsylvania had become a troublemaker early, spurning the example set by his brothers, who, like their father, lived decent, law-abiding lives. The youngest son took a different path. He enlisted in the army before the war with the British broke out, deserted, and later traveled north to Canada. Across the border he discovered the thriving expatriate underworld on the other side—the rabble of deserters, lowlifes, and jailbirds that Brock despised. It was also a haven for counterfeiters. Canadian-based engravers forged notes printed by American banks right above the border, drawing on a sophisticated network of smugglers to ship the product southward along roads, rivers, and canals into markets throughout the United States.

Like their colonial predecessors in the Oblong and elsewhere, counterfeiters understood the value of geography. From a moneymaker's point of view, a poorly guarded border between bickering neighbors offered the ideal location to base an operation. The bad blood between Britain and the United States in the early nineteenth century—not to mention three years of conflict during the War of 1812—made Canadian officials ill-inclined if not outright unwilling to crack down on the counterfeiting of American currency. Despite occasional moments of cooperation between the two countries, their strained relationship, combined with the rough terrain and the perpetual shortage of law enforcement, meant that money-makers ran a booming business in the Canadian townships.

One of these entrepreneurs was Philander Noble. Lewis met him while drifting up north, and they became close collaborators. An accomplished engraver, Noble had spent years between Vermont and Canada cutting plates and making fake cash. He took Lewis under his wing, mentoring the young deserter in the art of moneymaking. The apprenticeship proved important for Lewis: he began as a juvenile delinquent and graduated a master criminal.

The two men made an odd couple. Sixteen years older, Noble looked nothing like the tall, graceful Pennsylvanian. He was fat, bald, and a couple of inches shorter than his protégé. Like Lewis, however, he came from a small town with a frontier past: Westfield, Massachusetts, which for decades after its founding in the seventeenth century had the distinction of being the colony's westernmost settlement. Westfield was a farming community, but Noble, rather than working in the fields, became an artisan. His nimble fingers earned him a living as a silversmith, a clockmaker, and an inventor. In 1800, at the age of twenty-seven, he wrote a letter to his congressman, William Shepard, complaining that he had been hired to create a machine for grinding gun barrels but was cheated by his employer. "I performed the task which cost me many a sleepless night as well as very close & intense thought," Noble explained, and in return got only "a bare days wages." Even more infuriating, his boss took credit for inventing the device. Noble pressed Shepard to pass his story along to the secretary of war—if not to get more money, then "at least to place me in a favourable point of light to the publick."

For a young workman from western Massachusetts to think a high-level member of John Adams's cabinet would care about protecting his rights to a gun barrel grinder gives a sense of Noble's regard for himself. It's unlikely that Shepard followed up on the request, and within a few years, Noble took his metalworking skills into a trade that afforded better opportunities for wealth and recognition. He moved to Vermont and started carving copperplates to counterfeit currency.

The summer of 1807 found Noble huddled in a cave with three accomplices, each man engaged in a different task: Noble engraved plates while the others prepared the ink, fed paper into the rolling press, and forged the official signatures that appeared on the notes. While the criminals worked, a posse of twenty-six local men beat a path through the wilderness looking for them. The hideout lay in the mountains near Plymouth, a town in central Vermont at the bottom of a steep valley. Getting there required traversing tough ground under the hot sun and crawling part of the way on their hands and knees. It took the men hours to find the retreat, and they approached loudly enough for the counterfeiters to hear them coming.

Desperate to destroy the evidence, one of Noble's associates hurled some tools out of the cave's entrance—a precipitous fifteen-foot drop—and then leaped down after the debris to escape. He didn't get far: the men grabbed him, along with Noble and the other two criminals. Inside the cavern was more than enough incriminating evidence: plates, a rolling press, paper, and lots of counterfeit bills, some still wet with ink. Noble's handiwork, honed during his years as a craftsman, impressed even those who were happy to see him behind bars. After reporting the arrest "with sincere pleasure," a Vermont newspaper couldn't resist commenting on Noble's superb technique: "The engraving is very handsomely executed, and the bills so well done as to deceive tolerable good judges." The jail didn't hold Noble for long. Two years later, he resurfaced in Canada, arrested for counterfeiting once again.

THE MECHANICS OF MONEYMAKING had changed little in the almost sixty years between Noble's capture in Vermont and Owen Sullivan's first efforts in Boston. Both men inscribed copper sheets, and did it so well that they saw their workmanship praised by the same newspapers that demanded their arrest. But the financial universe that each engraver inhabited was completely different. Sullivan forged bills of credit printed by local governments. While a colony's money often circulated outside its borders, there were only as many currencies as there were colonies: Massachusetts money, Rhode Island money, and so on.

The bills strewn on the floor of Noble's cave in 1807, on the other hand, didn't display government insignia; they carried names like Bank of Vermont, Bank of New York, and Bank of Columbia. In the first few decades of the Republic, these banknotes had become America's de facto medium of exchange. They were denominated in dollars, the new nation's official unit of currency, derived from the Spanish silver dollars that had circulated on the American continent for centuries. Foreign currency still made up the bulk of the country's supply of coins, and although the U.S. Mint in Philadelphia had begun striking federal coins, it couldn't produce enough to meet the demand. Banknotes helped solve the problem by substituting paper dollars for hard dollars. In theory (although not always in practice), the bank's paper could be exchanged for precious metals at the banks, and while not technically legal tender, they served the same purpose as colonial bills of credit had decades earlier. Far from discouraging these institutions, state legislatures granted them charters, eager to stimulate their markets with infusions of capital.

Local governments had a practical reason for favoring this arrangement. The framers of the Constitution had hoped to put an end to the use of paper money by expressly forbidding the states to produce it. By chartering banks that printed the notes instead of doing it themselves, the states circumvented this ban. But there was another, even bigger loophole that let Americans retain their dependence on paper money: the distinction between banknotes and bills of credit. While the difference might seem minor, it was crucially important for the nation's first generation of leaders. When the delegates met in Philadelphia to draft the Constitution in 1787, the country had three banks—the Bank of North America, the Bank of New York, and the Bank of Boston. Their notes were considered highly reliable: unlike colonial bills or wartime continentals, they could always be redeemed for coin. As strident a critic of paper money as Thomas Paine enthusiastically endorsed the use of banknotes. While bills of credit substituted the shadow of paper for the substance of silver or gold, banknotes didn't raise any thorny metaphysical issues: they weren't money, Paine wrote, but "hostages to be exchanged for hard money." Instead of hauling around gold and silver, people could trade these useful hostages to make payments—IOUs that eased the flow of commerce without unhinging value from its foundation in precious metals.

Most of the Constitution's drafters shared Paine's sentiments. Although some delegates remained wary of banking, their arguments revolved around the constitutionality of granting bank charters, not on the potential effect of banknotes. No one on the convention floor seems to have seriously considered the possibility that banknotes would become a new form of paper currency even more volatile and complex than the colonial money it replaced. The final document to come out of Philadelphia, while strongly opposed to bills of credit, included not a single clause on banks or banknotes.

The silence was significant. It effectively postponed the debate over the nation's financial future, although not for very long. The first controversy erupted in 1790, and while it didn't deal with banknotes directly, it had serious implications for the fate of American banking. The argument centered on whether the federal government had the constitutional power to charter a national bank called the Bank of the United States. The Bank's chief supporter was Alexander Hamilton, easily the country's most sophisticated thinker on financial matters. He had been working on the idea for a while; in fact, he outlined it a decade earlier, as a twenty-four-year-old aide-de-camp to General Washington. In the winter of 1779–1780, when the British looked as if they would win the war, Hamilton was encamped in New Jersey with Washington and the ragged Continental army. The country was in an economic free fall: its soldiers poorly provisioned, unpaid, and close to mutiny; its citizens bankrupted by a glut of worthless continentals.

Hamilton's recovery plan involved creating a kind of superbank that could bolster the nation's finances, fund its flagging military, and restore public confidence. It would be a commercial bank owned partly by the government and partly by private investors, but also much more: it could borrow from foreign creditors, help collect taxes, and do anything else required to keep the state solvent. When Washington became president and appointed his old aide secretary of the treasury, Hamilton hoped to see his idea through.

As could be expected from the grumbling at the Constitutional Convention about the constitutionality of bank charters, Hamilton's proposal prompted a fierce dispute. Each side imputed a different meaning to the Constitution's silence on the issue. The Bank's opponents—Thomas Jefferson and James Madison, among others—said the federal government couldn't charter a bank, because its only powers were those specifically given by the Constitution; the states retained the rest. Hamilton disagreed, insisting that the federal government had the right to do whatever was necessary to govern effectively, so long as it wasn't expressly forbidden by the Constitution. At issue wasn't what the document said but what it left unsaid, and what the muteness meant. Hamilton submitted the bill in December 1790; Congress passed it the following February, and Washington, after much deliberation, signed it into law. The Bank's charter lasted twenty years. The argument surrounding it, however, continued for decades, until the Civil War put a bloody end to the power struggle between the central government and the states.

Although Hamilton got his Bank, the federal government never had a monopoly on banking. States had already chartered their own banks, and they would soon charter many more. At first, these institutions tended to be conservative. Most were run by wealthy merchants with a passion for scrupulous bookkeeping: they didn't issue more notes than they could redeem and lent money only on a limited, short-term basis. Someone who wanted a loan didn't just walk in and fill out an application; the directors carefully reviewed every request before deciding whether to grant it. Rules were strictly observed and credit closely held.

In the last decade of the eighteenth century, the ground began to shift. Demand for more banks and looser regulations grew. Just as in colonial days, the pressure came partly from farmers, who resented the merchants' monopoly on the money supply. But there were new voices as well: speculators, entrepreneurs, and investors who needed cheap credit to finance their ventures in an expanding domestic economy. Foreign trade, which for years had dominated American business, gradually gave way to profitable industries at home. Rivers that had irrigated farms for centuries now powered manufacturing mills; a construction boom in roads, bridges, and canals connected people and markets as the country pushed west, spurred by an influx of immigrants looking for land. The scale of American ambition had greatly increased since Benjamin Franklin's era. But one problem familiar to Franklin remained: initiative was abundant and available capital scarce. The solution was to print more money, which is exactly what the new banks did. As a result, the once stable relationship between banknotes and precious metals started to unravel as banks issued bills beyond what they could convert into coin. The new economy would be funded on faith, not silver and gold; on the hope that a series of risky undertakings—American independence, republican government, free markets, and the settlement of the West, among others—would pay off.

When Noble wrote his congressman about his gun barrel grinder in 1800, the United States had 29 banks. By the time Lewis broke out of jail during the bombardment of Fort George in 1812, the number exceeded 90, and within the next four years, reached almost 250. A key event in this financial explosion—contemporaries called it "bancomania"—was the closing of the Bank of the United States in 1811. As the nation's largest bank, it acted as a creditor to the smaller institutions scattered throughout the country and held many of their notes. By pressuring the state banks to pay their debts and redeem their bills, it helped keep them in line. For that reason, the Bank had many enemies, and after a heated fight, Congress voted not to renew its charter. The Bank's dissolution removed an important constraint on the nation's financial craze and opened the door to more banks and more paper.

Noble's experience as an engraver on the Canadian border gave him everything he needed to make the most of the money mania. It was a good time to be a counterfeiter, and for Lewis, it was a good time to learn. Decades later, a seventy-nine-year-old James Madison was asked whether he thought the states had the right to create banks. Madison replied that they did, so long as the states didn't make the banks' bills legal tender. The Constitution's authors, he explained, hadn't predicted that banknotes would become such "a great evil" and, even if they had, faced so many other hurdles in drafting a document that everyone could accept that they might have avoided addressing the issue anyway.

IN 1813, AS AMERICA STRUGGLED to finance a war against a vastly superior enemy without the benefit of a national bank, Noble and Lewis decided to head south to Pennsylvania. It's not clear when the two men teamed up; they had probably begun their partnership in Canada shortly before returning to America together. Lewis knew the way, since he had made the trip before, presumably to pass bad bills. But this time the counterfeiters weren't just looking for more markets for their notes; they needed a new headquarters for their operation. The northern border had become dangerous. As Lewis had learned at Niagara the previous fall, fleecing soldiers was a hazardous business: it risked provoking field commanders like Brock, whose summary justice made civilian courts look plodding and feeble in comparison. The trip to Pennsylvania required traveling hundreds of miles, from the lake-dotted landscape of Canada to the green hills and valley streams of the Allegheny country where Lewis grew up. Their destination was the town of Bellefonte, only one mountain ridge away from Lewis's birthplace on Bald Eagle Creek. Lewis wanted to keep his visit a secret. If he and Noble were going to scout the area for potential moneymaking hideouts, they would have to maintain a very low profile.

Around midday in late March, Lewis's older brother Thomas heard a knock on the door of his house in Bellefonte. Outside stood a heavyset bald man who identified himself as Philander Noble and asked for a place to stay. Lewis must have sent word ahead of time; it's hard to believe that Thomas would have let the shifty-looking stranger in otherwise. He arranged for Noble to stay with his mother, Jane, the twice-widowed Presbyterian, now in her sixties. As for Lewis, he came separately, after Noble. He lodged with Thomas or Jane but used an assumed name with others, hoping not to be discovered.

While a brilliant engraver, Noble was neither likable nor discreet. He lasted a week in Bellefonte before the locals hauled him before two justices of the peace on suspicion of being a British spy. The townsfolk's fears weren't unreasonable. They were fighting a war against an enemy who looked like them, who spoke the same language, and with whom they shared a long, porous border: the possibilities for infiltration, even in a community as strategically insignificant as Bellefonte, were enormous. The justices took the threat seriously. "[I]t is the duty of the Magistrates and Citizens of the United States to guard against the intrigues of the enemy," read their report. A mysterious new arrival from British Canada in a rural town in central Pennsylvania seemed intriguing enough to investigate. The witnesses the justices called to testify, however, could offer no evidence other than a vague feeling that Noble was a shady character, furtively conspiring with Lewis on something they knew nothing about. Lewis had already acquired a bad reputation since fleeing to Canada—for "his capers," as one witness put it, likely a reference to his counterfeiting— and his returning home with Noble in tow made people nervous. One man told the justices that Noble carried a gun; another said pointedly that he hadn't revealed anything "about who he was or what he was about." A third witness, summing up the general view, labeled Noble a "strange man."

It's doubtful that the citizens of Bellefonte even believed Noble was a spy. The likelier scenario is that they wanted to bring him in and used the espionage accusation as an excuse. But if they hoped to discover something else about Noble's activities, they would be disappointed: the inquiry produced nothing concrete. Thomas, for his part, cast doubt on the other witnesses by directly contradicting them when it came his turn to testify. "I do not know that this man has any connections with my brothers," he said of Noble, "nor I never heard him say he had." This was a blatant lie, uttered in the hopes of protecting his younger sibling.

Even though the justices had found no proof of his crimes, Noble, when called to speak, gave statements that sounded curiously like the nervous ramblings of a guilty man. Whoever transcribed them for the court's records had to copy his words in brisk cursive, punctuating the phrases and fragments with hastily scribbled dashes to mark his many abrupt shifts. He scurried from one topic to the next, giving an erratic account of his past while carefully omitting anything about his counterfeiting career. He said he came to Pennsylvania to buy land and denied collaborating with Lewis—he thought they had once met, but didn't remember being "particularly acquainted."

The next day, however, Noble took a different tack. No longer scattered and incoherent, he now told a story intended to cast himself in a more sympathetic light. First he made an important confession: not only did he know Lewis, he had journeyed with him part of the way from Canada to Pennsylvania. The tale of their crossing began the previous February, as British and American soldiers watched each other warily from opposite sides of the frozen St. Lawrence River, the long waterway dividing Canada from New York. Into this war zone stepped Noble and Lewis, who managed to slip through the British lines and walk one and a half miles across the ice to the other side. They reached the town of Ogdensburg, where they met the American commander, a spirited southerner named Captain Benjamin Forsyth, and warned him of an impending British attack. Forsyth provided the men with passes to enter the States—which Noble had since lost, he hastened to add—and they continued southward across the countryside.

If the travelers really did apprise Forsyth of the enemy's movements, their efforts didn't help much. Early in the morning of February 22, five hundred troops assembled on the Canadian shore, marched across the river's slippery surface, and after a fierce fight, captured Ogdensburg. Forsyth and his men fled to the woods, where he composed an angry dispatch to his superiors demanding reinforcements while the British set fire to his barracks. Of course, the point of Noble's story wasn't who won but his courageous act of patriotism: would a British spy risk his life aiding the Americans? Perhaps this persuaded the justices to drop their already tottering case; whatever they thought of Noble's tale, nothing else appears in the record after his second day of testimony.

Noble and Lewis couldn't admit the real reason for their trip. It wouldn't have comforted the justices to know that the men they suspected of treason had come to Pennsylvania to take part in a time-honored American tradition as deeply rooted as churchgoing or slavery. Noble and Lewis returned from Canada to forge money just as the nation's mushrooming financial sector began to look more and more like a massive counterfeiting enterprise. In the banking boom that began at the turn of the century and surged after the fall of the Bank of the United States, the bankers who printed notes and the criminals who forged them gradually became more or less indistinguishable. While their intentions differed, their product was often the same. Whether genuine or fake, the bills pretended to be something they weren't: placeholders—"hostages," in Thomas Paine's words—for precious metals.

The war with the British marked the turning point that pushed America's fragile finances over the edge. While Noble and Lewis tramped through the snow on their trek to the States, carts full of silver and gold spun their wooden wheels in the other direction, smuggled across the border by New England merchants trading with the British. This flourishing black market drained the nation's already strained supply of coined money, or specie; one contemporary estimated that $2 million worth of gold left the United States in early 1814 alone. The dwindling coin reserves only ratcheted up demand for credit, and Pennsylvania, where the shortage was acutely felt, responded dramatically. In March 1814, about a year after Noble and Lewis arrived in Bellefonte, the state legislature passed a bill chartering forty-one new banks in addition to the six that existed—an increase of almost 600 percent.

Horrified at the prospect of Pennsylvania being swamped with inflationary paper, Governor Simon Snyder vetoed the measure. He told the legislators that while "Eastern mercantile cupidity" had lost "immense sums of specie" doing business with the British, more banks would only make things worse. "Is there at this time an intelligent man in Pennsylvania," he wrote, "who believes that a bank-note of any description is the representative of specie?" The answer was yes, at least enough in the legislature to override Snyder's veto. While an extreme case, Pennsylvania wasn't alone. As Canada steadily siphoned off America's precious metals, states chartered more banks and the amount of paper money grew precipitously. From 1811 to 1815, the face value of notes in circulation almost doubled, rising from $66 million to $115 million.

Skyrocketing quantities of notes combined with shrinking stores of specie made a crisis inevitable. It came in August 1814, when the British invaded the Chesapeake and marched on Washington, DC. Under orders to retaliate for American rampages in Canada, the British officers staged a spectacle calculated to crush the enemy's spirit. They burned down the city's government buildings, including the White House, which blazed all night, leaving nothing but a smoldering shell. The psychological impact of torching the nation's capital was predictably severe, not only among American soldiers but also in the financial sector, which in its overextended state relied precariously on people's confidence. The razing of Washington destroyed that faith, setting off a panic that triggered a run on Chesapeake banks. In response, the banks suspended specie payments.

The freeze eventually spread throughout the country, until institutions everywhere stopped redeeming their notes for coin—everywhere but New

England, where reserves were greater and banks better regulated. While ostensibly a crisis, the affair must have come as a relief to bankers, who no longer had to sustain the expensive illusion that their notes represented silver and gold. Business continued as usual: although banknotes lost value, they continued to pass as money. Paine's hostages, after years of straining at their fetters, had finally been set free.

The federal government suffered the most. To fund the war, it levied duties on foreign trade and went deeply into debt by issuing bonds and printing Treasury notes. Since the Treasury accepted bank paper in payment of taxes and loans, it ended up losing a lot of money on the depreciated notes when banks stopped paying out coin in August. With escalating costs, deficient revenue, and no stable currency with which to pay its obligations, the Treasury hit rock bottom: it couldn't repay the interest on its debts, and by the end of the year, its notes had become worthless. Almost three decades since the delegates met in Philadelphia and vowed to prevent America's checkered financial past from repeating itself, the government was broke and the country awash with cheap paper. With no national bank to force the banks to resume payments, Americans found themselves in a purely faith-based economy. Moneymaking, once the exclusive province of disgruntled silversmiths and enterprising crooks, had gone mainstream.

ANYONE WHO GLIMPSED the four men scrambling uphill through the foliage could be forgiven for thinking they were homesteaders headed west. It was the fall of 1815, and the taverns overflowed with people who had waited until harvesttime to start their journey. The men traveled by wagon like pioneers; their cart might have carried food, bedding, and a closely kept bundle of cash to buy a plot of land wherever it was cheap enough. They ascended what locals called the Allegany range, a high ridge of the Alleghenies west of Bedford, the last major chain on the road to

Pittsburgh and the frontier beyond. The temperature cooled the higher they climbed, and the landscape grew more striking in scale, so that when the thick forests parted, the travelers caught dazzling views of blue mountains in the distance and green valleys sprawling below.

The scenery was familiar to Lewis, who walked alongside Noble and two cronies the counterfeiters had recruited, Rufus Crosby and James Smith. They were hiking to a camp in the wilderness, guiding a wagon weighed down by two locked trunks, each about three feet long. The travelers didn't unload their cargo until they reached the clearing where they had built their makeshift home. Around them lay all the necessities of frontier life: an ax, a butcher knife, a skillet, a canteen, a coffeepot, and various flasks of liquor. A nearby stream supplied the site with fresh water. Their hut consisted of a frame of saplings covered with a mat of branches and leaves. The roof wasn't sturdy enough to withstand the rain, and unfortunately, it rained often.

If the walls started leaking, they would travel to a tavern three miles away to find drier lodging. Its proprietor, Michael Miller, saw them frequently. When the men first appeared on the mountain in early September 1815, they told him they were a team of land surveyors planning to divide up an unsettled tract of twenty thousand acres into four-hundred-acre lots. Even Miller, whose profession exposed him to some odd characters, must have found the group a little strange. As always, Lewis cut the most attractive figure: polite, sociable, finely attired. James Smith was younger and shorter, with dark hair; Rufus Crosby could often be seen with a fiddle on his shoulder, which he played very well. Noble brought up the rear. He obviously ran the operation: the others called him "captain" and carried out his orders. He didn't endear himself to Miller, however—"a fat chunk of a man" was how the tavern keeper later described him. It didn't help that Noble spoke with a northern accent that immediately marked him as an outsider.

Miller might have had his doubts, but he had no solid grounds for suspecting anything illegal. All he saw them bring to the camp were provisions like beef, fish, and flour; the two mysterious trunks, when he peeked inside, contained nothing but bedclothes. But if he never caught sight of any counterfeiting tools, he didn't notice any surveying instruments either. There was something else that seemed curious. The men gave him a quart-size jug filled almost to the brim with ink, perhaps as a form of payment, or a token of their gratitude. The jug was so big that five months later, the tavern keeper still used it to write.

Producing counterfeits required ink, paper, plates, and a printing press. First Lewis and the others would ink the plate, place it in the press, and run paper through the contraption to produce sheets of fresh bills. When the sheets had dried, they could be cut into individual notes. Then the signatures of the bank's cashier and president would be forged on each bill, a process called "filling up" the notes. The final product didn't resemble the colonial money Sullivan had counterfeited decades earlier: the banknotes were wider, printed horizontally rather than vertically, and more visually sophisticated. They carried vignettes and various other design flourishes to dissuade counterfeiters, which made Noble's engraving task that much more difficult.

It had been more than two years since Bellefonte's citizens had accused Noble of espionage, and he had since learned to be more careful. A remote backcountry camp provided an excellent place to work, far from the prying eyes of local townsfolk. The counterfeiters kept everything secret. The container of ink given to Miller offered the only clue of their intentions; the tavern keeper never spotted any paper, plates, or a printing press. Aside from the inclement weather, the job went smoothly. They stayed for three weeks making fake bills before they packed up their wagon and took off, leaving no trace of their crime—just their butcher knife and hut remained.

Lewis and his collaborators were smart to take extra precautions. As they learned at Bellefonte, Noble inevitably aroused suspicion, and not even Lewis at his most appealing could entirely distract people from the pudgy engraver's eccentricities. But Noble's engraving expertise made him too valuable to lose, despite the risks his presence posed. Noble wasn't Lewis's only problem: circumstances had also made Pennsylvanians more vigilant. As the quantity of banknotes soared with the new bank charters in March 1814 and similar expansions in other states, so did the opportunities for moneymaking. Criminals could now do more than just forge an existing note. They could also defraud people with spurious, raised, and altered bills. Spurious money displayed the name of a real bank but used a different design: the passer counted on his victim's recognizing the bank without knowing what its notes looked like. Raised bills took genuine currency and made it more valuable by changing the denomination, and altered notes were printed from the plates of a bank that had gone bankrupt.

These creative swindles would not have been possible without America's growing financial complexity. In Owen Sullivan's era people only traded in a few currencies: their colony's and those of neighboring provinces. In David Lewis's day, by contrast, there were too many kinds of paper changing hands for the average American to be familiar with all of it. Detecting a bad bill required knowing the notes of hundreds of different banks, a daunting task for anyone, much less an ordinary shopkeeper. Newspapers did their part by publicizing known counterfeits and new publications, called "banknote reporters," gave readers detailed catalogs of fake money in circulation. But the banking world's vastness ensured that people's knowledge of it would always be incomplete, and even the slightest gap gave counterfeiters an opening.

The dizzying diversity of American currency didn't just make identifying fakes more difficult. It also created a headache for those honest citizens trying to exchange genuine money, as the relative values of different bills fluctuated constantly. A banknote's worth wasn't just indicated by the denomination printed on its surface; the more important factors were the reputation of the bank that issued it and the location of the person spending it. Generally, a bill cost more the closer you were to the institution where it originated, although some banks, namely, the more respected ones in eastern cities, preserved the value of their notes even at great distances. In Baltimore in 1818, for instance, notes from Boston, New York, and Philadelphia—called "eastern paper" or "city paper"—all passed at par. "Western paper," on the other hand—bills printed by banks in Bellefonte, Bedford, and Pittsburgh—was discounted, or "shaved," by 3 to 5 percent. Newspapers and banknote reporters kept people updated on the prices of different currencies, and the statistics published in their pages naturally encouraged speculation. A canny businessman could buy up western paper cheaply in Baltimore and make a profit when he arrived in Pittsburgh, where the same notes traded at a higher price. It may not have been counterfeiting, but it wasn't exactly honest either.

All of this meant that in the fall and winter of 1815, when Lewis started passing the notes that he and Noble forged at their campsite in September, he had to work harder than his colonial predecessors. Lewis carried counterfeits from three institutions: the Philadelphia Bank; the Baltimore-based Union Bank of Maryland; and the Hagerstown Bank, located in Maryland about six miles south of the Pennsylvania border. Not only did he need to muster every ounce of personal charm to cajole leery locals into believing his money was authentic, he also had to deal with varying values for different bills. Fortunately, he no longer had to worry about how people would respond to Noble, since after their September printing spree, the two drifted apart. The engraver likely returned to Canada, while Lewis stayed in Pennsylvania to make his fortune in his native state.

After splitting with Noble, Lewis flitted from one village to the next, trying to change his bogus cash for genuine money at stores and taverns along the way. He used a couple of aliases—David Philips and David Wilson—and avoided anywhere he might be recognized. If someone had plotted his route on a map of Pennsylvania, it would have cut across counties shaped like jigsaw pieces, divided by rivers or mountain ranges, sprinkled with hamlets separated by miles of jagged Allegheny terrain. From the tilled lowlands of Franklin County to the forested ridges of Mifflin County to the slate cliffs of Bedford County, Lewis spent the final few months of 1815 traversing a region almost as varied as the currency flowing through it.

ON THE LAST DAY of November, morning light filtered through the window of a shop in Franklin County to rest on the figure of James Shoaff lying in his bed. He awoke to the sound of a customer in his store: from his room he could hear a voice asking the clerk for a pocket comb. The man was insisting on buying it with city paper and wanted western paper in exchange. When Shoaff got up and walked into his shop, he met the stranger, who introduced himself as Philips and looked every bit the traveling gentleman. Philips presented the sleepy proprietor with a $100 bill of the Philadelphia Bank, and Shoaff, taking the note in his hands to examine it, immediately knew he had a problem. He had heard that there were counterfeits of this bank circulating, but Philadelphia paper, the most valuable in the state, would be hard to resist. Hoping to resolve his dilemma, Shoaff took the bill to a nearby tavern. There he got conflicting opinions: one man said to take the money; the other advised against it. Shoaff decided to compromise. Returning to the store, he refused to sell the customer the comb but agreed to change the $100 note for western paper. The shopkeeper added one crucial condition, however: he wouldn't trade the western bills at their usual discount but only at full face value. For $100 of Philadelphia paper, Shoaff paid out the same amount in western money.

Whenever currency changed hands, there was an opportunity to reap a profit. You didn't need to be a seasoned speculator to benefit from a smart exchange; everyone, including small-time vendors like Shoaff, was looking to cash in. When the man who called himself Philips took Shoaff's offer, the shopkeeper must have felt pretty pleased with himself: after a tough negotiation with a traveler eager to change money, he had gotten city paper cheap. What he couldn't know was that was exactly how Lewis wanted him to feel. The counterfeiter knew how to set the trap and let his mark's greed pull him deeper into the snare. He also had the self-possession to sit calmly while his soon-to-be victim scrutinized the bill and asked others for their opinion.

Sometimes Lewis relied less on charm than on swagger. When buying a black silk handkerchief from Thomas McClellan, a shopkeeper in McConnellsburg, he took a harder tone than usual. Lewis asked McClellan whether he would accept a large bill. "If it suits me," the merchant saltily replied. He would be glad to get it, Lewis shot back, and revealed one of his $100 notes from the Philadelphia Bank. While McClellan inspected it, Lewis lined up the ruse that would close the deal. He told the shopkeeper that he had better send the bill off to someone whose judgment he trusted. McClellan took the bait: his pride piqued, he declared that he could decide for himself and, after a brief examination, pronounced the money genuine.

Lewis had a masterful feel for the physics of persuasion: when to apply pressure, when to fall back, which levers to pull. Almost everyone he met at first regarded his money suspiciously but, more often than not, agreed to take it. He could have used a network of passers to circulate his bad bills and kept himself out of sight. But he couldn't stand to be invisible: he wanted to stand face-to-face with his prey and personally convince him that the note he held in his hands was authentic.

It was a dangerous approach. When he walked into Hill Wilson's tavern on New Year's Eve, he had spent so many counterfeits in the past weeks that it was only a matter of time before the law caught up with him. When Wilson and others confronted Lewis about buying a horse with fake money, he decided to drink gin with them for hours before the sheriff arrived. Perhaps he intended to get caught; without his arrest and subsequent trial at Bedford, he would have remained an unknown. The courtroom gave the citizens of central Pennsylvania their first opportunity to learn about Lewis, a local boy who had fled north as an army deserter and returned a moneymaker. The story line was irresistible, and Lewis, on the public stage for the first time, proved himself particularly well suited for the role.

I N THE FIRST COUPLE OF MONTHS OF 1816, horses pulling wagons toward Bedford trudged along frostbitten trails while their breath steamed in the cold air. Past the mountains the prospect opened up to reveal the town in the distance, a modest cluster of houses in the shadow of the Alleghenies, on the banks of a river that ran eastward through the bluffs. If the impression from afar was pleasantly rustic, the mood in Bedford was anything but tranquil. The travelers arrived to find a community whirling with frenzied activity. In a settlement of fewer than eight hundred residents, people walked with the impatient, purposeful stride of city dwellers. Philadelphia, New York, and Boston had never seemed so irrelevant.

Among its buildings of stone, brick, and timber, one topic alone dominated the conversation: counterfeiting. Since New Year's Day, David Lewis had sat in his cell at the courthouse jail near the center of town. The structure stood two stories high, built of immense limestone slabs that enclosed a courtyard where convicts were once pilloried and whipped. Despite its imposing stature, the courthouse was notoriously insecure, and every night, watchmen guarded the jail to prevent Lewis from escaping. A handful of other counterfeiters had been caught in the region, and Lewis, as the most conspicuous of the lot, would come to personify the moneymaking menace in the eyes of Bedford's citizens. The dapper criminal had to be tried before he could find a way to flee, and this was what gave Bedford its sense of urgency, unusual in a town accustomed to a more countrified pace. The newcomers streaming in were witnesses and informers, people who planned to testify against Lewis in court or denounce him in private. "You cannot conceive how busy a place it has been," noted an observer to a friend.

The man at the middle of the maelstrom was Samuel Riddle. A local attorney, he had the prestigious job of prosecuting Lewis, a responsibility he clearly enjoyed. Riddle was "in his element," wrote one resident, "much more busy than all the field marshalls at the battle of Waterloo." Tall and thin, he exuded tremendous energy; an arched nose protruded conspicuously from his face, lending his features the dignified air of a Roman statesman. Riddle was well liked, not only as a lawyer but also as a successful entrepreneur. He had started the first mines in the nearby Broad Top region, where he chiseled coal out of the seams, pulverized them, and sold the powder—not as fuel but as fertilizer, which he marketed to farmers with promises of richer harvests. One industry wasn't enough for Riddle; his other ventures included an orchard, a sawmill, and a peach brandy distillery. Perpetually seeking new outlets for his ambition, he never learned to stop taking risks.

Trying to bring Lewis to justice could easily have been a lost gamble. At first Riddle didn't have much of a case. Granted, Lewis had been apprehended at Hill Wilson's tavern for buying a horse with forged money and resisted arrest so violently that he almost killed the sheriff. But at the Bedford jail the prisoner confessed nothing. He claimed to be David Wilson Lewis from Philadelphia, and no evidence linked him to a broader moneymaking enterprise. Fortunately for Riddle, the authorities called someone in to confirm the criminal's true identity. Then the prosecutor began digging around for accomplices—people who had helped Lewis during his partnership with Noble in the fall of 1815, or during the subsequent months he spent passing the fake cash. The same day Lewis was locked in his cell, officers searched the house of his uncle William Drenning, who lived just south of Bedford. In his stable they found the horse that Lewis had bought with bad bills, as well as three pairs of saddlebags full of expensive goods likely purchased with counterfeit cash. Drenning and one of his sons were arrested; another son escaped. Four days later, the sheriff overtook him eleven miles from town.

As Riddle built his case, the drama surrounding Lewis's trial mounted. Riddle had a good reason for working as hard as he did. Lewis planned to put up a considerable fight: he hired excellent counsel, using the cash he had earned from exchanging forged bills for genuine notes. When he was arrested, Lewis had $1,900 in good money on him and, according to one report, another $1,500 deposited in the bank at Bedford. This was a sizable amount: in Philadelphia at the time, a gallon of brandy cost $2. The court ruled early on that it couldn't interfere with the defendant paying his lawyers, so Lewis spent freely: $200 during just his first week in jail.

His costly defense team consisted of George Burd and Charles Huston. Burd, known for his round face and affable demeanor, took second string to Huston. The older and more celebrated of the two, Huston ran a highly successful practice in Bellefonte. He had taught Latin and Greek before becoming a lawyer, and still dressed like a slovenly professor: "slouched hat, drab three-caped overcoat, green flannel leggings tied around the legs with black tape, homespun dress coat" was how one contemporary described his attire. In spite of his appearance, Huston awed judges and juries with his courtroom oratory, winning praise that allowed him to command high prices for his services. He belonged to the same postrevolutionary generation as Riddle; in fact, the men were born a month apart in 1771.

While Riddle and Huston wrangled over the prisoner's fate, his reputation lay in the ink-stained hands of Charles McDowell, the publisher of the *Bedford Gazette*. The newspaper's offices were next door to the courthouse where Lewis was held; inside, McDowell hastily set type for the next issue. He provided lively, detailed accounts of Lewis's adventures—at Hill Wilson's tavern, at the mountain campsite—that gave readers their first glimpse of the counterfeiter in action.

In the pages of the *Gazette*, Lewis went from being an obscure criminal to a leading culprit in a counterfeiting epidemic sweeping the countryside with such force that even "promising young men, of the most wealthy and respectable families," fell victim to it by joining the villains' ranks. According to McDowell's articles, Lewis belonged to an enormously sophisticated criminal organization with more than a hundred members active in Pennsylvania, New York, New Jersey, Ohio, and Virginia. They included expert engravers like Noble, wagon drivers who hauled large loads of forged notes, gamblers who passed bad bills at the betting table, and "affidavit men" paid to perjure themselves by supplying the counterfeiters with false alibis. An invisible army of moneymakers roamed the land, recruiting impressionable youth, funneling fraudulent paper into the pockets of honest Americans from their hidden retreats in the mountains.

The facts were far less dramatic. Counterfeiting was indeed widespread, but it thrived in diffuse networks, not large, coordinated ventures. A massive interstate conspiracy made up of a hundred criminals simply wasn't practical; the effort of managing such a gang would easily outweigh the benefits. John Reid, a counterfeiter captured at Hagerstown, gave a more reasonable estimate, putting the number of Noble and Lewis's network at twenty. But regardless of how many people Lewis and Noble collaborated with, their operation was more like a loose web than a tightly knit group. A little fantasy, however, went a long way in propelling Lewis to fame. Thanks to the sensationalism of McDowell's reports, the well-mannered moneymaker became known not only in Bedford but throughout Pennsylvania, as newspapers all over the state reprinted the *Gazette* articles.

Lewis's trial was set to begin on February 13, 1816. In fact, the court planned to hold three separate trials, as grand juries indicted the defendant on multiple charges of passing counterfeit currency. In the meantime, anticipation grew. Lewis passed the weeks confined in the courthouse jail while the men he had set in motion buzzed around him: Riddle mapped the line of attack, Huston prepared the defense, and McDowell stoked the suspense.

GETTING TO THE COURTROOM required going up an outdoor staircase that led to the second story of the building where Lewis was imprisoned. Up those steps climbed jurors and witnesses, shivering in the wind that swept across the valley. Inside the chamber sat Judge Jonathan Hoge Walker, who, at six feet four inches, towered over the proceedings but, in the judgment of a later historian, was "more remarkable for his size than for his brains." Riddle gave an impressive performance. He called twenty-seven witnesses, using their testimony to reconstruct Lewis's route through Pennsylvania over the past several months. He pieced together a portrait of the wilderness hideout where Lewis, Noble, and their two accomplices had spent weeks printing bogus bills the previous fall. He sketched Lewis's subsequent spending spree, bringing the victims before the court to talk about being swindled by the defendant. He even presented agents from banks whose bills Lewis had counterfeited to pronounce the notes forgeries.

The character that emerged from the dozens of statements, while undoubtedly a criminal, had an irrepressible appeal. Even witnesses who spoke against Lewis couldn't deny his charm: "sociable & good humoured" was how one tavern keeper put it. Lewis's playfulness was a large part of his allure. He was an inveterate gambler—a "sporting man," "active in playing cards," in the words of other witnesses—and he brought a gaming spirit to his counterfeiting career: relishing the risk, hoping to score. He was also generous. One witness, John Little, told the jurors a story about meeting Lewis in Morrison's Cove, a fertile expanse of low-land north of Bedford, at Christmastime. In the course of their conversation, Little admitted to being in debt and Lewis promptly gave him a forged $20 note as a present. Then they shared drinks and gambled all night until parting ways the following morning.

Lewis's years with Noble had taught him to avoid certain pitfalls. A tavern keeper testified that he once observed the defendant trying to persuade an old traveler from Kentucky to trade a large pile of silver for banknotes. The man declared he would only accept the bills if Lewis endorsed them by hand. The counterfeiter refused, saying he had injured his hand so badly he couldn't hold a pen, and the Kentuckian, dissatisfied by this answer, walked away. Although it cost him a bundle of silver, Lewis made the right decision. Signing a counterfeit note to verify its authenticity was perjury, and he didn't need another indictment on top of everything else.

Drawing on more than a month of hard work, Riddle produced definitive proof of Lewis's guilt. Huston couldn't hope to dispute such a substantial body of evidence with conflicting testimony, and in any case, he found only four witnesses to testify on Lewis's behalf. He nonetheless gave a spirited defense, using technicalities to try to dodge Riddle's well-supported accusations. He contested the court's jurisdiction, complained about irregularities in the spelling of a witness's name, and even cited English legal opinion in an unsuccessful effort to convince the judge that someone whose name had been forged couldn't be admitted as a witness. But the lawyer, for all his persistence, failed to clear his client. On February 13 and February 17, the jurors convicted Lewis on two of the three indictments for passing counterfeit money.

By protesting that a bank had been misnamed in the text of the indictment, Huston managed to get the first sentence reduced to a small fine and ten hours in the Bedford jail. The second, however, stuck. Lewis faced another fine and, far worse, six years in the Philadelphia penitentiary. The court specified that Lewis be transferred to the city prison "with all convenient speed under safe & secure conduct," no doubt fearing that the prisoner, after losing his bid for freedom, would take matters into his own hands.

About an hour after the sun rose on February 27, Lewis broke out of the Bedford jail. He had been locked inside for almost a full two months, and given the building's poor security, it's surprising he didn't make his getaway sooner. "He could easily have escaped," opined a Bedford attorney familiar with the affair, "but his lawyers assured him of an acquittal, and as he did not want to lose the fifteen hundred dollars in the bank, he stood trial." News of Lewis's flight had a predictably explosive effect on the town. After Riddle's artfully orchestrated conviction, the counterfeiter had vanished before the drama could come to its conclusion.

The *Bedford Gazette* was outraged. It accused Lewis's jailers of freeing him, presumably for a bribe, and blamed the state's "penny-wise Commissioners" for neglecting to build a better jail. "For the last five or six years we have not heard of any person detained in our prison, contrary to his wish," the newspaper fumed. The sheriff posted a $300 reward for Lewis, and personally led a fruitless attempt to find him. The *Gazette* demanded an official investigation into how Lewis escaped, and who, if anyone, abetted the criminal. The counterfeiter remained at large for months. In mid-May, the authorities caught him in Ohio, only to have him slip through their fingers again. Around the first of June, he was finally captured in New York and taken in chains to Philadelphia.

LEWIS ARRIVED IN PHILADELPHIA on June 8, 1816, just as the city was experiencing the worst cold wave in American memory. Three days before, a strong wind had come in from the northwest, driving the temperature down almost thirty degrees overnight. By the time Lewis got there, ice was so plentiful that fishermen brought chilled fish to summer market. The bizarre weather beset the entire country: farther north, snow fell throughout New England, reaching twelve inches in many places. The year as a whole was so frigid that Americans everywhere dubbed it "eighteen-hundred-and-froze-to-death." Some blamed sunspots, earthquakes, and a lunar eclipse for bringing on the cold; others prayed and fasted, begging God for forgiveness. Thousands of miles from Philadelphia, on the shores of Lake Geneva, the unusual climate kept Mary Wollstonecraft Godwin indoors, reading ghost tales by the fire with her future husband, Percy Bysshe Shelley, Lord Byron, and other friends. When they decided to write their own stories to pass the time, she produced the idea for her novel *Frankenstein*.

While passersby huddled for warmth, Lewis was hauled to the prison on Walnut Street at the center of town. Its facade stood two stories tall, built of rough-cut stone and capped with a copper weather vane shaped like a key, which spun wildly in the blustery weather. Compared to most American jails, the Philadelphia prison was striking for its size. The main entrance led through iron-grated doors to a long corridor linking two additional wings. Farther on was a courtyard that joined the compound's other structures, including workshops where inmates toiled at various trades, separate rooms for delinquent debtors, and a solitary-confinement block.

These buildings were the legacy of a vocal band of reformers who, decades earlier, had determined to make the Walnut Street Jail a prototype for a new kind of penitentiary. Colonial justice had emphasized corporal punishment and public humiliation; the new approach called for rehabilitating criminals by putting them to work, segregating debtors from serious offenders, and improving living standards. It also required regulating the conduct of wardens, who in earlier days had let alcohol and prostitutes flow freely through their jails. Although the reformers prevailed on the authorities to adopt the majority of these changes, they had less success with their most revolutionary demand: keeping prisoners in solitary confinement, letting them out only to work. Rather than shaming the convict in public—at the pillory or the whipping post at the center of town—the reformers wanted to sequester him, so he could reflect on his evil past and begin the lonely process of personal transformation. The plan simply wasn't practical. The state legislature eventually had sixteen such cells built, not nearly enough to hold its more than three hundred inmates. The jailers ended up using the cells to quarantine particularly tough convicts or to punish recalcitrant prisoners.

The Walnut Street Jail housed convicts from all over Pennsylvania. Small towns like Bedford—whose authorities couldn't afford to keep prisoners for long periods of time and whose jails were too weak to hold them anyway—dispatched their most troublesome criminals to Philadelphia. This eventually led to severe overcrowding that made conditions at the prison steadily worse. When Lewis arrived in the summer of 1816, the Walnut Street Jail had become almost precisely the opposite of what it was supposed to be. Instead of rehabilitating criminals, it hardened them; instead of segregating Pennsylvania's worst lawbreakers, it brought them together to conspire and enlist new recruits. People serving time for minor offenses rubbed shoulders with the state's most desperate felons, with the result that the prison undoubtedly produced more criminals than it reformed. Prisoners fought one another, provoked riots, assaulted jailers, and attempted increasingly brazen escapes. One convict sawed the irons off his leg, slipped through the bars on his window, and used a rope made from tied blankets to lower himself into the courtyard before vaulting over the wall.

The prison's criminal culture was familiar to Lewis. Twenty-eight years old, he already had years of experience as a lawbreaker, both in Canada and in the United States, and had seen his name in newspapers throughout Pennsylvania after his widely publicized trial. Even so, the Walnut Street Jail transformed him. It left his charisma and his poise intact but toughened his resolve and deepened his daring. He had always been a gambler. Prison made him eager to take greater risks; he emerged ready to commit bigger, more spectacular crimes.

The Walnut Street Jail's lawlessness not only emboldened Lewis, it also gave him a way to earn his freedom. As the prison descended into chaos, the jailers began relying on informers to help them keep order. Using informers had a double advantage: they supplied information that thwarted attacks and jailbreaks and, since they were usually pardoned, helped relieve congestion in the prison. Freeing inmates who squealed also saved lives, since other prisoners often tried to kill them. Determined not to serve his full six-year sentence, Lewis ingratiated himself with his keepers by informing on his fellow prisoners. In 1819, it finally paid off: after tipping off the jailers about a plan among inmates to escape, Lewis was recommended to the governor for amnesty.

When Lewis's pardon reached Governor William Findlay's desk in Harrisburg, he probably didn't think twice before signing it. He regularly freed inmates at the Walnut Street Jail who had been nominated for clemency; if he didn't, the overpopulation problem would have become even worse, and Findlay already had enough to worry about. He faced reelection the following year, and if the last contest was any indication, it wouldn't be easy. An early disciple of Thomas Jefferson and a loyal member of the Democratic-Republican Party, Findlay had narrowly won in 1817 after an especially bitter contest against a coalition of dissident Democrats, Federalists, and independents. The partisan rancor didn't subside when he took office, as the legislature immediately launched an inquiry into whether the new governor had embezzled public funds during his ten years as state treasurer. In the midst of managing this political whirlwind, granting another pardon would be a relief by comparison, a routine gesture. He couldn't have known that signing it would soon come back to haunt him.

ON SEPTEMBER 9, 1819, after three years and three months in the Walnut Street Jail, Lewis walked out a free man. A lot had happened while he was behind bars. He entered prison while America suffered the coldest summer on record; he left to find the nation in the grip of a depression. In Philadelphia, employment had fallen 78 percent across thirty different trades since 1816, affecting industries as varied as cotton manufacturing, pottery, and book printing. Thousands of out-of-work laborers roamed the streets desperate for food. As winter approached, fears grew that the newly destitute masses wouldn't be able to survive the season.

Lewis was witnessing what came to be called the Panic of 1819, the catastrophic conclusion to a period of prosperity that had lasted since the end of the War of 1812. The boom had been fueled by a surge in foreign trade, westward expansion, and a steady stream of currency and credit supplied by the nation's banks. Banks had stopped redeeming their notes for coin in 1814 during the financial uproar surrounding the British invasion of the nation's capital. When the war ended, the banks still hadn't resumed payment, which meant they could print more and more paper without bothering about whether they had enough silver and gold to back it. Flush with cheap money, Americans invested in a rapidly diversifying domestic economy, speculating in everything from real estate to road building to textile manufacturing.

In a sign of the times, the New York Stock & Exchange Board opened on Wall Street in 1817. The conservative business ethic of Alexander Hamilton's era, already under siege for decades, was in danger of being swept away by a horde of schemers and speculators. These men leveraged paper fortunes on stepladders of debt, prospering in an economy where actual cash was seldom exchanged. The engine ran on confidence: so long as people didn't try to redeem one another's promises to pay, banks could balance ever-greater piles of debt on a slim base of precious metals. America's growing financial sophistication, instead of producing real riches, had created a hallucination that everyone conspired to sustain.

This period of false prosperity also saw the federal government incorporate the Second Bank of the United States in the spring of 1816. Politicians like James Madison, who had loudly clamored for the first Bank's

demise in 1811, now supported chartering a new one: the dire state of
federal finances during the war and the deluge of irredeemable banknotes
that followed it had changed their minds. The Second Bank opened its
main branch a couple of blocks east of the Walnut Street Jail, in Carpenters' Hall, a colonial-era Georgian building planned by the same architect who designed the prison. Its redbrick walls and white cupola evoked
the receding memory of the Revolution: the delegates of the Continental
Congress had first met there in 1774. The same resolve that had won the
nation its independence would now be needed to rein in its financial disarray. The Bank scored an early victory in February 1817, when, along
with the Treasury Department, it persuaded most state banks to resume
the redemption of notes for coin, bringing a much-needed degree of sanity
to the economy. At least nominally, America had returned to a specie basis
for its currency.

The problem, of course, was that they weren't. The exchangeability of
bills for precious metals had grown increasingly theoretical: even banks
that had nominally resumed payment did everything they could to prevent people from redeeming their notes. The Bank couldn't continue

overextending itself for long, and by the summer of 1818, it was forced to take measures to stay solvent. It reduced the number of notes in circulation and, most important, called on the state banks to honor their bills.

This simple request triggered the calamitous chain of events that led to the Panic of 1819. As banks throughout the country scrambled to meet their obligations, many went bankrupt; those that remained afloat depleted their coin reserves, forcing them to limit note issues and curb lending. The violent contraction of currency and credit gave the economy a severe shock. Cash became scarce, interest rates rose, and prices fell sharply across the board. People who had gone deeply into debt expecting future profits now found themselves unable to repay their loans as their income dwindled. Merchants who traded in foreign goods saw the value of their products plummet; real estate speculators now held land worth a fraction of its former cost. Farmers who had borrowed to finance improvement projects suffered from a steep decline in agricultural prices. As money became harder to obtain, investment in manufacturing, construction, and transportation dried up. Laborers watched their wages plunge: an unskilled turnpike worker made seventy-five cents a day in 1818; a year later he earned only twelve cents a day. In many parts of Ohio and Indiana, the Panic essentially wiped out the money supply, as local banks failed and currency drained eastward to the cities. The situation became so severe that some communities resorted to the barter system, swapping goods the way America's first colonists had done centuries earlier, before the introduction of paper money.

Although the Panic affected Americans in very tangible ways, the trauma was also psychological. In a boom, everyone becomes a cheerleader; the abundance of easy money persuades people that the good times will continue forever. The bust abruptly shattered this illusion, and the emotions it provoked were as powerful as its economic impact. In the years after the War of 1812, American farmers overcame their traditional distrust of banks and took out large loans to develop their land. When the Panic struck, saddling them with intolerable debt, they erupted in anger, blaming everyone but themselves. While there had undoubtedly been unscrupulous characters who had exploited unsuspecting victims, the tide of righteous rage that tore through the country masked something deeper. The surge of inflated wealth couldn't have happened without the complicity of ordinary Americans; the fury they felt afterward was partly a way to vent their humiliation over being so easily fooled.

Perversely, the easiest target was the party least responsible: the Second Bank of the United States. By demanding that the state banks settle their outstanding balances, the Bank was simply doing its job. But, like sleepers rudely woken from a lovely dream, Americans lashed out at the Bank, denouncing it as a federal conspiracy to oppress the states and enrich eastern investors at the expense of hardworking citizens. The bankers in Philadelphia and politicians in Washington were too far away to bear the full brunt of people's bitterness, so a lesser cast of villains emerged: local landlords, tax collectors, financiers—anyone who stood to profit from someone else's labor without producing anything of his own.

The rising populist current couldn't have come at a better time for Lewis. As unemployment, bankruptcy, and foreclosures ravaged the country, crime acquired an aura of prestige. Not only was it a way for the dispossessed to make a living, but compared with the perfectly legal frauds perpetrated by the nation's banks, lawbreaking seemed honest. In difficult times, the outlaw often becomes a hero to the hopeless. He transcends the tedium of poverty: while the poor stand in soup lines or wander the streets looking for work, the outlaw takes what he wants instead of waiting for society to give it to him. It wasn't just his charisma or his daring that made Lewis a folk hero. What elevated him to the status of a legend was his metamorphosis into precisely the kind of populist icon that central Pennsylvania needed in 1819: a Robin Hood who protected the weak from the strong, who punished the avaricious and rewarded the needy. Lewis so skillfully cultivated the character of the righteous outlaw that people lionized him even as he robbed and swindled them. His success came at their expense, but at a time when communities across America were struggling, they could take pride in knowing that a native son of the Alleghenies was pocketing tremendous amounts of money—not as cowardly bankers and businessmen did but as a criminal, with bluster and bravado.

Lewis wasn't the Panic's only unlikely hero. John Adams, who turned eighty-four in 1819, proposed someone even more improbable: Thomas Hutchinson, the colonial leader who had tried to purge paper money from Massachusetts when Owen Sullivan was starting to forge bills and Adams was just a boy. Now, as the elderly Founding Father watched the country he helped create slide into a depression provoked by the fickleness of paper wealth, Hutchinson's judgment seemed prescient. A decade before the crash, Adams spelled out his thinking in a letter to a friend. "If I was the witch of Endor," he wrote, referring to a woman in the Old Testament who summons the spirit of a dead prophet, "I would wake the ghost of Hutchinson, and give him absolute power over the currency of the United States and every part of it." Despite hating Hutchinson's Loyalist politics, Adams admitted that the haughty merchant "understood the subject of coin and commerce better than any man I ever knew in this country." In the seven decades since Hutchinson proposed banning bills of credit in 1749, paper money had woven itself even more deeply into the fabric of American life. Adams feared for the stability of a nation that swung from boom to bust, and for the future of a citizenry so readily seduced by fraudulent fantasies of the good life.

ON A SUNDAY MORNING in October 1819, John McClelland bobbed gently in his saddle as he guided his horse down a mountain road east of Bedford. A Pittsburgh merchant, McClelland was carrying $1,500 in banknotes and gold to Philadelphia, where he planned to deposit the hefty sum in a bank. Transporting that kind of money across almost the whole length of Pennsylvania would be extremely dangerous, but unfortunately, there wasn't an easier way to transfer the funds. He still had two hundred miles to go before reaching Philadelphia, and the rugged Allegheny terrain, with its dense forests and secluded hollows, offered countless places for highwaymen to lurk—a thought that undoubtedly crossed McClelland's mind as he trotted along the turnpike.

At around nine o'clock, McClelland saw a man walking ahead on the path. A lone traveler on foot didn't seem like much of a threat, so the merchant kept his pace. Just as he got close enough to pass ahead, the man whirled around, pistol drawn. It was Lewis. He had blackened his face, presumably with ash or coal dust; a pair of blinking blue eyes and a streak of blond hair stood out against the dark skin. A careless moment could cost McClelland his life. As he dismounted at gunpoint, two accomplices also disguised in blackface darted out from the side of the road. One jumped on the horse and galloped away, while the other, sighting people coming up the path, helped Lewis force McClelland into the woods. They pushed the merchant to the ground and, thrusting their gun barrels against his chest, ordered him to remain absolutely silent. When the passersby had gone, the thieves stood McClelland on his feet and marched him to a camp about half a mile north of the road.

Just like the backcountry bivouac where Noble and Lewis had holed up four years earlier, the site had all the amenities of wilderness living: a fire, a pot, and a hut. The robbers hurled McClelland into the hovel, where he sat and watched them rifle through his saddlebags. The ringleader was clearly Lewis; the others were a pair of thuggish Irishmen named John Connelly and James Hanson. Connelly was tall and broad, with dark brown hair and a long, thin jaw that drew his face downward and gave it a sullen cast. Hanson was the shortest of the gang and apparently the most bloodthirsty; once back at the campsite, he proposed killing McClelland but was promptly vetoed by Lewis and Connelly.

During the several hours that they kept the merchant prisoner, the thieves took his money, his watch, and some of his clothing. Finally, at three o'clock in the afternoon, they departed, but not before instructing McClelland to stay in the hut until sunset. A short time later, Lewis returned alone. Handing the merchant his watch and $30, the robber said he planned to stick up a nearby stagecoach; if the heist succeeded, he promised to give McClelland back the rest of the money. Then Lewis left. The merchant didn't wait for the sun to set; he dashed to the nearest tavern and raised the alarm.

It was October 3, less than a month since Lewis's release from the Walnut Street Jail. The *Bedford Gazette*, whose publisher must have secretly rejoiced at the criminal's sensational return after a three-year absence, carried full coverage of the holdup, labeling it a "robbery of the most daring nature"—from the description provided by McClelland, the mastermind could be none other than "the noted David Lewis," "the celebrated counterfeiter." People remembered Lewis as a moneymaker, but he had since become more aggressive, and after leaving the Walnut Street Jail, he quit counterfeiting for robbery. The news of his attack on McClelland proved predictably embarrassing to Governor Findlay. The prisoner he had pardoned was running wild across the state terrorizing his constituents, and in Pennsylvania's fractious political climate, he couldn't afford to give his enemies more ammunition. But for whatever reason—perhaps the report took a while to reach Harrisburg, or Findlay had more pressing business—the governor didn't respond until four days after the incident, issuing a strongly worded proclamation that offered a $300 reward for the robbers' capture. "The reputation of the Government, the peace and security of its citizens, and the obligations of justice and humanity require that the perpetrators of offenses so atrocious should be brought to speedy and condign punishment," it read. Findlay had blundered again: by the time he made his announcement, the three men were already sitting in the Bedford jail.

The night after the robbery, a posse of well-armed townsfolk had tracked the gang to a small tavern a couple of miles outside Lewistown, a village on the Juniata River northeast of where they mugged McClelland. Not taking any chances, some of the vigilantes stood guard outside the building while the rest rushed inside. Luckily, the criminals had been sleeping and were taken by surprise, resulting in a bloodless capture; there were three pistols and two knives in their bedroom, which the vigilantes quickly secured. The posse ferried the dazed prisoners to Lewistown to give them a meal before locking them up for the night. Maybe it was the late hour or the satisfaction of a job well done, but one of the vigilantes carelessly left his gun on the table. Lewis, fully awake by now, noticed the pistol. He grabbed the gun—he had presumably been left unchained for dinner—and ran out the door and into the street. His captors followed. When they overtook him, Lewis raised the gun and pulled the trigger. As happened at Hill Wilson's tavern four years before, the weapon misfired— he tried again, with the same result. If Lewis hadn't yet killed anyone, it wasn't for lack of trying. The men knocked him unconscious, chained him in irons, and the next morning took all three prisoners to the Bedford jail.

Three years earlier, of course, he had been imprisoned in the exact same jail. Its formidable limestone facade housed the court that convicted him and the cell from which he had escaped shortly afterward. Back then he had been a counterfeiter; now he was a thief. Rather than defrauding people of their goods with bogus bills, he relieved them of their possessions at gunpoint. Instead of wheedling wary merchants into changing fake notes for genuine ones, he mugged them. Even though his tactics had grown more extreme, Lewis remained as affable as ever; in fact, he made a greater effort to endear himself to his victims. He wasn't just after money. In returning some of McClelland's cash and promising to restore the rest of it, Lewis had his reputation in mind. Whether his benevolence was genuine or affected didn't matter; the main thing for Lewis was that it made good copy in the local newspapers.

Just before daybreak on October 25, while Bedford's citizens slept soundly in their beds, Lewis and four others stood near the town's outskirts hacking at their shackles with an ax and a cleaver. The robber had languished in jail for three weeks; the group who escaped with him included Connelly, Hanson, and two runaway slaves who had shared their cell. Swinging sharp blades in the dawn's half-light, they might have severed their limbs instead of their cuffs. A shrill clanging sound rang with each strike, until the manacles finally broke. Their jailbreak had been expertly executed: the prisoners started a fire, first to burn off the fetters fastening them to the floor and then to scorch a large hole in the ground, which they expanded into a tunnel. Digging furiously, they burrowed under the building, came up outside, and sprinted southwest across the valley.

Winter had drained the landscape of color, casting the region's jagged topography in stark relief. Deep snow coated the earth, and on the forested slopes in the distance, the trees made black shapes against the white ground. If they wanted to get away, Lewis and his men needed to drag their aching bodies as far as they could over those slopes before the town awoke. Their legs were swollen and sore from almost a month in chains. The snow presented another obstacle, slowing them down and leaving footprints that would be clearly visible to anyone following them.

On the horizon ahead was Kinton Knob, a mountain that stood half a mile high. The five fugitives scaled the precipitous incline, pushing onward to the wooded glen on the opposite side, and then scurried downhill to take cover among the trees. By now they had been running for four and a half hours but didn't dare stop—especially once they heard the thundering hooves of the Bedford posse approaching. Hoping to hold off the vigilantes, Lewis loudly threatened to shoot; when that didn't work, the escapees dashed down a stream and up another ridge, with their pursuers close behind. The black runaways were caught first. Hanson, whose short legs weren't built for racing over rough terrain, fell next. "I don't give a damn for you or your militia!" the criminal yelled when one of the men ordered him to stop, but he was soon forced to surrender. Connelly, whose husky frame had taken him a long way but couldn't carry him any farther, climbed onto a steep ledge and refused to come down. One of the vigilantes crawled up the bluff and knocked him down with a club. Lewis had outpaced everyone else. But now, as the men with rifles rushed toward him in the snow, he decided to give up. He was exhausted, his clothes were shredded, and if he ran, he risked getting a bullet in the back. It was better to return to jail and bide his time until the next opportunity.

If the Bedford authorities had been smart, they would have tried Lewis quickly and shipped him off under heavy guard to Philadelphia. Instead, they appointed two watchmen to guard the courthouse building every night, as if this meager gesture would be enough to hold him. Lewis had become an escape artist, as notorious for his jailbreaks as for his crimes. So on the night of December 16, 1819, when the alarm went out through Bedford and the townsfolk convened by torchlight to find out what had happened, it couldn't have come as a surprise to learn that the prisoner had pulled off his second getaway in as many months. That morning, Connelly had found a way to pry off the latch that chained him to the floor using his handcuffs; once he had freed himself, he did the same for Lewis, Hanson, and the cell's other inmates.

They couldn't flee in broad daylight, so they had waited patiently until, near sunset, one of the guards arrived to serve supper. Connelly leaped to his feet and, wielding his cuffed hands as weapons, threatened to bash out the man's brains. Lewis took charge and the criminals seized control of the jail, finding a pair of pistols as well as an ax that they used to chop off the shackles on their wrists. Before fleeing, Lewis locked the guard and the head jailer and his family into the cell. He also forced one prisoner to remain in jail—a man named McCurdy, who had been imprisoned for stealing from a poor widow. Anyone depraved enough to commit such a crime, Lewis reportedly declared, wasn't "fit to associate with gentlemen."

Once out of the jail, the inmates scattered. Not all of them got away. Among those recaptured was Hanson, discovered the next morning within a mile of town, hobbling painfully because his feet had been injured in removing the irons. Lewis and Connelly had vanished, leaving their crippled colleague behind. In reporting the escape, one central Pennsylvania newspaper called the men "two of the most dangerous characters that perhaps ever were let loose on society," and included a description of Lewis so that readers might recognize him: "about 6 feet high, square shouldered, strait and well-made, reddish hair, lately cut—speaks quick & has a fierce look."

EVERY TUESDAY AND FRIDAY, Pittsburgh's postmaster loaded stacks of the *Pittsburgh Gazette* into a stagecoach that delivered the four-page publication to subscribers who each paid $3 a year. It was printed across the street, within sight of the stone piers that buttressed a newly built bridge over the Monongahela River.

Founded in 1786 as the first newspaper west of the Alleghenies, the *Gazette* had seen Pittsburgh evolve from a cluster of cabins to a trading and manufacturing hub of more than seven thousand people. By 1820, however, the town had fallen on hard times. Local industries, already hurting from a flood of cheap British imports, virtually collapsed in the aftermath of the Panic; the familiar clattering of the iron foundries, glassworks, and steam engine factories became barely audible, and the once cacophonous city center was, in the words of one *Gazette* contributor, "silent as Sunday." The *Gazette* itself was struggling. It had borrowed $4,000 to stay afloat, a burden that weighed heavily as the economic outlook darkened.

To this town of soup kitchens, insolvent debtors, and shuttered homes came stories of Lewis, brought over the road from the Alleghenies and told and retold in taverns until they reached the building on Front Street where the *Gazette* had its offices. The editors, high-minded men who shunned the sensationalist crime writing popular among most provincial papers, nonetheless found Lewis fascinating. "Many little traits in the character of Lewis are spoken of, and prove him to be a man of no common order," they wrote in January 1820, a month after his flight from Bedford. "With all his villainy, there is something magnanimous in his conduct." The *Gazette* praised him for sparing McClelland's life and spoke glowingly of his refusal to let McCurdy the widow-robber escape with the other inmates.

Even journalists who prided themselves on abstaining from breathless accounts of banditry couldn't help but admire Lewis. The gratifying spectacle of punishing someone who had stolen from a widow stirred everyone's sympathies. Widows and orphans had traditionally been the most helpless members of society, and during the depression, they suffered acutely. But they also became bywords for something that everyone endured to some degree: the misery caused by the ruthlessness of American capitalism. The same month that the *Pittsburgh Gazette* ran its report on Lewis, the Philadelphia-based *Weekly Aurora* published a letter addressed to the country's most despised financier, Langdon Cheves, the president of the Bank of the United States. "Bow down, and worship," its pseudonymous author wrote, "the great high priest of your tabernacle— the temple of Plutus, consecrated to deeds, which cause the widow's heart to mourn, the orphan's wants to go unsatisfied."

As Americans knew too well, there was more than one way to rob a widow. McCurdy's method happened to be illegal, but it merited as much moral outrage as the perfectly lawful heists perpetrated by savvier operators. People everywhere were being deprived of their livelihood and savings: landlords evicted tenants, stockbrokers fleeced shareholders, and creditors had debtors jailed if they couldn't pay. In such a world, an outlaw with a conscience exerted a powerful appeal. He could follow a higher code of conduct, one that valued the civility and decorum that had been conspicuously absent from a society overrun by profiteers. In the minds of his admirers, Lewis recalled a kinder, simpler era in American life, before a new generation started demolishing traditional notions of decency in its zeal to get rich at any cost.

Newspapers were only one way that his legend grew; the other route to fame was the spoken word. Folktales passed from one person to the next, the details varying slightly with each storyteller, until someone years later committed to print whatever version had survived. One day, Lewis came to the home of a destitute widow. She didn't have a single dollar to pay her rent, the woman confessed, so the constable would soon seize her cow, her last means of support. "I don't know what to do without her," she fretted. Lewis asked how much she owed, promptly handed over the exact amount, and then hid nearby. When the official arrived, the widow offered up the money and, satisfied, he continued on his way until Lewis appeared in his path and put a gun in his face. The robber retrieved the bills he lent the widow along with the rest of the cash the constable had on him, making a nice profit. His act of charity, Lewis allegedly declared, proved to be one of his smartest investments. More valuable than the money he stole from the constable, however, was the story of his benevolence toward the widow, which would help solidify his stature as a folk hero. Many of the people who heard the tale undoubtedly had experienced similar run-ins with merciless creditors; they could only hope that Lewis would miraculously emerge to deliver them from their debts.

Another story involved a German immigrant named Simmons, who one evening crossed a mountain path with a few hundred dollars in his pocket. As dusk fell, Simmons began to feel frightened. He knew that Lewis and his associates preyed on people who traveled the region's roads, and he feared they would stage an ambush under the cover of darkness. In his terror, every sound became the footstep of a pursuing robber, every shadow the silhouette of his attacker. When he came across a cabin by the side of the road, Simmons decided to stop and ask for lodging. The finely attired man who answered the door invited him inside, where a few other men sat smoking near a cheery fire. The cozy cottage set the German at ease, and warming himself at the hearth, he spilled his whole story: he revealed how much money he was carrying and explained his fear of being robbed. Before turning in for the night, his new friends treated him to a lavish dinner, and in the morning, gave him breakfast. Grateful for the hospitality, he asked his dapper host what he owed. "Nothing, sir," the man replied, "but you can inform your friends that you stopped with Robber Lewis and his colleagues!" This was how Lewis wanted his beneficiaries to repay their debt: by spreading stories of his generosity.

In January 1820, the Bedford court finally indicted Lewis *in absentia* for robbery and escaping from jail. When his name had last appeared in the Bedford docket four years earlier, it was for counterfeiting. Lewis had begun forging money as Pennsylvania's banks grew; he became a highwayman in a depression brought on by their overexpansion. Few people adapted so well to the mood swings of the American economy, and in 1820, while Pennsylvanians watched their economy disintegrate, he entered the final and most lucrative phase of his career.

THE DAY AFTER HIS THIRTY-SIXTH BIRTHDAY, Condy Raguet rose from his chair to deliver an address on the floor of the Pennsylvania Senate. It was January 29, 1820, and the most important moment of the young state senator's career. His path to Harrisburg had been unorthodox: he spent his early twenties in Haiti during the revolution, watching blacks and whites butcher each other and chronicling the bloody scenes for American publications. He later joined the army, where he reached the rank of colonel in the War of 1812. Raguet's real passion, however, wasn't journalism or soldiering but economics. He published a pamphlet about currency in 1815, the same year he won a seat in the state legislature. Now, standing in front of his colleagues in the Senate, he had his long-awaited chance to speak about his favorite subject.

No one in Pennsylvania understood the financial crisis better than Raguet. As the chairman of a special legislative committee charged with investigating the depression, he had pored over every shred of relevant data: unemployment figures, bankruptcy statistics, records from sheriffs' sales of foreclosed properties. He distilled this clutter of facts into an incisive report that detailed the downturn's effects and pinpointed its origins. Raguet was ruthlessly honest. Instead of reiterating popular tirades against the federal Bank in Philadelphia, which had become a punching bag for politicians everywhere, he put the blame squarely on the shoulders of Pennsylvania's legislators. The bill they passed in March 1814 chartering forty-one new banks had "inflicted upon the Commonwealth an evil of a more disastrous nature than has ever been experienced by its citizens," Raguet declared. The new financiers had persuaded Americans of all trades "to abandon the dull pursuits of a laborious life, for the golden dreams of an artificial fortune."

Raguet was right. The spirit of speculation that thrived during the boom years had caused a lot of damage, and the state's politicians bore a large share of the guilt. But not all of the banks they legislated into existence had joined the craze for cheap credit. Among the more responsible was the Bank of Chambersburg, a one-room operation that occupied an office in the president's home, overlooking two dirt streets that intersected at right angles to form the bustling town square. By 1820, when almost one-third of Pennsylvania's banks had gone bust, Chambersburg's bills passed at a discount of only 3 percent. By contrast, one county over in Carlisle, the Pennsylvania Agricultural and Manufacturing Bank saw its money marked down a full 45 percent. It wasn't just Chambersburg's bank that enjoyed a good reputation; the community as a whole was well respected. "A gentleman in conversation the other day remarked that he had visited nearly all the towns in Pennsylvania," reported a Carlisle newspaper, "but amongst the whole he would recommend Chambersburg for *steady habits*."

On a Wednesday night in late May 1820, a fight broke out in downtown Chambersburg. It happened near the jail, a brick building erected a couple of years earlier at great public expense and reputed to be the state's strongest. The jailer was locking the prisoners into their cells for the night when he heard his wife yelling: one of his employees had gotten into a scuffle with someone outside. He didn't have time to properly bolt the door, so he left the key in the latch, planning to return later to retrieve it. In his haste, the jailer failed to notice the strand of waxed string the inmates had threaded through the bars. Once he left, they lowered the cord and swung the slipknot tied on its end over the latch, unlocking it. Picking up the key, they rushed to the cell where the jail's most prized prisoner sat chained in irons: David Lewis, the notorious robber and counterfeiter.

Lewis had been there since April. After escaping from Bedford, he and Connelly ran free for months until a botched robbery attempt landed him in jail; Connelly fled, eluding arrest. Lewis's capture returned his name to newsprint after a brief lull. "His life has been so characterized with bold and daring acts of crime, that he has acquired a certain celebrity among persons of his own stamp," gushed the Philadelphia-based *Franklin Gazette*. He "has never embrued his hands in blood," it continued, "and in many instances he has exhibited a generosity not uncommon among bandits." The newspapers would have an even better story once Lewis broke jail. The version that appeared in Carlisle's *American Volunteer* reported that after the inmates freed Lewis, they picked the lock of the door to the women's quarters, and from there slipped into the courtyard and out to the street. By three in the morning, the courthouse bell was ringing and Chambersburg's citizens were awake. Shortly after daybreak, in a pine grove half a mile from town, a search party discovered Lewis's shackles and the chisel and ax he used to cut them off. They looked all day and night but found nothing else. Lewis had disappeared.

Six days later, William Findlay issued a reward for Lewis's arrest. This was the bandit's third jailbreak since the governor's pardon, and with the election in October almost four months away, the outlaw had once again made Findlay look weak and foolish. He didn't need more bad press: his tenure had been a disaster. His handling of Lewis reflected his governing style: he moved slowly, reacting to events rather than trying to influence them, and rarely took a strong stand. When the Panic hit in 1819, demanding forceful leadership from Harrisburg, Findlay met the greatest challenge of his career with a characteristically feeble response.

Findlay wasn't stupid and his ascent hadn't been easy. The son of a farmer, he descended from Scotch-Irish settlers, an ethnic group that had historically been poorer and less powerful than Pennsylvania's other two blocs, the Germans and the Quakers. Findlay drew his support from the same demographic as Lewis did: the Scotch-Irish farmers, laborers, and tradesmen who dominated the Allegheny and western counties. With their help, Findlay became the state's first Scotch-Irish governor. But anyone who expected his election to inaugurate a new era would be sorely disappointed. Findlay succeeded because he had thoroughly absorbed Pennsylvania's corrupt politics. The state constitution gave the governor the power to appoint almost every officer in the state, from his cabinet in Harrisburg all the way down to positions at the county level. With so many spoils to divide up, Findlay had little time for actual governing. He faced a difficult task: in addition to keeping his opponents at bay, he had to prevent his friends from becoming enemies if they didn't get the jobs they wanted. Although Findlay may have looked sluggish and impotent, he was actually in a frenzy of activity: dispensing favors, building alliances—doing everything except managing the state's affairs. Frustrated office-seekers turned against him and loudly accused him of graft. As Pennsylvania sank deeper into economic despair, its legislature spent three months wrangling over an ultimately unsuccessful effort to impeach Findlay, initiated by people angered by their exclusion from his patronage.

As Findlay's opponents scrambled for new ways to disgrace him, Lewis gave them just what they needed. Well-known throughout Pennsylvania for a crime spree made possible by Findlay's pardon, he regularly flouted the governor's authority. Even better, people read about Lewis in newspapers, and newspapers in those days were intensely partisan. Almost all editors were loyal to a particular party; their role wasn't to report the news impartially but to praise or condemn a certain candidate or cause. In an era when politics ruled journalism, it was only a matter of time before an anti-Findlay editor began using his coverage of Lewis for political ends. He could run an absorbing account of the robber's latest exploits that doubled as a polemic against Findlay's administration, thus entertaining and indoctrinating his readers at the same time.

John McFarland, the hotheaded Scotch-Irish editor of the *Carlisle Republican*, epitomized the combative newspapermen of his day. In the early nineteenth century, journalists abused public figures and rival newspapers with a ferocity that by today's standards would be considered defamatory. Their fights often spilled off the printed page and into the street. A competing publisher once brought charges against McFarland for whacking him with a cowhide, slashing him from "neck to heel." Similar skirmishes happened all the time: anyone brave enough to put his words into print had to be prepared to give or take a beating when the opportunity arose.

Like many of the governor's enemies, McFarland had once been a Findlay supporter but, months before the election in 1817, switched sides. The reasons for McFarland's apostasy were debated in the partisan press. One camp said the editor decided to support the governor's opponent in the upcoming race, and in retaliation, Findlay's people bought the paper where McFarland worked and forced him out. Another claimed that McFarland blamed Findlay when he didn't get appointed county treasurer; if the story was true, it wouldn't be the first time a personal grudge led to a political rivalry. By 1820, McFarland was publishing the *Carlisle Republican*, a four-page weekly that printed advertisements placed by local merchants, the discount rates for different banknotes, and broadsides against the incumbent in Harrisburg.

McFarland hammered Findlay relentlessly about Lewis, never missing an opportunity to remind his readers of the governor's negligence in freeing the convict from the Walnut Street Jail. "We have fallen indeed on evil times when the pardoning power of the Executive is thus ignorantly and improperly prostituted to the dangerous purpose of liberating infamous cut-throats, robbers, and counterfeiters, for the sake of acquiring a short-lived popularity, or obtaining the reputation of a false humanity," read one typical harangue. He alleged that Findlay visited Lewis in the Chambersburg jail to pay "his respects to this noted character"—a claim contested by other newspapers—and when Lewis escaped along with the other inmates, caustically noted that the jailbreak saved the governor "the trouble of signing their pardons." He even insinuated that Findlay had conducted secret dealings with the robber and aided his flight from Chambersburg. Hardly a week went by without another bulletin from the *Carlisle Republican*, its editorial voice amplified by the liberal use of italics and exclamation marks. The most imaginative of McFarland's attacks on Findlay was a poem written from Lewis's perspective entitled "Farewell to Chambersburg." In its final stanza, Lewis likens the governor to the jail's flimsy "nail-rod" locks that enabled his getaway:

> I laugh in my sleeve, whilst I bid you adieu—
> Farewell to your prison and Chambersburg too.
> Now, if prisoners you get, and wish them to stay,
> You will keep BILLY FINDLAY and nail-rods away.

LEWIS WAS ONLY TWENTY MILES away from McFarland's offices when those verses appeared in newsprint. He was hiding near Doubling Gap, a mountain pass north of Carlisle where a ridge of the Alleghenies bends back on itself like a hairpin. Indians and early settlers used it to travel between Pennsylvania's rugged central regions and the Cumberland Valley, the fertile stretch of land that by Lewis's time included Harrisburg, Carlisle, and Chambersburg. Later generations knew the Gap from old stories of Indian massacres that happened nearby and for its sulfur springs, which spouted water that smelled vile but was supposed to have a curative effect on anyone brave enough to bathe in it.

By this point Lewis had become an expert at wilderness living, and his camp at Doubling Gap reflected his years of experience. On a slope not far from the springs, mossy slabs of stone had been thrust against a rock to form an artificial cave large enough for four or five people. Inside were Lewis and the other prisoners from Chambersburg, as well as Connelly, who had joined the fugitives soon after their escape. They lived comfortably and ate well. What they couldn't steal they obtained from the Gap's residents, who, whether out of love or fear, gave the outlaws whatever they wanted—a shoemaker even made Connelly a new pair of shoes. A local named Robert, whose tavern stood on the opposite side of the road that passed through the Gap, regularly hiked to their hideout to bring provisions and the latest news from town. Thirty-three years later, Robert Moffitt, an old-timer living near the Gap, claimed to be this man. He reminisced fondly about his time with the bandits:

> Lewis was a great favorite with the ladies. Some of them used to
> furnish us with the comforts of life, and several times visited
> us at the cave. We had a number of little parties at the tavern,
> and had great times. A number of the mountain ladies would
> come, and some of the men, and we would every now and
> then have a dance . . . We did not rob in the neighborhood
> of the Gap, except to get such things as were necessary to
> live on. We lived on what we got in this way, and what was
> brought to us. I shall never forget.

If Robert had looked out his window on the night of June 15, 1820, he might have made out a figure working his way downhill from Lewis's cave in the darkness. Caesar Rodney, a man of mixed race whom newspapers referred to as the "yellow fellow," had broken out of jail with Lewis and accompanied him to Doubling Gap. But he soon began missing his wife—dancing with the mountain ladies apparently didn't help—and decided to return home to Bedford. While Lewis and the others slept, he crept out of the camp and began the long, difficult journey west. Seventy-five miles and several Allegheny ranges later, Rodney arrived in town and was promptly arrested. He confessed everything, describing Lewis's retreat and even offering to lead the authorities there. By the time they reached the Gap, however, the criminals had cleared out: "The cage was found but the birds were flown," announced the *Franklin Repository* from Chambersburg. All that remained were "symptoms of good living" found scattered around the cave, the *Repository* said, presumably leftovers from their last round of merrymaking. The locals didn't seem eager to cooperate. "We have been told that *suspicion* rests upon several of the inhabitants in the neighbourhood," reported the *American Volunteer*.

The few weeks Lewis spent carousing at Doubling Gap would be tranquil compared with what came next. Rather than retiring to another refuge deeper in the Alleghenies, he descended into the Cumberland Valley and began plundering the countryside at a feverish pace. Never before had he committed so many robberies in such a short period of time. Joined by Connelly and an escapee from the Chambersburg jail named Felix McGuire, Lewis raided homes, looted stores, and ransacked springhouses—storerooms that farmers used to refrigerate food by funneling running water up from the ground and into troughs that cooled the building's interior. As the summer weather set in, the criminals ate chilled meat and butter and drank cold milk to keep up their strength between burglaries.

Lewis's newly aggressive approach didn't suit his Robin Hood reputation. He wasn't helping the needy or punishing the greedy; he was pillaging everyday people's property. To the Pennsylvanians who had their farms and households ransacked by armed men, the tall, blond bandit leading the pack couldn't have seemed further from the romantic folk hero of legend. Of course, Lewis's depredations delighted the anti-Findlay crowd. The worse he behaved, the stronger their position. "The country is kept in continual alarm for which the citizens have to thank the humanity of William Findlay in letting loose so many hardened malefactors, to prey on society," declared the anti-Findlay *Harrisburg Chronicle*. In the *Carlisle*

Republican, McFarland noted that "the daily accounts of [Lewis's] nightly adventures" came mostly from the Cumberland Valley, near Harrisburg. The robber stayed close to the state capital, McFarland proposed, because there was a "remarkable connection" between him and Findlay—possibly a secret partnership, although the editor didn't try to explain why the governor would collude with someone who continued to be such an embarrassment to his administration.

As Lewis stepped up his attacks, people became increasingly vigilant for any sign of the robber. In late June, when the smell of something burning wafted down the banks of the West Branch of the Susquehanna River, nearby residents left their homes to investigate. It came from an area close to the confluence of the Susquehanna and Bald Eagle Creek, a waterway that drained the valley where Lewis had been born. As the locals approached, they found the source of the smell. On a summer day in a remote corner of the Alleghenies, miles from the nearest marketplace, a pile of expensive merchandise was on fire. And near this strange sight stood a suspicious-looking man who, once captured and committed to jail, identified himself as Felix McGuire, one of Lewis's cronies.

Lewis, Connelly, and McGuire had robbed $1,200 worth of goods a few days before from a wagon that broke down in the mountains south of Bellefonte. The men loaded the loot into a stolen canoe and paddled up Bald Eagle Creek but, once they reached the Susquehanna, decided to ditch the boat and continue overland. They had too much to carry, however, and needed to lighten their load. The bonfire they built, while practical from the fugitives' point of view, would undoubtedly be a grotesque spectacle to the Alleghenies' impoverished inhabitants, a savage act equivalent to destroying money or food at a time when people didn't have nearly enough of either.

The cost of leaving Lewis at large had become unacceptably high. In the midst of a depression, the citizens of the counties where Lewis operated couldn't afford to lose whatever assets they had left to a desperado who kept ravaging their communities. So they resolved to do something about it. On June 26, the day before the flaming merchandise was discovered, a posse assembled at Bellefonte. The townsfolk knew Lewis long before he made headlines in Bedford and Chambersburg; seven years earlier, they had accused Philander Noble of spying for the British, and while they never managed to convict him, they were determined to put a stop to his protégé. The group numbered around twelve and included a wide range of characters: a co-owner of the wagon whose cargo Lewis had incinerated, a one-armed war veteran, the county coroner, and, most likely, the county sheriff. The men rode northwest from their hometown toward a place past the Alleghenies that the *Bellefonte Patriot* called "a wild, unfrequented part of the world, inhabited only by beasts of prey."

Lewis and Connelly were well armed, skilled at avoiding arrest, and seasoned in wilderness survival. Capturing them would be difficult anywhere. In this case, the landscape presented its own challenges. The *Patriot* may have been a little dramatic in its description, but it was essentially accurate: the area above Bellefonte, north of the Alleghenies, was still mostly wilderness. Topographically the two regions looked completely different. The Alleghenies made broad strokes across central Pennsylvania; along their long, curved ridges were well-watered valleys that served as excellent sites for towns like Bellefonte and Bedford. Farther up, the terrain stayed mountainous but became more jagged. From above it resembled the veined surface of a leaf: rivers forked endlessly into branches, creeks, and streams, cutting ravines that broke up the land into smaller, saw-toothed pieces. Most of the area's inhabitants lived along these waterways, which in many places were obstructed by shoals and stray chunks of wood that fell from the dense pine forests lining the shore, making it harder for settlers to penetrate too deeply into the backcountry.

On Bennett's Branch of the Sinnemahoning Creek, not far from where a sawmill harnessed the channel's fast current to chop logs into lumber, lived Lewis's mother, Jane. Now seventy years old, she had married for the third and final time and, at an age when she might have sought an easier life, remained the tough Presbyterian frontierswoman that Lewis's father had courted more than a half-century earlier. The thinly settled country around the Sinnemahoning looked like the Pennsylvania that Jane remembered from her youth; perhaps more populated places like Bellefonte, which by 1820 still had fewer than five hundred residents, had become too crowded for her. The Bellefonte posse, convinced that Lewis and Connelly would try to hide with Jane, headed straight for her house. It took them three days to reach it, and on the evening of June 29, two of the men went ahead to speak with the old woman. Not only did they find no trace of Lewis, but Jane, loyal to her troublesome son ever since he had deserted from the army, told them nothing.

If she wouldn't lead them to the robbers, the troop from Bellefonte had little hope of success; adrift in an unfamiliar landscape, they could roam forever without finding the fugitives. The next day, the men marched up Bennett's Branch to where it joined Driftwood Branch, another tributary of the Sinnemahoning, and continued eastward along the water, swatting the gnats and mosquitoes that clung to their perspiring faces. They were five miles into the trek when they stumbled upon David Brooks, a local who told them he had recently seen someone who fit Lewis's description. Thrilled, the men enlisted him as a guide. Brooks led them back the way they came, traveling west on the Sinnemahoning and then north up Driftwood Branch as the sun sank steadily in the sky.

About an hour before sunset, they reached a steep bluff. Gunshots rang out below: peering down, they saw a house, with Lewis and Connelly shooting targets outside. The posse couldn't have hoped for a better setup: concealed from the criminals' view, they were perfectly positioned to launch a surprise attack. There was only one problem. According to Brooks, there were women and children inside the house who might get hurt in the firefight, and any civilian casualties would spoil the triumph of taking the villains. So, instead of charging down the cliff, the men instructed Brooks to tell another local they spotted nearby, William

Shephard, to walk over to the house and, without tipping off Lewis and Connelly, warn everyone to stay inside.

The plan failed miserably. As soon as Shephard finished talking to Brooks, he went right to the robbers and gave the alarm—perhaps he had been recruited as an accomplice, or sympathized with Lewis. The posse, realizing what had happened, sprinted down the bank, calling Lewis and Connelly by name and demanding their surrender. The criminals answered with threats—Connelly swore that he would blow them all to hell—and opened fire. The Bellefonte men let off a volley and the shootout began: guns crackling, smoke streaming from their barrels, bullets hurtling in all directions. Two of the balls hit Lewis: one pierced his left thigh, the other his right forearm, and with blood pouring from his wounds, the bandit dropped to the ground. Connelly, seeing his partner fall, turned around and ran. He tried to lose his pursuers in a grain field, but they hunted him down. A bullet had punctured his groin and exited through his right thigh, slicing open his lower belly. By the time the men found him, his intestines were bulging from his brawny body.

The posse treated the prisoners' injuries as best they could, purchased a canoe, and set off in haste toward Bellefonte. Lewis and Connelly lay in the boat, their flesh putrefying in the midsummer heat, while their captors navigated the meandering route home: down Driftwood Branch to the Sinnemahoning and then along the West Branch of the Susquehanna to the site where, a week earlier, the robbers had burned the goods they couldn't carry. The party landed there on July 2 and, instead of pushing on to Bellefonte, took the prisoners to a tavern and summoned three local doctors. Connelly was too far gone to save; he died that night. Lewis was in better shape. The bullets had wounded his leg and shattered his wrist, but he could travel. So the men, eager to bring him back alive, hauled their crippled captive the thirty remaining miles to Bellefonte and strode into town like conquering heroes.

They had reason to be proud. A dozen men from a small Allegheny town had done what no one else could, not even the governor in Harrisburg. The *Bellefonte Patriot* surged with hometown pride, praising the "gallant little band" as a model for all Pennsylvanians. "It is surely the duty of every good citizen, and every honest man, to hunt down such monsters," the *Patriot* wrote. But the townsfolk who got a glimpse of the prisoner could only be disappointed by what they saw. Bruised and broken, Lewis didn't look like the charismatic populist of myth or the terrifying desperado of recent news reports. And once secured in the town's jail, he didn't stage a memorable spectacle or attempt one of his daring jailbreaks. He sat in his filthy cell, refusing to make a statement of any kind, while his wounded arm grew black with gangrene. A doctor demanded that the limb be amputated, but Lewis resisted, and the gangrene spread. On July 12, he died in his cell. The Presbyterian minister who attended Lewis said he spent his painful last moments pleading with God to let him live.

NEWSPAPERS THROUGHOUT THE COUNTRY wrote about Lewis's capture and death. People in Philadelphia, New York, and Boston read about it; so did people living in smaller towns in Virginia, New Jersey, and South Carolina. Almost a thousand miles from Bellefonte, residents of Cahawba, Alabama's newly laid-out state capital, learned about Lewis's fate in the pages of the *Alabama Watchman*. Even for those who had never heard of the bandit, the showdown on the Sinnemahoning made for engaging reading. The only thing missing was a dramatic finish. Rather than dying defiantly on the battlefield, Lewis ended his life in a grimy cell, killed by a gruesome wound. Worst of all, he seemed to have lost the swagger that had made him a fascinating figure from his early career as a counterfeiter to his later days as a robber. His vicious thieving streak in the summer of 1820 had hurt his Robin Hood reputation, and he made no effort at the end of his life to restore his stature. For someone who had spent years cultivating his image, he went to the grave apparently indifferent to his legacy.

On August 1, 1820, twenty days after Lewis died, a curious notice appeared on page 3 of McFarland's *Carlisle Republican*. Before his death the prisoner suddenly became "very communicative," the editor said, and dictated the story of his life to a gentleman who visited him in jail. The *Republican* had gotten hold of the manuscript—"a true and correct statement of Lewis's own words"—and ran an excerpt, promising to print more in future issues. In the next couple of months, McFarland published another seven installments. He eventually put them together, in slightly edited and expanded form, into a sixty-page pamphlet that sold for fifty cents, entitled *The Confession or Narrative, of David Lewis*.

People familiar with the particulars weren't fooled. The idea that a prisoner dying of gangrene would narrate a lengthy memoir in fewer than ten days, and that his hastily transcribed words—scribbled on "several detached sheets in a hand writing somewhat difficult to read," McFarland noted—would turn up in a newspaper a hundred miles away, was pretty far-fetched. "David Lewis never uttered one sentence, word, or syllable of this FORGED confession," declared a letter published in the *American Volunteer* in September that refuted many of the narrative's claims. The next week's *Volunteer* reprinted a statement that had first appeared in the *Bellefonte Patriot*, cosigned by the county sheriff and town jailer, affirming that Lewis made no statement aside from the few words he had with the Presbyterian minister shortly before his death. The officials denounced McFarland's document as a "sheer fabrication."

The confession was a counterfeit, and McFarland—who may have written it, but more likely commissioned and edited it—knew that it wouldn't deceive everyone. Nonetheless its author tried to give the story a realistic touch by including a handful of events that contemporary readers would have recognized as factual, like Lewis's desertion from the army and his robbing spree with Connelly. The bulk, however, is total fantasy. Lewis speaks in florid, literary prose, recounting scenes with dazzling amounts of descriptive detail. He plays the quintessential picaresque hero: a charming rogue whose "rambling disposition" puts him on the path to becoming a counterfeiter and a thief at an early age. His adventures span several states and range from the plausible—cardsharping at Princeton— to the fantastic—swiping Mrs. John Jacob Astor's unattended purse at a Manhattan auction house.

Lewis's character is deeply emotional. He often launches into tearful interludes about how guilt-ridden and homesick he felt as an outlaw, regretting his criminal career almost as soon as it began. Toward the end of the story, he returns to his birthplace and, lamenting his lost innocence, starts sobbing: "This gentle fluid of humanity, while it ran from my inflamed eyes, only scalded my cheeks without relieving my bursting heart." Lewis's sentimentality, even in its most mawkish moments, is also what makes him sympathetic. Tormented by shame, he tries to soothe his conscience by striving to be as moral a criminal as possible. He checks the violent impulses of his rougher colleagues, rescuing a girl about to be raped in a dark alley by a thug named Bob Brimstone and intervening whenever Connelly wants to start killing people. But he can never bring himself to abandon his life of crime, and he concludes his confession in the Bellefonte jail, imploring the anonymous visitor transcribing his words to take a lock of his hair to his beloved mother, cut from her dying son's "unfortunate, but repentant" head.

McFarland printed the fake memoir to hurt Findlay. He timed its publication to inflict as much damage as possible on the incumbent's reelection chances; the final installment appeared in the *Carlisle Republican* on October 6, 1820, just four days before Pennsylvanians went to the polls. Given McFarland's bludgeoning editorial style, the confession's criticism of Findlay is surprisingly subtle. It only includes one specific reference to the governor, a derisive remark about "the weak side of Governor Findlay in favoring applications" from convicts seeking pardons. But it's full of angry diatribes against the Pennsylvania establishment that Findlay represents: an immoral political culture that lets the state's officeholders—appointed by the governor, of course—demand bribes and embezzle funds, and empowers predatory bankers to victimize unsuspecting country folk. When the Pennsylvania legislature charters forty-one new banks in March 1814, Lewis condemns the financial craze as "a legalized system of fraud, robbery and swindling"—although, as he himself admits, it's a boon for counterfeiters like him. Lewis never once mentions Findlay's name in these harangues, although the rampant venality he rails against reflects extremely poorly on the man sitting in the governor's seat in Harrisburg. And this was no doubt McFarland's intention: to disguise his personal attack on Findlay as a righteous call for reform.

By staying silent during his final days in jail, Lewis let McFarland's spurious confession speak for him. The narrative's fictional Lewis is much more virtuous than the historical Lewis ever was: he's a social crusader, a devoted son, an affectionate husband. The confession ascribes the less palatable parts of Lewis's career, like the ferocious string of robberies he committed just before his capture, to the influence of Connelly. The burly Irishman, whom Lewis calls his "evil genius," plays the role of a remorseless tough—a counterpoint to Lewis's idealism. And Lewis is not only the populist avenger familiar from the folktales; he's also a shrewd social critic, someone who understands the political and economic forces at work in the Pennsylvania countryside.

While contemporaries exposed McFarland's confession as a forgery, later generations weren't as discriminating. In fact, the document eventually came to be accepted as genuine: the pamphlet appeared in new editions in 1853 and 1890, and excerpts were reprinted in newspapers. Lewis became a fixture of Pennsylvania lore: decades later, local historians wrote hagiographies of the old outlaw. A "man of fine physique" and "a born leader," read one; "quite an Adonis," raved another. His posthumous celebrity proved remarkably persistent. Lewis was said to have buried a pile of gold somewhere in the Alleghenies during his lifetime, and almost a century after his death, people were still trying to find the treasure. As late as 1966, an owner of a Cumberland County feed mill named J. Raymond Baer remembered enough about Lewis to recount stories of the bandit's beneficence. "My father knew of him and thought he saw him one time," he said.

What's harder to gauge is McFarland's immediate impact on Findlay. The vitriol that characterized the contest in 1817 returned with a vengeance in 1820. The same candidates were running: the incumbent was William Findlay and the challenger was Joseph Hiester, a Revolutionary War hero. Neither represented a particular platform; all that distinguished them were the different political factions that backed them, motley coalitions vying for control of the Harrisburg patronage machine. The Panic had intensified the popular desire for reform, but instead of building their campaigns around specific policies, each side devoted its resources to denouncing the other as more corrupt. Mudslinging dominated the newspapers, leaving little room for real debate.

As if all the charges and countercharges weren't disorienting enough, the election also saw the disintegration of the party system. Findlay ostensibly belonged to Pennsylvania's ruling party, the Democratic-Republicans, but many members of his party defected to a rival camp, the Independent-Republicans, to support Hiester. The Federalists, who had almost disappeared on the national scene but still held pockets of Pennsylvania, split into pro-Findlay and pro-Hiester wings. And in each county, these groups splintered into smaller cliques with no particular party allegiance, cutting deals with one another to get their man elected to a local office. Lewis's confession, as another voice in this noisy carnival, may not have made much of a difference. But McFarland got what he wanted. Hiester won by fewer than two thousand votes.

WITHIN A YEAR OF HIS INAUGURATION, Governor Hiester had good news to report. In his annual address to the state legislature, he announced that the "pauperism" that plagued Pennsylvania in recent years was on the decline. By 1821, the country had begun a full economic recovery. Credit started to flow, the value of banknotes stabilized, and prices rose. Foreign exports and domestic manufacturing slowly revived. The Second Bank of the United States, after years of mismanagement, had finally found its footing under the stern stewardship of Langdon Cheves, who assumed the presidency in 1819. Cheves fired inept employees, curbed salaries and expenses, and, most important, overhauled the Bank's balance sheets. He restored its capital by demanding that state banks pay their balances and redeem their notes, and limited its liabilities by steadily reducing the number of the Bank's bills in circulation. Anchored by Cheves's sober leadership, the American economy looked as if it might grow at a more measured, manageable pace and avoid the pitfalls that produced the Panic.

But there were warning signs ahead. The factors that produced the banking boom in the first few decades of the Republic's existence only intensified in the coming years. Immigrants poured in, settlers pushed west, and the Industrial Revolution vastly expanded the scope of manufacturing and transportation. As the country accelerated in new directions, the materialism that had always been present in American life became dominant. The wise men of the eighteenth century—Benjamin Franklin and Alexander Hamilton, among others—were now seen as quaint; their thrift and restraint no longer seemed relevant in the aggressively acquisitive, steam-powered America of the future. The new economy, however, needed old-fashioned fuel: paper credit. The same tool that made it possible for colonists to trade goods and pay taxes in the seventeenth century would be used to build canals and textile mills in the nineteenth. But like steam, credit had to be handled carefully. In the right proportions, it could be a tremendous source of energy; too much, on the other hand, could set off an explosion.

Nicholas Biddle, who succeeded Cheves as the Bank's president in 1823, was not an obvious choice for the position. A lively, candid man with a round face and curly hair, Biddle belonged to a distinguished Philadelphia family but had little business experience to recommend him for the job. No one doubted his intelligence, however. Biddle had edited the authoritative version of Lewis and Clark's journey, served in the Pennsylvania legislature, and traveled throughout Europe, where he had devoted months to examining Greek and Roman ruins. Once, when attending a dinner party at Cambridge University with James Monroe, then the American minister to Britain, he delivered an eloquent disquisition on the differences between ancient and modern Greek. Monroe loved watching the young American put the Cambridge dons to shame. He remembered it twelve years later when, as president of the United States, he nominated Biddle to the Bank's governing board and later endorsed him for its presidency.

Biddle proved a fast learner. As the chief executive of the country's biggest corporation, he applied his considerable brainpower to mastering every aspect of the Bank's affairs. From the start he wanted the Bank to play a strong role in regulating the nation's currency. Like Cheves, he regularly redeemed the notes of state banks that ended up in the Bank's vaults. This had a dual effect: it forced the banks to keep enough coin in their coffers to back their bills and it steadily withdrew their paper from circulation. At the same time, Biddle increased the number of the Bank's notes, so that his bills gradually supplanted those of the state banks—and, crucially, preserved enough capital to ensure that his notes held their value.

In his first three years, Biddle had more than doubled the Bank's circulation, and by the late 1820s, his bills made up as much as a quarter of the country's total. The result was overwhelmingly positive: America's paper money became the most stable it had been in decades. In fact, the Bank's notes were so strong that they attracted a broad campaign by counterfeiters eager to cash in. Moneymaking gangs surfaced everywhere from Philadelphia to New Orleans to Matamoros, Mexico. Biddle called on the authorities to intervene, but the maze of different jurisdictions and inept law enforcement made it difficult to stem the tide of bad bills. By the end of 1827, the situation had gotten so bad that Biddle recalled all $20 and $100 notes to replace them with designs he hoped would be harder to forge.

Although counterfeiters posed a serious threat to the Bank, a graver menace would be the state banks and the array of interests that supported them. They came from prosperous states like New York as well as the wilder frontier regions of the South and West. What united them was their desire for looser credit. They resented Biddle's supervision of the economy; they wanted their local banks to be able to extend loans and print money without the Bank breathing down their necks. As the nation's rapid growth created new opportunities for investment and communities everywhere clamored for capital, the hostility toward Philadelphia's restraining influence grew. The rising entrepreneurial class needed to find a way to pry Biddle's fingers from the helm. They needed someone who could rally public opinion against the Bank and marshal its many enemies in a coordinated assault.

General Andrew Jackson was the man for the job. Culturally, he and Biddle couldn't have been more different. Unlike Biddle, Jackson enjoyed none of the benefits of a privileged upbringing. Born to Scotch-Irish immigrants in the backwoods of the Carolinas, he fought hard for his success. He became a national hero for defeating the British at New Orleans during the War of 1812, and his tactical finesse made him a formidable politician. After stints as a frontier lawyer, cotton planter, and senator, he mounted a bid for the presidency. Jackson's victory in 1828 marked a major realignment in American politics. He was the first president who hadn't been born in either Massachusetts or Virginia, and he brought a radically new spirit to the White House, defined by the whiskey-soaked individualism of the old Southwest. His admirers hailed him as the "People's President," a crusader for the common man against the ruling elite; his adversaries vilified him as "King Mob," a demagogue of the illiterate rabble. And while he drew support from the lower classes, he also found allies among the wealthy: southern slaveholders, western entrepreneurs, and many former Federalists.

Jackson's rise to power reflected the convergence of a number of forces working to upend the old order. As America evolved from a small patrician republic along the eastern seaboard into a boisterous democracy reaching deeper into the continent's interior, the nation now had a leader who knew the hardships of the West firsthand, a self-made man who could speak directly to the masses in a language they could understand.

Among Jackson's supporters was John McFarland, who had left the *Carlisle Republican* after Findlay's defeat and ended up at the *Allegheny Democrat* in Pittsburgh. As editor of the *Democrat* he campaigned for Jackson with typical zeal, at one point even inciting a crowd to burn an effigy of one of the general's foremost political foes, Henry Clay. McFarland's advocacy of Jackson was hardly surprising. Jackson was popular among the state's heavily Scotch-Irish western and mountain counties. And he shared certain traits with another of McFarland's favorites, David Lewis. The populist outlaw from the folktales and the fake confession exhibited many Jacksonian features: he championed the plight of the dispossessed and fought the moneyed interests, a story line that played well among Pennsylvanians deeply distrustful of the establishment. Like Jackson, Lewis represented the righteous struggle of people against power, although in both cases, their personal myths masked a much messier reality.

Jackson had campaigned on personality, not policy, and when he arrived in Washington, he brought with him a set of deeply held, often incompatible beliefs shaped by his personal experiences and prejudices. His feelings about finance were complex. On the one hand, he harbored an abiding hatred for all forms of banking and paper money. He believed that notes printed by state banks were not only unconstitutional but dangerous, and blamed them for the Panic of 1819 and the subsequent depression. Jackson wanted precious metals, not paper, to be the country's currency. But he also adhered to a winner-take-all individualism that made him reluctant to intervene in the marketplace. He had little sympathy for society's losers: he had struggled to overcome his humble origins and expected others to do the same. He opposed debt relief and promoted laissez-faire, which he hoped would produce a nation of self-made men like him—an economy free of monopolies, speculators, and government regulation.

Jackson's tangled financial thinking made it hard to predict how he would behave toward the Bank. Biddle, who voted for Jackson, expected their relationship to be cordial, and at first the president gave no indication that might make him think otherwise. The Bank printed paper money, of course, but it also exercised an important check on the state banks; it encouraged government supervision of the economy, but it also held the tide against the cheap-credit financiers that Jackson hated. Nonetheless, within months of assuming office, the president would come to despise the Bank. He saw it as an antidemocratic monopoly that concentrated power in the hands of the few at the expense of the many, an evil instrument of entrenched wealth.

Among the factors that drove him to this view was the influence of his Kitchen Cabinet, the intimate circle of advisers he consulted alongside his official cabinet. Many of them, like Martin Van Buren, had close ties to the state banks that wanted to liberate themselves from Philadelphia's control. In making their argument, they appealed to a range of sentiments: the old agrarian distrust of banking, the democratic dislike of monopolies, the defense of states' rights against federal power, and, perversely, the desire to replace all paper money with precious metals. The hard-money men who fought the Bank hoping to rid America of paper currency—Jackson counted himself among them—would be sorely disappointed; their efforts paved the way for more paper, not less. "I did not join in putting down the Bank of the United States," said their de facto spokesman, Senator Thomas Hart Benton of Missouri, "to put up a wilderness of local banks."

The opening act in what came to be called the Bank War occurred in December 1829, when Jackson questioned the institution's "constitutionality" and "expediency" in his first annual message to Congress. Over the course of the next few years, Jackson moved carefully, sometimes denouncing the Bank harshly, other times sounding conciliatory tones. These maneuvers confused Biddle and left him disorganized and defenseless when the deathblow came. While an expert administrator, he had no talent for politics. Rather than mobilizing the Bank's supporters in a spirited defense, he kept hoping that Jackson would change his mind, and remained naively open to compromise long after the battle lines had been indelibly drawn. It was when Biddle tried to go on the offensive, however, that he made his fatal mistake. In January 1832, he submitted the Bank's application for re-charter to Congress. The current charter didn't expire until 1836, but Biddle, on the advice of anti-Jackson politicians like Henry Clay, believed that forcing the issue on the eve of the presidential election would embarrass the president and improve the Bank's chances.

The plan backfired. Biddle had unwittingly ignited an all-out war with Jackson's seasoned political machine, and in the ensuing firestorm, he found himself rhetorically outgunned. The president and his propagandists skillfully spun the battle over the Bank to their benefit. The charter had enough votes in Congress to pass, but on July 10, 1832, Jackson vetoed it and delivered a message that made his case to the American people. "It is to be regretted that the rich and powerful too often bend the acts of government to their selfish purposes," he said. Government's responsibility, in Jackson's view, was to ensure that everyone competed freely according to his natural abilities without any artificial advantages. By making "the rich richer and the potent more powerful," the Bank gave its beneficiaries an unfair edge over the "humble members of society—the farmers, mechanics, and laborers."

Voters embraced Jackson's message. They didn't care that the president was wrong—that the Bank, far from enriching a conspiratorial cabal, had contributed tremendously to the overall health of the nation by stabilizing the currency and curbing bad banking practices. The finer points of financial policy weren't one of Jackson's strengths. But he knew how to win an election, and Biddle, by making the Bank a campaign issue, had handed him the perfect political weapon. Jackson elevated the debate over the Bank into a struggle for the soul of America, a stark choice between aristocracy and democracy. He tapped Americans' class anger toward the country's elites and offered them an appealing narrative: Jackson the rugged westerner versus Biddle the arrogant easterner. It worked. Four months after vetoing the Bank's re-charter, Jackson defeated his challenger at the polls, Henry Clay, by a wide margin. Emboldened by the victory, the president moved to finish off the Bank. In the fall of 1833, he began transferring the federal government's funds from Philadelphia into a handful of state banks whose directors were, almost without exception, staunch Jacksonians.

The day Jackson's treasury secretary announced the decision to strip the Bank of its government deposits, an incisive editorial appeared in the Philadelphia-based *National Gazette*. The Bank faced "two distinct sets of enemies," the writer declared, "the gang of counterfeiters" and "the junto of the Kitchen Cabinet." "The Kitchen Cabinet cost more than the counterfeiters," he continued, "because, having the whole patronage of the government at their disposal . . . they have the power to manufacture and circulate their counterfeits more readily than the humbler worthies of the copper-plate." Branding the president and his advisers moneymakers might seem like just another salvo in the Bank War, but it wasn't far from the truth. By destroying the Bank, they had done more to inundate the nation with worthless paper than even the most prolific counterfeiting operation. Without Biddle holding the reins, state banks could now print bills without bothering to redeem them. From 1833 to 1836, note issues increased 50 percent in the East, 100 percent in the West, and 130 percent in the South.

More paper, of course, also meant more opportunities for criminal moneymaking. Although the Bank had suffered from counterfeiters, it had the advantage of being able to coordinate a centralized strategy for dealing with them. Now that the money supply was in the hands of a rapidly growing number of banks—almost six hundred by 1836—it became impossible to organize a coherent plan for confronting the nation's thriving banknote forgers. It certainly didn't help that many of those who had cut their teeth counterfeiting the Bank's well-designed bills had been released by Jackson, who pardoned more of them than any preceding president—presumably on the principle that since the Bank was unconstitutional, forging its notes shouldn't be illegal.

The great irony is that the man most responsible for inaugurating an era of unregulated paper currency held the same hard-money views that had descended in a straight line from Thomas Hutchinson to the authors of the Constitution. In his farewell address in March 1837, Jackson made arguments that echoed the Massachusetts money war almost a century earlier, when Hutchinson tried to eradicate colonial bills of credit. Paper money had infected Americans with an "eager desire to amass wealth without labor," Jackson asserted, threatening not only to undermine economic stability but to endanger the nation's democratic institutions. Until paper had been replaced with precious metals, the "moneyed interest" would keep using it to exploit the "millions of freemen" who formed "the bone and sinew of the country." Before he left office, Jackson put these hard-money beliefs into practice with an executive order called the Specie Circular. A major source of government revenue came from the sale of public lands, mostly in the Mississippi and Ohio River valleys, and since the Bank's demise, speculation in those lands had greatly increased. In the hopes of dissuading speculators, the circular required that all payments for these purchases be in gold and silver, not paper notes.

Rather than strengthening the currency, the Specie Circular contributed to a catastrophe that highlighted the fragility of the economy Jackson had created. It heightened the demand for coin in the West, draining the banks of New York City, which in the aftermath of the Bank War had emerged as the country's new financial center of gravity. At the same time, the Treasury Department carried out a disorderly series of specie transfers among the state banks that held the government's deposits as part of an effort to distribute the federal surplus to the states. This produced an even greater outflow of precious metals from New York and other banking hubs, resulting in a credit crunch that culminated in the Panic of 1837.

In May, runs on New York's banks forced them to suspend payment of coin, and as the hysteria grew, the rest of the nation's banks did the same. Confidence plummeted and more than a quarter of America's banks went bust. Just as it had during the last Panic eighteen years earlier, the financial collapse inflicted a harsh human toll, especially in the cities where unemployment was acute. In the winter of 1836–1837, a mob of almost a thousand people gathered outside New York's City Hall and, enraged by skyrocketing food costs, went on a rampage through Manhattan. They ransacked stores and hurled barrels of flour and wheat into the street; when the mayor tried to intervene, they pelted him with rocks. The riot terrified the city's conservatives, reminding them of the French Revolution. But the real architect of the unrest was Jackson, whose laissez-faire legacy had made the economy vulnerable to the booms and busts of a violently mercurial market. When crisis struck, as it inevitably did, there was no national bank to restore order.

By the time Jackson left the White House, the country included twice as many states as it did when he first became president, and over the course of the next decade, it would extend across the continent to the Pacific coast. Some of the new states took laissez-faire to an extreme, enacting so-called free banking laws that enabled anyone who met certain conditions to start a bank immediately without obtaining a charter from the legislature. This radical democratization of finance reflected the idea that banking, as a trade like any other, should be open to everyone; it also meant the number of note-issuing banks could be essentially infinite. While some free bankers turned out to be responsible businessmen, the system created endless opportunities for fraud. In Michigan, the first state to pass such laws soon after its admission to statehood in 1837, stories circulated about "wildcat" banks built on remote patches of wilderness— on the theory that people couldn't redeem the banknotes if they couldn't find the bank—whose reserves consisted of kegs full of broken glass with a handful of coins sprinkled on top.

The uninhibited flow of paper credit that prevailed under free banking represented a triumph for the entrepreneurs who had helped kill the Bank. But they didn't succeed everywhere. While some states deregulated banking, others banned it entirely. In places like California and Oregon, where precious metals were plentiful, the prohibition didn't produce a currency shortage. But in the vast midwestern interior, settled by farmers whose distaste for finance dated at least as far back as Thomas Jefferson, the absence of legal banks deprived people of a medium of exchange. Despite these states' antibanking bias, they desperately needed money to trade goods and fund development. So paper currency found a way to flourish even where it wasn't permitted, as it always had in the past. Across the Mississippi in the territory of Wisconsin, the legislature, while firmly opposed to banks, chartered the Wisconsin Marine and Fire Insurance Company to receive deposits and make loans. The company gave its depositors certificates that passed like money: the bills enjoyed an excellent reputation and worked just as well as those of a chartered bank. When the legislators angrily responded by repealing the charter, the Wisconsin Marine and Fire Insurance Company decided to stay in business anyway, becoming one of the country's most important banks. It wasn't alone. Unincorporated banks sprang up across the country and printed notes that, while illegal, sometimes held their value better than those of their competitors.

Then there were the counterfeiters. Compared to the hundreds of free, wildcat, and unchartered banks sprouting across the countryside, counterfeiting was a straightforward swindle, the black margin to the various shades of gray that made up the financial spectrum. With so many kinds of paper money to forge, moneymakers thrived. They forged notes of existing banks, invented fictitious ones, or stole plates from defunct banks and resurrected their bills. As Americans surged west, they followed. In frontier towns they scammed pioneers who couldn't tell fake money from genuine; in cash-strapped settlements they put currency into the hands of people who didn't care if it was fake so long as it could circulate. Just as Owen Sullivan holed up in New York's swamps and David Lewis hid in Pennsylvania's mountains, so the next wave of counterfeiters found terrain that fit their trade, setting up shop in the wilder recesses of an expanding nation. There, far from the authorities' limited reach, they made money and distributed it to communities across America.

By the middle of the nineteenth century, the American economy was powered in large part by promises that couldn't be kept. These came from legitimate and illicit moneymakers—counterfeiters, chartered institutions, and unincorporated banks—that together financed the transformation of the country. Belief buttressed the currency, and it proved a powerful tool. Americans willed a nation into existence on an immense, unfamiliar continent, and this act of faith was made possible by a million smaller ones: the confidence that pieces of paper had value.

PART III

the

PATRIOT

O N FEBRUARY 22, 1862, damp flags fluttered along Pennsylvania Avenue as thousands of citizens walked toward the Capitol to commemorate the 130th anniversary of George Washington's birth. They passed beneath its unfinished dome in the wet, gloomy weather and joined the throng of people trying to get inside. Seated in the House of Representatives were the government's most powerful men: congressmen and senators, generals and commodores, cabinet members and Supreme Court justices. They had come to hear the secretary of the Senate read Washington's Farewell Address, the day's main event. In his final message as president, Washington had urged Americans to put aside their regional loyalties and unite as a nation—advice that, ten months into the Civil War, must have seemed powerfully prophetic to the sea of solemn faces gathered in the crowded hall.

Not all celebrations were as somber as the scene at the Capitol. In Philadelphia, a shopkeeper named Samuel Curtis Upham watched lively crowds surging through the streets to the celebratory sounds of cannon fire. He stood about five feet eight inches tall, with a high forehead and a square chin. His frank, alert face exuded common sense and sobriety, qualities that set him apart from the merrymaking mob. Women wore old dresses they didn't mind getting dirty and young toughs pushed strangers for fun, provoking good-natured shoving matches. When night fell, specially prepared lights illuminated the city. Merchants on Chestnut Street competed for the brightest, best-decorated storefront, adorning their windows with silk and satin banners dyed red, white, and blue. Upham was one of them: his shop stood at the intersection of Chestnut and Fourth, across from the Greek Revival building that had housed the Second Bank of the United States in its final years. He lit his store's narrow facade so brilliantly that it caught the eye of a passing journalist, and when Philadelphia's weary residents picked up the *North American and United States Gazette* that Monday, they found a description of it on the front page. Upham's facade featured one of the night's most impressive displays, the journalist wrote, "a blaze of glory from basement to apex."

On Monday morning, Upham woke up and went to work. He lived on the south side of town, about a mile and a half from his store at 403 Chestnut Street, where he sold stationery, newspapers, and cosmetics with names like Upham's Hair Dye. Perhaps in part because of the *Gazette*'s favorable report, business that day was brisk. One customer after another came in, and they all wanted the same thing: not the *Gazette* but its competitor, the *Philadelphia Inquirer*. Even after Upham ran out of copies, people kept stopping by to look for it. The *Inquirer* had attracted many new readers with its war coverage, which was so exhaustive that the Union government commissioned special editions to distribute to soldiers. Still, demand for the February 24, 1862, issue struck Upham as unusually high. Puzzled, he asked one of his patrons what made that day's *Inquirer* so sought-after.

The answer was on page 1. Just below the Gothic type of the newspaper's title, the editors had printed a copy of a $5 Confederate note. The *Inquirer*'s reproduction was primitive: the original had been beautifully executed in red and black ink, with finely textured etching that disappeared in the transfer to newsprint. But people didn't care: they had never seen rebel money before and were fascinated by it. Like the continental currency printed by American revolutionaries almost a century earlier, the Confederate bill was more than money: it was also propaganda. The design's dignified imagery and elaborate artistry were intended to give the new Southern nation an aura of legitimacy. It included the Roman goddess Minerva on one end and a robed statue of Washington on the other; in the center sat five cherubic women representing Agriculture, Commerce, Industry, Justice, and Liberty, right above the emblazoned words "Confederate States of America."

The note promised its redemption for coin "Six Months after the Ratification of a Treaty of peace between the Confederate States and the United States." This explicitly staked the money's value on a Southern victory—if the Confederacy didn't sign a treaty with the Union securing its independence, the note wouldn't be redeemed, which made everyone who used the money a stakeholder in the Confederate cause. The note could also be used to pay public debts like taxes. The *Inquirer*'s strongly pro-Union editors weren't impressed. Below their crude replica they remarked that the day's issue of the *Inquirer*, which cost two cents, was worth more than the $5 Confederate bill. "Those who entertain a contrary opinion," they added, "may hand us the small balance of $4.98, due after purchasing each copy of the paper."

Upham wasted no time. He raced to the *Inquirer*'s cast-iron headquarters, a block away from his store, and persuaded the publisher William W. Harding to sell him a plate of the note. Then he called on a nearby printer and ordered three thousand copies on French letter paper. When the bills were ready, he brought them back to his shop and sold them for a cent each. Along the bottom margin of the notes he included a thin strip that read in small print "Fac-simile Confederate Note—Sold Wholesale and Retail, by S. C. Upham, 403 Chestnut Street, Philadelphia." They sold extremely well. The novelty thrilled Philadelphians, most of whom expected the war to be brief and glorious. They wanted souvenirs of the rebellion before the Union crushed it.

Ever since the Civil War broke out, Upham had been looking for a way to cash in on the conflict. The year before, he printed envelopes stamped with dozens of different patriotic illustrations, ranging from reverential portraits of Union generals to witty visual gags that reflected Upham's mischievous sense of humor. Jefferson Davis, the president of the Confederacy, bore the brunt of most of these jokes, appearing as a jackass, a skunk, and a devil with a cloven hoof. One showed Davis hanging from the gallows with the text "A full length drawing of Jeff. Davis, Esq. *taken from life. Executed by U. States.*"

The Confederate notes, however, were something new. Upham had known that the South issued currency; he even poked fun at it in one of his envelopes, which displayed a pile of worthless Southern notes labeled "No Redemption" and "Wild Cat Marked Good." But it had never occurred to him to sell copies of the bills themselves, and the sensation surrounding the *Inquirer*'s reproduction clearly caught him by surprise. Confederate notes gave Upham the ideal product. His envelopes had faced competition from many stationers who peddled similar items; Southern money, on the other hand, was a commodity that no one sold openly but everyone wanted. He could corner the market, supplying his "facsimiles" to customers throughout the Union.

After the success of his first print run, Upham began expanding his inventory. He searched everywhere for more issues and denominations, and soon came across *Frank Leslie's Illustrated Newspaper*. An English-born engraver, Leslie published a popular weekly that carried vividly drawn woodcut scenes of the war, and in January 1862, he ran a copy of a $10 Confederate note. Upham bought the plate, printed more bills, and retailed them from his Chestnut Street storefront for the same price as the previous batch: one cent apiece. The new note, while less ornate than the last, made the same grandiose appeal to American iconography. The centerpiece depicted Lady Liberty and a bald eagle with their faces turned toward each other as if deep in conversation; at their feet lay a shield decorated with a Confederate flag.

Now with two plates in his possession, Upham diversified his catalog of Southern money at a rapid pace, promising to pay exorbitant rates in gold for more specimens. He insisted that his notes were souvenirs—"a curiosity . . . worth preserving," as the original *Inquirer* article put it. But as Upham's enterprise grew, it became clear that his merchandise served another, less innocent purpose. The tags along the bottom of the bills bearing his name and address could easily be clipped off, transforming the "facsimile" into a counterfeit note. Upham, the respectable small-business owner, devoted patriot, and upstanding member of Philadelphia's middle class, had become a moneymaker.

UPHAM MADE AN UNUSUAL ADDITION to the pantheon of American counterfeiters. Unlike Owen Sullivan or David Lewis, he didn't sequester himself in the wilderness; instead, he set up on a busy street in downtown Philadelphia, one of the nation's most densely populated cities, and hawked his counterfeits openly. He didn't perform daring stunts or stage spectacular jailbreaks. He wasn't a bandit; he was a shopkeeper driven by the logic of supply and demand. Southern notes, issued by a government that was emphatically not recognized by the Union, had no legal status in the North, which meant Upham could forge them with impunity. The British military had counterfeited American continentals during the Revolution; Upham, however, didn't belong to an official Union effort to undermine the Southern economy by flooding it with fake money. True to the American spirit of private enterprise, his operation came about as a for-profit business, not a government-sponsored campaign.

During the past several decades, Andrew Jackson's laissez-faire legacy had enabled many species of semi-legal financial fraud that bordered on counterfeiting. But the circumstances of the Civil War created a new kind of moneymaker: someone who could forge currency without breaking the law. This paradox of a profession was perfect for Upham, whose own personality contained more conflicts and contradictions than would have been apparent to those who knew him only as a middle-aged shopkeeper. In February 1862 he turned forty-three. His life had seen periods of great excitement and crushing tedium spread over a diverse series of careers. He had been both an accountant and an adventurer: he worked for years as a bookkeeper in Philadelphia, but had also sailed around Cape Horn to dig for gold in California. He was a meticulous man who loved putting numbers and names into lists; he embraced bourgeois values and believed deeply in democracy, capitalism, and self-reliance. But he also had a vision of a wider, sparkling world that couldn't be contained within the margins of a merchant's ledger, and occasionally this transcendent stirring would rise to the surface to challenge his otherwise orderly existence.

Upham was born in Montpelier, Vermont, in 1819. He grew up within sight of Camels Hump, one of the tallest peaks of the Green Mountains, and spent enough time looking at its distinctive silhouette to remember it clearly decades later, when he saw a similar summit off the coast of Brazil during his voyage to California. His parents, Samuel and Sally, were devout Methodists. His father, known locally as Honest Sam Upham, earned a living as a blacksmith and later as a farmer; his honesty appears to have been his most memorable trait, and he lived an undistinguished life in the shadow of his older brother William. William mangled his right hand in a cider press when he was fifteen, a gruesome accident that had the happy result of giving him an education. Since he couldn't work on a farm, he went to school. He became Vermont's best-known Upham: a successful lawyer and a staunchly antislavery senator whose death from smallpox in 1853 occasioned a moving eulogy from his friend William H. Seward, later Lincoln's secretary of state. "He had gotten nothing by fraud or guile," Seward said of Senator Upham, nine years before his nephew began forging money.

Few families traced their American ancestry as far back as the Uphams.

Five-shilling Massachusetts bill of credit, the first of its kind in America and the earliest government-printed paper money in the West. COURTESY OF Q. DAVID BOWERS AND THE PEABODY ESSEX MUSEUM, SALEM, MASSACHUSETTS

Counterfeit forty-shilling Rhode Island bill engraved by Owen Sullivan (obverse). HISTORY AND GENEALOGY UNIT, CONNECTICUT STATE LIBRARY

Counterfeit forty-shilling Rhode Island bill engraved by Owen Sullivan (reverse). HISTORY AND GENEALOGY UNIT, CONNECTICUT STATE LIBRARY

Woodcut of Owen Sullivan's execution in New York in 1756. © AMERICAN ANTIQUARIAN SOCIETY

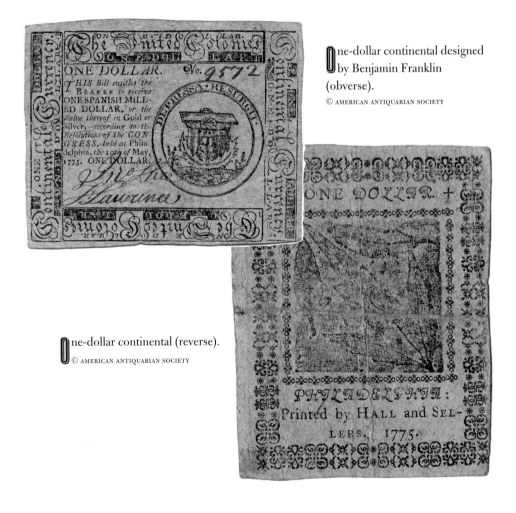

One-dollar continental designed by Benjamin Franklin (obverse).

© AMERICAN ANTIQUARIAN SOCIETY

One-dollar continental (reverse).

© AMERICAN ANTIQUARIAN SOCIETY

Six-dollar continental designed by Benjamin Franklin (obverse).

© AMERICAN ANTIQUARIAN SOCIETY

Six-dollar continental (reverse). © AMERICAN ANTIQUARIAN SOCIETY

Counterfeit fifty-dollar banknote of the kind David Lewis passed.
NATIONAL NUMISMATIC COLLECTION, SMITHSONIAN INSTITUTION

Detail of Samuel Curtis Upham (center), age fifty-eight, from a group portrait of the Associated Pioneers of the Territorial Days of California.

COURTESY OF THE BANCROFT LIBRARY, UNIVERSITY OF CALIFORNIA, BERKELEY, 1877. BANC PIC 1963.002:1882 (ENCLOSURE)—D.

Counterfeit five-dollar Confederate note printed by Samuel Curtis Upham, with his tag attached. IMAGE USED WITH PERMISSION FROM "A GUIDE BOOK OF COUNTERFEIT CONFEDERATE CURRENCY," © WHITMAN PUBLISHING, LLC. ALL RIGHTS RESERVED.

HALF PRICE! HALF PRICE!!

CONFEDERATE NOTES AND SHINPLASTERS

SELLING AT

ONE-HALF FORMER PRICES.

FOURTEEN DIFFERENT

REBEL NOTES, SHINPLASTERS AND POSTAGE STAMPS,

Perfect FAC-SIMILES of the originals, (printed in red, green and black ink,) sold by the 100 or 1,000 at the following reduced rates:—

50 cents per 100, or $4 per 1,000. One each of the fourteen different kinds sent post-paid to any address, on receipt of 25 cents.

☞ All orders by Mail or Express, promptly executed.

Address,

S. C. UPHAM, 403 Chestnut St. Philadelphia, Pa.

☞ **500,000 SOLD THE PAST THREE MONTHS.** ☜

☞ CARD TO THE PUBLIC.

As an individual in New York and a "shyster" in this city, lacking the brains to originate an idea or the liberality to pay for a respectable drawing or engraving, have recently gotten up "shocking bad" copies of several of my FAC-SIMILE REBEL NOTES and SHINPLASTERS, which they are endeavoring to foist upon the public, I have this day reduced the price of my FAC-SIMILE NOTES, SHINPLASTERS and POSTAGE STAMPS to 50 cents per 100 or $4 per 1,000, and shall be happy to receive and fill orders in large or small quantities at the above rates.

N. B.—BEWARE OF BASE IMITATIONS! Each and every FAC-SIMILE issued by me bears my imprint.

Philad'a, May 30, 1862.

S. C. UPHAM,
No. 403 CHESTNUT ST.

NOTICES OF THE PRESS.

"REBELDOM HIGHLY INDIGNANT.—'YANKEE TRICK.' The rebel papers contain the following:

"PHILADELPHIA CONFEDERATE BONDS.—Detective Goodrich, of the rebel Treasury Department, has exhibited to the editor of the Richmond *Dispatch* what he terms 'the last and grossest piece of Yankee scoundrelism, and an infernal means to discredit the currency of the Southern Confederacy.' 'It consists,' says the *Dispatch*, 'in well executed counterfeits of our five dollar Confederate notes, struck off in Philadelphia, where the news-boys are selling them at five cents a piece. This note is well calculated to deceive, and in nearly every particular is a fac-simile of the original. We caution persons receiving this money to be exceedingly careful, as there is no means of knowing to what extent they have been circulated.'

"The 'Yankee Scoundrel' who has counterfeited these *Valuable* notes is Mr. S. C. Upham, 403 Chestnut Street. He has issued fac-similes of seven kinds of rebel shinplasters and two denominations of their notes. He has also issued exact copies of rebel postage stamps of three kinds, the five and ten cent stamps issued by the Confederate Government, and the five cent stamp got up by J. S. Riddell, the postmaster at New Orleans, and bearing his name. Mr. Upham sells these fac-similes very cheap, but they certainly bring as much as the originals are worth."—*Philadelphia Evening Bulletin.*

☞ SAMUEL C. UPHAM, of Philadelphia, advertises that he will sell Confederate notes at easy prices. We at first thought that he had taken some of them for a very bad debt, but it appears he has executed fac-similes of them which he disposes of as mementos. The rates offered by MR. UPHAM are very moderate, and yet we assure all who are anxious to speculate, that his lithographed notes are worth just as much as those issued by Jeff. Davis.—*Louisville Journal.*

☞ *Confederate Bank Notes*, of the denomination of FIVE and TEN Dollars each, have been issued by S. C. Upham, No. 403 Chestnut Street, and are sold by him at the most remarkable discount on record. The engraving is fully equal to that of the originals, and the notes are perfect fac-similes of those prepared at Richmond.—*Philadelphia Inquirer.*

CONFEDERATE NOTES.—MR. S. C. UPHAM, 403 Chestnut Street, has published fac-similes of the $5 and $10 Confederate Notes, issued in Richmond, which will be curiosities ere long, when the rebellion is crushed. MR. UPHAM'S notes are as valuable, we dare say, as the originals.—*Philadelphia Press.*

MR. S. C. UPHAM, No. 403 Chestnut Street, Philadelphia, publishes fac-similes of the Confederate State notes, which are quite interesting to the curious.—*N. Y. Tribune.*

Confederate Money.—Mr. S. C. Upham, 403 Chestnut Street, has got out excellent fac-similes of the $5 and $10 notes of the "Confederate States of America," which he sells at prices even cheaper than they bring in Richmond and Memphis. They are curious and interesting, and will become more so as time advances.—*Phila. Evening Bulletin.*

N. B.—If you order by the 100, send 18 cents in addition to the price of each 100, to PRE-PAY postage.

☞ The $5 and $10 Notes, on Bank Note Paper, at $3 per 100, or $20 per 1,000.

Advertising circular from Samuel Curtis Upham, dated May 30, 1862.

THE LIBRARY COMPANY OF PHILADELPHIA

One-dollar United States Note, or greenback, with portrait of Treasury Secretary Salmon P. Chase (obverse). COURTESY OF THE AMERICAN NUMISMATIC SOCIETY

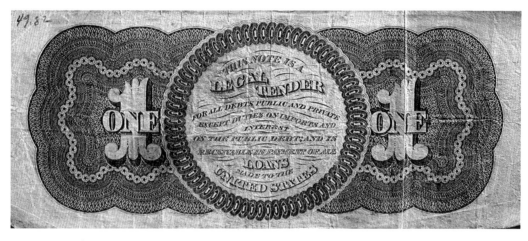

One-dollar United States Note (reverse). COURTESY OF THE AMERICAN NUMISMATIC SOCIETY

The patriarch, John Upham, sailed across the Atlantic in 1635, a mere fifteen years after the *Mayflower*, and settled in Weymouth, a colony on the Massachusetts coast. Over the course of the next couple of centuries, his descendants became farmers and doctors and congressmen—pillars of the establishment in communities across the country, earning the quiet esteem of their peers and, occasionally, the hatred of those who felt slighted. Charles Wentworth Upham had the misfortune of being a prominent Whig in Salem when Nathaniel Hawthorne, a Democrat, lost his job at the town customhouse for political reasons. The enraged author blamed Upham, and when his novel *House of the Seven Gables* appeared a few years later, it included a character that was said to be his revenge: Jaffrey Pyncheon, an eminent citizen and self-serving hypocrite who belongs to an old American family.

Samuel was a seventh-generation Upham and the fifth Samuel in a row. The Montpelier where he was born was a town of approximately two thousand people living in the foothills of the Green Mountains. It had become Vermont's capital in 1805, and the State House, an unpretentious wooden building three stories tall, dominated its center—especially at night, when tallow candles illuminated the facade. Inside hung a garish chandelier that seemed unrepublican to some of Montpelier's residents, whose mostly agrarian existence afforded few extravagances.

Montpelier's unhurried pace provided the young Upham with plenty of time for daydreaming about more exciting places. Elsewhere in the country, far from Blackberry Hill, Hogback Mountain, and the other imaginatively named inclines that surrounded his childhood home, life was moving faster. Factories and banks were being built; the twin engines of industrialization and finance were changing the way Americans had lived for generations. Some manufacturing came to Montpelier—cotton mills, a nail factory—but it couldn't keep up with Burlington, its faster-growing neighbor to the west. The first bank, the Bank of Montpelier, wasn't chartered until 1825, well after the banking mania had swept through the rest of the nation and helped trigger the Panic of 1819. Not everyone in Vermont shared Montpelier's ambivalence about printing money, however: counterfeiters had infested the state since the eighteenth century, producing stacks of fake cash along the rugged Canadian border. David Lewis and Philander Noble had been there the decade before Upham was born, and years later, the trade was still going strong. By the 1830s, Vermont's moneymakers had built sophisticated distribution networks to ferry their bills hundreds of miles along roads and canals to passers in Indiana and Virginia. As a boy, Upham probably saw at least one counterfeiter led in chains to Montpelier's granite jail.

At the age of twenty, Upham left home. He got as far away from Montpelier as he could: New York City. The industrial and financial currents that were making slow inroads in Montpelier were literally tearing New York apart. Thanks in part to the demise of the Second Bank of the United States in the 1830s, Manhattan had become the riotous epicenter of American capitalism, a victim of the extreme poverty and prosperity brought about by a laissez-faire economy. On Wall Street, brokers hustled for higher profits, while a mile up the island, newly arrived Irish immigrants cut one another's throats in tenement slums. For a young man from the countryside, New York would be a fast education. It certainly offered more opportunities for youthful indiscretion than Montpelier: saloons, opium dens, and brothels, to name a few. Upham got a job as a clerk, likely bookkeeping for one of the city's innumerable firms.

It wasn't until his late twenties that Upham settled into a more anchored life. He moved to Philadelphia, where he secured a well-paid position as an accountant for a lumber company and, in 1846, married a seventeen-year-old girl named Ann Eliza Bancroft. Within a couple of years, they had their first child: Marion, a daughter. But the restlessness that had burned within him since boyhood remained, waiting to flare up when the moment came. When, in the summer and fall of 1848, reports began to trickle in that gold had been discovered in California, Upham decided to go. His responsibilities as a father and husband could wait.

ON FEBRUARY 2, 1849, in a turbulent patch of the Atlantic somewhere off the coast of Florida, the *Osceola* cut powerfully through the waves, its two masts slanted obliquely across the horizon. The night before, a violent storm had blown in from the northeast, splitting the fore-topsail, and while the worst was over, the sea was still rough. On board, the brig's sixty-five passengers and fifteen crew members braced their stomachs for each heave of the hull, hoping to keep down their last meal. They were sailing to California via Cape Horn, the southernmost tip of South America, a voyage of twenty thousand miles. Three weeks into the trip, some were having second thoughts. Provisions of food and fresh water were already running low; gales struck the boat frequently. The captain was a stubborn old tyrant who yelled profanities at his mates and, worse, showed little concern for living conditions aboard the ship. Steerage, where most passengers were, looked like a tenement: forty-four people packed into a small, unventilated space littered with chicken coops and pigpens.

The richer travelers stayed above-decks, in cabins that got better air but sometimes flooded with seawater. This was where Upham sat, scribbling in his journal. It was his thirtieth birthday. "Have been a rolling-stone all my life, consequently have gathered no moss," he wrote. "And now in search of 'the golden fleece,' and may return shorn." He had earned enough as an accountant to buy a cabin berth, but even in his relatively comfortable quarters, the hardships of the journey had begun to take their toll. "Descriptions of a 'life on the ocean wave' read very prettily on shore," he reflected, "but the *reality* of a sea voyage speedily dispels the romance."

The romance had been intoxicating back in Philadelphia, when Upham started reading stories about California. At first they seemed too ridiculous to believe. On January 24, 1848, a carpenter named James W. Marshall had found pieces of gold in the American River while building a sawmill at Coloma, about 140 miles inland from San Francisco. The news took awhile to reach the eastern cities, but when it did, its impact was electric. The *New York Herald* raved about rivers "whose banks and bottoms are filled with pure gold"—the mythic El Dorado, sought by the Spaniards for centuries, had finally been found. Skeptics dismissed the rumors as a hoax. It seemed unlikely that California, a sparsely populated backwater that the United States had officially annexed in February 1848 after winning the Mexican-American War, would have so much untapped mineral wealth. But their doubts disappeared in December 1848, when President James K. Polk confirmed California's "abundance of gold" in his State of the Union address.

Polk's announcement officially launched what came to be known as the California gold rush. Hundreds of thousands of people from all over the country and the world—South America, Asia, Australia, Europe—went to California hoping to make their fortune. Contemporaries called it an "infection," a "fever," and they were right: what the gold rush resembled above all was an epidemic. Someone traveling across California might think the region had recently suffered from an outbreak of plague. The race to the mines had depopulated the countryside almost overnight, leaving behind the eerie spectacle of empty homes and half-sown fields. Captains who anchored their ships off the coast awoke to find their crews gone, the sailors having fled for the mines. The gold rush warped people's sanity, inducing a kind of delirium that made enormous risks seem completely justified. Australian sheepherders, Chinese peasants, and Philadelphia bookkeepers like Upham left home for a land they knew little about, with no guarantees that they would get rich or even survive the journey.

While global in scale, the gold rush epitomized the distinctly American desire to make something from nothing. Digging gold out of the ground required labor, of course. But extracting hundreds, even thousands, of dollars' worth of metal from the earth in a single day seemed more like alchemy than real work, and the migrants streaming into California wanted to become millionaires with a minimum of effort. The *Boston Courier* denounced their get-rich-quick mentality as an enemy to "industry, productive labor, thrifty habits." Paradoxically, this was the same argument that hard-money advocates from Thomas Hutchinson to Andrew Jackson had used against paper money: that by creating opportunities for acquiring wealth without labor, a paper economy ruined people's work ethic. If Hutchinson or Jackson had been alive in 1848, they might have had to revise their thinking. The gold rush proved there was nothing intrinsically moral about precious metals. Gold could encourage frenzied speculation just as well as paper. And, like the paper-fueled booms and busts that preceded it, the gold rush would end up enriching a small handful and bankrupting many more.

When gold fever reached Philadelphia in 1848, Upham surrendered without much of a fight. His daughter had been born in April, and departing for California meant leaving his wife at home alone with the child. But the temptation was too great—and perhaps, after two years of marriage, the banalities of domestic life felt a little stifling. Seized with enthusiasm, Upham spared no expense outfitting himself for the trip. He filled a chest with flannel and hickory shirts. He bought a pick, a spade, and a large tin pan. He even purchased a waterproof suit and tent, both made of rubber. Many of these items proved to be totally useless, but Upham couldn't help himself. An hour before midnight on January 15, 1849, he said good-bye to his wife and daughter and boarded the *Osceola*. The next morning, an iceboat began dragging the ship down the frozen Delaware River toward the open sea.

UPHAM'S CALIFORNIA ADVENTURE would be the defining experience of his life. The journals he kept during the trip formed the basis for a book he published in 1878, *Notes of a Voyage to California via Cape Horn,*

Together with Scenes in El Dorado, in the Years 1849–'50. An eyewitness chronicle of the gold rush era, it offers an indispensable portrait of the man who later in life became one of America's most intriguing counterfeiters.

In the book's preface, Upham calls his story "a narration of *facts*, not *fancies*," and true to his word, he includes many facts. He tended to wake up early on board the *Osceola*, usually around six. He would walk on deck to observe the ship's rigging and the winds. Before retiring for the night, he would note the temperature, the latitude, and the distance sailed in his journal. But Upham knew that the *Osceola* was more than the sum of these statistics. What makes his account an absorbing read is his eye for the ship's human drama, the scenes that ensue when eighty people are separated from civilization by miles of water and forced to interact for months under challenging conditions.

Life on the *Osceola* involved stretches of numbing boredom punctuated by moments of extreme terror. Most of the time there was nothing for the passengers to do. Their only exercise came from strolling about on deck, and they soon became lethargic; Upham gained so much weight on the trip that he could barely fit into his clothes. Then, after days of uninterrupted dullness, a storm would suddenly appear and wreak havoc. This schizophrenic pace must have been exhausting, and everyone dealt with it differently. Many got drunk, escaping the claustrophobic world of the *Osceola* in booze-fueled parties that Upham called "jollifications." One jollification had just gotten under way when a gale hit: "[W]ith the roaring of the elements and the carousing of the revelers," Upham wrote, "the night was rendered hideous." Others gambled, betting several hundred dollars on games of cards or dominoes. When a player ran out of money, he would cut the buttons off his coat and use those, or promise to buy the winner a pet monkey when they reached the next port. The most popular pastime, however, was fighting. Brawls provided an excellent way to relieve pent-up frustrations, especially when the weather heated up.

Although he faithfully recorded these activities in his journal, Upham preferred to spend his time reading and writing; his greatest vice was sipping a little whiskey to calm his nerves during a storm. His level disposition earned him the respect of his fellow passengers, who made him a mediator in their ongoing dispute with the captain. Captain James Fairfowl had been causing problems from the moment the brig set sail. He was a curmudgeonly Scot with big ears, imperious eyebrows, and an unfortunate tendency to take unreasonable positions from which he refused to back down. When the steerage passengers demanded to be served more potatoes, Fairfowl threatened to throw the food overboard.

On the night of May 13, 1849, Captain Fairfowl almost ran the *Osceola* into a reef off the Chilean coast. He was looking for Talcahuano, a popular port for whalers and passenger ships bound for California. After his near-collision, Fairfowl stayed close to the shore, hoping to find the right harbor. But the darkness obscured his view, and when day broke, a heavy fog fell. He piloted the *Osceola* into a small bay and dropped anchor. Once the haze lifted, he resolved to go ashore to try to figure out where they were, and gave the passengers permission to join him.

They learned that they were only twenty-seven miles from Talcahuano. As long as the wind kept blowing the *Osceola* toward the mouth of the bay, however, the ship couldn't leave. Upham didn't want to wait for the weather to change. He persuaded Fairfowl to let him and thirteen other passengers travel to Talcahuano on their own and reunite with the *Osceola* later. After the dreariness of life at sea, tramping through the Chilean countryside must have been invigorating, and Upham devoted long, colorful journal entries to it. He and his companions started down a muddy road lined with apple orchards, vineyards, and strawberry patches, stopping at huts along the way to sample the wine that people generously offered the travelers. Upham drank the wine, but immediately disliked the Chileans. He found them "idle, indolent," "a poor, flea-bitten, priest-ridden people" who were too lazy to develop their great natural resources. The men he admired the most in Chile weren't the Chileans but the American expatriates who had become local entrepreneurs—men like Brooks, a New Englander who had deserted from a whaling ship six years earlier and now ran a profitable hotel. Upham saw Americans everywhere: the Chilean coast seemed overrun with them.

It took the *Osceola* another sixty-nine days from Talcahuano to reach California. On August 2, 1849, the passengers glimpsed land through the fog, and three days later, they passed through the Golden Gate into a harbor teeming with ships unloading people and cargo from every part of the world. After seven difficult months, they had arrived in San Francisco. It was a "queer place," Upham wrote. San Francisco had grown rapidly in the past year, but it still seemed more like a large campsite than a proper town. Most of its five thousand residents lived in tents planted in the shifting sands along the beach or in the nearby dunes. They hadn't come to build a community—many didn't even share a common language—but to get rich as quickly as they could. Their ephemeral dwellings were regularly incinerated by fires, only to be rebuilt within weeks. When heavy rains fell in the winter of 1849–1850, the streets they hadn't bothered to pave flooded—Upham, who witnessed the deluge, saw men and mules drowning in "rivers of mud." San Francisco wasn't a destination but a transit point for people headed to the mines farther east. Its most permanent establishments were those that catered to the appetites of the mostly male newcomers, places where they could drink, gamble, and fornicate before trekking into the interior to look for gold.

Upham pitched his tent in a portion of the beach called Happy Valley. In his pocket was $6.75; he would need more money to make it to the mines, so he took a job at a lumberyard. Instead of recoiling from San Francisco's rawness, Upham enjoyed it. He felt it had a democratizing effect. "A graduate of Yale considers it no disgrace to sell peanuts," he noted approvingly. In California the aristocratic distinctions of the East meant nothing; men competed as equals, and succeeded through their own initiative and hard work. Determined to try his luck in the mines,

Upham booked passage in September aboard a ship that sailed up the San Joaquin River to Stockton, an inland town about ninety miles away. From there, he hired muleteers to take him to the Calaveras River and, armed with a pick, a crowbar, a spade, and a tin pan, began panning for gold. Upham would dig dirt from the riverbed and then place it in a pan with water, letting the heavier gold dust settle to the bottom and the rest wash off. On his first day, he extracted a quarter of an ounce of gold this way. He dedicated himself to the task, waking up at dawn and toiling for hours, moving boulders to locate richer lodes underneath.

The successful prospectors, he noticed, were those who took a patient, methodical approach. "Those who had expected to realize a fortune in a few days or weeks were sadly disappointed," Upham remarked. His persistence paid off, as when he found a patch of earth that held almost $400 worth of gold. But the job proved too physically demanding. In Philadelphia he had worked behind a desk, and he wasn't accustomed to strenuous manual labor. After nearly a month of mining, Upham's joints became so badly swollen that he could barely walk. He had no choice but to sell his tools and quit.

When Upham returned to San Francisco in November 1849, he couldn't believe how dramatically it had grown in his absence. "The saw and hammer of the carpenter could be heard in every square, and the voice of the crier and the auctioneer at the corner of nearly every street," he marveled. The campsite was becoming a city: the flimsy canvas tents had given way to sturdier wooden structures, built to accommodate an exploding population. Every day more gold-seekers showed up on the piers, and by the end of the year, around twenty-five thousand people lived in San Francisco. This influx created a huge demand for goods, and Upham came up with a plan. "I had a vision," he recalled, "and in that vision I saw—pickles." He bought cucumbers and vinegar from a ship newly arrived from Boston and cornered the market on pickles. Within a week he had netted $300, and soon started another profitable trade in tobacco pipes.

While he clearly had a gift for it, Upham hadn't sailed twenty thousand miles to sell pickles and pipes. If he couldn't dig for gold, he needed to find a satisfying way to spend his time or he might as well go home. So he closed his business and applied for a position signing up subscribers for a local newspaper, the *Pacific News*. Published by a pair of former gold prospectors who met in Chile on their way to California, the *News* appeared three times a week and cost twelve and a half cents. It carried reports from all over California as well as news from faraway capitals like Havana and Rome. San Francisco's isolated residents craved information from the outside world, and Upham had no trouble increasing the newspaper's circulation. The *News*'s publishers rewarded him by hiring him as their bookkeeper and providing him with a bunk in their offices where he could sleep.

Living and working in the rudimentary wood-frame building on Kearny Street that housed the *News* thrust Upham right into the hectic heart of early San Francisco. The newspaper was located north of the Plaza, which had been the town's center since its early days as a Mexican village. When something significant happened, like a fiery political speech or San Francisco's first theatrical performance, it took place in the Plaza. So many pairs of boots had trampled it that no grass could grow, and on the brown ground merchants had set up stalls to peddle items from the different continents represented by the swarm of ships in the harbor.

Upham loved newspapers. They appealed to his fondness for hard facts and engaging anecdotes. The *Pacific News* printed wholesale prices, election returns, and firsthand stories from the mines. It did for the citizens of San Francisco what Upham had been doing privately in his journal since departing Philadelphia: documenting what might otherwise go unrecorded. Upham liked the *News* but wanted to be more than an accountant. So in the spring of 1850, when a New Orleans printer named George Kenyon Fitch invited him to help publish a newspaper in Sacramento City, he agreed. They rented the second floor of a house near the American River and assembled the first issue of the *Sacramento Transcript*. Upham slept on the office counter, using a roll of paper for a pillow. He served not only as the newspaper's business manager but also as its local reporter. While Sacramento was only a fraction of the size of San Francisco, it didn't lack for excitement. In the summer after Upham arrived, a dispute over land titles escalated into a firefight between an angry mob of squatters and a group of armed citizens. The sheriff was shot dead, but the mayor survived.

Upham had come west for gold but found something else: a society in the process of being created. He felt exhilarated by the "almost magical" growth of Sacramento, watching its residents build the town's first levee or organize its first concerts. These weren't prospectors but pioneers, people who, like his ancestor John Upham, cleared the wilderness and planted the standard of civilization. Upham could have become one of them but he had a family waiting for him in Philadelphia, and in late August 1850, he decided to return home. He sold his stake in the *Transcript* and set off for San Francisco, where he began the voyage east. His friends at the newspaper were sorry to see him go. "We sincerely wish him a speedy return to his family," they wrote in their announcement of Upham's departure, "and success in the business in which he may hereafter engage."

WILLIAM LEWIS HERNDON HAD SPENT nearly his whole life at sea. He had joined the navy at fifteen, cruised the Gulf of Mexico in the Mexican-American War, and at thirty-eight, became the first American to explore the Amazon River. So in September 1857, when his ship, the *Central America*, sailed into a hurricane on its way from Panama to New York, he reacted calmly. The *Central America*, equipped with three masts and steam-powered paddle wheels on the port and starboard sides, had made the trip dozens of times before. Now it careened through mountains of swirling water, trying to keep its balance as the hull started to flood.

Herndon, a slim man with a red beard and round glasses, could be seen racing around the ship, raising his voice to be heard over the shrieking of the wind. He assembled bucket brigades to bail out the boat, but the water continued to rise, eventually extinguishing the fires in the steam engine's boilers. Herndon tried raising the sails, but the wind shredded them. He was adrift in a hurricane with no power to maneuver, and on the night of September 12, he stood on deck in dress uniform while the *Central America* sank. Moments later, the sea submerged him and everyone else on board. Some clung to floating debris but most thrashed about helplessly, crying or praying. One survivor saw hundreds of "human beings floating out on the bosom of the ocean, with no hope but death."

Four hundred and thirty-five people drowned in the wreck of the *Central America*. The story made headlines all over the country and inspired many artists' renderings of the ship's final moments. *Frank Leslie's Illustrated Newspaper* ran an engraving showing the *Central America*'s frantic passengers buried by a cresting wave, an image that captured the horror of the scene. While the human tragedy was considerable, lives weren't the only things lost. In the hold of the *Central America* was a large quantity of California gold, about $2 million worth, being transported to New York City banks. News of the disaster sent shock waves through Wall Street, and it couldn't have come at a worse time. The banks, facing a crisis of confidence that had been building since late August, had hoped to fortify their reserves with a fresh infusion of specie. Wall Street had become precariously dependent on regular shipments of gold from California, and the incident underscored the fundamental fragility of the nation's financial establishment. In the end, however, the banks weathered the disappointment fairly well, and the pangs of fear soon faded. But the sudden scare surrounding the *Central America* demonstrated how tense the situation was. And in the coming weeks, that tension would intensify into outright hysteria as the nation entered its next meltdown, the Panic of 1857.

To get from California to New York, the gold had sailed from San Francisco to Panama and crossed the isthmus before being loaded onto the

Central America. This was the same route Upham had taken home seven years earlier, a trip that lasted only thirty-eight days, far shorter than his voyage around Cape Horn. His time in California had transformed him, and he kept thinking about it long after returning to Philadelphia's comparatively tranquil cobblestone streets. Californians, he believed, were a "manly, vigorous, intelligent race of freemen" who lived independently, without the benefit of unfair privileges or monopolies. This ideal had a long history in American life, championed in some form from Thomas Jefferson to Andrew Jackson. By Upham's time, however, it had become more of a fantasy than a reality for many people, as the economy grew more complex and interconnected. The most striking examples of the trend could be found in the industrializing cities, where workers did back-breaking labor for little pay and had no illusions about being "freemen." By the middle of the nineteenth century, even the rural agrarians idolized by Jefferson felt their self-reliance slipping away. The economy had made them more vulnerable to forces beyond their control, a fact that became painfully evident in the Panic of 1857.

On August 24, 1857, one of New York City's most respected financial institutions—the local branch of the Ohio Life Insurance and Trust Company—failed. While it didn't issue notes, it had lent a lot of money and held large sums of deposits. It was also in debt to almost all the other New York banks, and its abrupt collapse frightened them. Then news emerged that most of the company's capital had been embezzled by its cashier, which proved even more unsettling: if fraud could be committed at a place as reputable as Ohio Life, it could happen anywhere. Worse, people might lose faith in the New York banks and demand their deposits or redeem their notes, creating a specie drain that could lead to more bankruptcies. So New York's bankers drastically curtailed their liabilities. They cut their lending, called in their loans, and pressed banks throughout the country to redeem notes that had accumulated in their coffers.

This contraction of credit, beginning in New York and radiating outward, shuttered businesses, crippled commerce and industry, and eventually forced almost every bank in the nation to suspend specie payments. The scale of the crisis surprised most Americans, who didn't expect a financial tremor in a faraway city to have much of an impact on their lives. Western farmers had an abundant harvest in 1857. But the crisis caused crop prices to plummet, so despite full granaries, they had a terrible season. Southern planters suffered a similar decline in demand for tobacco and cotton. Companies everywhere—New England textile mills, Wisconsin lumberyards, Pennsylvania coal mines—went bust or shed jobs. The pain was worst in New York City, where the number of unemployed reached as high as a hundred thousand. On November 5, 1857, four thousand people rallied at Tompkins Square near the East River to demand work. The crowds swelled in the following days, and after they marched through Wall Street and stormed City Hall, the mayor called in the police, the state militia, and federal troops. On the steps of the Merchants' Exchange, a blacksmith named Bowles declared that workingmen didn't intend to starve while millions of dollars' worth of specie sat idle in bank vaults.

Decades of laissez-faire hadn't produced a ruggedly egalitarian society of the kind Upham imagined in California. Instead, it had created a great scramble for wealth where some had power and others had none. As with previous panics, the Panic of 1857 capped an era of tremendous growth. The Mexican-American War from 1846 to 1848 had invigorated the economy and vastly increased the size of the country. The new territory came with significant natural resources—gold, most important—which further spurred the economy. At the same time, political instability in Europe caused a spike in immigration. The foreigners energized American industry with a flood of cheap labor. They also accelerated the migration westward, creating a booming real estate market and heightening demand for the railroads that had begun traversing the country. Railroad companies went deeply into debt to raise capital, borrowing from European creditors and issuing stocks and bonds that were traded on Wall Street.

Underwriting these ventures was a banking sector that almost doubled in size from 1850 to 1857. Paper money soared to perilous heights. By the 1850s, more than ten thousand different kinds of notes circulated, printed by incorporated and unincorporated banks, insurance firms, and railroad companies, among others. This made simple transactions mind-bogglingly complex. A baker selling a loaf of bread couldn't be expected to recognize most of the bills a customer might present as payment. His best option would be to consult a periodical like *Thompson's Bank Note Reporter*, which listed the latest values for different notes and catalogued known counterfeits. But the economy moved so fast that an edition of *Thompson's*, which subscribers received twice a week, could become obsolete almost as soon as it appeared. A bank might have failed, rendering its bills worthless, or a new type of forgery might have eluded detection. Even the most reliable sources of information couldn't keep up.

Counterfeiters had always exploited America's financial disarray, and the surge in paper money benefited them in obvious ways. The principle remained the same as it had for Owen Sullivan and David Lewis: the more bills changing hands, the better the chances a counterfeit would slip through unnoticed. But mid-nineteenth-century moneymakers also dealt with new developments that transformed their trade: the changing technology of banknote printing. Rather than engraving an entire note on a sheet of metal and then running it through a printing press, the modern technique involved breaking the bill's design down into interchangeable components—the name of the bank, for instance, or a picture of a bald eagle. These different parts were engraved on separate pieces of steel called dies and then assembled to print a banknote. The dies could be reused, swapped in or out as needed.

This made banknote printing faster and cheaper. Instead of hiring a skilled craftsman to carve a whole plate, a printer could pay him once to engrave the dies and then hire unskilled workers to manufacture the notes. It also made counterfeiting easier. When Owen Sullivan wanted to forge money, he had to inscribe a sheet of copper; now all a criminal had to do was obtain a handful of dies, which could easily be bought from failed banks or printing firms. There was no shortage of disgruntled banknote engravers willing to collaborate with counterfeiters. As banknote printing became industrialized and smaller firms consolidated into corporations, an earlier generation of craftsmen lost their jobs or were forced into menial wage labor. Counterfeiting gave them a way to earn the money they needed to survive. They could print genuine bills by day and forgeries by night.

Since New York City was the heart of America's banknote engraving industry, it had also become its counterfeiting capital by the 1850s. Many engravers lived in the working-class neighborhoods below Fourteenth Street, where they mingled with the crooks and con men who made up a thriving urban underworld centered in notorious slums like Five Points. Owen Sullivan and David Lewis had avoided cities, finding it easier to conceal their activities in the countryside. But as cities got bigger and denser in the nineteenth century, they became more conducive to crime. In 1857, New York had six hundred thousand people. Its alleyways, tenements, and vice dens provided moneymakers with countless places to hide, and the masses milling about Manhattan supplied plenty of potential victims. Passers targeted small establishments like oyster bars, bakeries, and tobacconists—places where they could buy a cheap item with fake cash and receive genuine bills in change. Usually they would wait until evening before spending counterfeits, since the forgeries were harder to detect in the half-light of a candle or a gas lamp than during the day. Passers didn't confine their activities to New York, however. Like legitimate banknotes, counterfeit bills were produced in Manhattan and then distributed throughout the country. Interstate networks of wholesalers and retailers channeled the paper into local markets, taking advantage of the nation's growing rail network to push their product farther and faster than ever before.

While the 1850s were lucrative for counterfeiters, they also saw escalating sectional tensions that ignited a war—one that would eventually threaten their livelihood. The strains between North and South had grown as the nation expanded. Tobacco and cotton, the South's main crops, exhausted farmland quickly, and many slaveholders found it cheaper to move west into virgin soil rather than spend money on fertilizer and irrigation. This contributed to the westward spread of slavery into new territories, an issue that inflamed Northern antislavery advocates. The angry debates that took place in Congress concerned the sovereignty of the federal government versus that of the states: the abolitionist hardliners believed Washington had the power to abolish slavery throughout the Union, while their opponents argued that slavery was left to each state to decide for itself. When the Civil War erupted, the federal government was forced to prove its sovereignty by putting down the rebellion. In order to do so, it would need to broaden the scope of its power. This included doing something about the nation's chaotic money supply, with significant consequences for counterfeiters.

WHEN UPHAM RETURNED to Philadelphia in the fall of 1850, he fathered two sons and started a newspaper. At their offices on South Third Street, in the heart of the downtown business district, he and his two co-publishers edited the first issue of the *Sunday Mercury*, which appeared on February 23, 1851. While Upham brought considerable experience to the job, the *Mercury* wasn't at all like the papers he had worked for in California. As a Sunday weekly, it didn't have to be as topical as Philadelphia's dailies. Its stories could be livelier, more literary—a gripping account of a doctor trying to save a young woman who had stabbed herself ("A Night in the Life of a Physician"), for instance, or a travelogue from the Orient ("Interior of a Persian Harem"). There were also poems, concert reviews, and a regular feature called "Higgledy Piggledies" that ran jokes and curiosities. The *Mercury*'s opinion pieces were earnest but rarely self-righteous; while it mocked reform movements like women's rights, it was never vicious.

A tone of reasonableness prevailed throughout, reflected in the crisp typography and the clean black lines dividing its columns.

Upham's newspaper catered to Philadelphia's middle class. It gave them entertaining weekend reading that didn't stray too far from their conservative, mercantile sensibility. The *Mercury*'s back page printed ads from local businesses with names like Tams & Ingram Plumbers, Gray's Typographical, and the Eighth Street Pie Bakery. These were Upham's readers. Like him, they were neither rich nor poor but small-time capitalists, the kind Benjamin Franklin had been a century before. The city had changed a lot since Franklin's era. While the colonial red brick could still be seen in the nicer neighborhoods, Philadelphia as a whole was becoming an industrial town like New York. Large factories sprang up on its outskirts, where workers made locomotives or umbrellas and lived in filthy shantytowns nearby. In the inner city, horse-drawn streetcars lined the roads, accelerating the pace of life and often colliding with pedestrians. As in New York, industry made some Philadelphians very wealthy and others destitute. In the middle were people like Upham. If they weren't millionaires, at least they didn't live in the slums. "[N]ever plead guilty of poverty," advised an article in the *Sunday Mercury*. "So far as this world is concerned, you had better admit that you are a scoundrel."

Philadelphians had strong economic ties to the South, which made them receptive to Southern concerns and resentful of the city's vocal abolitionist minority. But as the disputes of the 1850s deepened into something resembling insurrection, Philadelphia's sympathy wore thin. South Carolina seceded on December 20, 1860. By the time Lincoln took office in March, six more states had left the Union and Jefferson Davis had been named president of the new Confederate States of America. Then at four-thirty in the morning on April 12, 1861, Confederate batteries opened fire on federal troops garrisoned at Fort Sumter, outside Charleston, South Carolina.

Fort Sumter sparked an outpouring of patriotism throughout the North.

In Philadelphia, homes and shops and streetcars sprouted red, white, and blue; the hatred once reserved for abolitionists was now directed at the city's pro-Southern Democrats and anyone else perceived as insufficiently patriotic. The change of heart had nothing to do with slavery. The nation had been attacked and needed to retaliate. Upham shared this view. While stopping in Rio de Janeiro on his way to California, he had felt little compassion for the city's many slaves; they "appear to be well treated," he noted. Upham undoubtedly saw the Civil War as the majority of Northerners did, not as a crusade to end slavery but as a necessary effort to preserve the Union and punish the insidious forces of secession.

The North faced enormous logistical challenges. Lincoln inherited a feeble federal government, an army of fewer than twenty thousand men, and an empty Treasury, its credit exhausted by decades of mismanagement. The government had run a deficit every year since the Panic of 1857, and revenue from taxes and tariffs, its main source of income, had dropped precipitously. The Union needed ships, trains, weapons, tents, uniforms. The war would be expensive, and Lincoln didn't have time to figure out how to finance it. The man he counted on to deliver the funds was his treasury secretary: a tall, difficult man named Salmon Portland Chase.

Chase had no financial experience. He had been appointed to the Treasury for political reasons, as a reward for his support for Lincoln at the Republican convention. Neither of them could have anticipated how important a role it would become. Chase had grown up in Ohio, represented the state in the Senate, and served a term as governor. He belonged to the antislavery wing of the Republican Party, but his proud, patronizing attitude prevented him from going very far in politics. He had always been arrogant; even as a boy he had held himself apart from others, as if destined for greater things. His supreme confidence in himself, coupled with a relentless work ethic, brought him the success that he craved. He first made a name for himself in Cincinnati, as a defense lawyer advocating on behalf of fugitive slaves and those who harbored them.

The law suited Chase. He believed in the dispassionate justice of the courtroom, in process and precedent. His antislavery views had been formed in large part from his disgust for lynch mobs. In 1836, as local tensions over slavery grew, he met many of Cincinnati's antislavery activists through his abolitionist brother-in-law Isaac Colby. One day an anti-abolitionist mob came looking for one of Chase's friends at the hotel where he and his family had taken refuge. Chase planted his powerful frame in the doorway and refused to let them inside. This act of defiance helped sharpen his thinking on the issue. Even as he became convinced of the moral evil of slavery, however, his reverence for the law kept him from embracing the more radical positions of the abolitionist movement. Chase didn't think the federal government had the authority to abolish slavery in the South; the aim, he reasoned, should be to limit slavery to the states where it already existed. While he had opposed Andrew Jackson, whom he denounced as a vulgar "ignoramus," he shared Jackson's conviction that the power of the federal government should be limited. He also shared another of Jackson's beliefs, that gold and silver made the best currency.

After Fort Sumter, Chase secluded himself in the immense colonnaded structure that housed the Treasury and put together his plan to fix the nation's finances. He worked ten to twelve hours a day, patiently beating a path through the bureaucratic wilderness. Like most people, he didn't expect the war to go on for very long. True to his conservative nature, his measures were intended to raise the money required to suppress the rebellion without making any sweeping changes to the Treasury's dysfunctional machinery.

Chase presented his proposal to Congress in the summer of 1861. The legislation, signed by President Lincoln after little debate, allowed the Treasury to borrow as much as $250 million by issuing bonds and notes. Chase hoped to sell these not just to Wall Street but to ordinary Americans, who could show their support for the war by lending their government the money needed to fight it. So he printed paper obligations meant to be affordable to a range of investors: institutions, small-business owners, even families. There were bonds that matured in twenty years, interest-bearing Treasury notes exchangeable in three years for bonds or specie, and notes that bore no interest but were payable on demand. These "demand notes" were the most significant. They came in small denominations like five, ten, and twenty, which meant they could circulate as money.

Demand notes paved the way for a momentous shift. By issuing government debt in the form of notes small enough in value to be traded for goods and services, Chase had created a kind of federal paper currency. Uncomfortable with drastic departures from tradition, he moved cautiously, holding fast to his hard-money ways. His demand notes could technically be redeemed for coin at any time at one of the Treasury's branches, or "sub-Treasuries," around the country. This meant that as long as Americans had faith in the government's promises, they would keep passing the paper. But if their trust wavered, they could exchange the notes for precious metals—and if everyone tried to exchange notes at the same time, it would drain the Treasury's specie. Chase's money thus made the government's finances precariously dependent on the people, whose collective confidence had the power to make or break the credit of the nation.

A hundred miles south of Washington was Richmond, Virginia, the capital of the Confederacy, where Chase's counterpart struggled to finance the other side of the war. Treasury Secretary Christopher Gustavus Memminger had blue-gray eyes, white hair, and a sharp-featured face. His department occupied the first floor of a beautiful Italianate edifice that looked more like a Renaissance palazzo than a government building. On the second floor, Jefferson Davis and his secretary of state had their offices, and down the street stood the War Department's makeshift headquarters. Unlike most members of Davis's cabinet, Memminger wasn't a native-born Southerner. A German immigrant whose mother died soon after arriving in South Carolina, he grew up in an orphanage in Charleston, and would have remained there if Thomas Bennett Jr., a distinguished local citizen, hadn't adopted him.

A small, slightly built boy, Memminger had excelled in school, impressing his classmates with his tremendous self-discipline. Like Chase, he became a lawyer and then a politician, winning a seat in the South Carolina legislature. In the decades before the Civil War, Memminger played a moderating role in the disputes surrounding state sovereignty, urging South Carolina to remain in the Union until Lincoln's election persuaded him secession was necessary. His allegiance was always to his adopted state, not his adopted country. South Carolina had delivered him from poverty to prominence, and he was determined to repay the debt. No matter how zealously he embraced the Confederate cause, however, Memminger stayed somewhat of an outsider: a foreigner and an orphan in the keenly class-conscious aristocracy of the South.

If Chase's job was demanding, Memminger's was nearly impossible. He knew about finance from his time as chairman of the state legislature's Ways and Means Committee, where he had pushed banks to print fewer bills and maintain specie payments. But even with his expertise and earnestness, Memminger could only make so much of an unworkable situation. The Southern central government had very few ways to raise money. The states, emboldened by the recent reassertion of their sovereignty, resisted taxation, and tariffs from the overseas cotton trade dwindled with the Union naval blockade. So the Confederate Congress, starting in March 1861, authorized the issue of paper notes. These were, in theory, exchangeable for specie—either after a specific date or on demand—although the South suspended specie payments shortly after the war started. The Confederacy didn't have much in the way of precious metals; in fact, New York City's banks had more gold and silver in their vaults than all of the Southern banks combined. But Memminger had no alternative, so as war expenses rose, he printed more paper. With every new batch of Confederate notes, the possibility of ever being able to redeem them all became more remote. Nonetheless, the value they generated for the time being gave much-needed financial fuel to the fledgling Southern nation.

The Civil War would be fought not just with guns but with the paper promises of two governments—competing promises tied to two incompatible visions of America. At the age of forty-three, Upham became an unlikely combatant in this conflict. The forgeries he sold at the store he opened after leaving the *Sunday Mercury* challenged the legitimacy of the Southern government in a way his caricatures of Jefferson Davis never could. After decades of drifting from one occupation to another, Upham had found the perfect job, one that let him serve his country and his pocketbook at the same time.

T HE PRISONERS BEGAN ARRIVING AT FOUR in the morning, the ones who weren't too wounded to walk. It was June 28, 1862, the day after a decisive Southern victory at the Battle of Gaines' Mill, outside Richmond. That summer the Union army tried to take the Confederate capital and failed; the war, it seemed, would go on much longer than anyone had thought. Thousands of Yankees now filed into Richmond, not as conquerors but as captives, columns of exhausted men in ragged blue uniforms. Women heckled them as they passed. "This is another way to take Richmond," yelled one. The soldiers were headed for Libby Prison, a sprawling former warehouse overlooking the James River. They lined up in front, entering the clerk's office four at a time to be processed and then corralled into one of eight large, lice-infested cells.

Waiting outside with the others was Private Robert Holliday, Company F, Eleventh Pennsylvania Reserves. Holliday was hungry, and he knew he couldn't expect to eat well in prison. So he decided to buy some food. Reaching into his pocket, he pulled out a $10 Confederate note and called over a boy named James Ballou. Handing Ballou the bill, Holliday sent him to a nearby bakery to get bread.

An onlooker caught the exchange and, intercepting the boy, demanded to look at the note. It was one of Upham's fakes—"a counterfeit of the

Philadelphia manufacture," declared the *Daily Richmond Examiner* in its indignant report of the incident. Only a few months since he started printing his "facsimiles," the Philadelphia forger had become notorious in Richmond. The $5 bills he copied from the *Philadelphia Inquirer* had surfaced there as early as April, and caused a sensation at the Confederate Treasury Department. One of Treasury Secretary Christopher Memminger's men persuaded the editors of the *Richmond Daily Dispatch*, the most popular of the town's papers, to spread the word about the new counterfeits. "This note is well calculated to deceive, and in nearly every particular is a fac-simile of the original," they wrote, condemning the forgeries as "Yankee scoundrelism." As more of Upham's bills poured in, their outrage grew.

In May, the editors found an Upham reproduction with the bottom margin bearing his name and address still attached. "Who is this man Upham?" they asked. "A knave swindler, and forger of the most depraved and despicable sort." Within a couple of days, they came up with a better answer, having researched the mysterious counterfeiter's background. Upham, a name already "well known to many Virginians," had edited the *Sunday Mercury*, "in which profession he failed, owing to his lack of brains and low standing in society." Too stupid to make an honest living, Upham had since "taken to all sorts of low thieving and mean rascality."

The venom of these attacks reflected how much had changed in the past year. Before the Civil War, counterfeiters had been, at worst, nuisances to the banks whose notes they forged and, at best, heroes to those too poor or isolated to acquire genuine bills. They were idolized, ignored, and disliked, but rarely detested. Upham belonged to a new class of counterfeiters, those who forged the money of governments, not just banks. The stakes were much higher: these notes were backed by regimes prepared to send thousands of their citizens to the most gruesome deaths imaginable to secure their sovereignty. Their paper obligations were symbols of that sovereignty, rectangles emblazoned with images that reminded people from tiny towns in New Hampshire or North Carolina that they were part of a proud, powerful country. When Private Holliday tried to buy bread with a fake bill, it was an affront to the Southern nation as a whole. "The attempt to pass a counterfeit Confederate note is certainly an act of hostility against our government," said the *Daily Richmond Examiner*. Upham provoked such vitriol because he enabled people like Holliday to undermine the Confederacy's authority. The fact that he did it so openly—that he was brazen enough to put his name and address on his counterfeits— made Southerners even angrier. At 403 Chestnut Street in Philadelphia, a shopkeeper was selling stacks of fake Southern cash, and the Confederates couldn't do anything about it.

Upham's method had its advantages. Criminal moneymakers had developed ways to minimize risk through networks of smugglers, resellers, and passers. But Upham didn't need to be cautious; he could sell his products openly, and could market them as aggressively as any other commodity. While steadily enlarging his catalog of Confederate currency, he attracted new customers by placing full-page advertisements in various Northern publications. A broadside from March listed seven different "mementos of the Rebellion" for sale: $5 and $10 notes, plus several "shinplasters," fractional bills worth anywhere from five to fifteen cents, printed by Southern banks and companies. At the bottom of the ad, he reprinted testimonials excerpted from Northern newspapers like the *New York Tribune*. Under the heading "Notices of the Press," these promotional blurbs praised Upham's imitations for their high quality and low prices.

At first it seemed possible that Upham believed he was making innocent souvenirs. The endorsements included on his March flyer were careful to call the notes curiosities, not counterfeits. But as his business evolved from a modest retail operation into a high-volume wholesaling enterprise, there could no longer be any doubt about why people wanted his reproductions. At some point in his first few months of operation, he had shifted from selling souvenirs to selling counterfeits. A flyer published in late May claimed he had sold 500,000 facsimiles in the past three months. His inventory had grown to include fourteen varieties of Confederate notes, shinplasters, and postage stamps—and, for a premium, the notes could even be printed on real banknote paper. Ingeniously, Upham also began fulfilling orders through the mail. For fifty cents, plus eighteen cents for postage, customers throughout the Union could have a hundred of Upham's notes delivered. He had clearly outgrown the novelty market: no one needed a hundred souvenirs. Upham understood this—he added an article to his "Notices of the Press" from the *Richmond Daily Dispatch* denouncing his "well executed counterfeits." Incensed reports from Southern newspapers made good publicity, since it meant Upham's notes were having an effect. They so closely resembled genuine money that there was, as the *Dispatch* said, "no means of knowing to what extent they have been circulated."

While Upham owed his success partly to the quality of his imitations, what really distinguished him was his skill as a salesman. Thanks to the Civil War, he could treat moneymaking like a legitimate business, applying the lessons he had learned in his previous ventures. His marketing campaign would have been unthinkable for earlier counterfeiters like Owen Sullivan and David Lewis, who had to stay underground to keep out of jail. Of course, Upham didn't enjoy all the advantages of a legal trade; he couldn't patent his product, for instance. By the spring of 1862, counterfeiters in Philadelphia and New York had begun making cheap reproductions of his notes, forcing him to cut prices. "Beware of Base Imitations!" he announced in his May flyer. "Each and every fac-simile issued by me bears my imprint." His counterfeits, in other words, carried a personal guarantee that ensured their authenticity, a brand name that set them apart from the competition.

Upham faced lots of competition. Fake cash plagued the Confederacy from the beginning, supplied by Northern and Southern counterfeiting gangs as well as foreign sources. Moneymakers in Matamoros, Mexico, funneled their bills into the South via Texas; counterfeiters in Bermuda and Cuba hid their notes in the hulls of the Confederate blockade-runners that regularly evaded the Union navy to get Southern goods to overseas markets. The demand for fake Confederate money was driven not only by the usual small-time scammers but also by cotton smugglers, who ran a booming trade in Union-controlled border cities like St. Louis, Louisville, and Memphis. They could order a thousand of Upham's notes through the mail, sneak into the South to buy cotton with the counterfeits, and then return north to reap big profits. In 1862, cotton purchased in Helena, Arkansas, for fourteen cents per pound sold for more than three times that amount in St. Louis.

The biggest passers of counterfeit Confederate cash, however, were Union troops. They drew low wages, and fake notes obtained cheaply in the North offered an easy way to boost their income. They could use the money to buy provisions from Southern civilians, while also sabotaging the rebel economy. On their way to the battlefield, many soldiers from New England, New York, and New Jersey passed through Philadelphia, where they could stop by Upham's shop on Chestnut Street to buy a bundle of forged bills.

Without the Northern army carrying his counterfeits, Upham could never have penetrated the Southern market to the extent he did. They made ideal passers: they traveled constantly and didn't have to worry about being arrested. Moreover, a Southern merchant would presumably be more inclined to accept a bill from someone with a gun, even if he doubted the authenticity of the bill. In the summer of 1862, Upham's notes inundated northern Virginia, sown by Union forces marching south from Washington. Their commander, Major General John Pope, had issued a series of orders intended to intimidate Southern civilians. With Lincoln's approval, Pope essentially told his men to seize food from houses and farms—"subsist upon the country" were his exact words—rather than rely on their own supplies, and gave them broad latitude in confiscating the property of anyone deemed disloyal to the Union. The soldiers embraced Pope's message and pillaged the countryside. Their camps soon filled up with local livestock; freshly butchered meat provided a welcome change from typical military fare. Not all the troops took the Southerners' possessions by force, however: many found it easier to exchange fake cash for what they wanted. A Southern journalist observed that Pope's men were "fortified with exhaustless quantities of Philadelphia Confederate notes," which they used to buy everything from horses to sugar to tobacco. When one of the Yankees ended up a prisoner in Richmond, the Confederates searched him and found something that accounted for the flood of forged bills: an advertising circular for Upham's facsimiles.

Most Union commanders turned a blind eye to the counterfeit currency trade carried on by their troops. Their jurisdiction didn't just include the battlefield but, more important, the military-occupied border cities where moneymaking and other illicit activities thrived. In Memphis, authorities apprehended a man named Nathan Levi with $800 worth of fake Confederate notes. Levi was released because, in the words of one Massachusetts newspaper, "confederate notes were not money, and hence there were no counterfeits in the eye of the law." The military governor of Memphis at the time was William Tecumseh Sherman, a man who would later practice a more brutal kind of economic warfare, ravaging the Deep South in his March to the Sea. While not all commanders viewed counterfeiting as leniently, even those who disapproved of it appeared reluctant to discipline their own men. The same summer that Major General John Pope's men spent fake money in northern Virginia, Brigadier General Samuel W. Crawford imprisoned two youths, ages ten and thirteen, for passing bad bills in Culpeper, Virginia. The boys traded with the soldiers, and in all likelihood sold them stacks of fake Southern notes. At their arrest, the younger one cried and wiped his nose with his sleeve while the elder protested: he swore they only passed the money off on rebels, and said he knew at least one Union officer who did the same. They ended up in the town's brick jailhouse with Culpeper's other criminals.

The role of Union soldiers in circulating counterfeits drew enraged responses from Southerners. The *Richmond Daily Dispatch* had no doubts about who had brought Upham's notes into the South: the bills appeared "wherever an execrable Yankee soldier polluted the soil with his cloven foot." From the Confederate point of view, it made perfect sense that Yankees would take advantage of unsuspecting civilians. After all, they came from the grasping, acquisitive culture of the industrial North, where speculation and other predatory practices were widespread. The changes that had transformed Northern society in the past decades had left Southerners largely untouched: the Confederate states were mostly agricultural, with far fewer factories and banks. Their static, slave-based economy didn't foster the kind of entrepreneurial capitalism that prevailed in the North, and they often vilified Northerners as morally bankrupt profiteers. Wartime counterfeiting helped reinforce this stereotype. A diarist writing from New Orleans remarked that the Union army consisted of "[s]peculators and thieves," who "go to the battles with their pockets stuffed with counterfeit Confederate money."

As spurious notes streamed across the border in ever-greater quantities, Confederate leaders started to see the North's moneymaking operations as something more insidious than a handful of hustlers angling for a profit. They became convinced that the Union was waging a deliberate campaign of economic warfare against their currency. The signs seemed clear enough. If generals like Pope instructed soldiers to plunder Southern homes, surely they could also encourage their men to cripple the Confederate money supply by spreading counterfeits. Southerners focused on Upham in particular. His energetic salesmanship helped persuade the Confederates that Union officials were involved. For the Philadelphia shopkeeper to be able to advertise his forgeries in newspapers and send them through the mail meant the authorities must have given him

permission or, possibly, material support. How could the federal government not know?

ON MARCH 10, 1862, fourteen days after the *Philadelphia Inquirer*
published the $5 note that launched Upham's counterfeiting career,
another fascinating item appeared in the paper. The editors barely found
it newsworthy: they buried the story on the bottom half of the last page,
with the shipping news. According to the *Inquirer*'s sources in Washington, federal detectives had recently arrested a printer who had been
counterfeiting many Confederate notes of high denominations. The man
didn't put up a fight when the officers arrived; in fact, he was surprised to
see them. He had expected the government to let him continue his trade,
which, he explained, struck the rebels at their most vulnerable point, their
currency. "How is this?" asked a detective. "You see," the man replied,
"these are better than the original article; the originals are worthless; they
are unauthorized by law; so I am not counterfeiting. I have not attempted
to pass them for money, and really cannot see how I am doing wrong."
"Ah," said the detective, "of course you were not going to pass them, but
you are going to furnish them to the enemy."

The man conceded that a great deal of his forgeries had gotten across
the border, but insisted that his intentions were patriotic. He hoped to
destroy Southern confidence in Confederate money. When the detectives
investigated further, they discovered he had indeed sent several hundred
thousand fake dollars into the South. Unsure of how to proceed, they
decided to release him but confiscate his printing press, and referred the
case to Secretary of State William H. Seward. Seward couldn't figure out
what to do either, so he passed it along to Secretary of War Edwin M.
Stanton.

The counterfeiter almost certainly wasn't Upham. In March he hadn't
yet produced notes in such numbers, and the prices and denominations

provided in the *Inquirer* didn't match those of his first facsimiles. But the report offers a rare glimpse into the federal government's attitude toward Upham's line of work. Not only did Union officials know about Northern counterfeiting of Confederate notes, they seemed profoundly confused about how to deal with it. The counterfeiter's impassioned defense in the *Inquirer*—that Confederate money was illegal and thus free to be forged, and that in doing so, he wounded the enemy's economy—was convincing. Upham himself could have made the same argument. And Seward's decision to entrust the matter to the War Department suggests he was swayed by it: since counterfeiting had the potential to be useful to the Union military effort, he forwarded the case to the man responsible for running the war. The *Inquirer*, however, never explained how Stanton settled the issue.

If Seward or Stanton had wanted to aid Northern moneymakers, there were plenty of ways to do so. They could furnish counterfeiters with Southern plates and banknote paper seized from captured blockade-runners, organize groups of soldiers and spies to spread forged notes throughout the South, or just agree not to interfere with anyone trafficking in fake Confederate paper. But, contrary to Southern claims, there is no evidence of any officially sanctioned Union policy to promote the counterfeiting of Confederate money. Federal authorities most likely found it easier to ignore the forging of Southern bills than to take a position either for or against it. Certainly by the time Upham began manufacturing bills in bulk, the government didn't seem interested in preventing it.

Regardless, for a counterfeiting case to attract federal attention in the first place shows how involved Washington had become in monetary matters. Now that the government printed money, it took an active interest in protecting its paper from being forged. For both North and South, preserving the integrity of their obligations was a matter of national security: if too many counterfeits eroded faith in their currency, it couldn't be used to fund the war. In the Union this task acquired a new sense of urgency in early 1862, when Congress passed a law that, for the first time since the Revolution, made paper money printed by the government legal tender.

The legislation took effect on February 25, 1862, and represented nothing less than a revolution in American finance. It gave legal tender status to the demand notes already issued by the Treasury and to $100 million in additional bills called United States Notes. Both kinds of paper came to be known as greenbacks, from the colored ink on their reverse— Confederate Treasury notes, on the other hand, were called graybacks. Greenbacks weren't merely promises to pay coin but money in themselves, legally indistinguishable from gold and silver in almost every type of transaction. Their value didn't stem from their exchangeability into coin but from something more abstract: the credit of the United States. This was a bold expression of federal sovereignty. The introduction of demand notes the previous summer had planted the seed for a national currency; now those pieces of paper had become equivalent to precious metals simply because the government said so.

Such a dramatic step provoked sharp opposition, and the debate in Congress had been fierce. The belief that gold and silver were God-given measures of value, irreplaceable by a man-made material like paper, ran deep. It had a long history in American life, exerting a remarkably persistent power over people's minds even as the country shed its other superstitions. Some of the arguments made in Congress against legal tender were at least a century old. A representative from Illinois, Owen Lovejoy, compared the new notes to the Catholic doctrine of transubstantiation, a parallel that had been drawn 141 years earlier by a Protestant minister in Massachusetts denouncing colonial bills of credit. The point was the same in 1721 as in 1862: faith couldn't transform paper into gold any more than it could change bread into the body of Christ.

The strongest case against the Legal Tender Act of 1862 wasn't metaphysical but constitutional. The Constitution had a few things to say about money: it gave Congress the power to mint coins and explicitly forbade the states to issue bills of credit or designate anything other than gold and silver as legal tender. But it was silent on a range of issues, like whether the federal government could legislate a bank, print paper money, or make paper legal tender. This silence had been at the center of the country's most bitter constitutional struggles since the fight over Alexander Hamilton's first Bank of the United States in 1790–1791. Hamilton and his allies argued that the authority to create a bank was implied by the Constitution, which broadly empowered Congress to pass any laws "necessary and proper" for fulfilling its other duties. His enemies countered that the national government didn't possess any rights it wasn't specifically granted, those being reserved for the states. This latter interpretation eventually prevailed under the reign of Andrew Jackson, who used it to justify killing the Bank of the United States and curbing federal involvement in the economy. By 1862, however, the political climate had shifted. The principle of states' rights, which had long been a bulwark against federal power, was harder to defend now that it carried the taint of secessionism. Northern lawmakers were prepared to give the government what it needed to win the war. In order to do so, they abandoned Jackson's reading of the Constitution in favor of Hamilton's.

While Hamilton had encouraged a more robust federal role, making paper legal tender went much further than anything he proposed. It illustrated the impact of the Civil War, a conflict in which both sides radically departed from tradition while claiming to be faithful to the nation's founding vision. Southerners saw the right to secede as implicit in the Constitution, which they defined as a voluntary compact among sovereign states. This was no more extreme a view than the belief that the Constitution granted the federal government virtually unlimited power in wartime, a proposition that guided the Union's most drastic measures, like the suspension of habeas corpus and the use of military tribunals to try civilians.

To adapt the Constitution to the present emergency would require a more elastic approach to its language, even if this meant contradicting its original intentions. The delegates to the Constitutional Convention in 1789 didn't want the government printing paper money, much less making it legal tender. The catastrophe with the continentals had convinced them of the dangers of paper currency, and they were committed to putting the nation on a hard-money basis. But in the crisis brought on by the Civil War, the survival of the nation outweighed all other considerations. "If no other means were left to save the Republic from destruction," declared Pennsylvania congressman Thaddeus Stevens, a leading advocate of the Legal Tender Act, "I believe we have power, under the Constitution and according to its express provision, to declare a dictator."

Among the many Americans who didn't share Stevens's views was the man charged with implementing the law, Treasury Secretary Salmon Chase. As the war escalated, he overcame his earlier reservations about federal power, and in December 1861, he even called for a national paper currency; his demand notes certainly marked a step in that direction. But Chase stubbornly stuck by the notion that gold and silver provided the only sound basis for money, which naturally made him hostile to the idea of paper notes severed from specie. The Legal Tender Act was endorsed by leaders of his party, approved by Congress, and signed into law by Lincoln. So Chase accepted it, however reluctantly. Ironically, he probably bore more responsibility for the measure than anyone else in Washington: his actions over the last year had made it inevitable. To raise money for the war, Chase had borrowed from Northern banks. But rather than letting the banks credit the amount to the Treasury on their books, he insisted on being paid in gold. So the banks kept delivering shipments of specie at regular intervals, which Chase used to settle the government's debts and redeem its demand notes.

The qualities that made Chase a great antislavery lawyer—an indomitable will, unwavering faith in his own judgment—also made him an exasperating treasury secretary. As the bankers protested his policies, watching their coffers hemorrhage gold, Chase remained obstinate. He used his fiery courtroom rhetoric to bludgeon them into submission, famously saying that if they didn't agree to his proposals, he would return to Washington and print inflationary paper until it took "a thousand dollars to buy a breakfast." By December 1861, the disaster long predicted had arrived. The gold paid out by the government had vanished into the hands of hoarders and speculators. Faced with perilously low reserves, both the Northern banks and the Treasury suspended specie payments. Soldiers stopped receiving their wages; the military couldn't buy supplies. The financial foundation for the war effort was crumbling, and the Legal Tender Act offered the only way out.

Christopher Memminger, the Confederate treasury secretary, was a more sensible man than Chase but inherited a situation far more desperate. Not only was the South poorer than the North, its central government was much weaker. Marshaling the meager resources of a nation as deliberately decentralized as the Confederacy wouldn't be easy. As might be expected, Southerners had no sympathy for Hamilton's reading of the Constitution. Their heroes were Jefferson and Jackson, sworn enemies of the Bank of the United States. But, just as Hamilton's Northern disciples took his teachings to an extreme he couldn't have anticipated, so Southerners championed states' rights with a zeal surpassing that of their predecessors. The Confederate Constitution, adopted in March 1861, copied much of the original Constitution verbatim but made a few revolutionary changes, like removing the prohibition on states from issuing bills of credit. This meant Memminger's Treasury notes, the graybacks, had to compete not only with notes printed by banks and other companies but also with the circulating obligations of state governments. As if that weren't enough, the shortage of coin in the South produced another source of paper money in the form of fractional notes printed by individuals and businesses. A butcher or a baker might issue shinplasters worth a certain amount of beef or bread, and these bills, denominated in cents, functioned as a kind of currency. Shinplasters were so coarsely designed that almost any piece of paper could circulate; in 1862, residents of New Orleans joked that the label from an olive oil bottle would pass because it was "greasy, smelt bad, and bore an autograph."

None of these notes could be legal tender, not even the graybacks printed by Memminger at the Treasury. The Confederate Congress refused to enact legislation to that effect, since it would vest too much authority in the Richmond government and challenge the deeply entrenched belief that specie was the foundation for all money, even though the Confederacy had very little of it. The North had overcome its hard-money bias to meet the necessities of the war, but the South couldn't put aside its principles. So Memminger's bills, like everyone else's, could be refused without consequences. The Confederacy had seriously imperiled its survival by making it easier for everyone to print paper money and harder for its central government's notes to have value.

Memminger also dealt with daunting logistical problems. Since the North had most of the banks, it had most of the banknote engravers he needed to produce his notes. Before the bombardment of Fort Sumter in April 1861, the Confederacy contracted one of the North's largest engraving firms, the National Bank Note Company of New York, to print the first round of Confederate bills. But when the war began, the Union seized the plates and Memminger had to find a Southern source for the notes. Southern printers were less sophisticated than their Northern counterparts. Most of them used a faster, cruder process than the engraved-steel technique preferred in the North. Known as stone lithography, it satisfied Memminger's demand for high-volume production but produced lower-quality bills with serious design flaws. A careless lithographer could introduce changes by mistake, so that notes reproduced from an original would all be slightly different. To manufacture enough notes, Memminger had to employ a total of nine firms and a range of different designs. As a result, a single denomination could have hundreds of distinct varieties: the $20 bill of the September 2, 1861, issue, for instance, had 229.

Counterfeiters exploited the Confederacy's disorganized approach to making money. No Southerner could hope to remember what the hundreds of authorized notes looked like. Even judging a bill's authenticity by its craftsmanship was misleading, since the forgeries produced by skilled Northern moneymakers were often better executed than the originals. Memminger tried his best to address these problems, but there wasn't much he could do. The exigencies of war required escalating sums of paper money, no matter how poorly printed. "[W]e are well aware of the difficulty," he wrote in response to a Georgia judge who had complained about widespread counterfeiting, "but unfortunately are entirely unable to prevent it. . . . All that we could do," he explained, "was to put a death penalty upon the crime of counterfeiting," referring to a law from August 1861 that made forging Treasury notes punishable by death. Memminger must have felt discouraged. As a state legislator in South Carolina before the war, he had railed against banks for refusing to exchange their bills for coin. Now he produced more notes than they ever had, with no hope of redeeming them all and no power to prevent their being forged.

NEARLY A THOUSAND PEOPLE appeared outside the Richmond jail to get a glimpse of the condemned man, eager for a little entertainment on an otherwise dull day. On August 22, 1862, the war felt far away: no train or telegram brought news from the front, now more than a hundred miles north. The once imminent threat of Yankee invasion had passed, thanks to a string of Southern victories, and the sense of dread was slowly receding. At a quarter to eleven in the morning, the doors of the jailhouse swung open. The prisoner was Italian, about thirty years old, and handsome. He stepped calmly into the sunlight, removing his hat and bowing politely to the crowd before taking his seat on the wagon that carried his coffin. Soldiers formed a perimeter around the cart, and the procession set off, inching its way up Valley Street along the tracks of the Virginia

Central Railroad, a crucial Confederate supply line. Among the spectators who followed, a reporter noted in the next day's paper, were "a number of painted and overdressed females of doubtful respectability." When the cavalcade reached the gallows on the northern end of town, the prisoner ascended the scaffold and, at exactly noon, dropped four feet with the noose around his neck.

John Richardson, alias John Richards, alias Louis Napoleon, was the first and probably the only person executed for counterfeiting under the law Memminger mentioned in his letter. He was a Richmond resident of uncertain occupation: some said he sold fruit, others claimed he trafficked in illegal liquors. According to Richardson's own confession, his friend George Elam had convinced him to break into the offices of Hoyer and Ludwig, one of the companies that printed Confederate money. Elam used to work for the firm, so he knew his way around; once inside, the two men stole uncut sheets of $10 bills and printed hundreds of dollars of fake cash. Both were arrested for passing the notes, but the authorities settled on Richardson as the ringleader, sparing Elam's life. It would be easier to convict a foreigner of a capital crime than a native Southerner. Sure enough, the jury at Richardson's trial only took a few minutes to return a guilty verdict.

Executing an immigrant for counterfeiting suited the prevailing Southern view that moneymaking was a foreign plot. The *Richmond Daily Dispatch* made much of Richardson's origins, scolding the Italian for "skulking out of the service of the only land that ever gave him more than enough to keep life in him" by "striking at the very vitals of the Confederacy." Richardson's birthplace wasn't the only thing working against him, however: timing also played a role. August 1862 was a particularly ripe moment for a public display of justice to bolster people's flagging faith in Confederate currency. The counterfeiting epidemic had spread in recent months. Forged notes were found far from the Union border, in Atlanta, Savannah, Montgomery, and other cities of the Deep South.

At the Treasury's headquarters in Richmond, Memminger read alarming reports from agents throughout the country warning about the deteriorating situation. His assistant treasurer in Charleston, B. C. Pressley, described the city's frantic mood: "The panic and excitement here on the subject of the counterfeit bills is so great that I have not found time to write you without a crowd around asking my decision on bills which they hold." Fake cash contaminated the money supply to such a degree that Charleston's bank tellers had refused to accept certain denominations of Treasury notes. "Nearly all the money I have on hand is of the class which has been counterfeited," Pressley complained.

Memminger responded by withdrawing from circulation three kinds of Confederate currency that had been particularly widely forged. This affected three and a half million notes. It was a desperate act, solving Memminger's immediate problem while raising grave doubts about the government's ability to protect its currency. For the many Southerners who believed counterfeiting was a Northern conspiracy, the enemy had succeeded in decimating a significant portion of the money supply.

Meanwhile, the Yankee scoundrel at 403 Chestnut Street showed no signs of slowing down. His tireless publicity blitz continued to infuriate Southerners, who met with regular reminders of his growing success. In July 1862, authorities apprehended a young man named William P. Lee in Elizabeth City, North Carolina, carrying more than $750 in forged money and one of Upham's advertising circulars. Elizabeth City offered a natural point of entry for Upham's product. A coastal town overlooking an estuary in eastern North Carolina, it was blockaded by Union ships, and Yankee sailors often came ashore to trade.

Despite the heavy Northern presence in the area, Elizabeth City officials managed to arrest Lee and deliver him to Richmond to stand trial. Lee wasn't considered much of a threat. When he arrived in the Confederate capital, the *Daily Richmond Examiner* dismissed him as "an insignificant looking individual," undoubtedly "the dupe of others." The real culprit was Upham, who let pawns like Lee take the risks while sitting safely in his Philadelphia shop. For the *Examiner*, this latest instance of Upham's villainy proved beyond a doubt the existence of "a deep laid scheme on the part of the thieving, counterfeiting North through individuals, with the connivances of the Yankee Government, to undermine the Confederate currency." The editors demanded that the government execute a convicted counterfeiter to "evince the proper spirit . . . in its efforts to preserve the currency of the country from Yankee pollution." The authorities obliged a month later, by hanging Richardson. The sight of the Italian's corpse dangling from a rope made for a much more effective symbol of Confederate strength than the eagles and emblems that adorned its money. If the government couldn't legally compel anyone to take its notes, at least it could execute the criminals who forged them.

In August, while Memminger battled the rising tide of bad bills, Upham published his boldest broadside yet. He advertised thirty-five kinds of Confederate notes and stamps, and offered his customers a new service: the option to buy bills with the signatures omitted. This made his reproductions immeasurably more useful as counterfeits. All Treasury notes were signed by Memminger's clerks to verify their authenticity. Now Upham's clients could forge these inscriptions themselves in the spaces he left blank. He also erased the serial numbers from his facsimiles; those, too, could be written in to give the note the appearance of legitimacy. Upham's August flyer showed how far his business had come from "mementos of the Rebellion." Back in March, when a quick war seemed likely, it was conceivable that people would want keepsakes from the Southern revolt. Five months later, as both sides braced for a brutal conflict, they didn't need any more ways to remember the war. The maimed and mangled bodies filling Philadelphia's military hospitals were more than enough.

By the summer of 1862, the Civil War had become more than a struggle over secession. Lincoln's plan to crush the rebellion by seizing Richmond had failed, thwarted by the South's brilliant generals, Robert E. Lee and Stonewall Jackson, who pushed the Yankees back toward Washington. In late August, Lee humiliated the Union army at the Second Battle of Bull Run in northern Virginia and, five days later, put the North on the defensive by invading Maryland. The surprising resilience of the South forced Lincoln to rethink the war. He needed to undermine the enemy's ability to fight. This contributed to his decision to attack the cornerstone of the Southern economy, slavery. On July 17, 1862, Lincoln signed the Second Confiscation Act, providing for the liberation of slaves belonging to anyone involved in the rebellion. He soon planned to go even further with the Emancipation Proclamation, which threatened to emancipate the slaves of any rebellious state that didn't return to the Union by January 1, 1863. A declaration against slavery would rally international opinion to the Union side, thus depriving the Confederacy of a possible alliance with Britain or France. Lincoln presented the Proclamation on September 22, after Union forces halted Lee's advance through Maryland at the Battle of Antietam, an engagement that left twenty-three thousand men dead or wounded—the bloodiest single day in all of American military history.

Lincoln's embrace of emancipation fundamentally changed the equation for the South. At first the Confederacy was fighting for its independence; now it would be fighting for its way of life. As the catastrophic consequences of a Southern defeat became more apparent, safeguarding Southern currency became more important. Counterfeiting didn't just hurt the Confederate government—it undermined the struggle to save Southern civilization from annihilation. This sharpened the sense of panic provoked by the surge of fake bills in August 1862, and brought counterfeiting to the attention of the Confederacy's leading politicians. On August 18, President Jefferson Davis addressed the problem in a message to the Confederate Congress. The defeats recently suffered by the North, he wrote, had caused the enemy to resort to ruthless tactics, like confiscating slaves and counterfeiting Southern currency. According to Davis, fake Confederate notes were "publicly advertised for sale" and furnished to "the soldiers of the invading army" with the full "complicity" of the Union government. Later that same day, Memminger submitted a report to the House of Representatives that reiterated Davis's concerns and singled out Upham's role in the crisis: "[P]rinted advertisements have been found stating that the counterfeit notes, in any quantity, will be forwarded by mail from Chestnut street, in Philadelphia."

These warnings prompted intense debate in the Confederate Congress about how best to confront the moneymaking menace. Hoping to make the most of the mood, Memminger sent Vice President Alexander Hamilton Stephens his recommendations. He wanted the authority to post currency experts at Treasury branches around the country and at "principal places of trade" to help people distinguish genuine money from forged. To Memminger's considerable disappointment, Congress rejected the idea. The notion that counterfeiting was a Yankee ploy made lawmakers more concerned with preventing fake notes from coming into the country than with identifying those already there. On October 13, 1862, Congress enacted a law ordering death by hanging for any captured enemy soldiers found with counterfeit Confederate money. Four days later, Memminger vented his frustration to his subordinate B. C. Pressley, who had written him a letter urging better measures to combat counterfeiting. "I entirely concur in all views which you express," the secretary wearily replied, "and have tried in vain to get the concurrence of Congress." But, as the legislators had even refused him "the privilege of appointing experts to pronounce on the genuineness of Treasury notes," he was "unable to act as both your judgment and my own would advise." Once again, the secretary's hands were tied.

ON CHRISTMAS DAY 1862, firecrackers erupted all over Richmond— bright, sputtering bursts that left plumes of smoke lingering in the brisk air. John Beauchamp Jones could hear the explosions from his house. "[N]o little gunpowder is consumed in commemoration of the day," he wrote in his diary, a rare extravagance at a time when most Richmonders were narrowly scraping by. Jones worked as a clerk for the War Department, but even with a steady government paycheck he could scarcely support his wife and four children. The day before, he had sold his silver watch to buy a proper Christmas dinner and fuel to keep him and his family warm for a month. He consoled himself with the thought that his diary, filled with shrewd sketches of life in the capital, would someday become a best seller.

Jones was better off than many. He had a home, a job, and enough food to survive, although he lost twenty pounds during the war. Not everyone enjoyed the same advantages. Poverty, overcrowding, and crime racked wartime Richmond. "A portion of the people look like vagabonds," Jones observed. They wore "dingy and dilapidated clothes" and some seemed "gaunt and pale with hunger." Since Richmond had become the Confederate capital, the city's population had soared, from fewer than forty thousand in 1860 to roughly a hundred thousand three years later. Many of these new arrivals were soldiers, and they brought their favorite pastimes with them. Gambling houses opened; prostitutes solicited johns on the sidewalk and rode through the streets in open carriages. Murders, muggings, and brawls became more frequent. As the war dragged on, the ranks of Richmond's poor swelled: widows and orphans of dead soldiers, wives and children of those gone to fight, and refugees fleeing the fighting in the countryside.

What made life especially hard in Richmond was the skyrocketing cost of living. A Christmas turkey in 1862 sold for $11, an exorbitant sum for Jones and most others. The high prices were partly due to the shortages caused by the Union blockade and the large influx of people, which drove up demand. But they were also the result of a more pervasive and ultimately more poisonous problem: the weakness of Confederate money. Graybacks, after holding steady for months, had begun shedding their value in August 1862, a fateful month for Confederate currency. As Southerners saw their notes' purchasing power disappear, Memminger naturally took the blame. In his diary, Jones recalled hearing the publisher of the *Daily Richmond Enquirer* grumble about the secretary in December: "He says Mr. M.'s head is as worthless as a pin's head." Jones soon came to share the publisher's opinion, denouncing Memminger as "headstrong, haughty, and tyrannical." That the man responsible for running the Confederacy's finances into the ground was "no Carolinian by birth or descent" but a German-born immigrant made it even worse.

To his credit, Memminger was acutely aware of the dangers of paper money. He repeatedly alerted the Confederate Congress to the hazards of inflation, which could be put off but never avoided entirely. "Like the moon's attraction upon the ocean," he told them, "the time of high-water is postponed for a certain period . . . but, although there may be delay, the event is certain." Sometimes the legislators listened, periodically retiring large quantities of graybacks from circulation. But mounting expenses always forced them to authorize even more notes the next time, so that the overall volume of paper money continued to climb. The Confederacy's dependency on paper credit was self-reinforcing: as the value of graybacks fell and prices rose, Congress ordered more Treasury bills to meet the government's costs, further depreciating the currency.

Too much paper money wasn't the only thing causing the decline of the Confederate dollar. The value of Treasury notes relied to a great extent on something neither Memminger nor the Confederate congressmen could control: the public's perception of whether the South was winning the war. The better the Confederacy fared, the better chance it would keep its promise to exchange graybacks for specie, and thus the more desirable the bills. Some Treasury notes made this connection explicit, like the $5 bills that Upham first counterfeited, which promised their redemption six months after the ratification of a treaty between the Confederacy and the Union.

In the second half of 1862, the downturn picked up speed. On August 1, a gold dollar cost two Confederate paper dollars; by the end of the year, it cost $3.25, an increase of more than 60 percent. This precipitous drop in value coincided with a series of events that changed the Southern view of the war. The Battle of Antietam took place on September 17, Lincoln introduced the Emancipation Proclamation on September 22, and by November 4, most Northern states had voted in the congressional elections, leaving the Republicans in control of Congress. Taken together, these developments demonstrated the Union's will to fight. The North sacrificed thousands of men to eke out a narrow victory at Antietam, and then committed itself to waging total war by targeting the South's core institution. Continued Republican supremacy in Congress ensured that Lincoln's policies would remain in place, and eliminated any possibility of a negotiated peace. The consequences for the Southern money market were clear. A protracted struggle would prolong the redemption of graybacks, perhaps indefinitely. And, in the event of a Union victory, not only would Confederate currency be worthless but the entire economic system it was based on would be dismantled.

Upham posed a dual threat to the South's ailing currency. He helped depreciate graybacks by inflating the money supply and, in defying the Confederate government so publicly, undermined its credibility. Southern newspapers and politicians tried to use Upham as propaganda, publicizing his enterprise as another example of the enemy's depravity. "The people, among whom such a vice can be practiced, are not a people with whom we could *tolerate* association," declared the *Daily Richmond Enquirer.* "Such conduct but deepens the ditch which separates and increases the disgust which repels us." While this technique might fan anti-Northern feeling, it could just as easily backfire. By loudly condemning Upham, Southern opinion-makers risked drawing attention to how successfully his counterfeits had infiltrated the Confederacy. Since perception mattered as much as reality, such an impression would only further weaken the currency.

In late 1862, as Confederate values plummeted, a challenge to Upham's enterprise emerged. Winthrop E. Hilton was a New York City printer whose shop stood on Printing House Square, a triangular cluster of buildings opposite City Hall that housed some of the North's most powerful newspapers. The *New York Times* occupied an entire block at the southern end of the square, its ornate, olive-colored walls just opposite the smaller, less majestic headquarters of Horace Greeley's *New York Tribune*. Wedged between these giants of journalism was Hilton's office on Spruce Street, where he printed fake graybacks. Upham had never before encountered competition as formidable as Hilton's. The New Yorker used the same stone lithography method as the Confederacy's printers, resulting in almost perfect counterfeits. He had also learned Upham's lessons of self-promotion, and on October 4, 1862, advertised his "perfect facsimiles of Confederate Treasury notes" in *Harper's Weekly*. His rates were $4 per 1,000 bills, vastly underselling Upham, whose broadside a couple of months earlier had listed $40 per 1,000.

It didn't take long for Upham to respond. Two weeks later, he ran his own advertisement in *Harper's Weekly*, slashing his prices to match Hilton's. By January 1863, however, Hilton had adopted a new pricing model: rather than charging the same amount for each note, he factored in its face value. He now sold "$500 in Confederate Notes of all denominations" for $5. While this wasn't quite as good a deal as he had offered before, it showed that Hilton understood his customers. Someone trying to use the facsimiles as counterfeit money would be willing to pay more for a higher-denomination note. Hilton proved far more comfortable than Upham when it came to acknowledging the reason people bought his bills. In *Harper's Weekly* he boasted that his notes were "so exactly like the genuine that where one will pass current the other will go equally as well," a direct reference to passing counterfeits. On January 31, Upham countered with his best bargain yet: $20,000 in Confederate money of various denominations "sent, post-paid, to any address, on receipt of $5." For the same price as Hilton, he was offering forty times the face value, plus free postage.

For all its strengths, Upham's business model had a fatal flaw. The more counterfeits he sold, the less valuable Confederate notes became, depressing demand for his product. Of course, graybacks would depreciate without his help. But he hastened their decline, which would inevitably take a toll on his trade. By 1863, the future of his business looked grim. Hilton was forcing him to cut his prices even as the value of Confederate notes fell. Hemmed in by the flagging value of Confederate currency on one side and the competition of Hilton on the other, Upham couldn't hope to continue much longer. His fortunes were tied to those of the Confederacy, a peculiar situation for a Northern patriot.

I T WAS RAINING IN NEW YORK on New Year's Eve 1863, a hard, driving rain that pummeled the grimy streets. At the Astor House annual ball, guests danced under the glow of gaslights, the music rising above the rattling of the storm outside. U.S. Marshal Robert Murray stood less than a mile away, preparing to pull off the sting he had been carefully planning for a week. Murray's men had been tailing Upham's old competitor Winthrop E. Hilton around the clock, watching him commute between his office at Printing House Square and his home on Forty-ninth Street, compiling lists of his employees and business partners. Tonight, while the rest of the city was too drunk to notice, Murray would strike.

He split his men into two groups. One headed for Hilton's main shop at 11 Spruce Street; the other raided a location a few blocks away, above a saloon at the corner of Ann and Gold streets. It was there that the officers found Hilton and an accomplice named Williams, along with lithographic stones for printing $100, $50, and $5 Confederate notes. At two in the morning, Murray and his team stormed a third site, an apartment on Park Row across from the Astor House. They knocked down the door and discovered a cache of machines for printing money, including a geometric lathe, an expensive contraption that engraved highly detailed designs onto a steel plate. They also found millions of dollars' worth of freshly printed

Confederate notes and bonds. By the time Hilton's lawyers began looking for him the next day, their client was confined within the brick walls of Fort Lafayette, an island fortification off the southern coast of Brooklyn. There would be no trial. Hilton was a prisoner of war.

Upham had left the counterfeiting business four months before, in August 1863. By that time, Confederate currency was in a free fall. Runaway inflation and deepening distrust of the Richmond government had driven the price of gold in graybacks up 500 percent in the past year. That summer, the Battle of Gettysburg dealt the Confederacy a painful defeat, and when the news reached the South, it triggered another steep decline in the money market. With graybacks falling and Hilton continuing to give him stiff competition, Upham decided to abandon his facsimile trade, and avoided his rival's fate.

In an irony peculiar to the Civil War, federal authorities arrested Hilton not because he was a counterfeiter—forging Confederate notes was fine—but because they believed he was making genuine notes. They had recently unearthed evidence that the rebel government had hired Hilton to print its money, with his facsimile venture providing the perfect cover. The investigation began in December 1863, when New York City postmaster Abram Wakeman saw a suspicious envelope in the day's mail. It was addressed to Alexander Keith Jr. of Halifax, Nova Scotia—a known Confederate agent. Wakeman seized the letter and forwarded it to Secretary of War Edwin M. Stanton in Washington. Inside the envelope was something even more suspicious: an encrypted message, coded in strange symbols. Stanton's clerks at the War Department spent two days trying to decipher it before they gave the letter to a trio of young cryptographers from the telegraph office. These men were the Union's best codebreakers—the "Sacred Three," as they called themselves. It took them about four hours to crack the cipher. What they uncovered confirmed Wakeman's initial hunch: the letter was a covert Confederate communication from an operative in New York to his counterpart in Halifax, providing news on smuggling rifles into the South and other intrigues.

Two days later, another letter to the Halifax address appeared at the New York post office. The message had been encrypted with the same cipher, and the War Department cryptographers quickly decoded it. "Say to Memminger that Hilton will have the machines all finished and dies all cut ready for shipping by the first of January," it read. "The engraving of the plates is superb." The contraband would be shipped from New York to Halifax, from there to the Bahamas, and then brought into Florida by blockade-runner. "The main part of the work has been under the immediate supervision of Hilton," the letter continued, "who will act in good faith in consequence of the large amount he has and will receive." Determined to catch Hilton before he got the moneymaking materials to Halifax, Secretary Stanton ordered Murray to round up the printer and his collaborators. He also gave his three code-breakers a raise.

Murray's sweep went smoothly. He arrested everyone, even the machinist who had built Hilton's geometric lathe, a former Treasury Department employee living in New Jersey. The *New York Times* hailed the operation as "a great victory by our forces in the field," sure "to discourage the rebel leaders." To Hilton's friends, however, it came as a shock. He was a loyal Union man, they said, and an early supporter of Lincoln. A native of New Hampshire, he had arrived in New York ten years earlier and made a name for himself as an honest printer. They couldn't believe he would conspire with the rebels.

Although it would take months to learn the truth, they were right: Hilton was innocent. The first clue came in late January, when a Southern general in North Carolina saw a report of Hilton's capture in a Northern newspaper and passed the article along to Secretary Memminger in Richmond. "The Treasury has no connection whatever with the matter," Memminger replied, "but it would be well to leave the Yankee police under their present impressions." Hilton didn't work for the South: his notes were counterfeits. What Memminger didn't say, and perhaps didn't know, was that Hilton had been the victim of an elaborate Confederate conspiracy.

The details eventually leaked to the *New York World*, which published a long account on April 29, 1864, drawing on information gleaned from secret government documents. In late 1863, the South dispatched a team of undercover agents to New York in order to put a stop to Hilton, whose bad bills were pouring into the Confederacy at an alarming rate. The Southerners came up with a clever plan. They would write an encrypted letter incriminating Hilton, knowing it would be intercepted and decrypted by Union officials. For the hoax to work they needed someone close to the counterfeiter, so they tracked down one of his employees: George H. Briggs, a former Confederate spy who had defected to the North. In a room at the St. Nicholas Hotel on Broadway, one of the agents put a gun to Briggs's head and threatened to blow his brains out if he didn't help them jail his boss. They also enlisted James S. Chalker, a customhouse official who despised Hilton and desperately wanted to see him behind bars.

The Confederacy had eliminated a major counterfeiter by tricking the Union into thinking his forgeries were in fact genuine—the same deception perpetrated by Hilton on a wider scale in the South. It was a brilliant tactic, using the counterfeiter's logic against him. No doubt the agents would have targeted Upham instead if he had still been in business by the time they came North. His notes were certainly still coursing through the Confederacy, at least twenty-five different kinds in all. During the year and a half he spent counterfeiting, Upham made a lot of Southern money. In 1874, when a historian researching a book about Confederate currency asked him for specifics, he estimated he had printed about $15 million in bogus bills. If all of that ended up in the South, it would have made up almost 3 percent of the entire Confederate money supply—a significant chunk for a single counterfeiter. In his letter to the historian, Upham refused to admit his facsimiles had been anything other than curiosities. He insisted that Hilton had been the counterfeiter, not him. The New Yorker had ripped off his designs, he claimed, and then sold "large quantities to bogus Jew cotton brokers and other scalawags, who passed through the Confederate lines and purchased cotton from the Rebel planters."

More than a decade after their feud, Upham still hated Hilton. He had nothing to worry about: in the long run, the Philadelphian came out ahead. He was a better businessman, and when he ended his moneymaking venture, he had plenty to fall back on. In the fall of 1863, Upham sold his store at 403 Chestnut Street and opened a different kind of shop five blocks away. With no medical training whatsoever, he began hawking cures for almost anything. Upham's Bay Rum alleviated dandruff, burns, sores, fever, and headaches; his "Tish-Wang" Chinese lozenges treated gonorrhea, syphilis, and a host of other venereal diseases. He styled himself a chemist and called his store a laboratory, marketing his remedies as vigorously as he had his counterfeits. He took out ads in newspapers and distributed circulars with endorsements from satisfied customers. He patented his treatments and took measures to discourage bootleggers. "Beware of Counterfeits," one of his flyers warned.

Upham had moved from one swindle to another, from counterfeiting to quackery. He had nothing to recommend him but his talent as a salesman, which was considerable. His business thrived. He enjoyed an impeccable reputation, paid his debts on time, and had no trouble obtaining credit. Hilton, on the other hand, fell apart. By the end of the war, the authorities had released him and he became a printer again. But he struggled financially, and before long had ruined his credit by borrowing a large sum of money that he couldn't repay. In the summer of 1870 he went through bankruptcy, and seven years later he went out of business.

Hilton had been good at counterfeiting but not much else. Upham proved more versatile, hardened by a lifetime of hustling. If he could make a living peddling to the scrappy gold diggers of early San Francisco, he could do it anywhere. As Upham got older, he thought more and more about California. His memories of his time there were vivid, "so indelibly photographed upon the retina of the mind," he told a crowd of fellow forty-niners, "that nothing but death will efface them." He began writing about it: poems, songs, articles, and in 1878 a book, *Notes of a Voyage to California via Cape Horn, Together with Scenes in El Dorado, in the Years 1849–'50.* Upham didn't sentimentalize his days in California. He remembered how difficult it was to get rich, how many had left disappointed or had died in the effort. But he couldn't suppress his nostalgia for the most remarkable period of his life.

In 1876, America celebrated the hundredth anniversary of the Declaration of Independence by hosting its first world's fair in the city where the document was signed. From May to November, millions of visitors descended on Philadelphia's Fairmount Park to see the Centennial Exhibition. On the afternoon of September 9, Upham and the other members of the Associated Pioneers of the Territorial Days of California occupied one of the fair's pavilions to commemorate another, smaller anniversary: the twenty-six years since California's admission to the Union. Seven hundred people gathered in the wooden hall to hear songs, speeches, and letters of regret from absent dignitaries like President Ulysses S. Grant and General William Tecumseh Sherman. Upham wrote something special for the occasion: "Song of the Argonauts; or, the Days of 'Forty-nine." An opera singer performed it, intoning the wistful lyrics in a rumbling basso voice to a delighted crowd.

While Upham and his friends dwelt on the past, others at the exhibition focused on the future. Not far from the forty-niners' festivities was the show's most popular attraction: the Corliss steam engine, a machine that stood almost forty feet tall. Its giant flywheel, churning pistons, and fluttering valves powered the other exhibits in Machinery Hall, and made quite an impression on those who saw them. Elsewhere in the exhibition were other dazzling examples of American ingenuity. Thomas Edison demonstrated a telegraph capable of sending many messages simultaneously; Alexander Graham Bell unveiled an early version of the telephone; E. Remington and Sons displayed the first modern typewriter. These marvels drew many fascinated foreigners, who came away with a new respect for American engineering. Eleven years after the conclusion of the conflict that nearly cut the nation in two, the United States was a rising power on the world stage.

To Upham, the whirring gears and gadgetry must have been breathtaking. America in 1876 didn't look at all like the country he knew from his childhood in Montpelier or his adventures in California. Complex machines were changing how people lived and worked; a rising class of industrial tycoons were redefining what it meant to be an entrepreneur. Less than a decade later, on June 29, 1885, Upham passed away. Sixty-six years old, he died neither rich nor poor but somewhere in between, solidly middle class to the end. His brief obituary in the *Philadelphia Inquirer* didn't include a word about his moneymaking career: he wasn't remembered as a counterfeiter, but as a merchant, a writer, and a pioneer. He was killed by stomach cancer, in the privacy of his own home—a quiet, undramatic end for a man who had masterminded one of the most extraordinary counterfeiting schemes in American history.

UPHAM FOUND SUCCESS as a counterfeiter just as the golden age of American counterfeiting was coming to a close. While the Civil War made his enterprise possible, its effect on other moneymakers would be disastrous. The same government that let him forge Southern money used the war to tighten its control over Northern currency. For more than a century, criminals like Owen Sullivan and David Lewis had taken advantage of America's monetary chaos to make fake cash. Their ranks grew as the number of banks and the volume of paper money soared. Meanwhile, the federal government kept out of it, leaving the burden of policing the money supply to individual banks or states. With the arrival of the Civil War, however, Washington decided to enter the fray, putting counterfeiters on the defensive for the first time.

Initially the federal government shied away from taking a strong regulatory role. Its first steps, like the Legal Tender Act of 1862, strengthened national authority but didn't touch the heart of American finance, the approximately sixteen hundred state banks whose bills made up the circulating medium of the country. These banks had influential representatives in Congress, not to mention decades of precedent and a Supreme Court decision from the Andrew Jackson era, *Briscoe v. Bank of Kentucky*, protecting their right to print money. Now that the greenbacks in their vaults were considered as good as gold or silver, they could issue even more notes, stoking inflation.

Treasury Secretary Salmon Chase had a radical solution to the problem: a total overhaul of the banking establishment. He wanted Congress to create a system of federally chartered banks that printed a uniform national currency similar to the modern dollar. The banks would be required to buy government bonds to secure the notes, which would have the added benefit of fortifying the federal government's credit by providing a permanent market for its securities. The real appeal of the plan for Chase, however, had less to do with its usefulness than with his principles. He had opposed the Legal Tender Act because it violated his hard-money views; now he promoted national banking because he believed the Constitution demanded it. According to Chase, the Constitution empowered the federal government to regulate the currency, a responsibility that the states had unjustly usurped by granting charters to note-issuing banks. Bringing paper money under national control, Chase argued, would fulfill the Constitution's original intention.

The secretary's stubbornness had made him many enemies over the years. But it would prove an asset in his crusade for banking reform, a bruising fight that needed someone as headstrong as Chase to see it through. He had introduced the idea of a national bank system to Congress as early as December 1861, but didn't make a serious push for it until a year later, in December 1862. President Lincoln, who had long believed in the benefit of a national currency, gave his full support. Many Republicans, however, rejected Chase's plan—even those who otherwise advocated a strong federal government. Two of Congress's most outspoken proponents of the Legal Tender Act, Thaddeus Stevens of Pennsylvania and Elbridge Spaulding of New York, were particularly vocal in their opposition. Not coincidentally, they came from states with powerful banking interests.

To get the legislation passed, Chase campaigned ferociously. He courted congressmen, bankers, and journalists—anyone whose endorsement might tilt the balance in his favor. He insisted that the national banking bill was essential for winning the war. "Without it there may be success," he wrote the publisher of the *Chicago Tribune*, "but I don't see it." Actually, the plan would do little for the Treasury right away; its effect would mostly be felt in the long term. But by tying the national banking system to the Northern war effort, Chase hoped to make it harder to oppose him.

Chase's persistence could only take him so far. He needed a more persuasive spokesman, someone who could change minds. The man who rose to the occasion was John Sherman, the senator who occupied the Ohio seat vacated by Chase after his appointment to the Treasury. Nicknamed the "Ohio Icicle" for his frosty disposition, Sherman had a passion for finance. He also happened to be the younger brother of William Tecumseh Sherman, the great Union general, and he brought a comparable degree of strategic skill to the Senate floor on behalf of Chase's plan. In a series of incisive speeches in January and February 1863, he denounced the state banking system as volatile and inefficient, a haven for speculators and counterfeiters. "You cannot prevent the people from suffering largely from counterfeiting," he pointed out, "when you have sixteen hundred different banks, issuing each of them several different kinds of bills, under the laws of twenty-eight different States."

The disadvantages of the current system were obvious enough. But Sherman didn't stop there: he invoked the Founders. This wasn't in itself an unusual tactic. Among the famous names he cited for support, however, one in particular stood out: Thomas Jefferson. Jefferson seemed like an odd choice. He had upheld states' rights, fought Alexander Hamilton's Bank of the United States, and, along with most of his revolutionary colleagues, distrusted paper money. But he was also a nuanced thinker and, toward the end of his life, had reconsidered his financial views. During the War of 1812, when banks suspended specie payments, Jefferson conceded that bills printed by the federal government would be preferable to the paper of state banks. Sherman seized on this, quoting the statesman at length to recast the national banking proposal as a Jeffersonian idea.

Sherman's use of Jefferson was shrewd. It appealed to western agrarians, who worshipped Jefferson, as well as to current and former Democrats in Congress. Decades earlier, Andrew Jackson had exploited western antibanking sentiment to kill the Second Bank of the United States. Instead of eliminating all banks, as Jefferson would have wished, this removed one big bank and created many smaller, less scrupulous ones, particularly in the West. By the 1860s, the westerners who had supported Jackson were ready for change. Armed with Jefferson's words, Sherman helped them overcome their fear of paper money and the federal government and realize the benefits of a national currency. It was a masterpiece of political alchemy, using the language of Jefferson to help destroy the legacy of Jackson. On top of it all was a Hamiltonian twist: a federal government that protected its citizens by subduing the power of the individual states.

The Civil War gave Sherman valuable ammunition and, like Chase, he didn't hesitate to use it. He linked both state banks and secession to the "accursed heresy of State Sovereignty," and urged national banking as a necessary war measure. It wouldn't just help beat the South, he asserted, it would also ensure the future of the Union. A national currency would make people more dependent on the federal government, giving them a stake in its stability—Americans would "become inseparably united and consolidated" with the national leadership in Washington, and thus less likely to revolt against it. "The policy of this country ought to be to make everything national as far as possible," Sherman declared, "to nationalize our country so that we shall love our country."

Between Sherman's rhetoric and Chase's maneuvering, the national banking bill gradually gained traction in Congress. It passed narrowly: by two votes in the Senate and fourteen in the House. On February 25, 1863, Lincoln signed the National Currency Act into law. After the heat of the battle, what followed was anticlimactic. Sherman's desire to eliminate state banknotes didn't make it into the final legislation, so the new national banks were forced to compete with older, better-established rivals. By the end of 1863, only sixty-six banks had applied for federal charters. National banks scored a crucial victory in March 1865, when Congress, at Sherman's urging, levied a 10 percent tax on all state banknotes. State banks had no choice but to stop printing money, with national banknotes and greenbacks filling the vacuum. A month later, Confederate general Robert E. Lee surrendered at Appomattox Court House in Virginia, essentially ending the Civil War.

The United States emerged from the conflict completely transformed. The war had produced something that seemed unimaginable: a federal monopoly on paper currency. Although each national banknote carried the name of the institution that issued it, Chase commissioned private engravers to create uniform designs and print the actual bills. He insisted on including scenes from the country's common past on the notes, like the arrival of the Pilgrims and the Battle of Lexington, to underscore the national character of the new money. Never before in American history had the power to make paper money been held by a single authority.

Colonies, states, and banks had all printed currency. Paper was irresistible, a magical surrogate for precious metals. Its abrupt oscillations in value had sparked furious showdowns in eighteenth-century Massachusetts, aggravated relations between colonial Americans and Parliament, and jeopardized the Revolution by inundating the young country with inflationary continentals. In the nineteenth century, paper credit helped kindle both booms and busts, speeding the nation along its haphazard, collision-filled path to prosperity. Now the federal government was finally taking the reins, hoping to steady the economy and reaffirm its sovereignty at the same time.

Counterfeiters felt the effects right away. A national currency meant people could distinguish between genuine and fake money much more easily. They no longer had to recognize thousands of different bills, only the standardized designs of greenbacks and national banknotes. Simplifying the money supply put countless small-time swindlers out of business—gone were the days of banknote reporters with rambling inventories of arcane counterfeits. But it would take more than that to wipe out one of America's oldest criminal professions. Hard-core moneymakers wouldn't give up so easily. If the new currency made their jobs harder, it also made them potentially more lucrative. Greenbacks and national banknotes passed everywhere and held their value; forging them would be more profitable than counterfeiting the ratty bills of provincial banks.

This was evidently lost on Washington's lawmakers, who in the course of creating national banks and national money had somehow neglected to create a national agency to stop counterfeiting. For once the Constitution presented no problems: it explicitly empowered Congress to "provide for the Punishment of counterfeiting the Securities and current Coin of the United States." Instead, Congress chose to leave the task to existing law enforcement agencies. These included local authorities, who had neither the resources nor the motivation to tackle counterfeiting on a large scale, and federal marshals, who had fewer excuses but didn't do much better. Since marshals earned their living mostly from fees for making arrests and

delivering warrants, they had little incentive to build cases against counterfeiters. Counterfeiting was a notoriously tough crime to prosecute.
It required mapping distribution networks, recruiting informers—real
detective work, in other words. The nation's lawmen weren't sophisticated or well-organized enough to meet the challenge. But something
needed to be done: the credit of the United States was on the line. Without a coordinated campaign to protect the currency, counterfeiters had the
capacity to disrupt the new monetary regime.

In the absence of a congressional mandate, the anticounterfeiting offensive emerged more or less spontaneously from the turmoil of the Civil War.
It was spearheaded by a band of ambitious, adventurous men—opportunists
who carved out roles for themselves in the Union war machine by going
after counterfeiters with unrivaled zeal. They believed the ends justified
the means and, under the banner of an invigorated wartime government,
broke the law almost as often as the people they put away. In the process
they penetrated the counterfeiters' world, illuminating the hidden work-
ings of a centuries-old institution.

LAFAYETTE CURRY BAKER LOVED learning secrets. An intense man with
a brambly red beard and probing gray eyes, he first started prying into
other people's affairs in San Francisco, where he went in 1853, three years
after Upham's departure. He joined the Committee of Vigilance, a group
of armed citizens that seized control of the city in response to rising lawlessness and corruption. They lynched criminals and spied on residents,
giving Baker valuable espionage training. When the Civil War broke out,
he put his skills to use by traveling South as a secret agent, disguising himself as an itinerant photographer to gather information about Confederate
troop deployments. His daring impressed Secretary of State William H.
Seward, who hired him as a detective when he returned to Washington.

Northern intelligence was an uncoordinated cluster of "secret services" staffed by a motley cast of characters. Seward oversaw a spy network made up of informers, federal marshals, and city police. Other cabinet departments fielded their own detectives, as did individual generals—in the first year of the war, the famous private investigator Allan Pinkerton ran covert operations in Virginia for General George B. McClellan. Faced with this daunting tangle of agencies, Baker might have ended up as just another cog in the Union's unwieldy espionage machine. Instead, he broke through the bureaucracy and rose rapidly to the top, becoming the government's de facto intelligence czar. With a ruthlessness inherited from the San Francisco vigilantes, Baker went to extreme lengths to neutralize anything he perceived as a threat to national security.

In early 1862, about the same time Upham began printing his facsimiles, Seward transferred Baker to the War Department. It was there that he built his base of power, assembling an outfit called the National Detective Police. His team, which grew to include twenty-five agents and a whole cavalry regiment, didn't limit themselves to spying on the South. They became an all-purpose investigative unit, ferreting out corruption and disloyalty in the military, hunting down smugglers and traitors, even raiding Washington's brothels and gambling dens. They also kept an eye on the federal bureaucracy. In December 1863, allegations of impropriety at the Treasury led Secretary Chase to enlist Baker's services. The detective not only found workers pocketing money but, to Chase's chagrin, exposed a seedy sex scandal that rocked the capital. Baker accused Spencer M. Clark, the superintendent of the bureau that oversaw the national currency, of seducing his female employees. Chase suspended the man, but restored him when it came to light that Baker had coerced the women's testimony.

Baker had no scruples about violating people's civil liberties. He plucked suspects from their beds in the middle of the night and hauled them away in coaches with curtained windows, interrogating them for days on end. "Baker became a law unto himself," observed one Treasury official. "He instituted a veritable Reign of Terror." But he did his job remarkably well—almost too well, earning the enmity of the many people who profited from the graft he crusaded against. If Baker saw enemies everywhere, he wasn't entirely wrong: rampant fraud in the government and the military sapped urgently needed resources, and the country's innumerable Southern sympathizers could easily become a fifth column for the Confederacy. In Baker's mind, the gravity of the threat justified taking the gloves off, for as long as the national interest required it.

Whatever his vices or virtues, Baker was an innovator. He pioneered new interrogation techniques, compiled the nation's first police dossier, and kept photographs of criminals on file—an early example of the "mug shots" method attributed to Allan Pinkerton. He was also the first to confront counterfeiting on a national scale. In the summer of 1864, he broke up moneymaking enclaves in Missouri, Indiana, and Illinois, capturing ten forgers and several plates. A couple of months later, he struck again, this time in New York and New Jersey. Baker recognized the danger posed by counterfeiters—that they weren't just criminals but enemies of the state. He also understood that any realistic strategy for dealing with them would have to come from Washington. Only a broadly empowered federal agency could claw through the maze of different jurisdictions that counterfeiters manipulated to their advantage. Local police couldn't be trusted: their negligence over the last century had given forgers endless advantages. This was why Baker didn't turn the people he arrested over to local authorities. He shipped them to Washington in chains and installed them somewhere he knew would be secure.

When the prisoners emerged from the police van, they must have been surprised by what they saw. The Old Capitol Prison, where Baker kept his captives, looked shabby for a federal jail. It consisted of a row of ramshackle wooden structures tacked onto a blockish brick building, topped with a handful of chimneys standing stiffly at attention. The walls had been whitewashed, but the paint only came halfway up the facade, a pattern oddly reminiscent of the layered insides of a birthday cake. Its cells housed thousands of inmates, not only those swept up in Baker's raids but also a host of others: blockade-runners, spies, crooked Union officers, and captured Confederate soldiers. Many high-profile detainees spent time there, like Rose O'Neal Greenhow, a stylish Washington socialite turned Confederate agent who had charmed Northern officials into surrendering state secrets.

The prison's superintendent, William Patrick Wood, occupied a large corner office on the ground floor. A small, sturdy man, he shared Baker's appetite for intrigue. He used the Old Capitol as a launching site for clandestine actions in the South, often slipping across the front lines himself to snoop on the enemy, negotiate prisoner exchanges, and smuggle counterfeit Confederate money to Union hostages. It's unclear whether he had the authority to engage in these escapades; like Baker, though, he didn't mind stepping out-of-bounds. To his prisoners, Wood was something of a mystery. He could be gruff one moment, genial the next; a "strange compound, a perfect mass of contradictions" was how one inmate described him. Occasionally he erupted in anger, like when he beat a black man in the street for suggesting his gray suit looked like a Confederate uniform. While fickle and despotic, however, he wasn't a cruel warden. He wrangled with his superiors to improve the food and living conditions at the Old Capitol, and for his efforts won the grudging respect of many of his charges.

Wood liked to let people underestimate him. He dressed modestly and cultivated a folksy, unpretentious persona that masked cannier motives. In treating his prisoners humanely, he was earning their trust, softening them up for long, exhaustive interrogations. These sessions yielded useful scraps of intelligence that he would pass along to higher-ups at the War Department. Sometimes Wood and Baker would tag-team a suspect using a good cop–bad cop routine: the detective acting tough, the superintendent playing nice. While Wood had a lighter touch than the bullish Baker, he took a similarly dim view of due process. If a prisoner proved unwilling to talk, Wood would fabricate testimony incriminating him and read it aloud, browbeating him into confessing.

By questioning the counterfeiters who ended up in his custody, Wood learned their trade. In the summer of 1864, he joined Baker's raid on moneymaking gangs in the Midwest, and later embarked on several sweeps of his own, dragging the culprits back to the Old Capitol for rigorous examinations. He began building an invaluable body of knowledge about one of the least understood elements of the American underworld. Wood's growing expertise caught the attention of the Treasury Department, which in December 1864 hired him as an agent tasked with detecting forged government securities. He poured himself into the task, hiring a squad of detectives to help him. On July 5, 1865, the Treasury moved to make his posting more permanent, naming him the chief of a new departmental anticounterfeiting force called the U.S. Secret Service.

THE CHALLENGES THAT WOOD faced weren't new. Moneymakers had been dodging the law for a long time, and the ways they did it hadn't changed much. In the eighteenth century, Owen Sullivan had exploited the lack of coordination among the several colonies where he operated. He installed himself in the Oblong, a rugged piece of land between New York and Connecticut—two colonies with a history of bickering over their borders that weren't inclined to cooperate in flushing Sullivan out of his backwoods hideout. He traveled throughout the Northeast, distributing notes and plates, hopping jurisdictions before the authorities caught up. Law enforcement, in the eighteenth century as in the nineteenth, was mostly local, focused on policing individual communities, not dismantling broader criminal enterprises.

This wouldn't have been a problem if Wood had been allowed to bypass local authorities in pursuing counterfeiters wanted for federal crimes. But since the Treasury, not Congress, created the Secret Service, its operatives didn't have the power to make arrests or obtain search warrants. They had to collaborate with local police and federal marshals, who were not only fiercely territorial, but often had an interest in preserving the status quo. Many city cops cut lucrative deals with counterfeiters. So Wood, always eager to exceed his mandate, came up with a way to circumvent the process. He would arrange for one of his men to buy a packet of counterfeit cash, and station other operatives nearby to watch the transaction. Then they would swoop in on the seller, making a citizen's arrest on the basis of having observed a crime being committed. Other times Wood dispensed with this pretext altogether and seized suspects and evidence by force.

If the obstacles to catching counterfeiters weren't new, neither were the techniques for doing it. Wood's background in espionage helped: bringing down moneymaking rings required infiltrating them, the same way Union agents infiltrated the Confederacy during the Civil War. This meant using informants, a strategy that dated at least as far back as the colonial era. In 1752, a Providence court convicted Sullivan after his former partner Nicholas Stephens turned king's evidence against him. Informants like Stephens helped secure convictions by establishing intent: they could testify that the defendant knew the money was fake and intended to pass it. Informants also offered a way to gain access to the upper reaches of a counterfeiting operation. The authorities would arrest a passer, promise him money or immunity in exchange for cooperation, and then use him to burrow deeper into an organization, identifying distributors, manufacturers, and other principal players.

Wood absorbed these lessons thoroughly. He didn't just recruit counterfeiters as informants, he hired them as full-time employees. For a wage of $3 a day, they supplied information that led to arrests and convictions, and helped build cases against bigger targets further up the food chain. Criminals had various motives for collaborating with Wood. Sometimes they had no choice: they had been arrested and Wood gave them a chance to earn their freedom. Others wanted a regular paycheck to supplement their illicit income, or used the Secret Service to eliminate competitors while continuing to make fake money on the side. Wood didn't shrink from colluding with unsavory characters; many of his own operatives came from the same milieu. Almost half of the original Secret Service team had criminal records. Their firsthand knowledge of the underground economy opened doors that would have been closed to more law-abiding men. The downside was that many of them still acted like crooks. With little oversight from Wood, Secret Service operatives made illegal arrests, solicited bribes in exchange for protecting criminals, and sold bad bills they seized from counterfeiters.

Despite his men's questionable methods, Wood delivered results. In its first year, the Secret Service arrested more than two hundred counterfeiters. Wood's army of informants enabled him to chart the complex web of relationships among the people who printed, transported, and passed fake money throughout the country. He identified four major production points for counterfeit cash—New York, Philadelphia, St. Louis, and Cincinnati—and deployed most of his detectives there, hoping to stem the flow of bad bills at the source. Taking a cue from Baker, he began keeping extensive files on the nation's counterfeiters, documenting their criminal history, physical appearance, and known associations.

Moneymakers had historically been an elusive lot. They hid their identity with aliases, and the facts surrounding their lives tended to be murky, clarified only by the occasional rumor or newspaper report. In Pennsylvania during the early part of the nineteenth century, David Lewis became a folk hero on the basis of stories that were probably false or exaggerated. These tales portrayed Lewis as a Robin Hood figure who, in punishing the rich and protecting the poor, appealed to Pennsylvanians reeling from the economic injustices underscored by the Panic of 1819. Lewis wasn't the only counterfeiter to generate a mythology; the more enterprising criminals actively cultivated their mystique. By assembling a central database, Wood not only made it possible to track counterfeiters on a national level, he also helped demystify who they were and what they did.

In 1867, Wood took down a key counterfeiting hub, arresting thirty-eight dealers in upstate New York responsible for running fake cash into communities from New England to the Midwest. He did it by converting members of the ring into informants, patiently gathering evidence until he was ready to hit all his targets at once. But even as he was putting money-makers behind bars, his tactics were breeding a backlash that threatened to undermine his mission. With the Civil War over, people had less patience for Wood's heavy-handed style. After years of exercising broad authority, the federal government was in retreat; while the balance of power remained in Washington's favor, the courts pushed back against the excesses of the war era. As the chief of a federal law enforcement agency, Wood would have been unpopular just by virtue of what he represented. His behavior, however, made things considerably worse. Putting criminals on the pay-roll, and encouraging them to commit crimes in order to ensnare other, more important criminals, caused serious controversy. It involved subsi-dizing illegal activity with government money, a strategy that led to some memorable confrontations with outraged judges.

That summer, Wood helped defend a counterfeiter named William Brockway in federal court, and even took the witness stand on his behalf, because the man had worked for the Secret Service. The presiding judge, William Davis Shipman, was appalled. "We have thus had the unseemly spectacle before this Court of an officer of the Treasury Department encour-aging the defence of a prisoner, while the regular prosecuting officers were presenting proofs of his guilt," he said. He took particular offense at the alle-gation that Wood had promised Brockway immunity from prosecution—no one but the president of the United States, Judge Shipman declared, had the power of pardon. Wood's actions in court also prompted an indignant editorial from the *New York Times*, which recommended a congressional inquiry into the Secret Service's shady dealings with counterfeiters.

Wood made halfhearted attempts to rein in the agency, publishing a handbook in 1868 that set stricter rules for operatives, but his days were clearly numbered. When Ulysses S. Grant became president in 1869, he dismissed Wood, who by then was under indictment in New York for false imprisonment. In the following decades, the Secret Service gradually shed its scandalous reputation and became a well-respected part of the federal bureaucracy, waging a tremendously successful campaign against counterfeiters. At the end of the Civil War, counterfeit currency accounted for between one-third and one-half of the money in circulation; by 1911, the chief of the Secret Service announced that counterfeits made up less than one-thousandth of one percent of the paper money supply.

Wood's aggressive leadership laid the foundation for this dramatic decline. With the Secret Service safeguarding the nation's currency, counterfeiting lost its allure. It was no longer "an easy Way of getting Money," as Owen Sullivan once called it. Now a counterfeiter didn't know whom to trust: his closest associates could be government informants. If captured, he faced prosecution in a federal court and an average of eight to fifteen years in prison. The risks simply weren't worth it. While a few continued forging on a small scale, the national counterfeiting industry crumbled under the force of the federal assault.

Counterfeiting was a casualty of the Civil War, a victim of the federal consolidation of power undertaken by the North to preserve the Union. Before the war, Washington was a distant, barely perceptible presence in most Americans' lives. Afterward, people felt its power everywhere. Casting off the constraints imposed by Andrew Jackson and his disciples, the federal government thrust itself into the economic arena, becoming indispensable to everyday commerce. The pieces of paper printed under Washington's exclusive authority gave America's citizens a shared medium of exchange, uniting the currency as the war united the country. It was a belated victory for Alexander Hamilton and Nicholas Biddle, who had fought valiantly on behalf of their respective banks but never succeeded in fully nationalizing the money supply. The war accomplished what they couldn't. Energized by a strong national currency, the country embarked on a period of massive economic growth, rapidly maturing into the industrial powerhouse that Samuel Upham and millions of others saw on display at the 1876 Centennial Exhibition in Philadelphia.

The national notes were more than money. They were symbols of a new kind of nationhood, a common identity that transcended regional loyalties. People came to depend on their central government like never before, trusting Washington to regulate the country's currency and secure its value. In 1881, the Secret Service confiscated toy money from various firms in Manhattan, claiming the merchandise too closely resembled genuine bills. "Securities and Coins of all countries should be held sacred," the agency's chief declared. "[P]eople, especially manufacturers, should not seek to transform them into curiosities." As the one true moneymaker, the federal government would no longer tolerate even the slightest form of disrespect. Its notes had become sacrosanct, tokens of the nation-state's power to metamorphose slips of paper into money.

CONCLUSION

THE DECLINE OF THE AMERICAN COUNTERFEITER meant the end of a special kind of criminal. There would always be swindlers and cheats, new scams and hustles. But counterfeiters were different—they had played a leading role in America's long, fraught love affair with paper money. In a country where everyone wanted cash, they made it; they extracted wealth from thin air in a nation that had always lived beyond its means.

Paper currency first appeared on the continent in 1690, when Massachusetts printed bills of credit to fund a failed campaign to take Quebec from the French. The colony didn't have enough coin to pay the returning soldiers, so the legislature paid them in notes it promised to retire with future taxes. Soon bills of credit spread to other colonies, where they facilitated trade and financed more wars with the French. By the time the Revolution began, paper money had become a fixture of American life.

By postponing the present in anticipation of the future, paper promises helped America grow. No one could have expected the thirteen Atlantic colonies to become a united continental power stretching to the Pacific coast. It took a leap of faith, and a cascade of paper credit. The notes came not only from authorized sources—governments and banks, among others—but also from counterfeiters. If counterfeiters didn't intend to honor the promises printed on their bills, neither did many legal producers of money, who rarely had enough coin to back their paper. Counterfeiters acted as shadow financiers, contributing a significant portion of America's money supply. While they adapted to changing circumstances over the years, the core of their business remained intact: a persistent appetite for cash in a country that never seemed to have enough.

Owen Sullivan, David Lewis, and Samuel Upham each lived through very different eras, yet all three built their fortunes on America's addiction to paper money. Their careers mirrored the evolving confidence game of American capitalism, a machine that ran on various kinds of debt and deception, oscillating between manic exuberance and total collapse. In the decades after the Civil War, the rise of the Secret Service made the country's counterfeiters an endangered species. But the moneymaking mentality had so thoroughly suffused America's financial soul that even as counterfeiting declined, the spirit of Sullivan, Lewis, and Upham lived on. It could be seen on the trading floors where speculators bet money they didn't have on a mercurial stock market; it pervaded an economy where people piled up imaginary riches on precarious pyramids of debt.

While the federal government emerged from the Civil War with a stronger hand over the economy, national money and national banks wouldn't be enough to tame the country's financial madness. Panics still struck with relentless regularity: in 1873, 1884, 1890, 1893, and 1903. In 1907, an unsuccessful ploy by a Brooklyn-born mining tycoon to corner the stock of a copper company precipitated yet another crisis. The financier J. P. Morgan intervened, spearheading a bailout of struggling bankers and brokers that prevented the disaster from escalating—but not before the extent of the damage persuaded people that a more permanent solution to the problem needed to be found. In response, Congress created a commission to investigate the country's banking and currency laws. The group's findings ultimately led to the founding of America's first central bank since the fall of the Second Bank of the United States in 1836: the Federal Reserve, established by Congress in 1913. It consisted of twelve regional reserve banks, overseen from Washington by a six-person board. All national banks were required to join the system, and any state bank had the option to become a member.

The architects of the Federal Reserve hoped to avert future financial disasters by providing the economy with a lender of last resort, as Morgan had done during the Panic of 1907. They spoke of a lack of "elasticity" in the nation's currency—when demand for cash soared during a panic, the money supply couldn't grow to meet the need for liquidity. The Fed addressed this dilemma by giving the government a valve for regulating the flow of money into the economy. If the country required more currency, the Fed could lower the interest rate at which it lent money, easing credit by encouraging member banks to borrow. If it wanted to shrink the amount of currency in circulation, the Fed could raise the interest rate, curbing the growth of the money supply by making credit more expensive.

The formation of a central bank fortified federal control of America's money, accelerating the Hamiltonian trend put in motion by the Civil War. Even with the government taking a more active role, however, booms and busts persisted. Sixteen years after the creation of the Federal Reserve, the country suffered its worst financial meltdown in history: the crash of 1929, followed by the Great Depression. Like the Panic of 1907, the cataclysm prompted an overhaul of America's financial institutions. It also inaugurated a new chapter in the centuries-old saga surrounding the relationship between paper money and precious metals.

The United States had officially adopted the gold standard in 1900, after decades of furious wrangling over the currency regime inherited from the Civil War. Beginning in the 1870s, a populist coalition of workers and farmers urged the government to print more legal tender greenbacks, called United States Notes, without exchanging the bills for gold. They wanted an inflationary currency, which would devalue their debts and make cash more widely available. Their hopes were defeated when the government capped the quantity of greenbacks in circulation and, in 1879, made the notes freely convertible into gold. A new kind of federal currency appeared in 1914—Federal Reserve Notes—and these, too, were redeemable in gold, payable on demand at any reserve bank.

The Depression severed this link between the paper dollar and coin. Soon after assuming office in March 1933, President Franklin D. Roosevelt effectively took the nation off the gold standard, hoping to boost the price of American goods by driving down the dollar's value. The government withdrew gold from circulation, nationalized the country's gold reserves, and halted the convertibility of most federal money into precious metals. Roosevelt's radical move marked an important first step in the gradual transformation of the dollar into a purely faith-based currency. The deathblow came in 1971, when President Richard M. Nixon finished off the gold standard by closing the "gold window" that enabled foreign governments to exchange dollars for gold through the Treasury. Almost three hundred years since its first appearance in colonial Massachusetts, paper money had permanently liberated itself from precious metals. The worst fears of Thomas Hutchinson, Thomas Paine, and generations of hard-money Americans had been realized.

By 1971, the government had stopped printing greenbacks and national banknotes. Only Federal Reserve Notes remained, which are still the only paper dollars in use today. In the twentieth century, they spread throughout the world, taking on the role that gold had served for centuries: a secure store of value in countries where the domestic currency is too volatile to be trusted. Most Federal Reserve Notes are now held overseas—about $450 billion by the end of 2005, as much as 60 percent of the total amount in circulation.

As the dollar has become global, so has the counterfeiting of American currency. For decades, Colombia produced most of the fake money coming into the United States, supplying up to 70 percent of the counterfeit bills passed every year. A crackdown begun in the late 1990s by the Secret Service and the Colombian government brought this number down to 5 percent, but moneymaking hubs have sprung up elsewhere—notably Peru, which is now the region's major producer of counterfeit American cash. Like drug traffickers, Latin American counterfeiters have built underground networks for smuggling their product into the United States. While these bills are capable of fooling most people, experts can easily identify them as forgeries.

The most deceptive counterfeits on the market come from North Korea, whose government covertly forges American bills and then launders or wholesales them abroad. Printed with highly sophisticated intaglio presses—most likely at a secret factory about twenty miles from Pyongyang, the capital—the North Korean fakes are so difficult to detect they are known as supernotes. While North Korea officially denies involvement, the American government has openly accused the regime of counterfeiting, and continues to use both law enforcement and diplomacy to combat the spread of the supernotes. Nonetheless, the volume of supernotes in circulation is relatively small: about $45 million, according to a recent government estimate, not nearly enough to pose a serious threat to the American economy.

Overall, counterfeit currency accounts for a minuscule amount of the money in circulation: approximately one per ten thousand notes, both at home and abroad. This is partly due to the Secret Service, which projects a sizable international presence through its many overseas offices. But American money has also become much harder to forge. Today's printers embed notes with high-tech components that are considerably more effective at foiling counterfeiters than the complex leaf patterns Benjamin

Franklin used to deter colonial forgers. The new designs for Federal Reserve Notes introduced in 1996 include a security thread that glows in ultraviolet light and a special kind of ink that changes colors when viewed from different angles. The next generation of the $100 bill will feature another cutting-edge anticounterfeiting device: a strip composed of thousands of small lenses, which display three-dimensional images that change from bells to 100s as the viewer moves the note. A similar motion makes a larger bell to the right of the strip appear to vanish within a copper inkwell. The bills enter circulation on February 10, 2011.

As the gadgets the government uses to secure the national currency improve, counterfeiting will become more expensive and time-consuming. Only those with the resources to devote to such an undertaking will be able to continue producing passable fakes, employing expert technicians who bear little resemblance to the charismatic engravers of counterfeiting's golden age. Forging notes may even become obsolete, as criminals turn to more profitable swindles.

Perhaps the largest threat to counterfeiting is the uncertain future of paper money itself. In the twentieth century, paper definitively displaced precious metals; in Thomas Paine's words, "an apparition" took "the place of a man," an outcome he had warned against a decade after the Declaration of Independence. In this century, paper is being displaced by something even more ethereal. As financial institutions have grown more global and more intricate, money has become ghostlier than Paine could have imagined: traded as intangible signals, beams of light coursing through the filaments of the world's data network. With new technology come new ways to get rich quick, new schemes for creating wealth by cultivating confidence.

The counterfeiters from America's past understood the power of confidence better than anyone. They manufactured money backed by nothing but belief, using craftsmanship and charisma to earn their victims' trust. Today, their legacy can be felt on Wall Street, where people wield complex financial instruments like magic wands, spinning false fortunes out of the ether of global capitalism. These modern moneymakers probably don't realize they belong to an ancient American tradition—that centuries ago, their forefathers hunched over copperplates with inky fingers, trying to instill inanimate paper with the spark of faith that sustains the nation's economy to this day.

ACKNOWLEDGMENTS

The idea for this book came from Stephen Mihm's fascinating history of American counterfeiting, *A Nation of Counterfeiters: Capitalists, Con Men, and the Making of the United States*. After reading it I called Stephen, who graciously took the time to speak with me. Our conversation made me want to read everything I could find on the topic, and set in motion the research that eventually produced a book proposal. Without him, this book wouldn't have been written. At the time, I was working at a magazine called *Lapham's Quarterly*, helping to put together an issue about the history of money. It was a wonderful way to begin learning about America's financial past, and I'm grateful to the editor, Lewis Lapham, for letting me take part in such a worthwhile project.

When I first began researching this book, I wasn't sure what to expect. I cast a wide net, writing to archives, historical societies, and libraries around the country, and eventually visiting many of them in person. Everywhere I went I found people who were enormously generous with their time and their resources, and I'm deeply grateful to them for making my research possible. Thanks to Linda August and Nicole Joniec at the Library Company of Philadelphia, Christine Bertoni at the Peabody Essex Museum, Elizabeth Bouvier at the Massachusetts Supreme Judicial Court, Jeff Brueggeman of the Society of Paper Money Collectors, James

W. Campbell at the New Haven Museum & Historical Society, Kathleen A. Carrara at the Rutland Superior Court in Vermont, Don Carter of the Library and Archives Canada, Debbe Causey at the Daniel Library at the Citadel, Edward Dacey at the U.S. Military Academy Library at West Point, Richard Doty at the Smithsonian Institution's National Museum of American History, Elizabeth Hahn and Elena Stolyarik at the American Numismatic Society, John Hannigan at the Massachusetts Archives, Bonnie L. Hess at the Bedford County Archives, Cara Holtry at the Cumberland County Historical Society, Tab Lewis at the National Archives and Records Administration, Tanya Marshall and Catherine Sherman at the Vermont State Archives and Records Administration, Rhiannon McClintock at the Centre County Historical Society, Aaron McWilliams at the Pennsylvania State Archives, Jonah Parsons at F+W Media, Jaclyn Penny at the American Antiquarian Society, Benoît Pelletier Shoja of the New Hampshire State Archives, Andrew Smith at the Rhode Island Judicial Records Center, Mel E. Smith of the Connecticut State Library, Susan Snyder and Lorna Kirwan at the Bancroft Library, Abigail Thompson and the staff of the Baker Library Historical Collections at Harvard Business School, Malinda Triller at the Waidner-Spahr Library at Dickinson College, Dennis Tucker at Whitman Publishing, Abby Yochelson at the Library of Congress, the staff of the New York County Clerk's Office, the staff of the New York State Archives, and the staff of the Philadelphia City Archives. I'm especially grateful to Kitty Wunderly and the staff of the Centre County Library and Historical Museum in Bellefonte, Pennsylvania. Thanks also to Eric P. Newman, Elizabeth Sinclair, Q. David Bowers, Marc D. Weidenmier, Tom Carson, and Gladys Murray, who each made important contributions to my research.

Of the many authors whose work I relied on, three deserve special mention: Mark Dugan, Ned Frear, and George B. Tremmel. I'm indebted to them for sharing the results of their research and patiently pointing me in the right direction.

The New York Public Library's Frederick Lewis Allen Room gave me an ideal place to work. Thanks to Jay Barksdale and David Smith for letting me through the door; I can't imagine writing the book anywhere else. During my time at the library I made extensive use of the Irma and Paul Milstein Division of U.S. History, Local History and Genealogy and the Microforms Reading Room. Both collections were indispensable. Thomas Lannon of the Manuscripts and Archives Division provided expert research help.

My agent Joy Harris believed in this book from the beginning, and without her tireless enthusiasm and guidance, I couldn't have written it. My editors Laura Stickney and Vanessa Mobley improved the manuscript immeasurably. I'm grateful for their patience, dedication, and incisive editing. Rachel Nolan read a draft of the manuscript and made excellent suggestions that helped strengthen it. Patty O'Toole provided ideas and moral support at a crucial early stage. Mark Danner gave invaluable advice and encouragement throughout, as he always has in the past. Finally, I thank my parents, whose contributions are too significant to summarize in a couple of sentences. Their love, counsel, and eagle-eyed editing are present in every page of this book.

NOTES

The notes are organized by paragraph. For each note I've listed the page number, followed by the first few words of the paragraph.

INTRODUCTION

1, On a November night

The tomb raiders assaulted Lincoln's grave on November 7, 1876. The raid and arrest: *New York Times*, November 9, 1876; November 10, 1876; November 18, 1876; and November 22, 1876. See also the *Inter Ocean*, November 20, 1876.

3, American counterfeiters had

Early colonial currency: David R. Johnson, "Foreword," Kenneth Scott, *Counterfeiting in Colonial America* (Philadelphia: University of Pennsylvania Press, 2000 [1957]), pp. xi–xv; Scott, *Counterfeiting in Colonial America*, pp. 4–16; Richard Sylla, "Monetary Innovation in America," *Journal of Economic History* 42.1 (March 1982), pp. 21–26; Stephen Mihm, *A Nation of Counterfeiters: Capitalists, Con Men, and the Making of the United States* (Cambridge, MA: Harvard University Press, 2007), pp. 26–28.

3, Coins would have

British closing the Massachusetts mint: Sylla, "Monetary Innovation in America," p. 24.

3–4, A growing colonial

Spread of paper currency and tensions with the Crown: ibid., pp. 23–26, and Mihm, *A Nation of Counterfeiters*, pp. 31–33. Bills of credit: Robert E. Wright, *One*

Nation Under Debt: Hamilton, Jefferson, and the History of What We Owe (New York: McGraw-Hill, 2008), pp. 43–45.

4–5, Paper money had other

Crude quality of colonial currency and counterfeits: Scott, *Counterfeiting in Colonial America*, pp. 7–8.

5, When the Continental Congress

More than ten thousand kinds of notes: Mihm, *A Nation of Counterfeiters*, p. 3. Mihm computed his estimate by examining *Hodges' American Bank Note Safe-Guard*, an annual catalog of all circulating bills.

5–6, Paper helped entrepreneurs

Mary Peck Butterworth: Scott, *Counterfeiting in Colonial America*, pp. 64–67. Scene with Peter McCartney and *"I merely wished . . . "*: George Pickering Burnham, *Memoirs of the United States Secret Service* (Boston: Lee & Shepard, 1872), pp. 56–57. *"He was not an ordinary . . . "*: Allan Pinkerton, *Thirty Years a Detective* (New York: G. W. Dillingham, 1900 [1884]), p. 550. For more on McCartney's life, see Lynn Glaser, *Counterfeiting in America: The History of an American Way to Wealth* (Philadelphia: Clarkson N. Potter, 1968), pp. 132–143.

CHAPTER ONE

11, If you had spent

Colonial newspapers were full of sensational reports about weird or tragic events, and a single incident often inspired a handful of different accounts. Report of the twenty-eight-pound melon, the mulatto boy bitten by a rattlesnake, and the Irishman in yellow buckskin breeches: *Boston Gazette, or Weekly Journal*, August 15, 1749. Newspapers also served as a kind of bulletin board for merchants to advertise their wares. Choice Lisbon Salt and the Best Burlington Pork: *Boston Weekly News-Letter*, August 17, 1749; a Good Brick House: *Boston Gazette, or Weekly Journal*, August 1, 1749; a Healthy Strong Negro Man: *Boston Post Boy*, July 3, 1749; the pamphlet by Jonathan Edwards: *Boston Post Boy*, August 14, 1749.

12, One day in late August

The story of Sullivan's quarrel with his wife was well known; in particular, the phrase "forty-thousand-pound moneymaker" became closely linked to the counterfeiter, and in later newspaper reports accompanies his name as a kind of epithet. The best account of the incident: *Connecticut Gazette*, April 13, 1756, reproduced in Kenneth Scott, *Counterfeiting in Colonial Connecticut* (New York: American Numismatic Society, 1957), pp. 137–139. Sullivan also mentions the fight on p. 8 of his posthumously published confession, *A Short Account of the Life, of John——Alias Owen Syllavan . . .* , first printed in New York in 1756. The only available version is the reprint published by Green & Russell in Boston the same year; a copy is held by the American Antiquarian Society and available online through Readex Early American Imprints, Series I: Evans, 1639–1800; in quoting the confession, I use the pagination from the Boston reprint. Sullivan's occupation as a silversmith: from the record of his 1750 trial, found in the Massachusetts Supreme Court of Judicature Record Book, vol. 1750–1751, pp. 100–101, available on microfilm at the Massachusetts Archives.

12, The silversmith's name

Even by the standards of his time, Sullivan was a serious drinker. In *A Short Account*, p. 7, he blames his wife for his drinking: "she was given to take a Cup too much, and I for my Part took to the same." Later testimony from his criminal accomplices suggests the counterfeiter was rarely sober. Sullivan flaunting his fortune: *Connecticut Gazette*, April 13, 1756: "always flush of Money, tho' he lived in an expensive Manner, above his visable Income [*sic*]." The details of Sullivan's arrest on August 28, 1749: *Boston Weekly News-Letter*, August 31, 1749, and the Massachusetts SCJ Record Book, vol. 1750–1751, pp. 100–101.

12, They carried Sullivan

Relationship with Fairservice: Kenneth Scott, *Counterfeiting in Colonial America* (Philadelphia: University of Pennsylvania Press, 2000 [1957]), p. 187, and "Counterfeiting in Colonial New Hampshire," *Historical New Hampshire* 13.1 (December 1957), pp. 17–18. In his confession, Sullivan doesn't mention Fairservice by name but does boast that he engraved three plates in jail (two for forging New Hampshire money, and a third for Massachusetts bills) and struck off forged notes by hand, which he smuggled out to his accomplices. For more on the lax conditions of colonial jails, see Lawrence Friedman, *Crime and Punishment in American History* (New York: Basic Books, 1993), pp. 48–50.

13–14, Satisfied with the silversmith's services

Fairservice's counterfeiting operation: Scott, *Counterfeiting in Colonial America*, p. 187, and "Counterfeiting in Colonial New Hampshire," pp. 17–18. Bull Wharf, shown in Captain John Bonner's 1722 map of Boston, stood on the city's southern coast, near the Bull Tavern. The tavern's history: Samuel Adams Drake, *Old Boston Taverns and Tavern Clubs* (Boston: W. A. Butterfield, 1917), pp. 102–103. John Fairservice married Mary Lawrence on January 25, 1755, according to *A Volume of Records Relating to the Early History of Boston, Containing Boston Marriages From 1752 to 1809* (Boston: Boston Municipal Printing Office, 1903), p. 14. Their messy divorce: Nancy F. Cott, "Divorce and the Changing Status of Women in Eighteenth-Century Massachusetts," *William and Mary Quarterly* 33.4 (October 1976), pp. 586–614. *"criminal conversation . . . "*: from Fairservice's court testimony, quoted in Thomas A. Foster, *Sex and the Eighteenth-Century Man: Massachusetts and the History of Sexuality in America* (Boston: Beacon, 2006), p. 31.

14, In the meantime

Sullivan's trial: the Massachusetts SCJ Record Book, vol. 1750–1751, pp. 100–101, and Scott, *Counterfeiting in Colonial America*, p. 187. Notice of Sullivan's pillorying and whipping: *Boston News-Letter*, September 13, 1750, and *Boston Evening-Post*, September 14, 1750. The layout of colonial Boston, including the location of the pillory and the whipping post: Edwin Monroe Bacon, *Boston: A Guide Book to the City and Vicinity*, rev. ed. (Boston: Ginn and Company, 1922), pp. 4–8. The man who received twice as many stripes as Sullivan was one Monsieur Batter, known as the "French doctor," whose punishment is described in the *New-York Gazette*, September 24, 1750, and the *Boston Gazette*, September 18, 1750.

14–15, Being a counterfeiter

The approximate commodity prices: Ruth Crandall, "Wholesale Commodity Prices in Boston During the Eighteenth Century," *Review of Economics and Statistics* 16.6 (June 15, 1934), pp. 117–128. The actual amount people paid for goods like wheat and molasses varied widely; also, paper money emissions (or "tenors," as they were called) from different years traded at different values, which makes things even more complicated. Boston's population: Andrew N. Porter, *Atlas of British Overseas Expansion* (London: Routledge, 1991), p. 44. Thomas Wilson claimed to have seen Fairservice print 680 shillings in a single day; Wilson's testimony: Scott, *Counterfeiting in Colonial America*, p. 187, and "Counterfeiting in Colonial New Hampshire," pp. 17–18.

16–17, Sullivan couldn't have picked

The currency conflict in Massachusetts: Elizabeth E. Dunn, " 'Grasping at the Shadow': The Massachusetts Currency Debate, 1690–1751," *New England*

Quarterly 17.1 (March 1998), pp. 54–76, and Malcolm Freiberg, "Thomas Hutchinson and the Province Currency," *New England Quarterly* 30.2 (June 1957), pp. 190–208. The origins of Massachusetts paper currency: see Andrew McFarland Davis, *Currency and Banking in the Province of the Massachusetts-Bay*, pt. 1 (New York: Macmillan, 1901), pp. 8–23.

17, On May 1, 1749

The scene: Thomas Hutchinson, *The Diary and Letters of His Excellency Thomas Hutchinson*, ed. Peter Orlando Hutchinson (London: Sampson Low, Marston, Searle & Rivington, 1883), pp. 53–54. Report of the fire: *Boston Gazette*, May 2, 1749.

17–18, The house belonged

Hutchinson's early life: John Fiske, *Essays: Historical and Literary*, vol. 1 (New York: Macmillan, 1902), pp. 10–13, and Andrew Stephen Walmsley, *Thomas Hutchinson and the Origins of the American Revolution* (New York: NYU Press, 1999), pp. 9–11. After weeks of deliberation, Hutchinson's bill was finally approved on January 25, 1749; see Freiberg, "Thomas Hutchinson and the Province Currency," pp. 198–203.

18–19, It's possible that

History of colonial paper currency: Richard Sylla, "Monetary Innovation in America," *Journal of Economic History* 42.1 (March 1982), pp. 21–26. Depreciation of bills: Alvin Rabushka, *Taxation in Colonial America* (Princeton: Princeton University Press, 2008), pp. 364–366.

19, In 1744, a conflict

Nineteen new paper issues and the inflation that halved the currency's value: Freiberg, "Thomas Hutchinson and the Province Currency," p. 196.

19, Although the war

Louisbourg reimbursement and passage of the bill: ibid., pp. 195–199, 203. *"I am convinc'd . . . "*: ibid., p. 198.

20, The approaching elimination

Mood in Boston: Thomas Hutchinson, *The Diary and Letters*, p. 54, and Freiberg, "Thomas Hutchinson and the Province Currency," p. 200. *"Few Tokens of Joy . . ."* and the scene of the unloading: *Boston Evening-Post*, September 25, 1749, and *Pennsylvania Gazette*, October 5, 1749.

20–21, Instead of subsiding

"[W]e shall have . . .": Boston Evening-Post, August 21, 1749. *"Fraud, Injustice and Oppression . . . ": Boston Gazette*, December 12, 1749.

21, As the bickering

"Fear not Honestus . . . *": Boston News-Letter*, February 1, 1750.

22, Paper's proponents

Contrasting definitions of value: Dunn, "'Grasping at the Shadow,'" pp. 66–70. The Congregationalist preacher was John Wise. His 1721 pamphlet, "A Word of Comfort to a Melancholy Country," appears in Andrew McFarland Davis, ed., *Colonial Currency Reprints, 1682–1751*, vol. 2 (Boston: The Prince Society, 1911), pp. 159–223. *"necessary Evils . . .":* Davis, *Colonial Currency Reprints*, p. 192.

22–23, Paper money's most articulate

"The riches . . . ": Benjamin Franklin, "A Modest Enquiry into the Nature and Necessity of a Paper-Currency," *Benjamin Franklin: Writings*, ed. J. A. Leo Lemay (New York: Library of America, 1987), p. 127.

23, Increasing the quantity

Franklin's argument and the pamphlet's reception: Walter Isaacson, *Benjamin Franklin: An American Life* (New York: Simon & Schuster, 2003), pp. 63–64. The Pennsylvania legislature initially gave the commission for printing the money to Franklin's competitor Andrew Bradford; Franklin wasn't awarded a contract until 1731. *"This was another . . . ":* Benjamin Franklin, *The Autobiography of Benjamin Franklin* (New York: Macmillan, 1921), p. 69. Franklin's anticounterfeiting innovations: William N. Goetzmann and Laura Williams, "From Tallies and Chirographs to Franklin's Printing Press at Passy: The Evolution of the Technology of Financial Claims," *The Origins of Value: The Financial Innovations That Created Modern Capital Markets*, ed. William N. Goetzmann and K. Geert Rouwenhorst (Oxford: Oxford University Press, 2005), pp. 117–118.

24, The intangible nature

The Protestant minister's name was Thomas Paine—not the famous pamphleteer, although the men shared an aversion to paper money. *"Popish Doctrine of Transubstantiation . . . ":* Thomas Paine, "A Discourse Shewing That the Real First Cause of the Straits and Difficulties of This Province of the Massachusetts

Bay, Is Its Extravagancey, & Not Paper Money," quoted in Dunn, "'Grasping at the Shadow,'" p. 68. *"an abomination . . . "*: from an anonymous letter published in the *Independent Advertizer* on March 28, 1748, quoted ibid., p. 69.

25–26, The only account

The people and places Sullivan mentions in his narrative are corroborated by the available evidence; the characters that appear in the confession (Captain Gillmore, Captain Bradbury, et al.) existed at the times and locations that Sullivan places them. The proper names are usually spelled wrong (Sullivan's hometown Fethard appears as Fedard, Bradbury is spelled Bradbery), which suggests that Sullivan narrated the account while someone, most likely the printer, transcribed it by hand, writing out phonetically the names he didn't recognize. As it's impossible to confirm the truthfulness of much of the confession, I have relied on it only in part, mostly in sketching the otherwise unknown story of Sullivan's life before 1749. A word on the time line: based on the confession, I've calculated he was probably born in 1723, spent his childhood in Ireland in the 1720s and 1730s, and departed for America in 1742.

26, Sullivan started hearing

"[F]rom my youth . . . ": Sullivan, *A Short Account*, p. 3.

26–27, At the age of thirteen

Irish landscape: Constantine FitzGibbon, *The Irish in Ireland* (New York: W. W. Norton, 1983), pp. 220–221, and Mike Cronin, *A History of Ireland* (New York: Palgrave, 2001), pp. 88–93. *"miserable dress . . . "*: quoted in Redcliffe Nathan Salaman, *The History and Social Influence of the Potato* (Cambridge: Cambridge University Press, 1970 [1949]), p. 251. *"clothes so ragged . . . "*: quoted in Arthur P. I. Samuels, *The Early Life, Correspondence, and Writings of the Rt. Hon. Edmund Burke* (Cambridge: Cambridge University Press, 1923), pp. 172–173.

27, Anglo-Irish Protestants

Population growth: Liam de Paor, *The Peoples of Ireland: From Prehistory to Modern Times* (Notre Dame, IN: University of Notre Dame Press, 1986), p. 184. English economic restrictions on Ireland: Sean J. Connolly, *Religion, Law, and Power: The Making of Protestant Ireland, 1660–1760* (Oxford: Oxford University Press, 2002 [1992]), p. 107. Regular harvest failures and the 1740 famine: Daniel Webster Hollis III, *The History of Ireland* (Westport, CT: Greenwood, 2001), pp. 69–85.

27–28, A young face

Beggars and landless laborers: FitzGibbon, *The Irish in Ireland*, pp. 222–223. Sullivan ended up in Limerick County, about one hundred miles northwest from his hometown of Fethard (now Fethard-on-Sea).

28, Once he had recovered

"After I got well . . . ": Sullivan, *A Short Account*, p. 6.

29, In the fall

The *Sea-Flower* incident: in *A Report of the Record Commissioners of the City of Boston, Containing the Records of Boston Selectmen, 1736 to 1742* (Boston: Rockwell and Churchill, 1886), pp. 317–318, and *Boston Post Boy*, November 23, 1741.

29–30, Fifteen days

"Just arrived . . . ": *Boston Gazette*, December 1, 1741.

30, While an extreme case

Scene with the biscuits: Sullivan, *A Short Account*, p. 6.

30–31, The reason for

Conditions endured by indentured servants en route to America: Sharon V. Salinger, *"To Serve Well and Faithfully": Labor and Indentured Servants in Pennsylvania, 1682–1800* (Cambridge: Cambridge University Press, 1987), pp. 87–97.

31, If Sullivan came

In *A Short Account*, pp. 6–7, Sullivan reports that his seven-year indenture was sold to Captain Gillmore, whom he served in "chopping of Wood and clearing of Land" near the St. George River in Maine. James Gillmore's signature appears on a letter written on August 6, 1742, by several residents of the St. George region to Massachusetts governor William Shirley complaining of their cattle and horses being killed by Indians. The letter is included in the Massachusetts Archives Collection (1603–1799), vol. 31, p. 414, at the Massachusetts Archives. For more on the conflict over Maine, see George Bancroft, *History of the United States of America, From the Discovery of the Continent*, vol. 2 (New York: D. Appleton, 1895 [1837]), pp. 175–211, and Francis Parkman, *Pioneers of France in the New World* (Boston: Little, Brown, 1918 [1865]). Dummer's Treaty, in 1725, had brought about a period of relative peace between the English settlers and the Indians.

31–32, The next conflict

Charles VI's meal: Eduard Vehse, *Memoirs of the Court, Aristocracy, and Diplomacy of Austria*, vol. 2, trans. Franz Demmler (London: Longman, Brown, Green, and Longmans, 1856), p. 163. See also William W. Ford and Ernest D. Clark, "A Consideration of the Properties of Poisonous Fungi," *Mycologia* 6.4 (July 1914), p. 168. The beginning of the War of the Austrian Succession: Reed Browning, *The War of the Austrian Succession* (New York: St. Martin's Griffin, 1995), pp. 37–54. *"This plate of champignons . . . "*: Voltaire, *Memoirs of the Life of Voltaire: Written by Himself*, trans. unknown (London: G. Robinson, 1784), p. 49.

32, Despite heavy fighting

Delay in news reaching Boston and French surprise attack: George A. Rawlyk, *Nova Scotia's Massachusetts: A Study of Massachusetts–Nova Scotia Relations, 1630 to 1784* (Montreal: McGill-Queen's University Press, 1973), pp. 136–140. Gillmore's flight: Sullivan, *A Short Account*, p. 7. Jabez Bradbury was a commanding officer at the fort at St. George River from 1747 to 1756, according to the fort's payrolls held by the Massachusetts Archives: the Massachusetts Archives Collections (1603–1799), vol. 092, pp. 81–83, 88; vol. 093, pp. 51, 91–93, 152, 168; and vol. 094, p. 138. I'm grateful to John Hannigan of the Massachusetts Archives for finding this material.

32–33, Bradbury was a veteran

In 1755, Bradbury testified that he had been in Maine for thirty years; see Fannie Hardy Eckstrom, "Who Was Paugus?" *New England Quarterly* 12.2 (June 1939), p. 210. Bradbury's past and frontier milieu: Ronald Oliver Macfarlane, "The Massachusetts Bay Truck-Houses in Diplomacy with the Indians," *New England Quarterly* 11.1 (March 1938), pp. 48–65. Bradbury took command in 1742: Cyrus Eaton, *History of Thomaston, Rockland, and South Thomaston, Maine*, vol. 1 (Hallowell, ME: Masters, Smith, 1865), pp. 52–53. *"diliverd from this . . . "*: James Phinney Baxter, ed., *Documentary History of the State of Maine, Containing the Baxter Manuscripts*, vol. 24 (Portland, ME: Fred L. Tower, 1916), pp. 45–46. Bradbury and Shirley corresponded frequently in the 1740s and 1750s about Indian unrest in Maine.

33, While Sullivan and Bradbury's

The Louisbourg siege: Rawlyk, *Nova Scotia's Massachusetts*, pp. 154–155, 166–172.

34, Remarkably, though, the siege

The festivities: ibid., pp. 172–174. *"The churl and niggard . . . "*: *Boston Evening-Post*, July 8, 1745, quoted ibid., p. 174.

34, Not everyone greeted

The attack on the fort in July 1745: Samuel Gardner Drake, *A Particular History of the Five Years French and Indian War in New England and Parts Adjacent* (Albany: Joel Munsell, 1870), pp. 79–80, and Eaton, *History of Thomaston, Rockland, and South Thomaston, Maine*, pp. 55–56. The scalped corpse of the prisoner: from a letter from Bradbury to Shirley dated July 29, 1745, included in Charles Henry Lincoln, ed., *Correspondence of William Shirley: Governor of Massachusetts and Military Commander in America, 1731–1760*, vol. 1 (New York: Macmillan, 1912), p. 261.

34–35, Sullivan witnessed

In *A Short Account*, p. 7, Sullivan says he served Bradbury for two years from the time that the war broke out (in 1744), which means he didn't go to Louisbourg until 1746, the year after its capture. Military service by indentured servants: Richard B. Morris, *Government and Labor in Early America* (New York: Octagon Books, 1975 [1946]), pp. 282–290. *"took great Delight . . . "*: Sullivan, *A Short Account*, p. 7.

35, Perhaps for someone

Hardships of life in Louisbourg: Rawlyk, *Nova Scotia's Massachusetts*, pp. 175–177. Twelve hundred soldiers dying of sickness: from a letter by William Pepperrell, quoted ibid., p. 177.

35–36, During the two

"I unhappily Married . . ." and *"aggravating Tongue"*: Sullivan, *A Short Account*, p. 7.

36, Fortunately for Sullivan

The Treaty of Aix-la-Chapelle: Fred Anderson, *Crucible of War: The Seven Years' War and the Fate of Empire in British North America, 1754–1766* (New York: Vintage, 2001), pp. 35–36. Almost everything reverted to the map before the war, except for a few small concessions: for example, Prussia kept the Austrian territory of Silesia. The amount of the reimbursement was £183,649 2s. 7d., according to Rawlyk, *Nova Scotia's Massachusetts*, p. 177.

36–37, While the windfall delighted

The Louisbourg cross: Alison D. Overholt, "University Returns Louisbourg Cross to Canada," *Harvard Crimson*, June 30, 1995; John George Bourinot, "Once Famous Louisbourg," *Magazine of American History with Notes and Queries*, vol. 27, ed. Martha J. Lamb (New York: Historical Publication Co., 1892), p. 191.

37, Sullivan returned to

"I thought it . . . ": Sullivan, *A Short Account*, p. 8.

CHAPTER TWO

38, On a summer day

Descriptions of Providence: Charles Rappleye, *Sons of Providence: The Brown Brothers, the Slave Trade, and the American Revolution* (New York: Simon & Schuster, 2006), pp. 8–9; Lynne Withey, *Urban Growth in Colonial Rhode Island: Newport and Providence in the Eighteenth Century* (Albany: State University of New York Press, 1984), pp. 9–10; and William Eaton Foster, *Stephen Hopkins: A Rhode Island Statesman. A Study in the Political History of the Eighteenth Century*, pt. 1 (Providence: Sidney S. Rider, 1884), pp. 86–88. Meadows outside the town: Andrew Burnaby, *Travels Through the Middle Settlements in North America in the Years 1759 and 1760* (New York: A. Wessels, 1904 [1775]), p. 131.

38, When they had

Scene with Stephens: Owen Sullivan, *A Short Account of the Life, of John——Alias Owen Syllavan . . .* (Boston: Green & Russell, 1756), pp. 9–10. Stephens, whose full name is given in court documents as Nicholas Stephens Jr., was a laborer from Dighton, Bristol County, Rhode Island, according to his case entry in the Superior Court of Judicature, Court of Assize, and General Gaol Delivery, Providence County, Record Book 1, September Term, 1752, *Rex v. Stephens*, p. 97 (Judicial Archives, Supreme Court Judicial Record Center, Pawtucket, RI).

39, The Providence jail

The arrest of Sullivan's associates and *"he is now in the Country . . . ":* Boston Post Boy, August 17, 1752. See also Kenneth Scott, *Counterfeiting in Colonial Rhode Island* (Providence: Rhode Island Historical Society, 1960), pp. 31–33, and *Counterfeiting in Colonial America* (Philadelphia: University of Pennsylvania Press, 2000 [1957]), p. 188. Providence's taverns, churches, and inns: Rappleye, *Sons of Providence*, p. 8.

39, Colonial Americans had

The challenges of capturing and convicting counterfeiters in the colonial era: Scott, *Counterfeiting in Colonial America*, pp. 9–10.

39–40, Sullivan was caught

History and location of Providence jail: William R. Staples, *Annals of the Town of Providence, From Its First Settlement, to the Organization of the City Government, in June, 1832* (Providence: Knowles and Vose, 1843), p. 180. Providence's commerce with the West Indies: Gertrude Selwyn Kimball, *Providence in Colonial Times* (Boston: Houghton Mifflin, 1912), pp. 275–276. The wooden drawbridge: Rappleye, *Sons of Providence*, p. 8. Beds of oysters and clams on the eastern side of the river: Richard M. Bayles, ed., *History of Providence County, Rhode Island* (New York: W. W. Preston, 1891), pp. 134–135. Providence in mid-eighteenth century: Foster, *Stephen Hopkins*, pp. 87–88. Population estimates: Rappleye, *Sons of Providence*, p. 8; Bayles, *History of Providence County*, p. 3. Location of the shipyard: Foster, *Stephen Hopkins*, p. 88. For the overall layout of colonial Providence and its environs, see the 1750 map of the town included in John Hutchins Cady, *The Civic and Architectural Development of Providence, 1636–1950* (Providence: The Book Shop, 1957), p. 27.

40, By the time

"exceedingly well Counterfeited . . . ": *Boston Post Boy*, August 17, 1752. The report was reprinted in the *Boston Gazette, or Weekly Journal*, August 18, 1752, and the *New-York Evening Post*, August 24, 1752; shorter notices of the arrest are also found in the *Boston Evening-Post*, October 9, 1752, and the *New-York Gazette Revived in the Weekly Post-Boy*, October 16, 1752.

40–41, Providence provided

Political struggle between Providence and Newport: Mack E. Thompson, "The Ward-Hopkins Controversy and the American Revolution in Rhode Island: An Interpretation," *William and Mary Quarterly* 16.3 (July 1959), pp. 363–375. Rhode Island printed money by licensing "banks" to emit currency; see Henry Phillips, *Historical Sketches of the Paper Currency of the American Colonies, Prior to the Adoption of the Federal Constitution* (Roxbury, MA: W. Elliot Woodward, 1865), pp. 101–111.

41, When Sullivan arrived

Among those linked to Sullivan in 1752 were Joseph Stephens, a miller; Elias Smith, a yeoman; and John Rosier, a boatman; see Scott, *Counterfeiting in Colonial*

Rhode Island, pp. 32–34. A wide range of people engaged in counterfeiting in colonial America, running the gamut from mariners to carpenters to schoolmasters to tavern keepers, and the majority of them were amateurs, not professional criminals; see Kenneth Scott, *Counterfeiting in Colonial New York* (New York: American Numismatic Society, 1953), p. 198.

42, Sullivan's anger didn't

Sullivan's strategy for freeing his colleagues: Sullivan, *A Short Account*, p. 10; Scott, *Counterfeiting in Colonial America*, p. 188; *Connecticut Gazette*, April 13, 1756, reprinted in Scott, *Counterfeiting in Colonial Connecticut* (New York: American Numismatic Society, 1957), pp. 137–139.

42, A grand jury

Sullivan's case and *"a Transient Person . . . "*: the Superior Court of Judicature, Court of Assize, and General Gaol Delivery, Providence County, Record Book 1, September Term, 1752, *Rex v. Sullivan*, p. 94 (Judicial Archives, Supreme Court Judicial Record Center, Pawtucket, RI). Stephens's case and *"[F]or the sake . . . "*: ibid., *Rex v. Stephens*, p. 97.

43, In September 1752

Sullivan's and Stephens's punishment: *Connecticut Gazette*, April 13, 1756, reprinted in Scott, *Counterfeiting in Colonial Connecticut*, pp. 137–139. Counterfeiters were usually branded with the letter C, for "Counterfeiter," but Sullivan and Stephens merited a harsher penalty: R for "incorrigible Rogue," the same punishment given to runaway servants and slaves. They likely received the R because of Sullivan's previous conviction and his "transient" status; for more, see James Fitzjames Stephens, *A History of the Criminal Law of England*, vol. 3 (London: Macmillan, 1883), pp. 272–275, and Lawrence Friedman, *Crime and Punishment in American History* (New York: Basic Books, 1993), pp. 40–41. Location of the town pillory: the Federal Writers' Project, *Rhode Island: A Guide to the Smallest State* (Boston: Houghton Mifflin, 1937), p. 267. Rum distilleries: William Babcock Weeden, *Early Rhode Island: A Social History of the People* (New York: Grafton, 1910), p. 222.

43, Stephens's punishment was next

The scene: *Connecticut Gazette*, April 13, 1756, reprinted in Scott, *Counterfeiting in Colonial Connecticut*, pp. 137–139; Scott, *Counterfeiting in Colonial Connecticut*, pp. 188–189; Sullivan, *A Short Account*, p. 10.

43–44, Sullivan had escaped

"[T]hey pursu'd me . . . ": Sullivan, *A Short Account,* p. 10. His sentence in the Superior Court of Judicature Record Book specifies thirty days' imprisonment: relatively mild by today's standards, but severe enough to make Sullivan break out of jail.

44, Sullivan's performance

"a man of good Address . . . ": *Connecticut Gazette,* April 13, 1756, reprinted in Scott, *Counterfeiting in Colonial Connecticut,* pp. 137–139.

45, Sullivan had more

Punishment in colonial America: Friedman, *Crime and Punishment in American History,* pp. 25–26, 36–41, 48–50.

45–46, It was in Dutchess

There's no reliable estimate of how much counterfeit currency Sullivan made. In *A Short Account,* pp. 9–11, he admits to printing more than £27,000 of various colonies' money. That figure is probably too low, especially if it's supposed to reflect not just what Sullivan printed but the total amount of currency made from his plates. Since Sullivan left his plates in the hands of accomplices throughout the Northeast, there's no way of knowing how many notes they produced. In August 1755, a group in Newport admitted to printing about £50,000 from Sullivan's plates; if all of his accomplices made similar quantities, the total number could easily be in the hundreds of thousands. The Newport case: Scott, *Counterfeiting in Colonial America,* pp. 202–203.

46, Sullivan set up

The dimensions of the Oblong: C. J. Hughes, "Just Beyond New York's Suburbs, a Genuine Swamp," *New York Times,* June 30, 2006. According to Margaret E. Herrick, *Early Settlements in Dutchess County, New York* (Rhinebeck, NY: Kinship, 1994), p. 102, Connecticut ceded the Oblong to New York in exchange for property along Long Island Sound; Connecticut revived the dispute in the nineteenth century and the case wasn't formally resolved until 1881. Dover referred to a region spanning the present-day towns of Amenia, Dover, North East, Washington, Pawling, Beekman, and Clinton.

46–47, Dover presented a number

Settlement history of Dover and environs: Arthur T. Benson, "Glimpses of Dover History," *Dutchess County Historical Society Year Book 1921* (Poughkeepsie, NY:

Dutchess County Historical Society, 1921), pp. 18–25; "A Paper Read by Miss Mary Hoag at the Oblong Meeting House, Quaker Hill, Sept. 29, 1920," *Dutchess County Historical Society Year Book 1921*, pp. 13–14; Henry Noble MacCracken, *Old Dutchess Forever! The Story of an American County* (New York: Hastings House, 1956), p. 141; Herrick, *Early Settlements in Dutchess County*, p. 102.

47, Pioneers are usually

The wetlands of the Oblong: MacCracken, *Old Dutchess Forever!*, pp. 130–132. Wolves and panthers: Alfred T. Ackert, "Dutchess County in Colonial Days," a paper read before the Dutchess County Society in February 28, 1898, held by the New York Public Library's Irma and Paul Milstein Division of U.S. History, Local History and Genealogy.

47–48, If his choice

Dover Stone Church: Richard Francis Maher, "The Town of Dover," *The History of Dutchess County, New York*, ed. Frank Hasbrouck (Poughkeepsie, NY: S. A. Matthieu, 1909), pp. 279–280. Description of Sullivan's hideout: *Connecticut Gazette*, April 13, 1756, reprinted in Scott, *Counterfeiting in Colonial Connecticut*, pp. 137–139.

48, Sullivan also put

Oblong gang: *New-York Post-Boy*, March 29, 1756. The phrase "Dover Money Club" was probably a coinage of the authorities: according to Kenneth Scott, "The Dover Money Club," *New York Folklore Quarterly* 12.1 (Spring 1956), p. 17, the term surfaced as early as 1753, in connection with a mason from Stratford who obtained a large quantity of bills from the gang. Description of Joseph Boyce: *Boston Evening-Post*, September 10, 1744.

48–49, Without the Boyces

For more on the Boyce counterfeiting team, see Scott, *Counterfeiting in Colonial New York*, pp. 58–69. *"the place where this . . ."* and *"The Heads of this Confederacy . . . "*: ibid., pp. 58–59.

49, Despite their tough

Clarke's efforts: Scott, *Counterfeiting in Colonial New York*, pp. 62–66, and *Counterfeiting in Colonial America*, pp. 125–127. *"Endeavour'd to make . . . "*: from Clarke's affidavit, quoted in Scott, *Counterfeiting in Colonial New York*, p. 63.

50, A student of counterfeiting

Amateur character of colonial law enforcement: Friedman, *Crime and Punishment in American History*, pp. 27–30; and David R. Johnson, "Foreword," Scott, *Counterfeiting in Colonial America*, pp. xv–xvi.

50-51, Moneymaking was also

A vast majority of Americans lived in small, rural communities. On the eve of independence, only 7–8 percent of the population resided in towns of 2,500 or more inhabitants, according to John J. McCusker and Russell R. Menard, *The Economy of British America, 1607–1789* (Chapel Hill: University of North Carolina Press, 1991 [1985]), p. 250.

51, Anyone who wanted

Governor Gideon Wanton's rejected proposal to the Rhode Island assembly: Scott, *Counterfeiting in Colonial New York*, pp. 66–67.

51-52, The governor had good

The Boyces' specialty was Rhode Island currency: ibid., p. 66. The flow of money across colonies: Joseph Albert Ernst, *Money and Politics in America, 1755–1775: A Study in the Currency Act of 1764 and the Political Economy of Revolution* (Chapel Hill: University of North Carolina Press, 1973), pp. 35–36. *"Our chief Justices . . . "*: Scott, *Counterfeiting in Colonial New York*, p. 66.

52-53, The growing interconnectedness

The redemption period and the amount of outstanding paper bills: Malcolm Freiberg, "Thomas Hutchinson and the Province Currency," *New England Quarterly* 30.2 (June 1957), pp. 203–206. Paper money from other colonies flooding in: Ernst, *Money and Politics in America, 1755–1775*, p. 39. Oath about foreign money: Andrew McFarland Davis, *Currency and Banking in the Province of the Massachusetts-Bay*, pt. 1 (New York: Macmillan, 1901), p. 236.

53, What Hutchinson realized

Franklin's cartoon originally appeared in his newspaper, the *Pennsylvania Gazette*, in the spring of 1754. The image and motto resurfaced a couple of decades later, when American revolutionaries rallied for colonial unity against the British.

54, In the summer

Cady's brief career: Scott, *Counterfeiting in Colonial Connecticut*, pp. 108–110, and *Counterfeiting in Colonial America*, pp. 191–193.

54–55, Cady's case wasn't

Munroe and *"heard tell . . . "*: Scott, *Counterfeiting in Colonial Rhode Island*, pp. 36–37.

55, Stashing bills at

Newspapers instructed their readers how to detect counterfeit bills not only out of a sense of public service but for self-interested reasons as well. Since the newspapers' printers often printed the colony's money, they had an interest in removing forged currency from circulation. Warnings printed in 1754 in the *New-York Gazette* and the *New-York Mercury*: Scott, *Counterfeiting in Colonial New York*, pp. 82–84.

55–56, Sometimes the stress

Ide's case and *"being apprehensive . . . "*: Scott, *Counterfeiting in Colonial Rhode Island*, pp. 37–38.

56, While tramping across

Farming and fishing along the Merrimack: Kimball Webster, *History of Hudson, N.H.*, ed. George Waldo Browne (Manchester, NH: Granite State Publishing, 1913), pp. 18–21. The towns in the Merrimack region where Sullivan enlisted accomplices included Nottingham West (now Hudson), Merrimack, Londonderry, and Goffstown. The boundary dispute between New Hampshire and Massachusetts: Webster, *History of Hudson, N.H.*, pp. 137–139. Hutchinson's role: Malcolm Freiberg, "How to Become a Colonial Governor: Thomas Hutchinson of Massachusetts," *Review of Politics* 21.4 (October 1959), p. 648.

56–57, Few people knew

Rogers's physical appearance: Caleb Stark, *Memoir and Official Correspondence of Gen. John Stark* (Concord, NH: G. Parker Lyon, 1860), p. 387. Rogers's biography: Allan Nevins, "The Life of Robert Rogers," in Robert Rogers, *Ponteach or the Savages of America: A Tragedy* (Chicago: Caxton Club, 1914), pp. 17–22, 27–31, 33.

57, When Rogers went

Rogers's first encounter with Sullivan: Nevins, "The Life of Robert Rogers," p. 41, and Burt Garfield Loescher, *The History of Rogers' Rangers*, vol. 1 (Published by the author, San Francisco, 1946), pp. 17–18. The region's dense pine forests: Webster, *History of Hudson, N.H.*, p. 19.

57–58, Sullivan and Rogers

Rogers's travels: Nevins, "The Life of Robert Rogers," p. 34.

58, Whether by playing

According to Nevins, "The Life of Robert Rogers," p. 41, Sullivan didn't show up to buy the oxen because he became alarmed and fled the region. Sullivan may have disappeared briefly, but he certainly returned, because he had further contact with Rogers and others in the Merrimack Valley. *"Just Grounds to Suspect . . . "*: from the warrant, dated January 24, 1755, Provincial Court of New Hampshire #27267, held by the New Hampshire State Archives in Concord; for a transcription of the document, see Loescher, *The History of Rogers' Rangers*, pp. 264–265. Meshech Weare: Joseph Dow, *History of the Town of Hampton, New Hampshire, From Its Settlement in 1638, to the Autumn of 1892*, vol. 2 (Salem, MA: Salem Press Publishing and Printing, 1893), pp. 1030–1031.

58, The trial that took

The records of the 1755 trial: the Provincial Court of New Hampshire #27267, the New Hampshire State Archives.

58–59, Winn's wife hated

Winn's wife complained about Sullivan to Ezekiel Greeley, who volunteered the details in his examination. Greeley added that "the greater part of [Sullivan's] talk when sober" was about making money; other testimony confirmed the counterfeiter's frequent drinking. *"Damn you for a pack . . . "*: from the testimony of John McCurdy, included in the trial records. Sullivan's arrival in the Merrimack region and his collaboration with Winn: Kenneth Scott, "Counterfeiting in Colonial New Hampshire," *Historical New Hampshire* 13.1 (December 1957), pp. 19–20.

59–60, In his examination

"I saw a man . . . ": from Rogers's examination, dated February 7, 1755, included in the trial records.

60, Rogers was lying

In his testimony, John McCurdy claimed Rogers had more interactions with Lewis. For the justices' memorandum on the results of their investigation, see Loescher, *The History of Rogers' Rangers*, pp. 267–269.

60–61, In the spring

The skirmish, subsequently known as the Battle of Jumonville Glen: Fred Anderson, *Crucible of War: The Seven Years' War and the Fate of Empire in British North America, 1754–1766* (New York: Vintage, 2001), pp. 5–7, 52–59. Washington's men didn't kill all thirteen Frenchmen. Some of them, including their commander Joseph Coulon de Villiers de Jumonville, were slain by the Indians after they surrendered.

61, These were the first

The lead-up to the war: Anderson, *Crucible of War*, pp. 36–41, 112.

61–62, As with the last

Rogers and Frye: Nevins, "The Life of Robert Rogers," pp. 40–41, and Loescher, *The History of Rogers' Rangers*, pp. 18–19.

62, While in Portsmouth

Rogers's negotiation and Frye's complaint: Nevins, "The Life of Robert Rogers," pp. 41–42.

62, Rogers so successfully

Carty Gilman: Scott, "Counterfeiting in Colonial New Hampshire," pp. 26–27; Scott includes an image of the note to Gilman. *"Gilman, for God's sake . . . "*: quoted in Scott, *Counterfeiting in Colonial America*, p. 202.

62–63, Rogers presumably wanted

An overview of British forces and the reasons for training more irregular units: Daniel Marston, *The French-Indian War, 1754–1760* (Oxford: Osprey, 2002), pp. 16–21.

63, Rogers' Rangers

Expansion of the Rangers: Marston, ibid., p. 18. Rogers didn't invent ranging, but he certainly helped popularize and codify it. The "rules of ranging" used by the current U.S. Army have been modified and expanded since Rogers's day.

63–64, While Sullivan shared

Silence Dogood incident: Walter Isaacson, *Benjamin Franklin: An American Life* (New York: Simon & Schuster, 2003), p. 29. *"Let all men . . . "*: from the 1743 edition of *Poor Richard's Almanack,* in Benjamin Franklin, *Autobiography and Other Writings,* ed. Ormond Seavey (Oxford: Oxford University Press, 1998), p. 280.

64, Sullivan took the advice

Sullivan's pseudonyms: Scott, *Counterfeiting in Colonial Rhode Island,* pp. 31, 37, and *Counterfeiting in Colonial New York,* p. 81. The counterfeiter used the aliases John Pierson and Isaac Washington in Rhode Island, and the name Benjamin Parlon in New York. An example of an accomplice using an alias to deny knowing Sullivan was Joseph Munroe, a Massachusetts farmer caught passing counterfeit bills in Newport. Munroe confessed that a stranger named Smith had given him the notes, although Smith was clearly Sullivan. In *A Short Account,* Sullivan claims that his real name was John, and that he created the alias Owen Sullivan after running away from home in Ireland.

64–65, Sullivan's various names

Purchasing a barrel of Spanish wine: Scott, *Counterfeiting in Colonial Rhode Island,* p. 37. Buying drinks for everyone at the tavern: Scott, "Counterfeiting in Colonial New Hampshire," p. 20.

CHAPTER THREE

66, The sound of gunshots

The scene: Kenneth Scott, *Counterfeiting in Colonial Connecticut* (New York: American Numismatic Society, 1957), p. 117, and *Counterfeiting in Colonial America* (Philadelphia: University of Pennsylvania Press, 2000 [1957]), p. 198.

66–67, The crew was led

Sanford's hometown was near the present-day town of South Salem, New York, which was renamed to distinguish it from another Salem farther north. Sanford's career: Scott, *Counterfeiting in Colonial Connecticut,* pp. 116–117, and *Counterfeiting in Colonial America,* pp. 196–199. The story of Sanford's arrest is found in the Waterbury court records: New Haven County, Superior Court Files, Box 311, 1751–1754, Case #32, *Rex v. David Sanford,* in the Records of the Judiciary Department at the Connecticut State Library in Hartford. *"Say nothing . . . "*: from the testimony of Elisha Hall, one of the travelers, who gave an account of the incident to the court at Waterbury on January 26, 1754, included in the trial records. Sanford's raids: Mary Louise King, *Portrait of New Canaan: The History of a Connecticut Town* (New Canaan, CT: New Canaan Historical Society, 1981), p. 51. The Connecticut countryside: Daniel W. Teller, *The History of Ridgefield, Conn.: From Its First Settlement to the Present Time* (Danbury, CT: T. Donovan, 1878), p. 241.

67, Sanford's cronies shared

Joseph Nichols: Scott, *Counterfeiting in Colonial Connecticut*, pp. 117–118, and *Counterfeiting in Colonial America*, pp. 198–199.

67-68, Sanford's victims, knowing

The young men of Ridgefield secured the cooperation of the constable of Salem, and together they caught Sanford; see Scott, *Counterfeiting in Colonial Connecticut*, pp. 118–119. *"arming themselves . . . "*: Charles J. Hoadly, ed., *The Public Records of the Colony of Connecticut, from May, 1751, to February, 1757, Inclusive* (Hartford: Case, Lockwood & Brainard, 1877), p. 284. The resolution and *"Disclosing the wicked Design . . . "*: Scott, *Counterfeiting in Colonial Connecticut*, p. 119.

68-69, Sanford was a different

Damages inflicted by Sanford: Scott, *Counterfeiting in Colonial Connecticut*, p. 118.

69, In the four years

£400 reward for Sullivan: John Russell Bartlett, ed., *Records of the Colony of Rhode Island and Providence Plantations in New England*, vol. 5 (Providence: Knowles, Anthony, 1860), pp. 376–377. *"famous Villain* Sullivan . . . *"*: *Boston Evening-Post*, September 8, 1755. Sullivan's counterfeits in the lottery: Kenneth Scott, *Counterfeiting in Colonial Rhode Island* (Providence: Rhode Island Historical Society, 1960), p. 40. The situation in Rhode Island became so bad that the legislature banned the use of New Hampshire currency because it was too heavily counterfeited; see Bartlett, *Records of the Colony of Rhode Island*, pp. 508–509. The New York treasury decided to withdraw all notes bearing the date May 10, 1746; see Kenneth Scott, *Counterfeiting in Colonial New York* (New York: American Numismatic Society, 1953), pp. 86–87.

69-70, Colonial governments could

Beecher's testimony and the legislature's resolution: Scott, *Counterfeiting in Colonial New York*, pp. 88–89, and Hoadly, *The Public Records of the Colony of Connecticut*, p. 455. Beecher's speech wasn't transcribed, but a later memorial to the assembly, dated May 7, 1756, reports that he first encountered the Dover counterfeiters while traveling on "private business"; the memorial is excerpted in

Scott, *Counterfeiting in Colonial New York*, p. 88. Description of the Green: Charles Hebert Levermore, *The Republic of New Haven: A History of Municipal Evolution* (Baltimore: N. Murray, 1886), p. 235.

70, From New Haven

Limestone deposits in the Housatonic River valley: William North Rice and Herbert Ernest Gregory, *Manual of the Geology of Connecticut* (Hartford: Case, Lockwood & Brainard, 1906), pp. 87–91. Beecher's difficulties in New York and his complaint to the Connecticut legislature: Scott, *Counterfeiting in Colonial New York*, pp. 89–90. "*many difficulties . . .* ": Hoadly, *The Public Records of the Colony of Connecticut*, p. 462.

70–71, If he wanted

Beecher's hiring of deputies: Scott, *Counterfeiting in Colonial New York*, p. 90; although he enlisted eleven assistants, they worked for different periods of time, ranging from twenty-seven days at the most (Beecher's son) to six days at the least. Beecher ensnaring the tavern keeper: *Connecticut Gazette*, April 13, 1756, reprinted in Scott, *Counterfeiting in Colonial Connecticut*, p. 138.

71–72, Boggy ground squished

Beecher's final pursuit and Sullivan's capture: *Connecticut Gazette*, April 13, 1756, reprinted in Scott, *Counterfeiting in Colonial Connecticut*, pp. 138–139, and Owen Sullivan, *A Short Account of the Life, of John——Alias Owen Syllavan . . .* (Boston: Green & Russell, 1756), p. 11. The detail of the *Gazette*'s report suggests a member of Beecher's group, possibly even Beecher himself, spoke directly with the journalist. Kenneth Scott speculates that Beecher gave the *Gazette* an eyewitness account of Sullivan's arrest; this seems likely, as the newspaper was published in New Haven, where Beecher lived.

72–73, Sullivan was tired

Date of Sullivan's imprisonment: *Boston Gazette, or Weekly Journal*, March 29, 1756. Location of the New Haven jail: Levermore, *The Republic of New Haven*, p. 235.

73, It was March 17, 1756

For more on historical St. Patrick's Day celebrations, see Mike Cronin and Daryl Adair, *The Wearing of the Green: A History of St. Patrick's Day* (New York: Routledge, 2002), pp. 1–4, 21–22. "*famous Money Maker . . .* ": *Boston Gazette, or Weekly Journal*, March 29, 1756.

73-74, Beecher never revealed

"in the course of his . . . ": from Beecher's statement to the Connecticut General Assembly, dated May 7, 1756, quoted in Scott, *Counterfeiting in Colonial New York*, p. 88. Beecher's payment: ibid., pp. 90, 93. The businessman couldn't collect the official bounty, since Sullivan was tried and convicted in New York, so the Connecticut legislators paid Beecher a bonus taken from the forfeited bonds of counterfeiters caught in Fairfield. In addition to the *Boston Gazette, or Weekly Journal*, March 29, 1756, the *New-York Mercury*, March 29, 1756, praised Beecher's "extraordinary Address and Resolution."

74, At the end

Sullivan's transfer to New York: *Boston Evening-Post*, March 29, 1756. New York's counterfeiting laws: Scott, *Counterfeiting in Colonial New York*, pp. 202–203. Connecticut's counterfeiting laws: Scott, *Counterfeiting in Colonial Connecticut*, pp. 219–220.

74, The men charged

As late as 1783, the road from New Haven to New York was very rugged and even impassable at points; most people traveling to New York from the east rode overland to New Haven and boarded sloops for Manhattan. Country estates of colonial New York: Edwin G. Burrows and Mike Wallace, *Gotham: A History of New York City to 1898* (Oxford: Oxford University Press, 1999), pp. 178–179. Construction of palisades: ibid., p. 168. A 1755 map of New York, known as the Maerschalck or Duyckink Plan, shows the palisades along the northern border of town; the map is available in Allon Schoener, *New York: An Illustrated History of the People* (New York: W. W. Norton, 1998), p. 21.

75, The outbreak of war

Effect of war on the city's economy: Burrows and Wallace, *Gotham*, pp. 168–170. *"New York is growing . . . ":* from a letter by Benjamin Franklin to his friend William Parsons, dated June 28, 1756, quoted ibid., p. 168. New York's 1760 population: Michael G. Kammen, *Colonial New York: A History* (Oxford: Oxford University Press, 1996 [1975]), p. 279.

75-76, Despite a booming

The City Hall jail: Philip Klein, *Prison Methods in New York State: A Contribution to the Study of the Theory and Practice of Correctional Institutions in New York State,*

Ph.D. thesis (New York: Columbia University, 1920), p. 32. City Hall housed a range of official bodies, including the Common Council, the Assembly, the Mayor's Court, and the Supreme Court of Judicature. Sullivan's near escape: *New-York Mercury*, April 26, 1756. Sullivan's trial, conviction, and sentencing: Scott, *Counterfeiting in Colonial New York*, p. 91. The court records are available in the New York Supreme Court of Judicature Minute Book: April 1, 1754–January 22, 1757 (Engrossed), pp. 255, 261, and the New York Supreme Court of Judicature Minute Book: April 20, 1756–October 23, 1761 (Rough), pp. 10–12, 18–19; both items are held by the New York County Clerk's office in Manhattan. *"That the prisoner . . . "*: the New York Supreme Court of Judicature Minute Book: April 1, 1754–January 22, 1757 (Engrossed), p. 261.

76, The place of execution

The place of execution: William Nelson, "The Administration of William Burnet, 1720–1728," *The Memorial History of the City of New-York: From Its First Settlement to the Year 1892*, vol. 2, ed. James Grant Wilson, p. 165. Postponing of Sullivan's execution: *New York Gazette: or, the Weekly Post-Boy*, May 10, 1756, and *Boston Evening-Post*, May 17, 1756. *"He is certainly . . . "*: *New York Gazette: or, the Weekly Post-Boy*, May 10, 1756, quoted in Scott, *Counterfeiting in Colonial New York*, pp. 91–92.

76, The best route

The Bowling Green neighborhood and the artisanal wards on the west side: Burrows and Wallace, *Gotham*, pp. 175, 187–188. Trees along Broadway and Trinity Church: Andrew Burnaby, *Travels Through the Middle Settlements in North America in the Years 1759 and 1760* (New York: A. Wessels, 1904 [1775]), pp. 111–113.

77, First Sullivan boasted

The scene at the gallows: Sullivan, *A Short Account*, pp. 11–12, and *New-York Gazette: or, the Weekly Post-Boy*, May 17, 1756, reprinted in Scott, *Counterfeiting in Colonial Connecticut*, p. 141. Prices in New York: *New-York Mercury*, May 3, 1756.

77–78, A century later

Physiological effects associated with hanging: Charles Meymott Tidy, *Legal Medicine*, vol. 3 (New York: William Wood, 1884), pp. 241, 243–244.

78, Killing the moneymaker

"[I]t appears by . . . ": from the text of "An Act more effectually to Suppress and prevent the Counterfeiting of the Paper Currency of this Colony," quoted in Scott,

Counterfeiting in Colonial New York, p. 93. Beecher's efforts at capturing the remainder of the gang: Scott, *Counterfeiting in Colonial America*, pp. 208–209. Sullivan's products had a long shelf life: "It is not improbable that much of the counterfeit money circulating in the province in 1758 originated with the Dutchess County Gang," writes Scott in *Counterfeiting in Colonial New York*, p. 95.

78–79, Sullivan's posthumous paper

Sale of gallows speech: *New-York Mercury*, May 17, 1756. *"[t]aken from his own mouth"*: *Boston Evening-Post*, April 30, 1756. Sullivan's meager possessions when he stood trial are recorded in the New York Supreme Court of Judicature Minute Book: April 1, 1754–January 22, 1757 (Engrossed), p. 255.

79, Sullivan's career lasted

Printing large amounts of paper money to fund the war effort: Fred Anderson, *Crucible of War: The Seven Years' War and the Fate of Empire in British North America, 1754–1766* (New York: Vintage, 2001), p. 582.

79–80, Americans couldn't reform

British monetary policy toward the colonies: Joseph Albert Ernst, *Money and Politics in America, 1755–1775: A Study in the Currency Act of 1764 and the Political Economy of Revolution* (Chapel Hill: University of North Carolina Press, 1973), pp. 24–37, 39–40, and Bray Hammond, *Banks and Politics in America: From the Revolution to the Civil War* (Princeton: Princeton University Press, 1991 [1957]), pp. 25–26.

80, The legal tender

British creditors' concerns: Ernst, *Money and Politics in America, 1755–1775*, pp. 40–41. The peace treaty: Anderson, *Crucible of War*, pp. 505–506. Louisbourg's destruction: James D. Kornwolf with Georgiana W. Kornwolf, *Architecture and Town Planning in Colonial North America*, vol. 1 (Baltimore: Johns Hopkins University Press, 2002), pp. 307–308.

80–81, After the joy

The war's impact on the economy and the postwar depression: Anderson, *Crucible of War*, pp. 583, 588–591. The collapse of the Amsterdam firm Gebroeders Neufville in the summer of 1763 led to a panic throughout northern Europe.

81, In a case

"any bargains, contracts . . . ": Anderson, *Crucible of War*, p. 584. Currency Act of 1764: Hammond, *Banks and Politics in America*, p. 26, and Ernst, *Money and Politics in America, 1755–1775*, pp. 43–88, 90–133.

81–82, On a summer night

The scene of the attack: Malcolm Freiberg, "Thomas Hutchinson and the Province Currency," *New England Quarterly* 30.2 (June 1957), pp. 207–208, and Edmund S. Morgan, "Thomas Hutchinson and the Stamp Act," *New England Quarterly* 21.4 (December 1948), pp. 459–460. *"threatened me with destruction . . . "*: from Hutchinson's letter to Henry Seymour Conway, dated October 1, 1765, quoted in Freiberg, "Thomas Hutchinson and the Province Currency," pp. 207–208. Hutchinson's refutation of the Declaration of Independence was entitled "Strictures Upon the Declaration of the Congress at Philadelphia: In a Letter to a Noble Lord," published in London in 1776.

82–83, The revolutionaries' first

Charles W. Calomiris, "Institutional Failure, Monetary Scarcity, and the Depreciation of the Continental," *Journal of Economic History* 48.1 (March 1988), pp. 55–57, and Ralph Volney Harlow, "Aspects of Revolutionary Finance, 1775–1783," *American Historical Review* 35.1 (October 1929), pp. 46–68. On June 22, 1775, the Continental Congress resolved to print bills of credit "for the defence of America"; see Worthington Chauncey Ford, ed., *Journals of the Continental Congress, 1774–1789*, vol. 2 (Washington, DC: Government Printing Office, 1905), p. 103. For the July 29 resolution concerning the retirement and redemption of continentals, see Ford, *Journals of the Continental Congress*, vol. 2, pp. 221–223. Franklin's designs: Jennifer J. Baker, *Debt, Speculation, and Writing in the Making of Early America* (Baltimore: Johns Hopkins University Press, 2005), pp. 74–75, and Benjamin H. Irvin, "Benjamin Franklin's 'Enriching Virtues,'" *Common-place: The Interactive Journal of Early American Life* 6.3 (April 2006), http://www.common-place.org.

83–84, Despite Franklin's graceful

Legal tender policies: S. P. Breckinridge, *Legal Tender: A Study in English and American Monetary History* (Chicago: University of Chicago Press, 1903), pp. 66–67. *"treated as an enemy . . . "*: from a resolution passed on January 11, 1776, in Worthington Chauncey Ford, ed., *Journals of the Continental Congress, 1774–1789*, vol. 4 (Washington, DC: Government Printing Office, 1906), p. 49.

Continental losing half its value in three weeks and the March 1780 issue: Ron Chernow, *Alexander Hamilton* (New York: Penguin Press, 2004), p. 137.

84, Although Congress made

States' paper money issues during the war: Breckinridge, *Legal Tender*, pp. 68–71. British counterfeiting: Scott, *Counterfeiting in Colonial America*, pp. 253–263. *"counterfeit Congress-Notes . . . "*: from a newspaper advertisement dated April 14, 1777, quoted in Scott, *Counterfeiting in Colonial America*, p. 254. *"too illiberal . . . "*: from a letter by the British commander, General Sir William Howe, to Washington, dated February 5, 1788, and quoted in Lynn Glaser, *Counterfeiting in America: The History of an American Way to Wealth* (Philadelphia: Clarkson N. Potter, 1968), p. 43. Capture of British warships with counterfeits aboard: Scott, *Counterfeiting in Colonial America*, p. 255; and Glaser, *Counterfeiting in America*, pp. 41–42.

84–85, The currency crisis

"I am so angry . . . ": from a letter by an unidentified Pennsylvanian, reproduced in Henry Phillips Jr., *Continental Paper Money: Historical Sketches of American Paper Currency, Second Series* (Roxbury, MA: W. Elliot Woodward, 1866), pp. 104–105.

85, Antigovernment feeling spilled

Shays's Rebellion: John R. Alden, *A History of the American Revolution* (New York: Da Capo, 1989 [1969]), pp. 508–511; Chernow, *Alexander Hamilton*, pp. 224–225; and Hammond, *Banks and Politics in America*, pp. 96–97. After 1779, the Congress stopped large-scale printing of continentals.

85–86, The United States faced

Impact of continentals crisis and states' paper money on financial thinking: Hammond, *Banks and Politics in America*, pp. 91–99. *"to ruin commerce . . . "*: from a letter by Washington to Jabez Bowen of Rhode Island, dated January 9, 1787, quoted in George Bancroft, *A Plea for the Constitution of the U.S. of America: Wounded in the House of Its Guardians* (New York: Harper & Brothers, 1886), p. 88.

86, Thomas Paine took

"is like putting . . . ": from Thomas Paine, *Dissertations on Government, the Affairs of the Bank, and Paper Money* (1786), in Thomas Paine, *Thomas Paine Reader*, ed. Michael Foot and Isaac Kramnick (London: Penguin Books, 1987), p. 193.

86, At the Constitutional Convention

Debate at the Constitutional Convention: Hammond, *Banks and Politics in America*, pp. 91–95. *"a friend to paper money"*: Max Farrand, ed., *The Records of the Federal Convention of 1787*, vol. 2 (New Haven: Yale University Press, 1911), p. 309.

86–87, Opposition was predictably

"if not struck out . . ." and *"reject the whole . . . "*: Farrand, *The Records of the Federal Convention*, p. 310.

CHAPTER FOUR

91, On New Year's Eve

St. George's United Methodist Church in Philadelphia was founded in 1769 and remains the oldest continuously used Methodist church in America. The Methodist vigil was called a "watch night"; see Karen B. Westerfield Tucker, *American Methodist Worship* (Oxford: Oxford University Press, 2001), pp. 65–67. Postwar growth in foreign trade and surge in patriotism: C. Edward Skeen, *1816: America Rising* (Lexington, KY: University Press of Kentucky, 2003), pp. 18–19, 27. War's effect on westward expansion: Donald R. Hickey, *The War of 1812: A Forgotten Conflict* (Urbana: University of Illinois Press, 1989), pp. 303–304. *"Come, let us . . . "*: from a hymn written by Charles Wesley, included in *Hymnal of the Methodist Episcopal Church With Tunes* (New York: Phillips & Hunt, 1882), p. 354.

91–92, About two hundred

The story of New Year's Eve at Bloody Run: Hill Wilson's testimony at Lewis's 1816 trial, *Commonwealth v. David Lewis*, Court of Oyer and Terminer, Bedford County (January and February Terms, 1816). The testimony appears in the fifty-eight pages of trial transcript recorded by someone working for Charles Huston, Lewis's defense lawyer, and currently held by the Centre County Library and Historical Museum in Bellefonte, Pennsylvania. The pages are difficult to read, but portions of them are transcribed in a pair of articles written for a special edition of *Centre County Heritage* devoted entirely to Lewis: Douglas Macneal, "Uttering, Publishing and Passing—Counterfeiting in 1816" and "A Suspicious Camp, an Arrest in Bedford, and Showdown on the Sinnemahoning," both in *Centre County Heritage* 24.2 (Fall 1987). All dialogue is taken from Wilson's statements.

92, Lewis was a man

Physical description of Lewis: *American Volunteer*, May 9, 1816, and the record of Philadelphia's Walnut Street Jail, where Lewis arrived as a prisoner in June 1816, both quoted in Mark Dugan, *The Making of Legends: More Stories of Frontier America* (Athens, OH: Swallow Press/Ohio University Press, 1997), pp. 34–35.

92, Wilson the tavern keeper

Wilson was anxious because he feared how Lewis might react. "I felt uneasy," he explains in his testimony, "because [Lewis] was suspected."

93, The sheriff later

"Lewis said he . . . ": from the testimony of Thomas Moore, the sheriff, included in the fifty-eight-page trial transcript.

94, Lewis had every

Description of the jail: *History of Bedford, Somerset and Fulton Counties, Pennsylvania* (Chicago: Waterman, Watkins, 1884), pp. 196–197. Scenic details of Bedford: Fortescue Cuming, *Cuming's Tour to the Western Country (1807–1809)*, vol. 4 of *Early Western Travels*, ed. Reuben Gold Thwaites (Cleveland: A. H. Clark, 1904 [1810]), p. 65. The coalfields were located at Broad Top Mountain, in northeastern Bedford County. Samuel Riddle, a lawyer who played a major role in Lewis's prosecution, was the first to mine coal there and ship it commercially; see John Woolf Jordan, ed., *A History of the Juniata Valley and Its People*, vol. 1 (New York: Lewis Historical Publishing Company, 1913), p. 306.

94, Lewis was virtually

"a man calling . . . ": American Volunteer, January 18, 1816.

94–95, Despite his apparent

The facts of Lewis's childhood and early life are hard to come by, not only because of the ever-present problem of a thin paper trail, but also because of a spurious confession that appeared after his death in 1820. The confession, which purported to be written by Lewis in his jail cell in Bellefonte but which was in fact forged, offered false information about his life that subsequent genealogists incorporated into their histories. One resident of central Pennsylvania was so enraged by the confession's inaccuracy that he wrote a letter, published in the *American Volunteer*, September 21, 1820, offering many corrections. He gave Lewis's birthplace as "*Bald-Eagle Valley*, on the banks of the Bald-Eagle creek, about half a mile below the Bald-Eagle Nest." This is corroborated by records showing that Lewis Lewis, David Lewis's father, lived in the region that later became Upper Bald Eagle township in 1787—roughly a year before the counterfeiter's birth—according to John Blair Linn, *History of Centre and Clinton Counties, Pennsylvania* (Philadelphia: Louis H. Everts, 1883), p. 23. The year of Lewis's birth is debated, but 1788 is the best estimate. Mac E. Barrick, in "Who Was Lewis the Robber?" *Cumberland County History* 6.2 (Winter 1989), p. 55, gives 1788 as his birth year after looking at the records of the Philadelphia penitentiary that he entered in 1816, which listed him as twenty-eight years old. Lewis Lewis's life: Rosalie Jones Dill, *Mathew Dill Genealogy: A Study of the Dill Family of Dillsburg, York County, Pennsylvania, 1698–1935*, pt. 2 (Spokane, WA: 1935), pp. 17–18. The vigilantes that stormed Philadelphia, known as the Paxton Boys: Walter Isaacson, *Benjamin Franklin: An American Life* (New York: Simon & Schuster, 2003), pp. 210–213. The 1774 war was called Lord Dunmore's War, after the Virginia governor (John Murray, fourth Earl of Dunmore) who provoked it; see John Grenier, *The First Way of War: American War Making on the Frontier, 1607–1814* (Cambridge: Cambridge University Press, 2005), pp. 148–151.

95, Surveying was a

Colonial land surveying: William E. Burns, *Science and Technology in Colonial America* (Westport, CT: Greenwood, 2005), pp. 101–102. Lewis Lewis's surveying career: Dill, *Mathew Dill Genealogy*, pp. 17–18.

95–96, Despite the danger

Lewis's landholdings and list of possessions sold after his death: Dill, *Mathew Dill Genealogy*, pp. 18, 21.

96, Lewis Lewis's background

Lewis Lewis's education and pedigree: ibid., pp. 17, 19–20. Jane Dill's reputation for horsemanship and Presbyterianism: ibid., p. 21. The marriage: ibid., p. 18.

96, By the time

Eight children: ibid., pp. 23–25. The cooling of the Pennsylvania frontier: C. Hale Sipe, *The Indian Wars of Pennsylvania: An Account of the Indian Events, in Pennsylvania, of the French and Indian War, Pontiac's War, Lord Dunmore's War, the Revolutionary War and the Indian Uprising from 1789 to 1795* (Lewisburg, PA: Wennawoods, 1995 [1929]), pp. 709–715. Bald Eagle Creek's name: Paul A. W. Wallace, *Indians in Pennsylvania* (Harrisburg: Commonwealth of Pennsylvania,

2005 [1961]), p. 173. The naming of Bloody Run: Charles Augustus Hanna, *The Wilderness Trail*, vol. 1 (New York: G. P. Putnam's Sons, 1911), pp. 277–278.

97, Lewis never had

Lewis Lewis died sometime before 1790, according to Dugan, *The Making of Legends*, p. 20. Jane's remarriage and *"loving wife, Jane"*: Dill, *Mathew Dill Genealogy*, p. 17. Jane's arrival in Clearfield: Roland D. Swoope Jr., *Twentieth Century History of Clearfield County, Pennsylvania, and Representative Citizens* (Chicago: Richmond-Arnold, 1911), p. 28.

97–98, In the fall

Physical description of Brock: Robert Malcolmson, *A Very Brilliant Affair: The Battle of Queenston Heights, 1812* (Annapolis: Naval Institute Press, 2003), p. 35. Brock's early life: Mary Beacock Fryer, *Bold, Brave, and Born to Lead: Major General Isaac Brock and the Canadas* (Toronto: Dundurn, 2004), pp. 31–32. Brock's efforts to transfer out of Canada: Ven Begamudré, *Isaac Brock: Larger Than Life* (Montreal: XYZ Publishing, 2005), p. 112. Overview of Brock's career: Wesley B. Turner, "Brock, Isaac," *Encyclopedia of the War of 1812*, ed. David Stephen Heidler and Jeanne T. Heidler, (Annapolis: Naval Institute Press, 2004 [1997]), pp. 62–63.

98, On the other

Standoff across the river: Hickey, *The War of 1812*, p. 86. Relationship between Prevost and Brock: John K. Mahon, *The War of 1812* (New York: Da Capo, 1991 [1972]), p. 19, and Malcolmson, *A Very Brilliant Affair*, pp. 47, 75. *"[T]he population, believe me . . . "*: quoted in Malcolmson, *A Very Brilliant Affair*, p. 76. *"the most abandoned . . . "*: quoted in Mahon, *The War of 1812*, p. 19.

98–99, One of these

The account of Lewis's capture and near execution comes from his mentor Philander Noble, who in 1813 was arrested and examined on suspicion of being a British spy in Bellefonte, Pennsylvania. Noble's testimony, along with the writ of mittimus ordering his arrest and testimony from others, appears in the Bellefonte Court of Common Pleas (or Quarter Sessions) records from April 1813 under the heading "United States v. Philander N. Noble," although it's unlikely the case ever went to trial. These documents are held by the Centre County Library and Historical Museum in Bellefonte, Pennsylvania; for a transcription and discussion of their contents, see Douglas Macneal, "Amplification: David Lewis in Centre County in 1813," *Centre County*

Heritage 26.1 (Spring 1989), pp. 27–33. In what follows, I'll be referring extensively to the testimony from Noble's espionage hearing, because it provides a rare glimpse of Lewis's early career. Brock as disciplinarian: Malcolmson, *A Very Brilliant Affair*, p. 35.

99, Fortunately for Lewis

The Battle of Queenston Heights: Hickey, *The War of 1812*, pp. 86–87, and Turner, "Brock, Isaac," p. 63. A vivid firsthand account of the assault and Brock's death is a letter from an officer named Sir John Beverley Robinson, found in Charles Walker Robinson, *Life of Sir John Beverley Robinson* (Toronto: Morang, 1904), pp. 33–39.

99, The battle that

Lewis told Noble he escaped from jail when it was set on fire from the cannonading across the river. This would have been in mid-November, when an artillery duel erupted after the expiration of a brief armistice; see Mahon, *The War of 1812*, pp. 82–83. The exchange of fire continued through November 21, and left six men dead, a few wounded, and extensive property damage. Eyewitness account of the destruction from the American side: E. Cruikshank, ed., *The Documentary History of the Campaign upon the Niagara Frontier in the Year 1812, Part IV, October, November and December* (Welland, ON: Lundy's Lane Historical Society, n.d.), pp. 233–235.

99–100, Lewis was twenty-four

Children of Jane Dill and Lewis Lewis: Dill, *Mathew Dill Genealogy*, pp. 23–25. The story of Lewis's desertion from the army has a complicated provenance. In the writ of mittimus ordering Noble's arrest in 1813, the justices wrote, "David Lewis is generally understood and known to have deserted some years ago from the Army of the United States and eloped to the said province of Upper Canada." A witness at Noble's espionage hearing, William Robinson, offered further confirmation: "The old woman his mother told me that he had been condemned to be shot but that she had got him cleared." Finally, Sheriff Moore, when posting a reward for Lewis's capture in 1816, claimed that Lewis "has been in the Army of the United States, from which he deserted." All of this strongly suggests that Lewis deserted, although it's not known exactly when or from which company, as no records exist of the court-martial. Mark Dugan contacted the National Archives in Washington, DC, and the archivists couldn't find Lewis's case, although the files are incomplete before 1809. Thriving counterfeiting trade along the Canadian border: Stephen Mihm, *A Nation of Counterfeiters: Capitalists, Con Men, and the Making of the United States* (Cambridge, MA: Harvard University Press, 2007), pp. 64–66.

100, Like their colonial

Enforcement problem along Canadian border: Mihm, *A Nation of Counterfeiters*, pp. 64–66. Mihm's discussion focuses on Stephen Burroughs, a famous counterfeiter who operated in present-day Quebec. According to the Randolph, Vermont, newspaper the *Weekly Wanderer*, July 27, 1807, Lewis's mentor Philander Noble was a close associate of Burroughs.

100, One of these

Noble was in Vermont as early as July 1807, when he was arrested for counterfeiting near Plymouth. He bounced back and forth across the border: in September 1809, he was in Canada, arrested at Niagara, the same place where Lewis almost lost his life. See *Weekly Wanderer*, July 27, 1807; *Vermont Precursor*, July 31, 1807; *Otsego Herald*, November 4, 1809; and *Connecticut Herald*, November 14, 1809. A small report from the *Weekly Wanderer*, February 23, 1810, provides a possible lead of Lewis's whereabouts during this period: the article states that David Lewis, "a transient person," has been sentenced to prison in Burlington for seven years for passing counterfeit bills. It's impossible to know whether this is the same David Lewis that grew up in Pennsylvania, but the timing and location certainly makes it plausible.

100–101, The two men

Noble's physical appearance: *American Volunteer*, May 9, 1816, quoted in Dugan, *The Making of Legends*, p. 23. His date of birth (April 1772) and occupation: Lucius Manlius Boltwood, *History and Genealogy of the Family of Thomas Noble, of Westfield, Massachusetts* (Hartford: Case, Lockwood & Brainard, 1878), p. 648. Westfield's history: Josiah Gilbert Holland, *History of Western Massachusetts: The Counties of Hampden, Hampshire, Franklin, and Berkshire*, vol. 1 (Springfield, MA: Samuel Bowles, 1855), p. 66. "*I performed the task . . .* ": from Noble's 1800 letter to William Shepard, reproduced in John H. Lockwood, *Westfield and Its Historic Influences 1669–1919: The Life of an Early Town, with a Survey of Events in New England and Bordering Regions to Which It Was Related in Colonial and Revolutionary Times*, vol. 2 (Westfield, MA: printed by the author, 1922), p. 188.

101, For a young

In his testimony at his 1813 espionage hearing, "United States v. Philander N. Noble," Noble claims to have moved to Vermont in 1803. He was certainly there by 1807, when he was arrested near Plymouth.

101–102, The summer of 1807

The scene: *Weekly Wanderer*, July 27, 1807, and *Vermont Precursor*, July 31, 1807. *"with sincere pleasure . . . "*: *Weekly Wanderer*, July 27, 1807. Noble's arrest and conviction in Upper Canada in 1809: *Otsego Herald*, November 4, 1809.

102, The mechanics of moneymaking

The *Vermont Precursor,* July 31, 1807, mentions "four coppers prepared for engraving" discovered in the counterfeiters' hideout.

102–103, The bills strewn

The banknotes that Noble forged: *Weekly Wanderer*, July 27, 1807, and *Vermont Precursor*, July 31, 1807. Origins of American banks and banknotes: Bray Hammond, *Banks and Politics in America: From the Revolution to the Civil War* (Princeton: Princeton University Press, 1991 [1957]), pp. 3–171. "The notes the banks issued were," he writes on p. 71, "in form if not in essence, just another variety of paper money."

103, Local governments had

Though the first note-issuing banks predated the Constitution's ban on the states printing paper money, the prohibition forced the states to use banks to get currency into circulation, even if the notes couldn't be made legal tender. The conservative banking world of 1787: Hammond, *Banks and Politics in America*, pp. 74–77, 105. *"hostages to be . . . "*: from Thomas Paine's *Dissertations*, quoted ibid., p. 61.

103–104, Most of the Constitution's

Banking at the Constitutional Convention: Hammond, *Banks and Politics in America,* pp. 103–106.

104, The silence was significant

Hamilton's idea for the Bank of the United States: ibid., pp. 40–42, 114–115.

105, As could be

Debate over the Bank: ibid., pp. 114–122. The Senate passed the bill on January 20, 1791; the House passed it on February 8, 1791. Washington used as much time as allowed by the Constitution to decide whether or not to veto it. His secretary of state, Thomas Jefferson, and his attorney general, Edmund Randolph, told him it was unconstitutional.

105, Although Hamilton got

The conservative mercantile banks: ibid., pp. 74–77.

105–106, In the last

The changing face of the American banking world and the economy as a whole: ibid., pp. 67–74, 145–149.

106, When Noble wrote

There were 29 banks in 1800, 90 in 1811, and 246 in 1816, according to Hammond, in *Banks and Politics in America*, pp. 144–146. Checks exerted by Bank: ibid., pp. 198–199. Debate over renewing Bank's charter: ibid., pp. 222–226. An overview of the banking boom triggered by the Bank's fall: Mihm, *A Nation of Counterfeiters*, pp. 110–111.

106–107, Noble's experience

"a great evil": from James Madison's reply to Charles Jared Ingersoll, dated February 2, 1831, included in M. St. Clair Clarke and D. A. Hall, eds., *Legislative and Documentary History of the Bank of the United States: Including the Original Bank of North America* (Washington, DC: Gales and Seaton, 1832), p. 778.

107, In 1813, as

America's wartime financial woes: Hickey, *The War of 1812*, pp. 113–119, 222–225. Lewis returned to Bellefonte at least twice before moving back to Pennsylvania permanently in 1813: at Noble's espionage hearing, "United States v. Philander N. Noble," Thomas Lewis testified that he had seen his brother in Bellefonte in the summer of 1812, and Isaac Buffington declared that he had seen Lewis in Bellefonte during the winter of 1810–1811.

107–108, Around midday in

The details of Noble's arrival are drawn from Thomas Lewis's and Aaron Ellis's testimony at Noble's espionage hearing. In his testimony in "United States v. Philander N. Noble," Noble claimed that Lewis "sent a line" through Noble to his wife, and that she then handed the message to Thomas Lewis—perhaps this note contained instructions regarding Noble. Who was Lewis's wife? In his testimony, Aaron Ellis declared that "Margarate Lewis," who lived with Jane Leathers (formerly Jane Lewis), "says she is the wife of David Lewis." But there is no reference in the genealogical record to David Lewis's marriage, and the name Margarate or Margaret Lewis doesn't surface again in Lewis's paper trail. Perhaps they weren't legally married; in any case, nothing firm exists about their relationship.

108, While a brilliant

Noble and Lewis first arrived in Bellefonte on March 28, 1813; a week later, April 4, 1813, Noble was brought before two justices of the peace, William Petrikin and Elisha Moore, for examination on suspicion of being a British spy. *"[I]t is the duty . . . "*: from the writ of mittimus ordering Noble's arrest. *"his capers"*: Isaac Buffington's testimony at Noble's hearing, "United States v. Philander N. Noble." The claim that Noble had a gun: Aaron Ellis's testimony. *"about who he was . . . "*: William Robinson's testimony. *"strange man"*: Isaac Buffington's testimony.

108–109, It's doubtful that

"I do not know . . . ": Thomas Lewis's testimony, "United States v. Philander N. Noble." Two other witnesses, William Robinson and Isaac Buffington, claimed Thomas was present when they saw Lewis and Noble together, and one of those times was at Thomas's own house (the other was at his mother's).

109, Even though the

A glance at the handwriting of the original record gives a sense of Noble's scattered speaking style—it was clearly written in haste, and Noble's abrupt conversational jumps didn't make transcribing his words any easier. In their writ of mittimus, the justices acknowledged the chaotic quality of Noble's testimony, declaring that he had "stated many contradi[cti]ons in the account he gives of himself and of his business."

109, The next day

Noble had two days of testimony in "United States v. Philander N. Noble": April 4, 1813, and April 5, 1813. On April 4, he didn't tell the full story of his journey to Canada but did offer a few sentences on crossing the St. Lawrence River with someone named Brown—omitting Lewis, of course. On April 5, he admitted that

Lewis was present along with Brown, and gave a much more detailed account of the trip. It's unknown who Brown was, as he doesn't seem to have accompanied them to Bellefonte. Benjamin Forsyth: Richard V. Barbuto, "Forsyth, Benjamin," *Encyclopedia of the War of 1812*, p. 191. Width of the St. Lawrence: C. P. Lucas, *The Canadian War of 1812* (Oxford: Clarendon, 1906), p. 83.

109-110, If the travelers

The Battle of Ogdensburg: Lucas, *The Canadian War of 1812*, pp. 82-84. At his espionage hearing, "United States v. Philander N. Noble," Noble alleged that he and Lewis came to Ogdensburg "a few days" before the British attack; if the story is true, this would be around February 19, 1813. Although nothing else exists in the record after Noble's last day of testimony, the case was almost certainly dropped for lack of evidence. A conviction would mean death; the engraver was alive and well two years later, when he and Lewis counterfeited currency at a mountain campsite.

110, Noble and Lewis

Contemporary observers commented on the resemblance between bankers and counterfeiters. Mihm, in *A Nation of Counterfeiters*, pp. 8-9, quotes Hezekiah Niles—the Baltimore-based editor whose *Weekly Register* was a popular newsmagazine—and John Quincy Adams discussing the similarity between the two.

110-111, The war with

Illicit trade with the British: Hickey, *The War of 1812*, p. 224. Bill authorizing new Pennsylvania banks: Hammond, *Banks and Politics in America*, p. 165.

111, Horrified at the prospect

"*Eastern mercantile cupidity . . .* ": quoted in Henry Adams, *History of the United States of America During the Second Administration of James Madison*, vol. 2 (New York: Charles Scribner's Sons, 1921), p. 16. Snyder vetoed the measure on March 19; it was passed over his objections on March 21. Soaring number of notes in circulation: Hickey, *The War of 1812*, p. 224.

111-112, Skyrocketing quantities of

Invasion of the Chesapeake and razing of Washington: Hickey, *The War of 1812*, pp. 195-202. Subsequent panic and bank suspension: Hammond, *Banks and Politics in America*, pp. 227-230, and Hickey, *The War of 1812*, pp. 224-225.

112, The federal government

Efforts to fund the war are outlined in Curtis P. Nettels, *The Emergence of a National Economy, 1775–1815* (Armonk, NY: M. E. Sharpe, 1989 [1962]), pp. 331–333. Federal government's financial distress: Hickey, *The War of 1812*, pp. 222–225; Hammond, *Banks and Politics in America*, pp. 227–230; and Edwin J. Perkins, "Financing the War of 1812," *Encyclopedia of the War of 1812*, p. 184. Suspension of specie payments didn't end until February 1817, and even then, resumption wasn't universal and banknotes continued to circulate at a discount depending on the institution; see Hammond, *Banks and Politics in America*, pp. 246–250.

112–113, Anyone who glimpsed

Scenic details of the Allegany range: James Flint, *Flint's Letters from America, 1818–1820*, vol. 9 of *Early Western Travels, 1748–1846*, ed. Reuben Gold Thwaites (Cleveland: A. H. Clark, 1904 [1822]), pp. 74–77; Thaddeus Mason Harris, *Journal of a Tour into the Territory Northwest of the Alleghany Mountains*, vol. 3 of *Early Western Travels, 1748–1846*, ed. Reuben Gold Thwaites (Cleveland: A. H. Clark, 1904 [1805]), pp. 325–329; and Morris Birkbeck, *Notes on a Journey in America, From the Coast of Virginia to the Territory of Illinois* (London: Severn, 1818 [1817]), pp. 30–35. Traveling in September 1818, Flint observed large numbers of westward-bound homesteaders, "chiefly occasioned by people in the eastern States having reaped and disposed of their crops at this season, and on that account finding it a convenient time for removing to the western country." A word on the geography: what was known as the Allegany range is located about fifteen miles west of Bedford and labeled on a map of Pennsylvania in the 1814 edition of Mathew Carey's *General Atlas*, http://www.mapsofpa.com/19thcentury/1814carey.jpg. The Alleghenies, on the other hand, is a term that was used by people in Lewis's day to refer to the entire mountainous region in central Pennsylvania, which forms a part of the massive Appalachian Mountains system.

113, The scenery was

The account of the campsite: from testimony at Lewis's 1816 trial by Michael Miller, a local tavern keeper who saw the counterfeiters frequently, and Jacob Kinsey, a German immigrant who stumbled across the hideout on a hunting trip. Their statements appear in the fifty-eight handwritten pages of trial transcript; portions of their testimony are transcribed in Macneal, "A Suspicious Camp, An Arrest in Bedford, and Showdown on the Sinnemahoning," pp. 36–38.

113, If the walls

Details drawn from Michael Miller's testimony. Miller stated that Lewis and Smith first came to his tavern on September 5, 1815; three days later they were joined by Noble and Crosby, who brought the wagon and trunks. Noble "talked a little like a Yanky," according to Miller. Description of James Smith: *American Volunteer*, May 9, 1816.

113-114, Miller might have had

"They gave me the Jug almost full—I write with it steady," said Miller at Lewis's trial. The trunks no doubt held counterfeiting tools. One witness at Lewis's trial, Elie Beatty, speculated that a trunk of that size "would contain paper and plates to print 50,000 Dolls. of 100s, 50s, and 20s."

114, It had been

Miller testified the counterfeiters stayed for three weeks: from September 5 to September 26, 1815. He visited the camp three weeks after they left, and found that almost nothing remained, except for the knife and the hut.

114, Lewis and his

Different types of bad bills: Macneal, "Uttering, Publishing and Passing—Counterfeiting in 1816," p. 31, and Lynn Glaser, *Counterfeiting in America: The History of an American Way to Wealth* (Philadelphia: Clarkson N. Potter, 1968), p. 273.

115, These creative swindles

Newspapers had printed information about how to detect counterfeit bills since the colonial era, and the tradition continued into the nineteenth century: Baltimore editor Hezekiah Niles was particularly outspoken, and used his *Weekly Register* to draw attention to the problem. The first banknote reporter/counterfeit detector probably appeared in 1805, printed by the publishers of the Boston-based newspaper the *Centinel*. The format proved enormously popular, and beginning in the 1820s, banknote reporters came into wide use; see Glaser, *Counterfeiting in America*, pp. 87–89, and Mihm, *A Nation of Counterfeiters*, pp. 235–253.

115-116, The dizzying diversity

Fluctuating values of different notes: Mihm, *A Nation of Counterfeiters*, pp. 248–250, and Macneal, "Uttering, Publishing and Passing—Counterfeiting in 1816," pp. 28–29. Rates in Baltimore in 1818: Macneal, "Uttering, Publishing and Passing—Counterfeiting in 1816," p. 29. For an example of a local newspaper publishing discount rates, see the Reading, Pennsylvania-based *Berks and Schuylkill Journal*, February 8, 1817. Opportunities for currency speculation were no secret; a letter to the *Weekly Aurora*, July 14, 1817, describes a scheme for exploiting the exchange rate between Philadelphia and Cincinnati paper.

116, All of this

The notes Lewis, Noble, and company counterfeited: *American Volunteer*, January 18, 1816, and testimony from Lewis's 1816 trial. Noble disappeared after he and Lewis parted ways at the end of September 1815. According to an article in the *Bedford Gazette*, April 13, 1816, reprinted in the *American Volunteer*, May 9, 1816, the engraver returned to Canada.

116–117, After splitting with

Lewis's aliases: testimony from several witnesses at his 1816 trial. A rough time line of Lewis's journey: Douglas Macneal, "A Brief Chronology of Firm Dates in David Lewis's Life," *Centre County Heritage* 24.2 (Fall 1987), pp. 23–24. For a map of the counties that Lewis traveled through, see the map in the 1814 edition of Mathew Carey's *General Atlas*, http://www.mapsofpa.com/19thcentury/1814carey.jpg. Descriptions of the different counties: Charles B. Trego, *A Geography of Pennsylvania* (Philadelphia: Edward C. Biddle, 1843), pp. 183–187, 247–248, 295–296.

117, On the last

Account drawn entirely from James Shoaff's testimony at Lewis's 1816 trial, as recorded in the fifty-eight pages of trial transcript.

118, Sometimes Lewis relied

Account drawn entirely from Thomas McClellan's testimony at Lewis's 1816 trial, as recorded in the fifty-eight pages of trial transcript.

CHAPTER FIVE
120, In the first

Description of Bedford: Fortescue Cuming, *Cuming's Tour to the Western Country, 1807–1809*, vol. 4 of *Early Western Travels*, ed. Reuben Gold Thwaites (Cleveland: A. H. Clark, 1904 [1810]), p. 65, and *North View of Bedford, PA* (1840), a drawing by Augustus Kollner. Town's chaotic mood in early 1816: Ned Frear, *Davey Lewis* (Frear Publications, 1999), pp. 11–13. Frear, the former publisher of the *Bedford Gazette* (published since 1805 and still in print), includes excerpts from old, hard-to-find issues of the *Gazette* and snippets of letters written by local lawyers. There are no exact population figures for Bedford in 1816: the 1810 census was destroyed in a fire, and the 1820 census puts the population of Bedford borough at 789.

120–121, Among its buildings

Bedford's houses: Cuming, *Cuming's Tour to the Western Country*, p. 65. Courthouse jail: *History of Bedford, Somerset and Fulton Counties, Pennsylvania* (Chicago: Waterman, Watkins, 1884), pp. 196–197, and Mark Dugan, *The Making of Legends: More Stories of Frontier America* (Athens, OH: Swallow Press/Ohio University Press, 1997), p. 40. Nightly guard at the jail: from a letter by David Mann to John Tod, dated January 18, 1816, in the "John Tod Papers, 1783–1838," Manuscript Group 126, "John Tod Papers, 1783–1838," Box 6: General Correspondence, 1816–1818, in the Pennsylvania State Archives in Harrisburg. Ned Frear uncovered the letters written by Bedford lawyers about the case to John Tod, and draws on them extensively in his *Davey Lewis*. *"You cannot conceive . . . ":* from a letter by James Carson to John Tod, dated January 15, 1816, in the "John Tod Papers, 1783–1838"; in the same letter, Carson says that "secret spies," or informers, were coming to Bedford in droves. "Proof is pouring in from every direction," declared the *Bedford Gazette*, quoted in Frear, *Davey Lewis*, p. 11.

121, The man at the

"in his element . . . ": from a letter by James Carson to John Tod, dated January 15, 1816, in the "John Tod Papers, 1783–1838." Description and background of Samuel Riddle: G. T. Ridlon, *History of the Ancient Ryedales and their Descendants in Normandy, Great Britain, Ireland, and America, from 860 to 1884* (Manchester, NH: published by the author, 1884), pp. 211–212. Riddle's coal business: John Woolf Jordan, ed., *A History of the Juniata Valley and Its People*, vol. 1 (New York: Lewis Historical Publishing Company, 1913), p. 306.

121–122, Trying to bring

Lewis identifying himself as David Wilson Lewis from Philadelphia: *Bedford Gazette*, quoted in Frear, *Davey Lewis*, p. 10. William Drenning's arrest: *Bedford Gazette*, quoted in Frear, *Davey Lewis*, p. 10. Drenning's son: *Poulson's American Daily Advertiser*, January 25, 1816.

122, As Riddle built

Lewis having $1,900 at the time of his arrest: *American Volunteer*, January 18, 1816. $1,500 in the bank: according to a local attorney named J. W. Sharpe, quoted in Frear,

Davey Lewis, p. 26. In the docket book for the trial held by the Pennsylvania State Archives in Harrisburg—*Commonwealth v. David Lewis*, Numbers 2, 3, 4, Docket of the 4th District, Court of Oyer and Terminer, Bedford County, Pennsylvania (January and February Terms, 1816)—the court states on January 5, 1816, that it cannot interfere with the defendant's decision to pay one of his lawyers, George Burd, Esq., $200. Philadelphia prices: *Grotjan's Philadelphia Public Sale Report*, January 1, 1816.

122, His costly defense

Burd and Huston as defense lawyers: Douglas Macneal, "Introducing David Lewis," *Centre County Heritage* 24.2 (Fall 1987), pp. 3–5. Description of Burd: Anne Royall, *Mrs. Royall's Pennsylvania, or Travels Continued in the United States*, vol. 1 (Washington, DC: Published by the author, 1829), p. 247. Huston: *Commemorative Biographical Record of Central Pennsylvania: Including the Counties of Centre, Clearfield, Jefferson and Clarion: Containing Biographical Sketches of Prominent and Representative Citizens, Etc.* (Chicago: J. H. Beers, 1898), pp. 23–24; *The Scotch-Irish in America: Proceedings and Addresses of the Eighth Congress, at Harrisburg, PA, June 4–7, 1896* (Nashville, TN: Scotch-Irish Society of America, 1897), pp. 167–168. *"slouched hat . . . "*: quoted in Macneal, "Uttering, Publishing and Passing—Counterfeiting in 1816," p. 34.

122–123, While Riddle and Huston

The *Gazette*'s history: *History of Bedford, Somerset and Fulton Counties*, pp. 226–227. For examples of the *Gazette*'s reports, see *Bedford Gazette*, January 4, 1816, reprinted in *Kline's Weekly Carlisle Gazette*, January 17, 1816, and *Bedford Gazette*, January 5–6, 1816, reprinted in *Poulson's American Daily Advertiser*, January 25, 1816.

123, In the pages

McDowell's articles: *Bedford Gazette*, January 11, 1816, reprinted in *Kline's Weekly Carlisle Gazette*, January 31, 1816, which includes the quote about "promising young men"; and *Bedford Gazette*, April 13, 1816, reprinted in *American Volunteer*, May 9, 1816.

123, The facts were

Reid's estimate: *American Volunteer*, January 18, 1816. The Carlisle-based *Volunteer* reprinted reports from the *Bedford Gazette*, as did the Philadelphia-based *Poulson's American Daily Advertiser* and several other papers throughout the state.

123–124, Lewis's trial was

Lewis's indictments: Dugan, *The Making of Legends*, p. 30, and available in greater detail in the Bedford court docket book.

124, Getting to the courtroom

Description of Judge Walker: quoted in Frear, *Davey Lewis*, p. 17. See the fifty-eight-page trial transcript for Riddle's line of attack.

124–125, The character that

"sociable & good humoured": from John H. Bridenthal's testimony, included in the fifty-eight pages of trial transcript. *"sporting man"*: from Moses Power's testimony. *"active in playing cards"*: from Henry Leeder's testimony. The date of Little's encounter with Lewis is uncertain: Little claimed it was on Christmas Day, while John Bridenthal said it was the day after. Little's story about gambling with Lewis was corroborated at the trial by John H. Bridenthal's testimony.

125, Lewis's years with

The tavern keeper was Christian Romer, who ran a tavern at the foot of Sideling Hill, and testified that he saw Lewis on December 12. Lewis even tried to convince Romer to sign the bills for him, but the tavern keeper refused.

125, Drawing on more

Number of witnesses on each side: Dugan, *The Making of Legends*, p. 30. For more on Huston's technique, see *Lancaster Journal*, March 13, 1816. A summary of Lewis's convictions and acquittals: Macneal, "Introducing David Lewis," pp. 3–5.

125–126, By protesting that

Motion filed by Huston about misspelling: Dugan, *The Making of Legends*, p. 31. *"with all convenient . . . "*: from the Bedford court docket book, dated February 22, 1816.

126, About an hour

Lewis escaping at 8:00 a.m.: from a letter by Joseph Morrison to John Tod, dated February 27, 1816, in "John Tod Papers, 1783–1838." The sun rose that day at 6:52 a.m., according to the U.S. Naval Observatory Astronomical Applications Department, Naval Oceanography Portal, http://www.usno.navy.mil. *"He could easily . . . "*: from a letter by J. W. Sharpe, Esq., quoted in Frear, *Davey Lewis*, p. 26.

126, The *Bedford Gazette*

Impact of Lewis's escape on the town and *Gazette* reports: Frear, *Davey Lewis*, pp. 22–25. *"penny-wise Commissioners . . . ": Bedford Gazette*, April 13, 1816, reprinted in *American Volunteer*, May 9, 1816. Reward for Lewis: *American Volunteer*, May 9, 1816. News of the sheriff's failed expedition and the demand for an inquiry: *Bedford Gazette*, March 18, 1816, reprinted in Dugan, *The Making of Legends*, p. 33. Lewis's capture: Dugan, *The Making of Legends*, p. 34.

126–127, Lewis arrived in

Lewis's date of arrival: Dugan, *The Making of Legends*, p. 34. The weather and its impact: C. Edward Skeen, *1816: America Rising* (Lexington, KY: University Press of Kentucky, 2003), pp. 1–4, 7–11. Temperature estimates: *Poulson's American Daily Advertiser*, June 12, 1816; June 5 was reportedly 82 degrees, and June 6 and 7 were approximately 52 degrees. Plentiful ice: J. Thomas Scharf and Thompson Westcott, *History of Philadelphia, 1609–1884*, vol. 2 (Philadelphia: L. H. Everts & Co., 1884), p. 938. Mary Shelley and the origins of *Frankenstein*: M. K. Joseph, "Appendix A: The Composition of *Frankenstein*," in Mary Wollstonecraft Shelley, *Frankenstein, or, The Modern Prometheus* (Oxford: Oxford University Press, 1998), pp. 224–227.

127, While passersby huddled

Description of the jail: James Mease and Thomas Porter, *Picture of Philadelphia, Giving an Account of Its Origin, Increase and Improvements in Arts, Sciences, Manufactures, Commerce and Revenue*, vol. 1 (Philadelphia: Robert Desilver, 1831), pp. 179–180, and Negley K. Teeters, *The Cradle of the Penitentiary: The Walnut Street Jail at Philadelphia, 1773–1835* (Philadelphia: Pennsylvania Prison Society, 1955), pp. 18–19, 93.

127–128, These buildings were

The band of reformers was called the Philadelphia Society for Alleviating the Miseries of Public Prisons, founded in 1787; see Teeters, *The Cradle of the Penitentiary*, pp. 29–35. Implementation of reforms: Cyndi Banks, *Punishment in America: A Reference Handbook* (Santa Barbara, CA: ABC-CLIO, 2005), pp. 36–37; Mitchel P. Roth, "Walnut Street Jail," *Prisons and Prison Systems: A Global Encyclopedia* (Westport, CT: Greenwood, 2006), pp. 292–293; and Teeters, *The Cradle of the Penitentiary*, pp. 36–44. The average number of prisoners from 1815 to 1824 was 331, according to LeRoy B. DePuy, in "The Walnut Street Prison: Pennsylvania's First Penitentiary," *Pennsylvania History* 18.2 (April 1951), p. 136.

128 The Walnut Street Jail housed

Decline of the Walnut Street Jail: DePuy, "The Walnut Street Prison: Pennsylvania's First Penitentiary," pp. 141–142; Teeters, *The Cradle of the Penitentiary*, pp. 96–103. Convict who sawed the iron off his leg: Teeters, *The Cradle of the Penitentiary*, p. 100.

129, The Walnut Street Jail's lawlessness

Use of informers: Teeters, *The Cradle of the Penitentiary*, p. 95. The text of the Walnut Street authorities' recommendation: The *Franklin Gazette*, June 5, 1820, published a response to allegations that Findlay pardoned Lewis for self-serving political reasons. Dated August 30, 1819, it read "The inspectors are induced to consider the said David Lewis as a suitable object for the clemency of the Governor, and respectfully recommend him to his excellency, for pardon of his offences, and remission of his fine, in consideration of his communicating information of an attempt to force the prison, by those confined in the same room with him."

129, When Lewis's pardon

Policy of freeing cooperative prisoners: Dugan, *The Making of Legends*, p. 35, and *American Volunteer*, July 6, 1820. Election of 1817 and its aftermath: Isaac Sharpless, *Two Centuries of Pennsylvania History* (Philadelphia: J. B. Lippincott, 1900), pp. 276–278, and Philip S. Klein and Ari Hoogenbloom, *A History of Pennsylvania: Second and Enlarged Edition* (University Park, PA: Pennsylvania State University, 1980), p. 133. Biography of William Findlay: William C. Armor, *Lives of the Governors of Pennsylvania, with the Incidental History of the State, From 1609 to 1873* (Norwich, CT: T. H. Davis, 1874), pp. 323–332.

129–130, On September 9, 1819

Date of Lewis's departure: Dugan, *The Making of Legends*, p. 35. Unemployment figure: from a city report commissioned in August 1819, summarized in Edward S. Kaplan, *The Bank of the United States and the American Economy* (Westport, CT: Greenwood, 1999), p. 67. Portions of the report were printed in local newspapers; see *Grotjan's Philadelphia Public Sale Report*, September 13, 1819, and the *Weekly Aurora*, September 13, 1819.

130, Lewis was witnessing

The Panic of 1819: Murray N. Rothbard, *The Panic of 1819: Reactions and Policies* (Auburn, AL: Ludwig von Mises Institute, 2007 [1962]), pp. 1–35; Kaplan, *The Bank of the United States*, pp. 67–75; and Samuel Rezneck, "The Depression of

1819–1822, A Social History," *American Historical Review* 39.1 (October 1933), pp. 28–47.

130–131, This period of false

Madison's about-face and the broader shift in Democratic-Republican financial policy: Bray Hammond, *Banks and Politics in America: From the Revolution to the Civil War* (Princeton: Princeton University Press, 1991 [1957]), pp. 230–241. Still standing today, Carpenters' Hall headquartered the first Bank from 1791–1797 and the Second Bank from 1817–1821; Robert Smith was the architect who designed Carpenters' Hall and the Walnut Street Jail, along with a handful of other important colonial-era buildings in Philadelphia. Resumption of specie payments in February 1817: Hammond, *Banks and Politics in America*, pp. 246–250, and Kaplan, *The Bank of the United States*, pp. 60–61.

131, Despite a strong start

The Bank's poor management and reasons for its contraction: Rothbard, *The Panic of 1819*, pp. 10–18; Kaplan, *The Bank of the United States*, pp. 69–70; and Hammond, *Banks and Politics in America*, pp. 251–258, 272–276.

132, This simple request

Effects of the contraction: Rothbard, *The Panic of 1819*, pp. 17–24. Urban unemployment and plummeting real estate prices: Rezneck, "The Depression of 1819–1822," pp. 30–34. Panic's origins: Stephen Mihm, *A Nation of Counterfeiters: Capitalists, Con Men, and the Making of the United States* (Cambridge, MA: Harvard University Press, 2007), pp. 111–112. Panic's impact on Ohio, Indiana, and other frontier areas of the Midwest: Mihm, *A Nation of Counterfeiters*, pp. 167–168. Reversion to a barter system: Rothbard, *The Panic of 1819*, p. 22.

132–133, Although the Panic

Agrarian rage provoked by the Panic: Hammond, *Banks and Politics in America*, pp. 258–259, 279–285.

133, Perversely, the easiest

The widespread anger over the spirit of speculation in general and the Bank in particular is evident from the newspapers of the period, particularly Hezekiah Niles's popular *Weekly Register*. Anti-Bank sentiment: Samuel Rezneck, "The Depression of 1819–1822, A Social History," pp. 36–40. Many state legislatures, responding to the outrage, passed taxes on the Bank's branches, until the Supreme Court, in *McCulloch v. Maryland*, established the legal precedent shielding the Bank from state taxation.

133–134, The rising populist

The social and economic foundations of the outlaw myth: E. J. Hobsbawm, *Bandits* (London: Weidenfeld and Nicolson, 1969), pp. 13–49, 72–83, 109–115. Origins of Lewis's Robin Hood reputation: Mac E. Barrick, "Lewis the Robber in Life and Legend," *Pennsylvania Folklife* 17.1 (August 1967), p. 13.

134, Lewis wasn't the

"If I was the witch . . . ": from a letter by John Adams to Joseph Ward, dated October 24, 1809, quoted in Malcolm Freiberg, "Thomas Hutchinson and the Province Currency," *New England Quarterly* 30.2 (June 1957), p. 190. In a later letter to John Taylor, dated March 12, 1819, Adams reminisces about having "seen a paper currency annihilated at a blow in Massachusetts" and discusses the dangers of paper money; see John Adams, *The Works of John Adams, Second President of the United States: With a Life of the Author, Notes and Illustrations*, vol. 10, ed. Charles Francis Adams (Boston: Little, Brown, 1856), pp. 375–377.

134–135, On a Sunday morning

McClelland's story is drawn entirely from two reports in the *Bedford Gazette*, both reprinted in the *American Volunteer*, October 14, 1819. The robbery took place on Sunday, October 3, 1819, on the turnpike at Sideling Hill in Bedford County.

135, At around nine o'clock

The robbers having their faces blackened: from Governor Findlay's proclamation of an award for their arrest, found in George Edward Reed, ed., *Pennsylvania Archives, Fourth Series*, vol. 5 (Harrisburg: State of Pennsylvania, 1900), pp. 148–149.

135, Just like the backcountry

Physical description of Connelly: *American Volunteer*, December 30, 1819; *Pittsburgh Gazette*, December 24, 1819; and William M. Hall, *Reminiscences and Sketches, Historical and Biographical* (Harrisburg: Meyers Printing House, 1890), p. 264. Hanson's height and bloodthirstiness: *American Volunteer*, October 14, 1819.

136, It was October 3

"*robbery of the most daring nature . . . *": *Bedford Gazette*, reprinted in *American Volunteer*, October 14, 1819. "*The reputation . . . *": from Findlay's announcement, included in Reed, *Pennsylvania Archives, Fourth Series*, vol. 5, pp. 148–149.

137, The night after

The taking of Lewis and his cronies: Dugan, *The Making of Legends*, pp. 37–38; *York Recorder*, quoted in Frear, *Davey Lewis*, p. 33.

138, Just before daybreak

The story of the October 25 escape is drawn entirely from the *Bedford Gazette*, quoted in Frear, *Davey Lewis*, pp. 34–36, and the *American Volunteer*, November 11, 1819.

138, Winter had drained

Painful swelling produced by Lewis's irons: *Pittsburgh Gazette*, December 24, 1819, and *Bedford Gazette*, quoted in Frear, *Davey Lewis*, p. 37.

138–139, On the horizon

The elevation of Kinton Knob is 2,642 feet, slightly taller than half a mile (2,640 feet). According to the *Bedford Gazette* reports, the posse spotted the criminals in the forest near Milligan Cove, a glen southwest of Kinton Knob, around 11:00 a.m. The sun rose in Bedford on October 25, 1819, at 6:35 a.m., according to the U.S. Naval Observatory Astronomical Applications Department, Naval Oceanography Portal, http://www.usno.navy.mil.

139, If the Bedford authorities

The December 16 jailbreak: *American Volunteer*, December 30, 1819.

139, They couldn't flee

"*fit to associate . . . *": *Pittsburgh Gazette*, January 14, 1820, also reprinted in *American Volunteer*, January 27, 1820.

140, Once out of the jail

Hanson's recapture and "*two of the most . . . *": *American Volunteer*, December 30, 1819.

140, Every Tuesday and Friday

The *Pittsburgh Gazette*: J. Cutler Andrews, *Pittsburgh's Post-Gazette: "The First Newspaper West of the Alleghenies"* (Boston: Chapman & Grimes, 1936), pp. 1, 55–61. Location of the newspaper's offices: Sarah H. Killikelly, *The History of Pittsburgh: Its Rise and Progress* (Pittsburgh: B. C. & Gordon Montgomery, 1906), p. 129. Layout of early Pittsburgh: the 1784 Survey & Town Plan by George Woods, http://www.mapsofpa.com/pitts/1784fromhopkins.jpg. The bridge opened in 1818, built of wood and iron and supported by stone piers; see George Thornton Fleming, *History of Pittsburgh and Environs*, vol. 2 (New York: American Historical Society, 1922), p. 177. Impact of the Panic on Pittsburgh: Richard C. Wade, *The Urban Frontier: The Rise of Western Cities, 1790–1830* (Urbana: University of Illinois Press, 1996 [1959]), pp. 161–169.

140, Founded in 1786

"silent as Sunday": Wade, *The Urban Frontier*, p. 168. Population of Pittsburgh: Joseph F. Rishel, *Founding Families of Pittsburgh: The Evolution of a Regional Elite, 1760–1910* (Pittsburgh: University of Pittsburgh Press, 1990), p. 46.

140–141, To this town

The *Gazette*'s high-minded editors and aversion to sensationalist crime stories: Andrews, *Pittsburgh's Post-Gazette*, pp. 58–61, 108. *"Many little traits . . . "*: *Pittsburgh Gazette*, January 14, 1820. As Mark Dugan points out in *The Making of Legends*, p. 40, the *Pittsburgh Gazette* article, reprinted throughout Pennsylvania, was the first to give Lewis "the mantle of a folk hero/bandit."

141, Even journalists who

"Bow down . . . ": *Weekly Aurora*, January 10, 1820. Newly aggressive spirit in business: Hammond, *Banks and Politics in America*, pp. 177, 252–253.

142, Newspapers were only

It's impossible to know when the folk stories first appeared. Since they don't appear in the spurious confession published after his death, they must have developed separately, and then passed down through the generations until they found their way into print. When C. D. Rishel reprinted Lewis's fake confession in 1890, he published a number of the folktales that had been included in the 1853 reprint of the confession; see C. D. Rishel, ed., *The Life and Adventures of David Lewis, the Robber and Counterfeiter, the Terror of the Cumberland Valley* (Whitefish, MT: Kessinger, 2006 [1890]), pp. 22–32. The widow story is perhaps the best known; Rishel's version appears on pp. 24–25, although the victim in his account is identified only as an "elderly female, of respectable appearance." William M. Hall, whose *Reminiscences and Sketches* also appeared in 1890, gives the story on pp. 250–251, noting that the victim was a "poor widow." The story proved remarkably durable through the decades. In 1966, Mac E. Barrick interviewed J. Raymond Baer, the owner of a Cumberland County feed mill, who told the widow story as it had been told to him by his father; see Mac E. Barrick, "Lewis the Robber in Life and Legend," p. 10.

142–143, Another story involved

Simmons's story: Rishel, *The Life and Adventures of David Lewis*, pp. 27–29.

143, In January 1820

Lewis's *in absentia* indictment: Dugan, *The Making of Legends*, p. 40. Text of the indictment: *Commonwealth v. David Lewis, John Conley & James Hanson*, Court of Oyer and Terminer, Bedford County, Pennsylvania (January Term, 1820), held by the Pennsylvania State Archives in Harrisburg.

CHAPTER SIX

144, The day after

Raguet: James M. Willcox, *A History of the Philadelphia Saving Fund Society, 1816–1916* (Philadelphia: J. B. Lippincott, 1916), pp. 11–12; Harold Milton Ellis, *Joseph Dennie and His Circle: A Study in American Literature From 1792 to 1812* (Austin: University of Texas, 1915), p. 203; and J. Thomas Scharf and Thompson Westcott, *History of Philadelphia, 1609–1884*, vol. 2 (Philadelphia: L. H. Everts & Co., 1884), pp. 1136, 1433. Raguet's articles on Haiti appeared in the Philadelphia-based *Poulson's American Daily Advertiser* and the periodical *Port Folio*. The pamphlet he published in 1815 was *An Inquiry into the Causes of the Present State of the Circulating Medium of the United States.*

144–145, No one in Pennsylvania

Significance of Raguet's report: Murray N. Rothbard, *The Panic of 1819: Reactions and Policies* (Auburn, AL: Ludwig von Mises Institute, 2007 [1962]), pp. 100–101. The committee was appointed on December 10, 1819, and its findings, "Report on the Causes and Extent of the Present General Distress," were read on January 29,

1820. Extracts are available in Appendix H of Condy Raguet, *A Treatise on Currency and Banking*, 2nd ed. (Philadelphia: Grigg & Elliot, 1840), pp. 289–306. *"inflicted upon the Commonwealth . . . "*: Raguet, *A Treatise on Currency and Banking*, p. 298. Excerpts from the memorials mailed to Raguet describing the distress in every part of Pennsylvania: Philip Shriver Klein, *Pennsylvania Politics, 1817–1832: A Game Without Rules* (Philadelphia: Historical Society of Pennsylvania, 1940), p. 108.

145, Raguet was right

Chambersburg and its bank: George Patterson Donehoo, *A History of the Cumberland Valley in Pennsylvania*, vol. 1 (Harrisburg: Susquehanna History Association, 1930), p. 312; the Chambersburg Community Development Committee, *Chambersburg: Its Record and Its Prospect* (Chambersburg, PA: Chamber of Commerce, 1945), pp. 20–21, 82–85; and Thaddeus Mason Harris, *Journal of a Tour into the Territory Northwest of the Alleghany Mountains*, vol. 3 of *Early Western Travels, 1748–1846*, ed. Reuben Gold Thwaites (Cleveland: A. H. Clark, 1904 [1805]), pp. 368–369. The text of the legislative bill chartering the Bank of Chambersburg along with many others is found in the *Lancaster Journal*, March 25, 1814. Discount rates: *Grotjan's Philadelphia Public Sale Report*, January 10, 1820. Almost a third of Pennsylvania's banks going bankrupt: Emma Lapsansky, "Building Democratic Communities, 1800–1850," in *Pennsylvania: A History of the Commonwealth*, ed. Randal M. Miller and William Pencak (University Park and Harrisburg, PA: Pennsylvania State University Press and the Pennsylvania Historical and Museum Commission, 2002), p. 165. *"A gentleman in . . . "*: *Carlisle Republican*, January 4, 1820.

145–146, On a Wednesday night

Jailbreak: *American Volunteer*, June 1, 1820. The jailbreak occurred on the night of Wednesday, May 24, 1820, and the early morning of Thursday, May 25. Description of the Chambersburg jail: the Chambersburg Community Development Committee, *Chambersburg*, p. 20. Cost of jail's construction: *Spirit of the Times & Carlisle Gazette*, May 4, 1818. Jail's reputation as strongest in the state: *American Volunteer*, April 27, 1820.

146, Lewis had been

According to the *American Volunteer*, April 27, 1820, Lewis and Connelly tried to rob a Cumberland County resident named Mr. Beshore on April 19; Lewis was captured but Connelly escaped. *"His life has been . . . "*: *Franklin Gazette*, April 29, 1820. Search for escapees: *American Volunteer*, June 1, 1820.

146, Six days later

The text of Findlay's proclamation, issued on May 31, 1820: George Edward Reed, ed., *Pennsylvania Archives, Fourth Series*, vol. 5 (Harrisburg: State of Pennsylvania, 1900), pp. 218–219. Findlay's incompetence and his response to the Panic: Klein, *Pennsylvania Politics*, pp. 96–99.

146–147, Findlay wasn't stupid

Biography of Findlay: William C. Armor, *Lives of the Governors of Pennsylvania, with the Incidental History of the State, From 1609 to 1873* (Norwich, CT: T. H. Davis, 1874), pp. 323–332. Pennsylvania's competing ethnic blocs: Klein, *Pennsylvania Politics*, pp. 5–13, 26. Election results of 1817: ibid., pp. 95–96. Patronage system established by state constitution of 1790: ibid., pp. 24–25. Findlay's impeachment proceedings: ibid., pp. 101–104. The inquiry proceeded from December 8, 1819, to February 3, 1820, and on February 16, Findlay was cleared of all charges.

147–148, As Findlay's opponents

Pennsylvania's partisan press: Klein, *Pennsylvania Politics*, pp. 59–63.

148, John McFarland, the

The era's rowdy newspapermen: ibid. McFarland: William H. Burkhart, *Cumberland Valley Chronicles: A Bicentennial History* (Shippensburg, PA: Shippensburg Historical Society/The News-Chronicle Company, 1976), pp. 154–155, and David Wilson Thompson, *Early Publications of Carlisle, Pennsylvania, 1785–1835* (Carlisle, PA: Sentinel, 1932), pp. 67–68. *"neck to heel"*: from the text of the indictment, quoted in Thompson, *Early Publications of Carlisle, Pennsylvania*, pp. 67–68.

148, Like many of the

The *Lancaster Weekly Journal*, June 4, 1817, claimed that Findlay's followers bought the Chambersburg newspaper after McFarland decided to support Findlay's opponent in the 1817 election; the *Weekly Aurora*, July 14, 1817, seconded this, adding that John Findlay, the governor's brother, was the one who had arranged the purchase. The *American Telegraph*, August 20, 1817, claimed that McFarland turned against Findlay because he hadn't been appointed the county treasurer when Findlay was state treasurer.

148-149, McFarland hammered Findlay

"We have fallen . . . ": *Carlisle Republican*, April 25, 1820. *"his respects . . . "*: *Carlisle Republican*, May 2, 1820. *"the trouble of signing . . . "*: *Carlisle Republican*, May 30, 1820. The suggestion that Findlay collaborated with Lewis: *Carlisle Republican*, July 4, 1820. The *Free Press*, June 1, 1820, contests the claim that Findlay visited the Chambersburg jail, writing that the governor, during his trip to the town, hadn't come "within one square" of the building. *"I laugh in my . . . "*: *Carlisle Republican*, June 13, 1820.

149, Lewis was only

Doubling Gap: H. H. Hain, *History of Perry County, Pennsylvania, Including Descriptions of Indian and Pioneer Life from the Time of Earliest Settlement* (Harrisburg: Hain-Moore Company, 1922), pp. 26–27, and C. D. Rishel, ed., *The Life and Adventures of David Lewis, the Robber and Counterfeiter, the Terror of the Cumberland Valley* (Whitefish, MT: Kessinger, 2006 [1890]), pp. 16–21.

149-150, By this point

Criminals' camp and lifestyle: *Bedford Gazette*, quoted in Ned Frear, *Davey Lewis* (Frear Publications, 1999), p. 39, and reprinted in *Free Press*, June 29, 1820; and *Poulson's American Daily Advertiser*, July 1, 1820. *"Lewis was a great . . . "*: reproduced in a footnote in Rishel, *The Life and Adventures of David Lewis*, p. 69. The statement is attributed to "R.M."; according to Frear, *Davey Lewis*, pp. 38–39, this "R.M." was the same Robert Moffitt whose tavern stood near the Doubling Gap hideout.

150-151, If Robert had

Rodney's escape and the *"yellow fellow"*: *Free Press*, June 29, 1820; *Poulson's American Daily Advertiser*, July 1, 1820; and *American Volunteer*, June 29, 1820. Rodney's returning home to his wife: *Baltimore Patriot & Mercantile Advertiser*, June 30, 1820, and Frear, *Davey Lewis*, p. 42. *"The cage was found . . . "*: *Franklin Repository*, June 27, 1820; "Caesar had described everything correctly," the *Repository* noted. *"We have been told . . . "*: *American Volunteer*, June 29, 1820.

151, The few weeks

Lewis and his band had fled the Doubling Gap camp by June 17, 1820, when they unsuccessfully tried to rob Eberly's home in Cumberland County; see *Harrisburg*

Chronicle, June 24, 1820, quoted in Mark Dugan, *The Making of Legends: More Stories of Frontier America* (Athens, OH: Swallow Press/Ohio University Press, 1997), pp. 46–47. The Eberly robbery attempt set off a spree that continued until roughly Sunday, June 25; see Dugan, *The Making of Legends*, pp. 46–48. Springhouses: Byron D. Halsted, ed., *Barns and Outbuildings and How to Build Them*, 2nd ed. (Guilford, CT: Lyons, 2008 [1881]), pp. 170–176.

151–152, Lewis's newly aggressive

"The country is kept . . . ": Harrisburg *Chronicle*, June 24, 1820, quoted in Dugan, *The Making of Legends*, p. 46. *"the daily accounts . . . "*: *Carlisle Republican*, July 4, 1820.

152, As Lewis stepped

Bonfire: *American Volunteer*, July 20, 1820. The *Volunteer* article seems to have been based in whole or in part on an article from the *Bellefonte Patriot*, July 8, 1820.

152, Lewis, Connelly, and McGuire

The robbery and the journey up Bald Eagle Creek: *American Volunteer*, July 20, 1820, and John Blair Linn, *History of Centre and Clinton Counties, Pennsylvania* (Philadelphia: Louis H. Everts, 1883), p. 61. Cost of stolen goods: Frear, *Davey Lewis*, p. 47.

152–153, The cost of leaving

Posse: *American Volunteer*, July 20, 1820, and Dugan, *The Making of Legends*, p. 49. *"a wild, unfrequented . . . "*: *Bellefonte Patriot*, quoted in Frear, *Davey Lewis*, p. 47.

153, Lewis and Connelly

Description of the region just north of the ranges in central Pennsylvania: I. D. Rupp, ed., *History and Topography of Northumberland, Huntingdon, Mifflin, Centre, Union, Columbia, Juniata and Clinton Counties, Pa.* (Lancaster, PA: Gilbert Hills, 1846), pp. 354–357, and Samuel Maclay, *Journal of Samuel Maclay, While Surveying the West Branch of the Susquehanna, the Sinnemahoning and the Allegheny Rivers, in 1790* (Williamsport, PA: John F. Meginness, 1887 [1790]), pp. 17, 35–36.

153–154, On Bennett's Branch

Sawmill: Maclay, *Journal of Samuel Maclay*, p. 24. After Frederick Leathers died, Lewis's mother, Jane, married a third time, to Reese Stevens; see Rosalie Jones

Dill, *Mathew Dill Genealogy: A Study of the Dill Family of Dillsburg, York County, Pennsylvania, 1698–1935*, pt. 2 (Spokane, WA: 1935), p. 17. By 1820, Jane and Reese Stevens lived in the valley of Bennett's Branch. David's brother Thomas Lewis also moved into the area in late 1817, near the village of Benezette on Bennett's Branch; see Dugan, *The Making of Legends*, p. 49. It's possible that Lewis visited his brother, although it's unknown if he even visited his mother. The 1820 census puts the number of residents in Bellefonte at 433. The posse's members questioning Jane: *American Volunteer*, July 20, 1820.

154, If she wouldn't

There are three slightly different accounts of the posse's pursuit of Lewis. I rely for the most part on the version in the *American Volunteer*, July 20, 1820, which, as noted above, is drawn from the *Bellefonte Patriot*, July 8, 1820. There are two later accounts, published in 1883 and 1890, respectively: Linn, *History of Centre and Clinton Counties*, p. 62, and Michael A. Leeson, ed., *History of the Counties of McKean, Elk, Cameron and Potter, Pennsylvania, with Biographical Selections*, vol. 2 (Chicago: J. H. Beers, 1890), pp. 384–385. Linn—who claims to have based his account on the testimony of a member of the posse—and Leeson—who spoke with a local resident named John Brooks—both report that the posse met William Shephard while traveling on the river, and that Shephard, along with Brooks, helped guide them to the robbers. Prevalence of mosquitoes and gnats along Bennett's Branch during the summer: Maclay navigated the same waterway in June 1790; see *Journal of Samuel Maclay*, p. 22. Heat and hardship: Frear, *Davey Lewis*, p. 51.

155, The plan failed

Both the *American Volunteer*, July 20, 1820, and Linn, *History of Centre and Clinton Counties*, p. 62, offer this version of the shootout. But Leeson, in *History of the Counties of McKean, Elk, Cameron and Potter*, pp. 384–385, in his most significant departure from the other accounts, includes this remarkable sentence: "Connelly seized his gun when the alarm was given, Lewis surrendered, and was shot in the arm afterward." This would mean that Lewis was deliberately injured by the posse when he was defenseless—although Leeson doesn't mention the wound in Lewis's leg. Leeson's account, based on the testimony of a local resident who claimed to have seen the shootout and published seventy years after the events took place, is probably the least reliable of the three. It's entirely possible, however, that the posse shot Lewis down in cold blood and then suppressed the true story. Detail about

Connelly's entrails: Linn, *History of Centre and Clinton Counties*, p. 62, and Frear, *Davey Lewis*, p. 51.

155, The posse treated

The *American Volunteer*, July 20, 1820, attributes Connelly's death to a "mortification" of the wound, meaning gangrene or necrosis; he died "in gloomy sullenness," the article added. Lewis's wounds: *American Volunteer*, July 20, 1820, and Linn, *History of Centre and Clinton Counties*, p. 62. Reception of posse in Bellefonte: Frear, *Davey Lewis*, p. 51.

155–156, They had reason

"gallant little band . . . ": *Bellefonte Patriot*, July 8, 1820, reprinted in *American Volunteer*, July 20, 1820. Doctor's examination: Linn, *History of Centre and Clinton Counties*, p. 62. Lewis's silence before his death is confirmed by a statement cosigned by Bellefonte's sheriff and jailer—John Mitchell and Joseph Williams—who said Lewis made "no manner of confession whatever, of his past life, other than what he made to the Minister of the Gospel who attended him," published in the *Bellefonte Patriot*, September 13, 1820, and reprinted in the *American Volunteer*, September 28, 1820. Lewis's last hours: from a letter by the attending minister, Reverend Linn, published in the *Bellefonte Patriot* and quoted in Frear, *Davey Lewis*, pp. 53–54. The location of Lewis's grave is a matter of dispute: the *American Volunteer*, July 27, 1820, claims Lewis was buried at Bellefonte, while Mark Dugan maintains he was buried with his family at the Milesburg cemetery about five miles away.

156, Newspapers throughout the

The *Bellefonte Patriot* report of Lewis's capture was reprinted in Philadelphia, Boston, and Norfolk, Virginia; the notice of his death was reprinted in Morristown, New Jersey, and Charleston, South Carolina. The *Alabama Watchman*, September 15, 1820, reported Lewis's arrest and his fatal injury. In the *Patriot* account of the pursuit that was widely reprinted, Lewis and his band are called "monsters," an indication of how much damage Lewis had done to his reputation in his final months.

157, On August 1, 1820

First installment of the confession: *Carlisle Republican*, August 1, 1820. Subsequent installments that year ran on August 15, August 22, September 5, September 12, September 19, September 30, and October 6. McFarland published the full confession as a pamphlet on October 25, 1820, and copyrighted it. A copy of the first edition is held by the Waidner-Spahr Library, Archives and Special Collections at Dickinson College in Carlisle, Pennsylvania.

157, People familiar with

"several detached sheets ... ": *Carlisle Republican,* August 8, 1820. When McFarland complained about the illegible handwriting as an excuse for not printing another installment, he was probably stalling for time until the next chunk of the confession had been written. *"David Lewis never uttered ... ":* from a letter by a Centre County resident to a Cumberland County resident, printed in the *American Volunteer,* September 21, 1820. *"sheer fabrication":* *American Volunteer,* September 28, 1820.

157-158, The confession was

Authorship controversy: Douglas Macneal, "Settling the *Confession*'s Hash," *Centre County Heritage* 24.2 (Fall 1987), pp. 16–17, and Dugan, *The Making of Legends,* pp. 55–56. For an excellent overview of the confession, which charts the text's passage through different genres—romance, satire, and melodrama—see Macneal, "Settling the *Confession*'s Hash," pp. 13–14. *"rambling disposition":* Rishel, *The Life and Adventures of David Lewis,* p. 39.

158, Lewis's character is deeply

"This gentle fluid ... ": Rishel, *The Life and Adventures of David Lewis,* p. 75. *"unfortunate, but repentant":* ibid., p. 84.

158-159, McFarland printed the

"the weak side ... ": ibid., p. 63. *"a legalized system ... ":* ibid., p. 62. For another tirade against finance, see ibid., pp. 39–40.

159, By staying silent

"evil genius": ibid., p. 71.

159-160, While contemporaries exposed

Judging from the preface to his 1890 edition, *The Life and Adventures of David Lewis,* C. D. Rishel seems to have thought the confession was genuine. The preface to the 1853 edition, which Rishel includes, casts more doubt on the confession's authenticity but stops short of labeling it a forgery. Excerpts from the confession appeared in the Carlisle-based *Evening Sentinel,* April 29, 1898; May 6, 1898; and

May 19, 1898—with no doubt as to their accuracy. *"man of fine physique"* and *"a born leader"*: William M. Hall, *Reminiscences and Sketches, Historical and Biographical* (Harrisburg: Meyers Printing House, 1890), p. 269. *"quite an Adonis"*: Linn, *History of Centre and Clinton Counties*, p. 62. There are many newspaper reports of Pennsylvanians trying to find Lewis's treasure or other relics belonging to him. See Bellefonte's *Democratic Watchman*, November 17, 1893; Centre Hall's *Centre Reporter*, July 1, 1897, and October 28, 1909; and Bellefonte's *Centre Democrat*, January 11, 1912. *"My father knew of him . . . "*: quoted in Mac E. Barrick, "Lewis the Robber in Life and Legend," *Pennsylvania Folklife* 17.1 (August 1967), p. 10.

160, What's harder to gauge

The familiar accusations of corruption were made against Findlay; the pro-Findlay camp attacked Hiester by questioning his Revolutionary War credentials and accusing him of voting to give himself a pay raise while in Congress. Election of 1820: James A. Kehl, *Ill Feeling in the Era of Good Feeling: Western Pennsylvania Political Battles, 1815–1825* (Pittsburgh: University of Pittsburgh Press, 1956), pp. 199–204, and Klein, *Pennsylvania Politics*, pp. 107–112. Political culture of the era: Klein, *Pennsylvania Politics*, pp. 65–66.

160, As if all the

1820 election returns: Klein, *Pennsylvania Politics*, p. 408. The total for Hiester was 67,905, and the total for Findlay was 66,308.

160–161, Within a year

"pauperism": from Hiester's message, dated December 5, 1821, included in George Edward Reed, ed., *Pennsylvania Archives, Fourth Series*, vol. 5, pp. 280–281; the full message is on pp. 280–296. Nation's recovery: Rothbard, *The Panic of 1819*, p. 25. Cheves's policies and legacy: Edward S. Kaplan, *The Bank of the United States and the American Economy* (Westport, CT: Greenwood, 1999), pp. 69–75, and Bray Hammond, *Banks and Politics in America: From the Revolution to the Civil War* (Princeton: Princeton University Press, 1991 [1957]), pp. 276–277, 302–304.

161, But there were

Economic shift: Hammond, *Banks and Politics in America*, pp. 319, 326–329. Hammond draws the comparison between steam and credit frequently in his book, most clearly on pp. 35–36. Of course, not everyone succumbed to the get-rich-quick mentality: Albert Gallatin, who served as treasury secretary from 1801 to 1814, became a prominent spokesman for a saner, more managed approach to growth. Arthur M. Schlesinger Jr., *The Age of Jackson* (Boston: Little, Brown, 1945), pp. 9–44, also discusses the country's transformation in this period, with an eye to the rise of Jackson.

161–162, Nicholas Biddle, who

Biddle's biography: Thomas Payne Govan, *Nicholas Biddle: Nationalist and Public Banker, 1786–1844* (Chicago: University of Chicago Press, 1959), pp. 2–27, 49–77, and Hammond, *Banks and Politics in America*, pp. 287–291. For a portrait of Biddle, see the engraving by J. B. Longacre and T. B. Welch after an oil painting by Rembrandt Peale.

162, Biddle proved a fast

First phase of Biddle's tenure: Hammond, *Banks and Politics in America*, pp. 300–325, 374–375, and Kaplan, *The Bank of the United States*, pp. 81–83. According to Kaplan, when Biddle became president in January 1823, the Bank's note circulation was $4.4 million; it had increased to $6.7 million by June 1825 and $9.6 million one year later.

162–163, In his first three

Stephen Mihm, in *A Nation of Counterfeiters: Capitalists, Con Men, and the Making of the United States* (Cambridge, MA: Harvard University Press, 2007), p. 116, writes that by the late 1820s the Bank's circulation exceeded $10 million and made up between a fifth and a quarter of all paper money in circulation. Counterfeiting of the Bank's money and Biddle's response: ibid., pp. 113–125.

163, Although counterfeiters posed

Rising entrepreneurial forces: Hammond, *Banks and Politics in America*, pp. 274–285. Under Cheves, the Bank took delinquent state banks to court. The Supreme Court sided with the Bank, entrenching Philadelphia's power but deepening the hostility of the state banks.

163–164, General Andrew Jackson

Jackson's life before the presidency: Sean Wilentz, *Andrew Jackson* (New York: Times Books, 2005), pp. 13–34. Failed bid for presidency in 1824 and election of 1828: ibid., pp. 35–54. Background of Jackson's rise: Schlesinger, *The Age of Jackson*, pp. 30–44. The terms "People's President" and "King Mob" were prompted by his 1829 inauguration, a legendary drunken celebration attended by thousands of ordinary people; see Robert V. Remini, *The Life of Andrew Jackson* (Perennial Classics, 2001 [1988]), pp. 179–182.

164, Among Jackson's supporters

McFarland started the *Allegheny Democrat* in May 1824; he died in 1827. Inciting a crowd to burn Henry Clay in effigy: Klein, *Pennsylvania Politics*, pp. 185–187. Jackson's popularity among the Scotch-Irish in Pennsylvania: ibid., pp. 249–250.

164–165, Jackson had campaigned

Jackson's views on banking: Hammond, *Banks and Politics in America*, pp. 346–350. Jackson's view of the Panic of 1819: Rothbard, *The Panic of 1819*, pp. 127–129.

165, Jackson's tangled financial

Biddle's early relationship with Jackson: Hammond, *Banks and Politics in America*, pp. 369–373, and Govan, *Nicholas Biddle*, pp. 111–121.

165, Among the factors

Reasons for Jackson's assault on the Bank: Hammond, *Banks and Politics in America*, pp. 328–346, 351–366, 442–445; Govan, *Nicholas Biddle*, pp. 122–168; Mihm, *A Nation of Counterfeiters*, pp. 125–129; and Schlesinger, *The Age of Jackson*, pp. 79–94, 115–131. For a pro-Jackson point of view, see Wilentz, *Andrew Jackson*, pp. 74–85. *"I did not join . . . "*: quoted in Hammond, *Banks and Politics in America*, pp. 364–365.

166, The opening act

Full text of Jackson's first annual message to Congress, delivered on December 8, 1829: Andrew Jackson, *Messages of Gen. Andrew Jackson: With a Short Sketch of His Life* (Concord, NH: John F. Brown and William White, 1837), pp. 39–68. Lead-up to the Bank War: Hammond, *Banks and Politics in America*, pp. 369–404.

166, The plan backfired

"It is to be regretted . . ." and *"the rich richer . . . "*: Jackson, *Messages of Gen. Andrew Jackson*, p. 167; for the full text of the veto message, see pp. 147–168.

166–167, Voters embraced Jackson's

Veto message's popularity, the election of 1832, and the transfer of government deposits: Wilentz, *Andrew Jackson*, pp. 85–88; Schlesinger, *The Age of Jackson*, pp. 90–94, 97–102; and Hammond, *Banks and Politics in America*, pp. 405–423.

167, The day Jackson's

"two distinct sets... ": National Gazette, September 26, 1833, quoted in Mihm, *A Nation of Counterfeiters*, pp. 141–142. Swift increase in notes and banks: Hammond, *Banks and Politics in America*, p. 453.

168, More paper, of course

Jackson's pardoning of counterfeiters: Mihm, *A Nation of Counterfeiters*, pp. 133–134.

168, The great irony

"eager desire... ": Andrew Jackson, "Farewell Address (March 4, 1837)," *The Statesmanship of Andrew Jackson*, ed. Francis Newton Thorpe (New York: Tandy-Thomas, 1909), pp. 506–507. *"moneyed interest... ":* ibid., p. 512; for the full text of the farewell address, see pp. 493–515. Specie Circular: Hammond, *Banks and Politics in America*, pp. 452–455, and Schlesinger, *The Age of Jackson*, pp. 129–131.

168–169, Rather than strengthening

The origins of the Panic of 1837 are disputed. Wilentz, in *Andrew Jackson*, pp. 119–120, casts doubt on the central role of the Specie Circular in precipitating the crisis. For an overview of the competing explanations for the Panic of 1837, see Peter L. Rousseau, "Jacksonian Monetary Policy, Specie Flows, and the Panic of 1837," *Journal of Economic History* 62.2 (June 2002), pp. 457–488. Rousseau, after reviewing new documentary evidence from government archives, concludes that two factors were principally to blame: the Specie Circular and "a series of 'supplemental' interbank transfers of public balances ordered by the Treasury under the Deposit Act of 23 June 1836 to prepare for the 'official' distribution of $28 million of the $34 million federal surplus." The Deposit Act mandated the distribution of the federal surplus to state banks based on each state's representation in Congress; Jackson had serious reservations about the bill but signed it into law.

169, In May, runs on

Suspension of coin payments in New York and the Panic's impact: Mihm, *A Nation of Counterfeiters*, pp. 151–156, and Schlesinger, *The Age of Jackson*, pp. 217–226. New York riot: Schlesinger, *The Age of Jackson*, pp. 219–220, and "An Eyewitness Account of the Flour Riot in New York (February 1837)," *Voices of a People's History of the United States*, ed. Howard Zinn and Anthony Arnove (New York: Seven Stories, 2009 [2004]), pp. 198–200.

169–170, By the time

Nation doubling in size during Jackson's administration: Hammond, *Banks and Politics in America*, p. 326. Free banking: ibid., pp. 572–604, 617–630; Mihm, *A Nation of Counterfeiters*, pp. 180–186; and Kevin Dowd, "U.S. Banking in the 'Free Banking' Period," *The Experience of Free Banking*, ed. Kevin Dowd (London: Routledge, 1992), pp. 206–230. The first free banking law was passed in Michigan a few months after it gained statehood in January 1837; eighteen other states had passed similar laws by 1860. Stories of wildcat banks: Hammond, *Banks and Politics in America*, p. 601.

170, The uninhibited flow

Efforts by states to ban or severely restrict banking: Hammond, *Banks and Politics in America*, pp. 605–617. Wisconsin Marine and Fire Insurance Company and prevalence of unincorporated banks: ibid., pp. 613–614, 625–626.

170–171, Then there were

Western counterfeiters: Mihm, *A Nation of Counterfeiters*, pp. 158–208. Practice of resurrecting notes of bankrupt banks and other moneymaking techniques: ibid., pp. 286–294. On p. 156, Mihm writes, "While a banker in the East might be compared to a counterfeiter, it was not uncommon for a counterfeiter in the West to be likened to a banker, thanks to the public service he provided by pumping much-needed money into a developing economy."

CHAPTER SEVEN

175, On February 22, 1862

Scene in Washington: *Philadelphia Inquirer*, February 26, 1862; *North American and United States Gazette*, February 24, 1862; Edward Bates, *The Diary of Edward Bates, 1859–1866*, ed. Howard K. Beale (Washington, DC: Government Printing Office, 1933), pp. 235–236; Albert Gallatin Riddle, *Recollections of War Times: Reminiscences of Men and Events in Washington, 1860–1865* (New York: G. P. Putnam's Sons, 1895), pp. 183–186; and Ernest B. Furgurson, *Freedom Rising: Washington in the Civil War* (New York: Knopf, 2004), p. 158. President Lincoln was absent from the ceremonies at the Capitol because of the recent death of his son Willie.

175–176, Not all celebrations

There are two images of Upham. The first is an engraving by David Scattergood, from a photograph by Gilbert & Bacon, included as the frontispiece to Samuel Curtis

Upham, *Notes of a Voyage to California via Cape Horn, Together with Scenes in El Dorado, in the Years 1849–'50* (New York: Arno, 1973 [1878]). The second is a group portrait taken in 1877 of the Associated Pioneers of the Territorial Days of California, held by the Robert B. Honeyman Jr. Collection of Early Californian and Western American Pictorial Material, the Bancroft Library, University of California, Berkeley. Physical description of Upham: from his 1879 passport application, accessed through an online database on Ancestry.com, *U.S. Passport Applications, 1795–1925*, drawn from microfilm records housed at the National Archives. Philadelphia celebration: *Philadelphia Inquirer*, February 24, 1862, and *North American and United States Gazette*, February 24, 1862. *"a blaze of glory . . . "*: *North American and United States Gazette*, February 24, 1862. For views of the facade of 403 Chestnut Street, see the images taken from Philadelphia business directories reproduced by the Philadelphia Architects and Buildings Project, http://www.philadelphiabuildings.org.

176, On Monday morning

Upham's home and work addresses: *McElroy's Philadelphia City Directory for 1862* (Philadelphia: E. C. & J. Biddle, A. McElroy, 1862), available on microfilm at the Philadelphia City Archives. Upham discusses how he started printing reproductions (significantly, he doesn't use the word "counterfeits") of Confederate notes in a letter dated October 12, 1874, to author William Lee, who includes it in *The Currency of the Confederate States of America, a Description of the Various Notes, Their Dates of Issue, Varieties, Series, Sub-Series, Letters, Numbers, Etc.; Accompanied with Photographs of the Distinct Varieties of Each Issue* (Washington, DC: Published by the author, 1875), pp. 24–25. The *Inquirer*'s history: J. Thomas Scharf and Thompson Westcott, *History of Philadelphia, 1609–1884*, vol. 3 (Philadelphia: L. H. Everts, 1884), pp. 1992–1994.

176–177, The answer was

The $5 bill was printed by the Southern Bank Note Company at New Orleans and belonged to the September 2, 1861, issue of Confederate notes. The original had been engraved in steel, but the *Inquirer* had to reproduce it in woodcut, causing the quality to deteriorate; see Brent Hughes, *The Saga of Sam Upham: "Yankee Scoundrel,"* rev. ed. (Inman, SC: Published by the author, 1988), p. 8.

177, The note promised

"Those who entertain . . . ": *Philadelphia Inquirer*, February 24, 1862. I'm grateful to Marc D. Weidenmier and George B. Tremmel for clarification on this point.

177, Upham wasted no time

Story of Upham's first print run: from his letter to William Lee, reproduced in *The Currency of the Confederate States of America*, pp. 24–25. It's unclear exactly when Upham began his facsimile trade. While the $5 note appeared in the *Philadelphia Inquirer* on February 24, 1862, he claims in his 1874 letter to Lee that he didn't begin printing facsimiles until March 12, 1862. Since twelve years had passed, his memory may be mistaken on this point. The *Inquirer* building: Scharf and Westcott, *History of Philadelphia, 1609–1884*, vol. 3, p. 1993.

178, Ever since the

There was a thriving trade in patriotic envelopes in the early years of the war. The Print Department of the Library Company of Philadelphia has thousands of these items in its "Civil War Envelope Collection, 1861–1865," with a wide assortment printed by Upham, including *"A full length drawing of Jeff. Davis . . ."*

178, After the success

Upham's letter to William Lee describes him finding the note in *Frank Leslie's Illustrated Newspaper*, although Upham misremembers when the bill appeared: it ran in the January 11, 1862, edition.

179, Now with two

"a curiosity . . . worth preserving": *Philadelphia Inquirer*, February 24, 1862.

180, Upham was born

Upham's birth and childhood: F. K. Upham, *Upham Genealogy: The Descendants of John Upham of Massachusetts* (Albany, NY: J. Munsell's Sons, 1892), pp. 349–351. Upham's parents: ibid., pp. 240–241. Upham recalls his childhood home near the Green Mountains in S. C. Upham, *Notes of a Voyage to California via Cape Horn*, p. 54. Upham's uncle William: F. K. Upham, *Upham Genealogy*, pp. 235–240, and Walter Hill Crockett, *Vermont: The Green Mountain State*, vol. 3 (New York: Century History Company, 1921), pp. 332–333, 381–384. *"He had gotten nothing . . . "*: William H. Seward, *The Works of William H. Seward*, vol. 1, ed. George E. Baker (New York: Redfield, 1853), p. 388.

180–181, Few families traced

John Upham: Albert G. Upham, *Family History: Notices on the Life of John Upham* (Concord, NH: Asa McFarland, 1845), pp. 5–20. John Upham's descendants:

F. K. Upham, *Upham Genealogy*. Charles Wentworth Upham: ibid., pp. 201–218. Dispute between Charles Wentworth Upham and Nathaniel Hawthorne: Bryan F. Le Beau, "Foreword," Charles Wentworth Upham, *Salem Witchcraft* (Mineola, NY: Dover Publications, 2000), pp. xxvi–xxviii.

181, Samuel was a seventh-generation

The population of Montpelier in 1820 was 2,308, according to the federal census. State House: Abby Maria Hemenway and Eliakim Persons Walton, *The History of the Town of Montpelier* (Montpelier: A. M. Hemenway, 1882), p. 285. Early settlement of Montpelier: Daniel Pierce Thompson, *History of the Town of Montpelier* (Montpelier: E. P. Walton, 1860), pp. 38–58, 74–83.

181–182, Montpelier's unhurried pace

Montpelier's early manufacturing and founding of bank: Hemenway and Walton, *The History of the Town of Montpelier*, pp. 274–277, 281. History of town jail: Thompson, *History of the Town of Montpelier*, p. 108. Counterfeiting trade between Canada and the northern United States: Stephen Mihm, *A Nation of Counterfeiters: Capitalists, Con Men, and the Making of the United States* (Cambridge, MA: Harvard University Press, 2007), pp. 66–102.

182, At the age

Upham's early life: F. K. Upham, *Upham Genealogy*, pp. 349–351. Heady era of Wall Street: Charles R. Geisst, *Wall Street: A History: From Its Beginnings to the Fall of Enron* (Oxford: Oxford University Press, 2004 [1997]), pp. 35–47. Slum life in New York: Luc Sante, *Low Life: Lures and Snares of Old New York* (New York: Farrar, Straus and Giroux, 2003 [1991]), pp. 23–30.

182–183, It wasn't until

Upham's marriage: F. K. Upham, *Upham Genealogy*, p. 349. His wife's name is given as Ann Eliza Bancroft in Raymond Finley Hughes, *Hughes Family of Cape May County, New Jersey, 1650–1950* (Salem, MA: published by the author, 1950), p. 80, and in Paul Sturtevant Howe, *Mayflower Pilgrim Descendants in Cape May County, New Jersey* (Cape May, NJ: Albert R. Hand, 1921), p. 171. The Paul Sturtevant Howe genealogy says she was born in Fishing Creek, New Jersey, on April 22, 1829. Upham's daughter Marion was born on April 8, 1848, according to F. K. Upham, *Upham Genealogy*, p. 351.

183, On February 2, 1849

All descriptions of life aboard the *Osceola* are drawn from S. C. Upham, *Notes of a Voyage to California via Cape Horn*, pp. 23–217; a sketch of the *Osceola* in a gale appears on p. 113. The ship sailed 19,308 miles from Philadelphia to San Francisco, according to Upham's final tally on p. 217. See also Charles R. Schultz, *Forty-niners 'Round the Horn* (Columbia, SC: University of South Carolina, 1999).

183, The richer travelers

"Have been a rolling-stone . . . ": S. C. Upham, *Notes of a Voyage to California via Cape Horn*, pp. 33–34.

183-184, The romance had been

Marshall's discovery and origins of the gold rush: H. W. Brands, *The Age of Gold: The California Gold Rush and the New American Dream* (New York: Doubleday, 2002), pp. 1–24, 69–72. *"whose banks and bottoms . . . ":* *New York Herald*, September 17, 1848. *"abundance of gold":* from President Polk's 1848 State of the Union address, quoted in Brands, *The Age of Gold*, p. 70.

184, Polk's announcement officially

Gold rush: Brands, *The Age of Gold*, pp. 43–71. *"infection":* quoted ibid., p. 44. *"fever":* quoted ibid., p. 43.

184-185, While global in scale

"industry, productive labor . . . ": *Boston Courier*, quoted ibid., p. 71.

185, When gold fever

Packing for the trip and boarding the *Osceola*: S. C. Upham, *Notes of a Voyage to California via Cape Horn*, pp. ix–xi, 23.

186, In the book's

"a narration of facts . . . ": ibid., p. x.

186, Life on the *Osceola*

Four months after departing, Upham had already gained fifteen pounds. *"[W]ith the roaring . . . ":* ibid., p. 115.

186-187, Although he faithfully

I'm grateful to Elizabeth Sinclair, a genealogist in Texas, for providing me with a photograph of a painting of Captain James Fairfowl.

187-188, They learned that

"idle, indolent . . . ": S. C. Upham, *Notes of a Voyage to California via Cape Horn,* p. 157.

188, It took the *Osceola*

The *Osceola* left Talcahuano harbor on May 27, 1849, and passed through the Golden Gate on August 5, 1849. *"queer place":* ibid., p. 221. Population of San Francisco in summer of 1849: Frank Soulé, John H. Gihon, and James Nisbet, *The Annals of San Francisco* (New York: D. Appleton, 1854), p. 226. San Francisco in 1849: ibid., pp. 243-263; Brands, *The Age of Gold,* pp. 247-256; and S. C. Upham, *Notes of a Voyage to California via Cape Horn,* pp. 218-226, 265-268. *"rivers of mud":* ibid., p. 268.

188-189, Upham pitched his tent

"A graduate of Yale . . . ": S. C. Upham, *Notes of a Voyage to California via Cape Horn,* p. 226.

189, The successful prospectors

"Those who had expected . . . ": ibid., p. 250. Upham's short-lived mining career: ibid., pp. 229-253.

189, When Upham returned

"The saw and hammer . . . ": ibid., p. 257. Population growth: Soulé, Gihon, and Nisbet, *The Annals of San Francisco,* p. 244. *"I had a vision . . . ":* S. C. Upham, *Notes of a Voyage to California via Cape Horn,* p. 259.

190, While he clearly had

The *Pacific News*: S. C. Upham, *Notes of a Voyage to California via Cape Horn,* pp. 259-261, 385-390. Copies of the *Pacific News* are available on microfilm in the Newspaper & Current Periodical Reading Room at the Library of Congress.

190, Living and working

The Plaza: Soulé, Gihon, and Nisbet, *The Annals of San Francisco,* pp. 259, 271-272, 279-280; Zoeth Skinner Eldredge, *The Beginnings of San Francisco, from the*

Expedition of Anza, 1774, to the City Charter of April 15, 1850, vol. 2 (San Francisco: Published by the author, 1912), p. 598; and S. C. Upham, *Notes of a Voyage to California via Cape Horn*, p. 257. On p. 271, Upham notes that the first theatrical performance in San Francisco took place in January 1850, in Washington Hall opposite the Plaza.

190–191, Upham loved newspapers

The *Sacramento Transcript*: S. C. Upham, *Notes of a Voyage to California via Cape Horn*, pp. 275–278, 390–391. The newspaper was located on Second Street, between J and K streets. Copies of the *Transcript* are available on microfilm in the Newspaper & Current Periodical Reading Room at the Library of Congress. Squatter war: ibid., pp. 333–351.

191, Upham had come

"almost magical": ibid., p. 307. *"We sincerely wish . . . "*: from the farewell to Upham printed in the *Transcript*, reproduced ibid., pp. 352–353.

191, William Lewis Herndon

Herndon's life: Normand E. Klare, *The Final Voyage of the* Central America, *1857: The Saga of a Gold Rush Steamship, the Tragedy of Her Loss in a Hurricane, and the Treasure Which Is Now Recovered* (Spokane, WA: Arthur H. Clark Company, 1992), pp. 29–36. The storm: ibid., pp. 63–119.

191–192, Herndon, a slim man

"human beings . . . ": quoted ibid. p. 114. See also Gary Kinder, *Ship of Gold in the Deep Blue Sea* (New York: Grove, 1998).

192, Four hundred and thirty-five

Body count: Klare, *The Final Voyage of the* Central America, p. 247. The image in *Frank Leslie's Illustrated Newspaper* appeared on the front page of the October 3, 1857, issue. Public response to disaster: Klare, *The Final Voyage of the* Central America, pp. 146–147; financial fallout from the loss of gold discussed on pp. 195–202. According to the *New York Herald*, September 19, 1857, the news of the shipwreck caused alarm on Wall Street on the morning of September 18, 1857, but the panic had mostly abated by the afternoon.

192–193, To get from California

Gold's route: Klare, *The Final Voyage of the* Central America, pp. 39–62. Upham's return to Philadelphia: S. C. Upham, *Notes of a Voyage to California via Cape*

Horn, pp. 354–380. *"manly, vigorous . . . "*: ibid., p. 308. America in 1857: George Washington Van Vleck, *The Panic of 1857: An Analytical Study* (New York: Columbia University Press, 1943), pp. 1–21, and Kenneth M. Stampp, *America in 1857: A Nation on the Brink* (Oxford: Oxford University Press, 1992 [1990]), pp. 15–45.

193, On August 24, 1857

Origins of the Panic: Bray Hammond, *Banks and Politics in America: From the Revolution to the Civil War* (Princeton: Princeton University Press, 1991 [1957]), pp. 707–712; Van Vleck, *The Panic of 1857*, pp. 60–73; and James L. Huston, *The Panic of 1857 and the Coming of the Civil War* (Baton Rouge: Louisiana State University Press, 1987), pp. 14–18.

193–194, This contraction of credit

The Panic taking Americans by surprise: Huston, *The Panic of 1857*, pp. 14–19. Widespread suffering: Van Vleck, *The Panic of 1857*, pp. 74–77, and Stampp, *America in 1857*, pp. 224–228. Protests in New York: Edwin G. Burrows and Mike Wallace, *Gotham: A History of New York City to 1898* (Oxford: Oxford University Press, 1999), pp. 849–850.

194, Decades of laissez-faire

Country's transformation in the years before 1857: Hammond, *Banks and Politics in America*, pp. 671–673, 698–709. Period of growth before the Panic: Van Vleck, *The Panic of 1857*, pp. 29–37, and Stampp, *America in 1857*, pp. 214–215.

195, Underwriting these ventures

Rapid growth of the banking sector: Stampp, *America in 1857*, p. 217. *Thompson's Bank Note Reporter* was quite popular: by 1855, it had a circulation of 100,000, according to Mihm, in *A Nation of Counterfeiters*, p. 239; on p. 3, Mihm estimates that by the 1850s, more than ten thousand different kinds of paper were circulating.

195, Counterfeiters had always

Transformation of banknote printing: Mihm, *A Nation of Counterfeiters*, pp. 262–304.

195–196, This made banknote

Impact of the new technology on counterfeiting: Mihm, *A Nation of Counterfeiters*, pp. 277–304, and David R. Johnson, *Illegal Tender: Counterfeiting and the Secret*

Service in Nineteenth-Century America (Washington, DC: Smithsonian Institution, 1995), pp. 9–13, 43–44.

196, Since New York City

Moneymaking underworld of lower Manhattan: Johnson, *Illegal Tender*, pp. 7–17, 43–45, 60–64, and Mihm, *A Nation of Counterfeiters*, pp. 209–235. Population of New York in 1857: Stampp, *America in 1857*, p. 40.

196–197, While the 1850s

Westward movement of slaveholders: Van Vleck, *The Panic of 1857*, pp. 30–33. Sectional tensions of the 1850s: Stampp, *America in 1857*, pp. 110–143.

197–198, When Upham returned

Upham's first son, Samuel Zenas, was born on August 9, 1851, followed by Charles Henry on January 15, 1856, according to F. K. Upham, *Upham Genealogy*, p. 351. The *Sunday Mercury*: Scharf and Westcott, *History of Philadelphia, 1609–1884*, vol. 3, p. 2022. Copies of the *Mercury* are available in bound volumes at the Newspaper and Current Periodical Reading Room at the Library of Congress. "A Night in the Life of a Physician" appeared in the March 12, 1854, edition; "Interior of a Persian Harem," on February 26, 1854.

198, Upham's newspaper catered

Advertisements from the *Mercury*'s back page are taken from the February 5, 1854, edition. Transformation of Philadelphia: Russell F. Weigley, "The Border City in Civil War, 1854–1865," *Philadelphia: A 300-Year History*, ed. Russell F. Weigley, Nicholas B. Wainwright, and Edwin Wolf, 2nd (New York: W. W. Norton, 1982), pp. 366–381. *"[N]ever plead guilty . . . "*: *Sunday Mercury*, March 19, 1854.

198, Philadelphians had strong

Mood in Philadelphia prior to Fort Sumter: Weigley, "The Border City in Civil War, 1854–1865," pp. 383–394.

198–199, Fort Sumter sparked

Impact of Fort Sumter on Philadelphia: ibid., pp. 394–396. *"appear to be well treated"*: S. C. Upham, *Notes of a Voyage to California via Cape Horn*, p. 89.

199, The North faced

Stunted state of the federal government: Hammond, *Banks and Politics in America*, pp. 718–720; Bray Hammond, *Sovereignty and an Empty Purse: Banks and Politics in the Civil War* (Princeton: Princeton University Press, 1970), pp. 18–26; Mihm, *A Nation of Counterfeiters*, p. 309; and Frederick J. Blue, *Salmon P. Chase: A Life in Politics* (Kent, OH: Kent State University Press, 1987), p. 143.

199, Chase had no

Chase's early life and career as a lawyer and politician: Blue, *Salmon P. Chase*, pp. 1–40, 61–133, and Hammond, *Sovereignty and an Empty Purse*, p. 33.

200, The law suited

Cincinnati lynch mob: Blue, *Salmon P. Chase*, pp. 28–30. Chase's views on slavery: ibid., pp. 45–46. His opinion of Jackson: ibid., pp. 11–12, 40–41. At his inaugural address as governor of Ohio in 1856, Chase announced that coin provided "the best practicable currency," quoted ibid., p. 150.

200, After Fort Sumter

Chase's heavy work schedule: ibid., pp. 137–138, 207.

200–201, Chase presented his

Chase's measures: Hammond, *Sovereignty and an Empty Purse*, pp. 37–47; Blue, *Salmon P. Chase*, pp. 144–145; and Mihm, *A Nation of Counterfeiters*, pp. 310–311.

201–202, A hundred miles

Memminger's physical appearance: Henry D. Capers, *The Life and Times of C. G. Memminger* (Richmond: Everett Waddey, 1893), pp. 23–24. For a photograph of Memminger, see Judith Ann Benner, *Fraudulent Finance: Counterfeiting and the Confederate States: 1861–1865* (Hillsboro, TX: Hill Junior College Press, 1970), p. 40. The Confederate Treasury occupied the Richmond customhouse, which was designed by Ammi B. Young, the same architect who had overseen the recent expansion of the Treasury in Washington. The other non-native-born member of Davis's cabinet was Judah P. Benjamin, born a British subject in the West Indies.

202, A small, slightly built

Memminger's early life: Capers, *The Life and Times of C. G. Memminger*, pp. 7–36; for his career as a lawyer and politician, see pp. 136–289. See also Hammond, *Sovereignty and an Empty Purse*, pp. 258–259.

202–203, If Chase's job

Difficulty of Memminger's position: Mihm, *A Nation of Counterfeiters*, pp. 319–321. Confederacy's first Treasury notes: Richard Cecil Todd, *Confederate Finance* (Athens: University of Georgia Press, 1954), pp. 90–93.

CHAPTER EIGHT

204, The prisoners began

The scene: *Daily Richmond Examiner*, June 30, 1862, and Joseph Gibbs, *Three Years in the "Bloody Eleventh": The Campaigns of a Pennsylvania Reserves Regiment* (University Park, PA: Pennsylvania State University Press, 2002), pp. 127–130.

204–205, An onlooker caught

"a counterfeit of the Philadelphia manufacture": *Daily Richmond Examiner*, June 30, 1862. *"This note is well calculated . . . "*: *Richmond Daily Dispatch*, April 15, 1862.

205, In May, the editors

"Who is this man Upham? . . . ": *Richmond Daily Dispatch*, May 31, 1862. *"well known to many Virginians . . . "*: *Richmond Daily Dispatch*, June 2, 1862. The *Dispatch* probably had the largest readership in the South, according to Ford Risley, *The Civil War: Primary Documents on Events from 1860 to 1865* (Westport, CT: Greenwood, 2004), p. 5.

205–206, The venom of

"The attempt to pass . . . ": *Daily Richmond Examiner*, June 30, 1862.

206, Upham's method had

Upham's advertising campaign: George B. Tremmel, *A Guide Book of Counterfeit Confederate Currency: History, Rarity, and Values* (Atlanta, GA: Whitman, 2007), pp. 40–41. On p. 40, Tremmel reproduces the March broadside.

206–207, At first it seemed

A copy of the May flyer, dated May 30, 1862, is held by the Books & Other Texts Department of the Library Company of Philadelphia.

207–208, Upham faced lots

Origins of counterfeit Confederate notes: Judith Ann Benner, *Fraudulent Finance: Counterfeiting and the Confederate States: 1861–1865* (Hillsboro, TX: Hill Junior College Press, 1970), pp. 26–35, and Tremmel, *A Guide Book of Counterfeit Confederate Currency*, pp. 23–28. Illicit cotton trade, including figure about prices: Stuart D. Brandes, *Warhogs: A History of War Profits in America* (Lexington, KY: University Press of Kentucky, 1997), pp. 92–95.

208, The biggest passers

Role of soldiers in passing counterfeits: Benner, *Fraudulent Finance*, pp. 26–30, and Tremmel, *A Guide Book of Counterfeit Confederate Currency*, p. 26. Philadelphia was a railway transfer point for soldiers from New England, New York, and New Jersey heading south, according to Russell F. Weigley, "The Border City in Civil War, 1854–1865," *Philadelphia: A 300-Year History*, ed. Russell F. Weigley, Nicholas B. Wainwright, and Edwin Wolf, 2nd (New York: W. W. Norton, 1982), pp. 398–399.

208–209, Without the Northern

Pope's command and the influx of counterfeits: Benner, *Fraudulent Finance*, pp. 28–29. *"subsist upon the country"*: from Pope's General Order No. 5, quoted in John J. Hennessy, *Return to Bull Run: The Campaign and Battle of Second Manassas* (Norman, OK: University of Oklahoma Press, 1999 [1993]), p. 14; see pp. 14–20 for more on Pope's orders. *"fortified with exhaustless . . . "*: Edward Alfred Pollard, *Southern History of the War: The Second Year of the War* (New York: Charles B. Richardson, 1864), p. 94; on the same page, in a footnote, Pollard quotes an Upham circular found on a Yankee prisoner. Aside from northern Virginia, the Ozarks region between Missouri and Arkansas was another major entry point for counterfeit Confederate money passed by Union soldiers; see John Bradbury, "'The Bank of Fac Simile': Economic Warfare in the White River Valley, 1862–1863," *White River Valley Historical Quarterly* 32.3 (Spring 1993), pp. 7–8.

209–210, Most Union commanders

Nathan Levi's arrest and *"confederate notes were not money . . . "*: *Lowell Daily Citizen and News*, September 16, 1862. Accusations that Sherman knowingly allowed soldiers in his jurisdiction to pass counterfeits: Benner, *Fraudulent Finance*, p. 31. Case in Culpeper, Virginia: George Alfred Townsend, *Campaigns of a Non-Combatant, and his Romaunt Abroad During the War* (New York: Blelock, 1866), pp. 244–245. Another Union officer who didn't approve of counterfeiting was Brigadier General

Milo S. Hascall, who issued an order in Ohio threatening to punish his men for passing fake bills; quoted in Tremmel, *A Guide Book of Counterfeit Confederate Currency*, p. 70.

210, The role of Union

"wherever an execrable . . . ": *Richmond Daily Dispatch*, May 31, 1862. A key factor in the Southern view of Northern economic practices was the Panic of 1857, which reaffirmed the belief among Southerners that their economy was beholden to irresponsible Yankee speculators; see Kenneth M. Stampp, *America in 1857: A Nation on the Brink* (Oxford: Oxford University Press, 1992 [1990]), pp. 229–230. *"[s]peculators and thieves . . . "*: from a diary entry dated February 16, 1863, included in Julia Ellen LeGrand Waitz, *The Journal of Julia LeGrand, New Orleans, 1862–1863*, ed. Kate Mason Rowland and Agnes E. Croxall (Richmond: Everett Waddey, 1911), pp. 131–132.

211, On March 10, 1862

The article, including all quotes: *Philadelphia Inquirer*, March 10, 1862.

211–212, The counterfeiter almost

I'm grateful to George Tremmel for corresponding with me about the *Inquirer* article. He made a persuasive case that the unnamed counterfeiter in the report couldn't have been Upham.

212, If Seward or Stanton

Union sponsorship of counterfeiting is the subject of endless speculation. Brent Hughes, in *The Saga of Sam Upham: "Yankee Scoundrel,"* rev. ed. (Inman, SC: Published by the author, 1988), p. 12, sketches a potential scenario whereby federal officials gave English banknote paper seized from Confederate blockade-runners to Upham in order to aid his business. Paper wouldn't be the only material officials could provide; Confederate plates also fell into Union hands, according to Benner, *Fraudulent Finance*, p. 12. However, as Stephen Mihm points out in *A Nation of Counterfeiters: Capitalists, Con Men, and the Making of the United States* (Cambridge, MA: Harvard University Press, 2007), p. 325, no evidence exists to support the theory that Union authorities conspired to aid Upham or any other counterfeiter of Southern currency.

213, The legislation took

Impact and significance of the Legal Tender Act: Bray Hammond, *Sovereignty and an Empty Purse: Banks and Politics in the Civil War* (Princeton: Princeton

University Press, 1970), pp. 225–229. The law specified that the greenbacks couldn't be used to pay import duties or the interest on government bonds and notes; in those cases, payment had to be in coin.

213, Such a dramatic

Debate in Congress over legal tender: ibid., pp. 179–224. Representative Lovejoy's argument: Mihm, *A Nation of Counterfeiters*, p. 313.

214, While Hamilton had

For more on the radical nature of the expanded federal role, see Hammond, *Sovereignty and an Empty Purse*, pp. 25–26, 226–227. Union's suppression of civil liberties: Clinton L. Rossiter, *Constitutional Dictatorship: Crisis Government in the Modern Democracies* (Princeton: Princeton University Press, 1948), pp. 224–239. The Confederacy also suspended habeas corpus, although to a more limited degree.

214–215, To adapt the Constitution

"If no other means . . . ": from an address by Thaddeus Stevens, dated January 22, 1862, quoted in Hammond, *Sovereignty and an Empty Purse*, p. 193.

215, Among the many

Chase's stubbornness on the specie issue and opposition to the Legal Tender Act: ibid., pp. 60–186, and Frederick J. Blue, *Salmon P. Chase: A Life in Politics* (Kent, OH: Kent State University Press, 1987), pp. 145–150.

215–216, The qualities that

December crisis: Hammond, *Sovereignty and an Empty Purse*, pp. 131–163. *"a thousand dollars . . . "*: from a letter by Chase to John T. Trowbridge, quoted ibid., p. 82.

216–217, Christopher Memminger

Financial plight of the South: ibid., pp. 254–260, and Mihm, *A Nation of Counterfeiters*, pp. 319–321. Proliferation of shinplasters and *"greasy, smelt bad . . . "*: Benner, *Fraudulent Finance*, pp. 16–17. Some of the Confederate notes bore interest; the March 1861 issue bore an annual interest rate of 3.65 percent, or one cent a day for each one hundred dollars, due in one year. Memminger hoped that people would consider them an investment and hold them rather than spend them.

217, None of these

Confederacy's resistance to making paper notes a legal tender: Hammond, *Sovereignty and an Empty Purse*, pp. 255–257.

217, Memminger also dealt

Memminger's logistical problems: Mihm, *A Nation of Counterfeiters*, pp. 321–323, and Benner, *Fraudulent Finance*, pp. 5–10. Stone lithography technique and its disadvantages: Tremmel, *A Guide Book of Counterfeit Confederate Currency*, pp. 3, 309–310. Number of different engraving firms and note varieties: Benner, *Fraudulent Finance*, pp. 11–12. It wasn't until the December 2, 1862, issue of Confederate Treasury notes that Memminger issued only one design for each denomination, according to Tremmel, *A Guide Book of Counterfeit Confederate Currency*, p. 17.

218, Counterfeiters exploited the

"[W]e are well aware . . . ": from a letter by Memminger to Ebenezer Starnes, dated August 20, 1861, included in Raphael P. Thian, *Correspondence of the Treasury Department of the Confederate States of America, 1861–'65*, appendix, pt. 4 (Washington, DC, 1879), pp. 176–177. I'm grateful to George Tremmel, Bob Schreiner, and Tom Carson for digitizing the works of Raphael P. Thian.

218–219, Nearly a thousand

Absence of news from the front: *Richmond Daily Dispatch*, August 22, 1862. Scene at the jailhouse and the gallows and *"a number of painted . . . ": Richmond Daily Dispatch*, August 23, 1862. Relative calm in Richmond after McClelland's failed Virginia campaign: Emory M. Thomas, *The Confederate State of Richmond: A Biography of the Capital* (Austin: University of Texas Press, 1971), pp. 100–102; on p. 22, Thomas includes a detailed map of Civil War–era Richmond showing the route of the Virginia Central Railroad.

219, John Richardson, alias

Richardson's backstory, trial, and sentencing: Benner, *Fraudulent Finance*, pp. 40–42, and *Richmond Daily Dispatch*, 1862: April 2, 7; May 8, 22; August 14, 18, 21, 22, and 23. Richardson was convicted in the Eastern District of Virginia on April 5, 1862, and sentenced to "be hanged by the neck until he be dead," according to William Morrison Robinson, *Justice in Grey: A History of the Judicial System of the Confederate States of America* (Cambridge, MA: Harvard University Press, 1941),

p. 206. Robinson discusses the cases of other convicted counterfeiters; many were pardoned or saw their sentences commuted by Jefferson Davis.

219–220, Executing an immigrant

"skulking out of . . . ": Richmond Daily Dispatch, April 7, 1862. Counterfeiting crisis: Tremmel, *A Guide Book of Counterfeit Confederate Currency*, pp. 5–7, and Benner, *Fraudulent Finance*, p. 15. *"The panic and excitement . . . "*: from a letter by B. C. Pressley to Memminger, dated August 25, 1862, included in Raphael P. Thian, *Correspondence of the Treasury Department of the Confederate States of America, 1861–'65*, appendix, pt. 5 (Washington, DC, 1880), pp. 604–605. See also various letters to Memminger on subject of counterfeiting on pp. 601–607.

220, Memminger responded by

Memminger's measures: Tremmel, *A Guide Book of Counterfeit Confederate Currency*, pp. 6–7.

220, Meanwhile, the Yankee

Arrest of William P. Lee: *Daily Richmond Examiner*, July 26, 1862. Union presence in Elizabeth City: Alex Christopher Meekins, *Elizabeth City, North Carolina, and the Civil War: A History of Battle and Occupation* (Charleston: History Press, 2007), pp. 42–43.

220–221, Despite the heavy

All quotes: *Daily Richmond Examiner*, July 26, 1862. While the government in Richmond couldn't legally compel people to accept its Treasury notes, individual states passed laws that monetized graybacks by requiring banks to accept them on deposit and use them to settle interbank balances. They were also made receivable in payment for state taxes and dues; see Gary Pecquet, George Davis, and Bryce Kanago, "The Emancipation Proclamation, Confederate Expectations, and the Price of Southern Bank Notes," *Southern Economic Journal* 70.3 (January 2004), pp. 618–619.

221, In August, while

Upham's August flyer is reproduced in Tremmel, *A Guide Book of Counterfeit Confederate Currency*, p. 41.

221–222, By the summer

The Second Battle of Bull Run took place on August 28–30, 1862, and Lee ordered his troops to cross the Potomac into Maryland on September 4, 1862; see James

M. McPherson, *Crossroads of Freedom: Antietam* (Oxford: Oxford University Press, 2002), pp. 81–90. Lead-up to emancipation: David Herbert Donald, *Lincoln* (New York: Simon & Schuster, 1995), pp. 373–376. The Battle of Antietam: Harry Hansen, *The Civil War: A History* (New York: Signet Classic, 2002 [1961]), pp. 249–263, and Drew Gilpin Faust, *This Republic of Suffering: Death and the American Civil War* (New York: Knopf, 2008), pp. 66–69.

222–223, Lincoln's embrace of

Shifting perception of the war in the South: Pecquet, Davis, and Kanago, "The Emancipation Proclamation," pp. 622–623. *"publicly advertised . . . ":* from Davis's message, included in *Journal of the Congress of the Confederate States of America, 1861–1865*, vol. 5 (Washington, DC: Government Printing Office, 1905), p. 297; for the full message, see pp. 297–299. *"[P]rinted advertisements . . . ":* from Memminger's report, included in Raphael P. Thian, *Reports of the Secretary of the Treasury of the Confederate States of America, 1861–'65*, appendix, pt. 3 (Washington, DC, 1878), p. 76.

223, These warnings prompted

Debate in Confederate Congress: Tremmel, *A Guide Book of Counterfeit Confederate Currency*, pp. 8–10. *"principal places of trade":* from a letter by Memminger to Alexander Hamilton Stephens, dated August 26, 1862, included in Thian, *Reports of the Secretary of the Treasury of the Confederate States of America, 1861–'65*, appendix, pt. 3, pp. 81–82. Approval of death penalty for captured enemy soldiers with counterfeit money: Tremmel, *A Guide Book of Counterfeit Confederate Currency*, p. 10. *"I entirely concur . . . ":* from a letter by Memminger to B. C. Pressley, dated October 17, 1862, included in Raphael P. Thian, *Correspondence of the Treasury Department of the Confederate States of America, 1861–'65*, appendix, pt. 4, p. 367.

223–224, On Christmas Day

The scene and *"[N]o little gunpowder . . . ":* John Beauchamp Jones, *A Rebel War Clerk's Diary at the Confederate States Capital*, vol. 1 (Philadelphia: J. B. Lippincott, 1866), pp. 224–225. See also Joseph G. Dawson, "Jones, John Beauchamp," *American National Biography Online*, February 2000, http://www.anb.org/articles/16/16-00879.html. Weather in December 1862 in Richmond: Robert K. Krick, *Civil War Weather in Virginia* (Tuscaloosa: University of Alabama Press, 2007), pp. 78–80.

224, Jones was better

"A portion of the people . . . ": Jones, *A Rebel War Clerk's Diary*, p. 200. Transformation of Richmond into a rowdy capital: Thomas, *The Confederate State of Richmond*, pp. 65–70; Thomas discusses the winter of 1862 on pp. 111–112 and the city's population on pp. 24, 128. For more on prostitution in wartime Richmond, see *Richmond Daily Dispatch*, May 13, 1862. Rise of gambling, prostitution, and crime: Ernest B. Furgurson, *Ashes of Glory: Richmond at War* (New York: Knopf, 1996), pp. 99–100.

224–225, What made life

Rising prices: Thomas, *The Confederate State of Richmond*, pp. 73–74, 87, 113–114. Cost of a Christmas turkey in 1862: Jones, *A Rebel War Clerk's Diary*, p. 224. Steady decline of the grayback: Marc D. Weidenmier, "Turning Points in the U.S. Civil War: Views from the Grayback Market," *Southern Economic Journal* 68.4 (April 2002), pp. 886–889. Drawing on quotations from Southern newspapers, Weidenmier charts the grayback price of a gold dollar over the course of the war. On August 15, 1862, after holding steady at two Confederate dollars per gold dollar since May 2, the price of gold in graybacks begins to increase. *"He says Mr. M.'s head . . . "*: Jones, *A Rebel War Clerk's Diary*, p. 211. *"headstrong, haughty . . . "*: ibid., p. 242.

225, To his credit

Memminger's efforts to warn Congress: Richard Cecil Todd, *Confederate Finance* (Athens: University of Georgia Press, 1954), pp. 109–120. *"Like the moon's . . . "*: from a report by Memminger delivered on January 10, 1863, quoted ibid., p. 110. Vicious cycle of Confederate paper credit: Mihm, *A Nation of Counterfeiters*, pp. 328–329. For more on Confederate inflation and the vilification of Memminger, see Furgurson, *Ashes of Glory*, pp. 190–191.

225, Too much paper

The link between war news, Southern expectations, and Confederate values has been well documented: see Pecquet, Davis, and Kanago, "The Emancipation Proclamation," pp. 616–630, and Weidenmier, "Turning Points in the U.S. Civil War," pp. 875–890.

225–226, In the second

Prices of a gold dollar in graybacks: Weidenmier, "Turning Points in the U.S. Civil War," p. 887. Impact of Antietam, the Emancipation Proclamation, and the Northern congressional elections on the value of the grayback: ibid., pp. 875–885, and Pecquet, Davis, and Kanago, "The Emancipation Proclamation," pp. 617–629. As Weidenmier shows, the value of the grayback didn't perfectly track Confederate war fortunes: it didn't always rise with a battlefield victory and fall with a battlefield defeat. However, the evidence does suggest that the grayback's decline from August 1862 onward reflected the hardening Southern view of the war as a longer, costlier conflict—and the corresponding spike in skepticism over whether the Confederate government would ever be able to exchange its notes for specie. Even if the notes couldn't be redeemed for coin, a negotiated peace would have left Southern state governments intact; their courts could uphold the legality of the grayback and make arrangements for its retirement. This possibility also became more remote as the war went on.

226, Upham posed a

Upham's effect on grayback depreciation: Marc D. Weidenmier, "Bogus Money Matters: Sam Upham and his Confederate Counterfeiting Business," *Business and Economic History* 28.2 (Winter 1999), pp. 313–324. *"The people, among whom . . . ": Daily Richmond Enquirer*, October 9, 1862.

226–227, In late 1862

Hilton's shop was located at 11 Spruce Street. Hilton's career: Tremmel, *A Guide Book of Counterfeit Confederate Currency*, pp. 54–55. Printing House Square: Lee E. Gray, "Type and Building Type: Newspaper/Office Buildings in Nineteenth-Century New York," *The American Skyscraper: Cultural Histories*, ed. Roberta Moudry (Cambridge: Cambridge University Press, 2005), pp. 86–89, and Sarah Bradford Landau and Carl W. Condit, *Rise of the New York Skyscraper, 1865–1913* (New Haven: Yale University Press, 1996), pp. 50–52. A color lithograph of Printing House Square in 1866 by Endicott & Co. can be seen in the New York Public Library Digital Gallery, http://digitalgallery.nypl.org. *"perfect fac-similes . . . ": Harper's Weekly*, October 4, 1862.

227, It didn't take

Upham's response ad: *Harper's Weekly*, October 18, 1862. *"$500 in Confederate . . ."* and *"so exactly like . . . ": Harper's Weekly*, January 10, 1863. *"sent, post-paid . . . ": Harper's Weekly*, January 31, 1863.

CHAPTER NINE

229, It was raining

Weather in New York on New Year's Eve: *New York Herald*, January 1, 1864. Astor House ball: *New York Herald*, January 1, 1864, and *New York Times*, January 1,

1864. Background and description of the Astor House: Edwin G. Burrows and Mike Wallace, *Gotham: A History of New York City to 1898* (Oxford: Oxford University Press, 1999), pp. 600–601. Murray's operation and the details of Hilton's arrest: *New York Times,* January 3, 1864, and January 4, 1864; see also *New York World,* January 4, 1864.

230, Upham had left

Upham stopped printing notes on August 1, 1863, according to his October 12, 1874, letter to William Lee, included in William Lee, *The Currency of the Confederate States of America, a Description of the Various Notes, Their Dates of Issue, Varieties, Series, Sub-Series, Letters, Numbers, Etc.; Accompanied with Photographs of the Distinct Varieties of Each Issue* (Washington, DC: Published by the author, 1875), p. 24. A gold dollar cost two grayback dollars on August 8, 1862, and by August 7, 1863, the same amount of gold cost twelve grayback dollars; see Marc D. Weidenmier, "Turning Points in the U.S. Civil War: Views from the Grayback Market," *Southern Economic Journal* 68.4 (April 2002), pp. 887–888. On p. 883, Weidenmier discusses the impact of Gettysburg on the grayback.

230–231, In an irony

One of the three code-breakers, David Homer Bates, wrote an article for *Harper's* in 1898 about the case: David Homer Bates, "A Rebel Cipher Dispatch. One Which Did Not Reach Judah P. Benjamin," *Harper's New Monthly Magazine,* vol. 97 (New York: Harper & Brothers, 1898), pp. 105–109. Aside from Bates, the "Sacred Three" also included Arthur B. Chandler and Charles A. Tinker; see Christopher Andrew, *For the President's Eyes Only: Secret Intelligence and the American Presidency from Washington to Bush* (New York: HarperCollins, 1995), p. 19.

231, Two days later

"Say to Memminger . . . ": Bates, "A Rebel Cipher Dispatch," p. 109.

231, Murray's sweep went

Murray's sweep and *"a great victory . . . ": New York Times,* January 4, 1864. Pleas of Hilton's friends: *New York World,* April 29, 1864. One of Hilton's friends, A. J. Williamson, wrote President Lincoln a letter, dated June 29, 1864; see George B. Tremmel, *A Guide Book of Counterfeit Confederate Currency: History, Rarity, and Values* (Atlanta, GA: Whitman, 2007), p. 58.

231–232, Although it would

"The Treasury has no connection . . . ": from Memminger's letter to Major General Whiting, dated January 21, 1864, included in Raphael P. Thian, *Correspondence of the Treasury Department of the Confederate States of America, 1861–'65,* appendix, pt. 4, pp. 570–572.

232, The details eventually

The long, somewhat convoluted story appeared in the *New York World,* April 29, 1864.

232–233, The Confederacy had

In 2001, a portfolio of twenty-five of Upham's facsimiles was discovered at an auction in Pottstown, Pennsylvania. The portfolio was prepared by Upham for his friend George William Childs, a journalist and the publisher of the *Philadelphia Public Ledger.* See George B. Tremmel, "The Rosetta Stone of Sam Upham," *Paper Money* 45.2 (March/April 2006), pp. 138–152, and *A Guide Book of Counterfeit Confederate Currency,* pp. 48–53. The historian was William Lee; Upham's letter of October 12, 1874, appears in Lee, *The Currency of the Confederate States of America,* pp. 24–25.

233, More than a decade

Upham's move: Tremmel, *A Guide Book of Counterfeit Confederate Currency,* pp. 36–37. Upham's new location was 25 South Eighth Street. *McElroy's Philadelphia City Directory for 1865* (Philadelphia: E. C. & J. Biddle, A. McElroy, 1865), available on microfilm at the Philadelphia City Archives, lists Upham's shop on Eighth Street as selling "patent medicines." He advertised Upham's Bay Rum on the back page of a pamphlet of one of his poems, "Columbia's Centennial Greeting," published in 1876; the item is held by the Broadsides Collection of the American Antiquarian Society, accessible online through Readex American Broadsides and Ephemera, Series I, 1760–1900. In the ad, he lists his South Eighth Street address as his "principal depot and laboratory." A broadside advertising "Tish-Wang," from 1863, is held by the Graphics Arts Collection of the American Antiquarian Society, also accessible online through Readex American Broadsides and Ephemera, Series I, 1760–1900. The "Tish-Wang" ad includes the warning "Beware of Counterfeits."

233, Upham had moved

Upham's credit record and business reputation: "Upham, Samuel C.," Pennsylvania, vol. 140, p. 78, R. G. Dun & Co. Collection, Baker Library Historical Collections,

Harvard Business School. Hilton's record: "Hilton, Winthrop," New York, vol. 194, p. 749, R. G. Dun & Co. Collection, Baker Library Historical Collections, Harvard Business School. It's not clear when Hilton was released from prison. According to an online database accessed through Ancestry.com, *Civil War Prisoner of War Records, 1861–1865*, drawn from microfilm records housed at the National Archives, Hilton was captured on December 31, 1863, in New York City, and released by order of General Dix in April 1864. Either the date of his release is incorrect or he was transferred to another facility, because A. J. Williamson wrote his letter to Lincoln on Hilton's behalf on June 29, 1864, when the printer was still imprisoned.

233–234, Hilton had been

"so indelibly photographed . . . ": from a speech by Upham at the "Second Annual Re-union and Banquet of 'The Associated Pioneers of the Territorial Days of California,'" dated January 18, 1877, included in the appendix to Samuel Curtis Upham, *Notes of a Voyage to California via Cape Horn, Together with Scenes in El Dorado, in the Years 1849–'50* (New York: Arno, 1973 [1878]), p. 435; for the full speech, see pp. 432–436. The appendix includes a range of Upham's writings on California, including "Ye Ancient Yuba Miner, of the Days of '49," an unsentimental and darkly funny poem about the gold rush days.

234, In 1876, America

1876 Centennial: Dorothy Gondos Beers, "The Centennial City, 1865–1876," *Philadelphia: A 300-Year History*, ed. Russell F. Weigley, Nicholas B. Wainwright, and Edwin Wolf, 2nd (New York: W. W. Norton, 1982), pp. 465–470. Associated Pioneers celebration: S. C. Upham, *Notes of a Voyage to California via Cape Horn*, pp. 400–423.

234–235, While Upham and

Technology of the Centennial: Beers, "The Centennial City, 1865–1876," p. 469, and Linda P. Gross and Theresa R. Snyder, *Philadelphia's 1876 Centennial Exhibition* (Charleston: Arcadia, 2005), p. 73.

235, To Upham, the

Upham's death certificate, obtained from microfilmed records at the Philadelphia City Archives, provides the details; his occupation is listed as "Manufacturer, Chemist." His will and the inventory of his estate: Brent Hughes, *The Saga of Sam*

Upham: "Yankee Scoundrel," rev. ed. (Inman, SC: published by the author, 1988), pp. 15–17. Obituary: *Philadelphia Inquirer,* July 1, 1885.

236, Initially the federal

Sixteen hundred state banks: Bray Hammond, *Sovereignty and an Empty Purse: Banks and Politics in the Civil War* (Princeton: Princeton University Press, 1970), p. 291. *Briscoe v. Bank of Kentucky*: Bray Hammond, *Banks and Politics in America: From the Revolution to the Civil War* (Princeton: Princeton University Press, 1991 [1957]), pp. 566–571. Inflationary effect of greenbacks: Hammond, *Sovereignty and an Empty Purse,* p. 300.

236, Treasury Secretary Salmon

Chase's national banking idea: Hammond, *Sovereignty and an Empty Purse,* pp. 285–292, and Frederick J. Blue, *Salmon P. Chase: A Life in Politics* (Kent, OH: Kent State University Press, 1987), pp. 157–159. As Chase acknowledged, national banking would give "little direct aid" to the war effort right away; "the constitutional supremacy of the nation over states and citizens" provided the real impetus for the measure; see Hammond, *Sovereignty and an Empty Purse,* p. 292.

236–237, The secretary's stubbornness

Abraham Lincoln had believed in the necessity of a national currency since 1839, when he gave a speech defending the Bank of the United States: "no duty is more imperative on [the federal] government," he said, "than the duty it owes the people of furnishing them a sound and uniform currency"; see Hammond, *Sovereignty and an Empty Purse,* pp. 24–25. As a result, Lincoln energetically supported Chase's national banking measure. Republican opposition: ibid., pp. 296–297, 303–309.

237, To get the legislation

Chase's campaign: ibid., pp. 293–295, and Blue, *Salmon P. Chase,* pp. 159–160. *"Without it . . . ":* Hammond, *Sovereignty and an Empty Purse,* p. 293.

237–238, Chase's persistence could

Sherman's background: Allan Burton Spetter, "Sherman, John," *American National Biography Online,* February 2000, http://www.anb.org/articles/05/05-00704.html. For Sherman's speeches, see John Sherman, *Selected Speeches and Reports on Finance and Taxation, From 1859 to 1878* (New York: D. Appleton, 1879), pp. 32–79; *"You cannot prevent . . ."* appears on p. 42.

238, Sherman's use of Jefferson

Sherman's strategy: Hammond, *Sovereignty and an Empty Purse*, pp. 300–301, 326–327.

238–239, The Civil War

"accursed heresy of . . . ": *New York Times*, February 3, 1863, quoted ibid., p. 326. *"become inseparably united . . . "*: *New York Times*, February 2, 1863, quoted in Mihm, *A Nation of Counterfeiters*, p. 333. *"The policy of this country . . . "*: Sherman, *Selected Speeches and Reports on Finance and Taxation*, p. 70.

239, Between Sherman's rhetoric

The bill passed the Senate 23 to 21, and the House 78 to 64; see Hammond, *Sovereignty and an Empty Purse*, pp. 328, 332. Sluggish growth of national banks and tax on state banknotes: ibid., pp. 345–347. The National Currency Act was later superseded by a revised version of the law, passed June 3, 1864.

239–240, The United States emerged

Design and printing of national banknotes: Mihm, *A Nation of Counterfeiters*, pp. 335–338.

240, Counterfeiters felt the

Impact on counterfeiting: ibid., p. 347.

240–241, This was evidently

Incompetence of local authorities and U.S. marshals in tackling counterfeiting: David R. Johnson, *Illegal Tender: Counterfeiting and the Secret Service in Nineteenth-Century America* (Washington, DC: Smithsonian Institution, 1995), pp. 40–41, 85–86, 109.

241, Lafayette Curry Baker

Baker's physical appearance: Jacob Mogelever, *Death to Traitors: The Story of General Lafayette C. Baker, Lincoln's Forgotten Secret Service Chief* (New York: Doubleday, 1960), p. 17, and J. H. Harris, "Introduction," in Lafayette Curry Baker, *History of the United States Secret Service* (Philadelphia: published by the author, 1867), p. 20. Baker's San Francisco days and early espionage career: Mogelever, *Death to Traitors*, pp. 29–80.

241–242, Northern intelligence was

Union intelligence confusion: Johnson, *Illegal Tender*, p. 67, and Andrew, *For the President's Eyes Only*, pp. 16–17.

242, In early 1862

Rise of the National Detective Police: Mogelever, *Death to Traitors*, pp. 85–95, 109–117, and C. Wyatt Evans, "Lafayette Baker and Security in the Civil War North," *North and South* 11.1 (September 2008), pp. 44–51. Treasury investigation: Mogelever, *Death to Traitors*, pp. 248–278; Ernest B. Furgurson, *Freedom Rising: Washington in the Civil War* (New York: Knopf, 2004), pp. 292–293; and Baker, *History of the United States Secret Service*, pp. 310–327. After the war, a woman named Loreta Janeta Velazquez published a memoir in which she claimed to have been a Confederate double agent in Baker's employ; among other things, she said Baker used counterfeit Confederate currency to fund covert activities in the South. It's still unknown whether her account is a fraud; see Tremmel, *A Guide Book of Counterfeit Confederate Currency*, pp. 72–84.

242–243, Baker had no scruples

Baker's curtained coaches: Mogelever, *Death to Traitors*, p. 117. "*Baker became a law . . .*": Lucius Eugene Chittenden, *Recollections of President Lincoln and His Administration* (New York: Harper & Brothers, 1904 [1891]), p. 346.

243, Whatever his vices or virtues

Baker's innovations: Mogelever, *Death to Traitors*, p. 111. Counterfeiting raids: Mihm, *A Nation of Counterfeiters*, p. 343, and *New York Times*, August 11, October 9, and October 14, 1864.

243–244, When the prisoners

Old Capitol Prison: Curtis Carroll Davis, "The 'Old Capitol' and Its Keeper: How William P. Wood Ran a Civil War Prison," *Records of the Columbia Historical Society, Washington, DC*, vol. 52 (Washington, DC: Historical Society of Washington, DC, 1989), pp. 207–208, 212–214.

244, The prison's superintendent

Wood's appearance and character as warden: ibid., pp. 211–212, 214–219. "*strange compound . . .*": from the diary of Catherine V. Baxley, a prisoner of Wood's, quoted ibid., p. 234.

244-245, Wood liked to let

Wood's interrogations: ibid., pp. 220–222, and Mihm, *A Nation of Counterfeiters*, pp. 341–342.

245, By questioning the

Wood's path to the Secret Service: Mihm, *A Nation of Counterfeiters*, pp. 344–346, and Johnson, *Illegal Tender*, pp. 70–71.

245-246, This wouldn't have been

Obstacles faced by the Secret Service and Wood's solutions: Johnson, *Illegal Tender*, pp. 72–77.

246-247, Wood absorbed these

Putting counterfeiters on the payroll: ibid., pp. 122–124, and Mihm, *A Nation of Counterfeiters*, p. 354. Criminal background of Secret Service operatives and questionable methods: Johnson, *Illegal Tender*, pp. 76–77.

247, Despite his men's

Arresting more than two hundred counterfeiters: Johnson, *Illegal Tender*, p. 76. Wood's analysis of the national counterfeit market: ibid., pp. 129–132. Extensive files on counterfeiters: Mihm, *A Nation of Counterfeiters*, p. 347.

248, In 1867, Wood

Raid: Johnson, *Illegal Tender*, p. 132. Backlash to Wood's tactics: ibid., pp. 156–157.

248, That summer, Wood

Wood's defense of Brockway: *New York Times*, June 27, 1867. *"We have thus . . . "*: *New York Times*, July 2, 1867. Indignant editorial: *New York Times*, June 28, 1867.

249, Wood made halfhearted

Secret Service's first handbook: Johnson, *Illegal Tender*, pp. 77–78. Gradual rehabilitation of the agency: ibid., pp. 79–108, 114–115. Counterfeit currency accounting for one-third and one-half of money supply: Philip H. Melanson with Peter F. Stevens, *The Secret Service: The Hidden History of an Enigmatic Agency* (New York: Carroll & Graf, 2002), p. 4. Less than one-thousandth of one percent: *New York Times*, January 29, 1911, and Mihm, *A Nation of Counterfeiters*, p. 373.

249, Wood's aggressive leadership

Crisis of confidence among counterfeiters and tougher sentencing: Johnson, *Illegal Tender*, pp. 135, 140, 149. Decline of counterfeiting industry: ibid., pp. 174–180.

250, The national notes

Campaign against toy money and *"Securities and Coins . . . "*: ibid., p. 177.

CONCLUSION

252-253, While the federal government

Regular panics: Wesley C. Mitchell, "Business Cycles," in National Bureau of Economic Research, *Business Cycles and Unemployment: Report and Recommendations of a Committee of the President's Conference on Unemployment* (New York: McGraw-Hill, 1923), pp. 5–6. The Panic of 1907 and the founding of the Federal Reserve: Kenneth Weiher, *America's Search for Economic Stability: Monetary and Fiscal Policy Since 1913* (New York: Twayne, 1992), pp. 19–22, and William G. Dewald, "The National Monetary Commission: A Look Back," *Journal of Money, Credit and Banking* 4.4 (November 1972), pp. 930–935.

253, The architects of the Federal

The Fed and the money supply: Weiher, *America's Search for Economic Stability*, pp. 22–23, and Liaquat Ahamed, *Lords of Finance: The Bankers Who Broke the World* (New York: Penguin Press, 2009), pp. 11–15.

253-254, The United States had

Congress passed the Gold Standard Act in 1900, legally cementing the gold standard that had been effectively in place since 1879. The struggle over greenbacks and the gold standard: Stephen Mihm, *A Nation of Counterfeiters: Capitalists, Con Men, and the Making of the United States* (Cambridge, MA: Harvard University Press, 2007), pp. 363, 369. The Federal Reserve Note: Arthur L. and Ira S. Friedberg, *Paper Money of the United States: A Complete Illustrated Guide with Valuations*, 18th ed. (Clifton, NJ: Coin & Currency Institute, 2006), p. 126.

254, The Depression severed

Roosevelt's monetary policies: Lester V. Chandler, *American Monetary Policy, 1928–1941* (New York: Harper & Row, 1971), pp. 272–295, and Weiher, *America's Search for Economic Stability*, pp. 79–82. Nixon closing the gold window: Daniel Yergin and Joseph Stanislaw, *The Commanding Heights: The Battle Between*

Government and the Marketplace That Is Remaking the Modern World (New York: Simon & Schuster, 1998), pp. 62–64.

254, By 1971, the government

Number of dollars held overseas: U.S. Department of the Treasury, *The Use and Counterfeiting of United States Currency Abroad*, pt. 3 (Washington, DC: U.S. Government Printing Office, September 2006), p. 9.

255, As the dollar has become

Counterfeiting in Latin America, Colombia, and Peru: U.S. Department of the Treasury, *The Use and Counterfeiting*, pp. 60–65. Decline of Colombian counterfeits and rise of Peru: Josh Meyer, "The Nation; Fake Dollars from Peru Trouble U.S.; Millions in Counterfeit Notes Have Been Seized in the Last Year," *Los Angeles Times*, September 13, 2009, and "Printing Money; Crime in Peru," *Economist*, May 9, 2009.

255, The most deceptive

North Korea and the supernotes: Stephen Mihm, "No Ordinary Counterfeit," *New York Times Magazine*, July 23, 2006; Dick K. Nanto, "North Korean Counterfeiting of U.S. Currency," U.S. Congressional Research Service (RL 33324), June 12, 2009; and Bill Gertz, "N. Korea General Tied to Forged $100 Bills; Report Details 'Supernotes,'" *Washington Times*, June 2, 2009.

255–256, Overall, counterfeit currency

Amount of counterfeit currency in circulation: U.S. Department of the Treasury, *The Use and Counterfeiting*, p. 75. New security features of 1996 notes: Mihm, "No Ordinary Counterfeit." New $100 bill: "U.S. Government Unveils New Design for the $100 Note," Press release from the Department of the Treasury, the Federal Reserve Board, and the U.S. Secret Service (April 21, 2010), http://www .newmoney.gov/media/release_04212010.htm; and Jeannine Aversa and Martin Crutsinger, "Government goes high-tech to redesign $100 bills," Associated Press, April 22, 2010.

INDEX